Teacher Edition

SCIENCE

Fusion

fusion [FYOO • zhuhn] a combination of two
or more things that releases energy

HOLT McDOUGAL

HOUGHTON MIFFLIN HARCOURT

Professional Development

Houghton Mifflin Harcourt and NSTA, the National Science Teacher's Association, have partnered to provide customized professional and development resources for teachers using *ScienceFusion*.

The Professional Development Resources in the NSTA Learning Center include:

—do-it-yourself resources, where you can study at your own pace.

—live and archived online seminars.

—journal articles, many of which include lesson plans.

—fee-based eBooks, eBook chapters, online short courses, symposia, and conferences.

Access to the NSTA Learning Center is provided in the *ScienceFusion* Online Resources.

Acknowledgments for Covers

DNA molecule (bg) ©Carl Goodman/Meese Photo Research; *false color x-rays on hand* (l) ©Lester Lefkowitz/Getty Images; *primate* (cl) ©Bruno Morandi/The Image Bank/Getty Images; *red cells* (cr) ©Todd Davidson/Getty Images; *fossils* (r) ©Yoshihi Tanaka/amana Images/Getty Images.

Interior, digital screens: *giraffes* ©Corbis.

Contents in Brief

About the Program

Teaching Tools

Units at a Glance

Resources

Consulting Authors

Michael A. DiSpezio
Global Educator
North Falmouth, Massachusetts

Michael DiSpezio is a renaissance educator who moved from the research laboratory of a Nobel Prize winner to the K–12 science classroom. He has authored or coauthored numerous textbooks and written more than 25 trade books. For nearly a decade, he worked with the JASON Project under the auspices of the National Geographic Society, where he designed curriculum, wrote lessons, and hosted dozens of studio and location broadcasts.

Over the past two decades, he has developed supplementary material for organizations and shows that include PBS's *Scientific American Frontiers*, *Discover* magazine, and the Discovery Channel. He has extended his reach outside the United States and into topics of crucial importance today. To all his projects, he brings his extensive background in science and his expertise in classroom teaching at the elementary, middle, and high school levels.

Marjorie Frank
*Science Writer and
Content-Area Reading Specialist*
Brooklyn, New York

An educator and linguist by training, a writer and poet by nature, Marjorie Frank has authored and designed a generation of instructional materials in all subject areas, including past HMH Science programs. Her other credits include authoring science issues of an award-winning children's magazine; writing game-based digital assessments in math, reading, and language arts; and serving as instructional designer and coauthor of pioneering school-to-work software

for Classroom Inc., a nonprofit organization dedicated to improving reading and math skills for middle and high school learners. She wrote lyrics and music for *SCIENCE SONGS*, which was an American Library Association nominee for notable recording. In addition, she has served on the adjunct faculty of Hunter, Manhattan, and Brooklyn Colleges, teaching courses in science methods, literacy, and writing.

iv

Michael R. Heithaus

Director, School of Environment and Society
Associate Professor, Department of Biological Sciences
Florida International University
North Miami, Florida

Mike Heithaus joined the Florida International University Biology Department in 2003. He has served as Director of the Marine Sciences Program and is now Director of the School of Environment and Society, which brings together the natural and social sciences and humanities to develop solutions to today's environmental challenges. While earning his doctorate, he began the research that grew into the Shark Bay Ecosystem Project in Western Australia, with which he still works. Back in the United States, he served as a Research Fellow with National Geographic, using remote imaging in his research and hosting a 13-part *Crittercam* television series on the National Geographic Channel. His current research centers on predator-prey interactions among vertebrates, such as tiger sharks, dolphins, dugongs, sea turtles, and cormorants.

Donna M. Ogle

Professor of Reading and Language
National-Louis University
Chicago, Illinois

Creator of the well-known KWL strategy, Donna Ogle has directed many staff development projects translating theory and research into school practice in middle and secondary schools throughout the United States. She is a past president of the International Reading Association and has served as a consultant on literacy projects worldwide. Her extensive international experience includes coordinating the Reading and Writing for Critical Thinking Project in Eastern Europe, developing an integrated curriculum for a USAID Afghan Education Project, and speaking and consulting on projects in several Latin American countries and in Asia. Her books include *Coming Together as Readers; Reading Comprehension: Strategies for Independent Learners; All Children Read;* and *Literacy for a Democratic Society.*

Program Reviewers

Content Reviewers

Paul D. Asimow, PhD
*Professor of Geology
and Geochemistry*
Division of Geological and Planetary Sciences
California Institute of Technology
Pasadena, CA

Laura K. Baumgartner, PhD
Postdoctoral Researcher
Molecular, Cellular, and Developmental Biology
University of Colorado
Boulder, CO

Eileen Cashman, PhD
Professor
Department of Environmental Resources Engineering
Humboldt State University
Arcata, CA

Hilary Clement Olson, PhD
Research Scientist Associate V
Institute for Geophysics, Jackson School of
Geosciences
The University of Texas at Austin
Austin, TX

Joe W. Crim, PhD
Professor Emeritus
Department of Cellular Biology
The University of Georgia
Athens, GA

Elizabeth A. De Stasio, PhD
*Raymond H. Herzog Professor
of Science*
Professor of Biology
Department of Biology
Lawrence University
Appleton, WI

Dan Franck, PhD
Botany Education Consultant
Chatham, NY

Julia R. Greer, PhD
*Assistant Professor of Materials Science and
Mechanics*
Division of Engineering and Applied Science
California Institute of Technology
Pasadena, CA

John E. Hoover, PhD
Professor
Department of Biology
Millersville University
Millersville, PA

William H. Ingham, PhD
Professor (Emeritus)
Department of Physics and Astronomy
James Madison University
Harrisonburg, VA

Charles W. Johnson, PhD
*Chairman, Division of Natural Sciences,
Mathematics, and Physical Education*
Associate Professor of Physics
South Georgia College
Douglas, GA

Tatiana A. Krivosheev, PhD
Associate Professor of Physics
Department of Natural Sciences
Clayton State University
Morrow, GA

Joseph A. McClure, PhD
Associate Professor Emeritus
Department of Physics
Georgetown University
Washington, DC

Mark Moldwin, PhD
Professor of Space Sciences
Atmospheric, Oceanic, and Space Sciences
University of Michigan
Ann Arbor, MI

Russell Patrick, PhD
Professor of Physics
Department of Biology, Chemistry, and Physics
Southern Polytechnic State University
Marietta, GA

Patricia M. Pauley, PhD
Meteorologist, Data Assimilation Group
Naval Research Laboratory
Monterey, CA

Stephen F. Pavkovic, PhD
Professor Emeritus
Department of Chemistry
Loyola University of Chicago
Chicago, IL

L. Jeanne Perry, PhD
Director (Retired)
Protein Expression Technology Center
Institute for Genomics and Proteomics
University of California, Los Angeles
Los Angeles, CA

Kenneth H. Rubin, PhD
Professor
Department of Geology and Geophysics
University of Hawaii
Honolulu, HI

Brandon E. Schwab, PhD
Associate Professor
Department of Geology
Humboldt State University
Arcata, CA

Marllin L. Simon, Ph.D.
Associate Professor
Department of Physics
Auburn University
Auburn, AL

Larry Stookey, PE
Upper Iowa University
Wausau, WI

Kim Withers, PhD
Associate Research Scientist
Center for Coastal Studies
Texas A&M University-Corpus Christi
Corpus Christi, TX

Matthew A. Wood, PhD
Professor
Department of Physics & Space Sciences
Florida Institute of Technology
Melbourne, FL

Adam D. Woods, PhD
Associate Professor
Department of Geological Sciences
California State University, Fullerton
Fullerton, CA

Natalie Zayas, MS, EdD
Lecturer
Division of Science and Environmental Policy
California State University, Monterey Bay
Seaside, CA

Teacher Reviewers

Ann Barrette, MST
Whitman Middle School
Wauwatosa, WI

Barbara Brege
Crestwood Middle School
Kentwood, MI

Katherine Eaton Campbell, M Ed
Chicago Public Schools-Area 2 Office
Chicago, IL

Karen Cavalluzzi, M Ed, NBCT
Sunny Vale Middle School
Blue Springs, MO

Katie Demorest, MA Ed Tech
Marshall Middle School
Marshall, MI

Jennifer Eddy, M Ed
Lindale Middle School
Linthicum, MD

Tully Fenner
George Fox Middle School
Pasadena, MD

Dave Grabski, MS Ed
PJ Jacobs Junior High School
Stevens Point, WI

Amelia C. Holm, M Ed
McKinley Middle School
Kenosha, WI

Ben Hondorp
Creekside Middle School
Zeeland, MI

George E. Hunkele, M Ed
Harborside Middle School
Milford, CT

Jude Kesl
Science Teaching Specialist 6–8
Milwaukee Public Schools
Milwaukee, WI

Joe Kubasta, M Ed
Rockwood Valley Middle School
St. Louis, MO

Mary Larsen
Science Instructional Coach
Helena Public Schools
Helena, MT

Angie Larson
Bernard Campbell Middle School
Lee's Summit, MO

Christy Leier
Horizon Middle School
Moorhead, MN

Helen Mihm, NBCT
Crofton Middle School
Crofton, MDL

Jeff Moravec, Sr., MS Ed
Teaching Specialist
Milwaukee Public Schools
Milwaukee, WI

Nancy Kawecki Nega, MST, NBCT, PAESMT
Churchville Middle School
Elmhurst, IL

Mark E. Poggensee, MS Ed
Elkhorn Middle School
Elkhorn, WI

Sherry Rich
Bernard Campbell Middle School
Lee's Summit, MO

Mike Szydlowski, M Ed
Science Coordinator
Columbia Public Schools
Columbia, MO

Nichole Trzasko, M Ed
Clarkston Junior High School
Clarkston, MI

Heather Wares, M Ed
Traverse City West Middle School
Traverse City, MI

Power up with

SCIENCE FUSiON

Print

The **Write-in Student Edition** teaches science content through constant **interaction** with the text.

Labs and Activities

Digital

The parallel **Digital Curriculum** provides **e-learning digital lessons and virtual labs** for every print lesson of the program.

Energize your students through a multimodal blend of Print, Inquiry, and Digital experiences.

Unit Assessment

Formative Assessment

Strategies RTI
Throughout TE

Lesson Reviews SE

Unit PreTest

Summative Assessment

Alternative Assessment
(1 per lesson) RTI

Lesson Quizzes

Unit Tests A and B

Unit Review RTI
(with answer remediation)

Practice Tests
(end of module)

Project-Based Assessment

See the Assessment Guide for quizzes and tests.

Go Online to edit and create quizzes and tests.

See RTI teacher support materials.

The **Hands-on Labs** and **Virtual Labs**

provide meaningful and exciting inquiry experiences.

The **Write-in Student Edition** teaches science content through constant **interaction** with the text.

Write-in Student Edition

360° of Inquiry

The *ScienceFusion* write-in student edition promotes a student-centered approach for

- **learning and applying inquiry skills in the student edition**

- **building STEM and 21st Century skills**

- **keeping digital natives engaged and interactive**

Research shows that an interactive text teaches students how to relate to content in a personal, meaningful way. They learn how to be attentive, energetic readers who reach a deep level of comprehension.

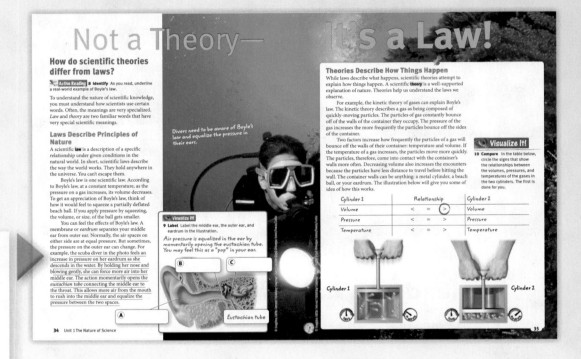

Big Ideas & Essential Questions

Each unit is designed to focus on a Big Idea and supporting lesson-level Essential Questions.

Connect Essential Questions

At the close of every unit, students build enduring understandings through synthesizing connections between different Essential Questions.

Active Reading

Annotation prompts and questions throughout the text teach students how to analyze and interact with content.

S.T.E.M.

STEM activities in every unit ask students to apply engineering and technology solutions in scenario-based learning situations.

Think Outside the Book

Students may wish to keep a Science Notebook to record illustrations and written work assignments. Blank pages at the end of each unit can also be used for this purpose.

Visualize It!

As concepts become more abstract, Visualize It! provides additional support for conceptual understanding.

Labs and Activities

The **Hands-on Labs** and **Virtual Labs** provide meaningful and exciting inquiry experiences.

360° of Inquiry

Labs and Activities

S.T.E.M. Engineering & Technology

STEM activities in every unit focus on
- **engineering and technology**
- **developing critical thinking and problem solving skills**
- **building inquiry, STEM, and 21st Century skills**

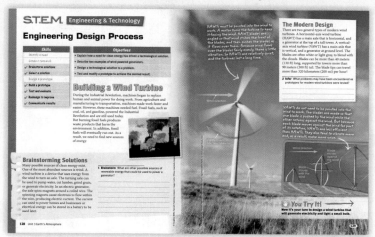

Scenario-Based STEM Activity

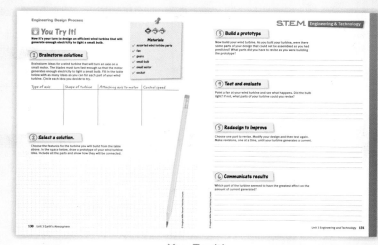

You Try It!

Hands-On and Virtual

Three levels—directed, guided, and independent—of labs and activities plus lesson level Virtual Labs give students wall-to-wall options for exploring science concepts and building inquiry skills.

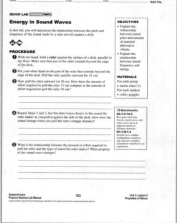

Hands-On Labs and Activities

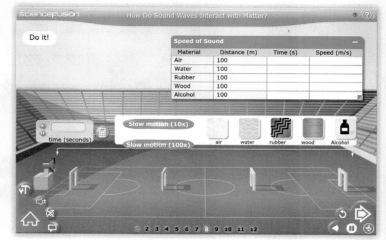

Virtual Lab

About *Science Fusion*   **xi**

The parallel-to-print **Digital Curriculum** provides

e-learning digital lessons and virtual labs

for every print lesson of the program.

360° of Inquiry

Digital Lessons and Virtual Labs

Digital Lessons and Virtual Labs provide an e-Learning environment of interactivity, videos, simulations, animations, and assessment designed for the way digital natives learn. An online Student Edition provides students anytime access to their student book.

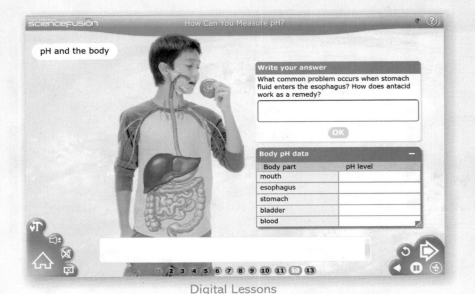

Digital Lessons

Online Student Edition

Video-Based Projects

Virtual Labs

Also available online:

- **NSTA** *SciLinks*
- **Digital Lesson Progress Sheets**
- **Video-Based Projects**
- **Virtual Lab Datasheets**
- **People in Science Gallery**
- **Media Gallery**
- **Extra Support for Vocabulary and Concepts**

Assessment

All paths lead to a full suite of print and online
Assessment Options right at your fingertips.

Classroom Management Integrated Assessment Options

The *ScienceFusion* assessment options give you maximum flexibility in assessing what your students know and what they can do. Both the print and digital paths include formative and summative assessment. See the **Assessment Guide** for a comprehensive overview of your assessment options.

Teacher Online Management Center

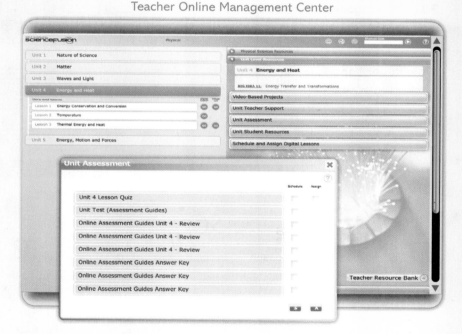

Print Assessment

The print **Assessment Guide** includes

- **Lesson Quizzes**
- **Unit Tests**
- **Unit Performance Assessments**

Online Assessment

The **Digital Assessment** includes

- **assignable leveled assessments for individuals**
- **customizable lesson quizzes and unit tests**
- **individual and whole class reporting**

Customizing Assessment for Your Classroom

Editable quizzes and tests are available in ExamView and online at ⊙ **thinkcentral.com.** You can customize a quiz or test by adding or deleting items, revising difficulty levels, changing formats, revising sequence, and editing items. Students can also take quizzes and tests directly online.

Choose Your Options

with two powerful teaching tools— a comprehensive **Teacher Edition** and the **Teacher Online Management Center.**

Classroom Management   Teacher Edition

Lesson level teaching support, includes activities, probing questions, misconception alerts, differentiated instruction, and interpreting visuals.

- Lessons organized around a 5E lesson format

- Comprehensive support—print, digital, or hands-on—to match all teaching styles.

- Extension strategies for every lesson give teacher more tools to review and reinforce.

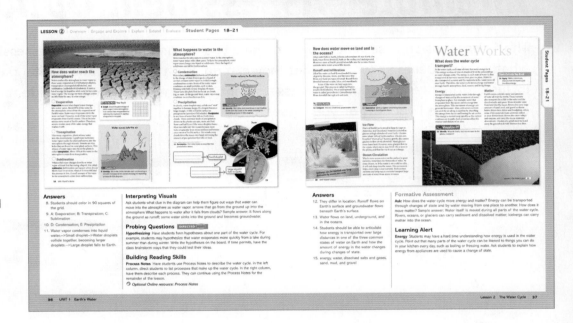

☑

- Easy access to NSTA's e-professional development center, *The Learning Center*

- SciLinks provide students and teachers content-specific online support.

☑

Additional support for STEM activities focuses on 21st century skills and helping students master the multi-dimensional abilities required of them in the 21st century.

☑ **RTI Response to Intervention**

Response to Intervention is a process for identifying and supporting students who are not making expected progress toward essential learning goals.

☑ **Probing Questions**

Lesson level questions and suggestions provide teachers with options for getting students to think more deeply and critically about a science concept.

☑ **Professional Development**

Unit and lesson level professional development focuses on supporting teachers and building educator capacity in key areas of academic achievement.

☑ **Learning Alert** **MISCONCEPTION**

The Learning Alert section previews Inquiry Activities and Lessons to gather and manage the materials needed for each lesson.

Classroom Management
Online teaching and planning

ScienceFusion is a comprehensive, multimodal science program that provides all the digital tools teachers need to engage students in inquiry-based learning. *The Teacher Online Management Center,* at ⊙ thinkcentral.com, is designed to make it easier for teachers to access program resources to plan, teach, assess, and track.

▶ Program resources can be easily previewed in PDF format and downloaded for editing.

▶ Assign and schedule resources online, and they will appear in your students' inboxes.

▶ All quizzes and tests can be taken and automatically scored online.

▶ Easily monitor and track student progress.

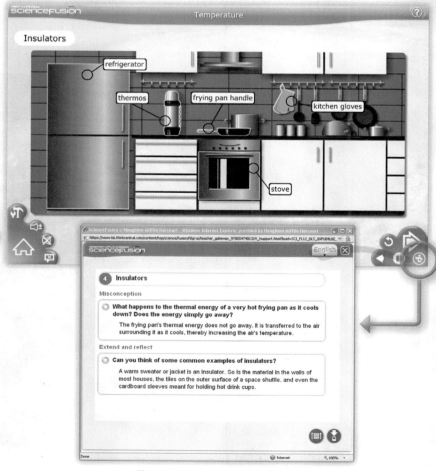

Teacher Resource Questions

Teaching with Technology Made Easy

ScienceFusion's 3,000+ animations, simulations, videos, & interactivities are organized to provide

▶ flexible options for delivering exciting and engaging digital lessons

▶ Teacher Resource Questions, for every lesson, to ensure that the important information is learned

▶ multimodal learning options that connect online learning to concepts learned from reading, writing, and hands-on inquiry

Student Edition Contents

Butterfly wings are covered in tiny, colorful scales, which protect the membranes of the wings.

If all dogs belong to the same species, why do all the breeds look so different from one another?

Assignments:

Program Scope and Sequence

ScienceFusion is organized by five major strands of science. Each strand includes Big Ideas that flow throughout all grade levels and build in rigor as students move to higher grades.

ScienceFusion Grade Levels and Units

	GRADE K	GRADE 1	GRADE 2	GRADE 3
Nature of Science	**Unit 1** Doing Science	**Unit 1** How Scientists Work	**Unit 1** Work Like a Scientist	**Unit 1** Investigating Questions
STEM		**Unit 2** Technology All Around Us	**Unit 2** Technology and Our World	**Unit 2** The Engineering Process
Life Science	**Unit 2** Animals **Unit 3** Plants **Unit 4** Habitats	**Unit 3** Animals **Unit 4** Plants **Unit 5** Environments	**Unit 3** All About Animals **Unit 4** All About Plants **Unit 5** Environments for Living Things	**Unit 3** Plants and Animals **Unit 4** Ecosystems and Interactions

GRADE 4	GRADE 5	GRADES 6-8
Unit 1 Studying Science	**Unit 1** How Scientists Work	**Module K** Introduction to Science and Technology **Unit 1** The Nature of Science **Unit 2** Measurement and Data
Unit 2 The Engineering Process	**Unit 2** The Engineering Process	**Module K** Introduction to Science and Technology **Unit 3** Engineering, Technology, and Society
Unit 3 Plants and Animals **Unit 4** Energy and Ecosystems	**Unit 3** Cells to Body Systems **Unit 4** Living Things Grow and Reproduce **Unit 5** Ecosystems **Unit 6** Energy and Ecosystems	**Module A** Cells and Heredity **Unit 1** Cells **Unit 2** Reproduction and Heredity **Module B** The Diversity of Living Things **Unit 1** Life over Time **Unit 2** Earth's Organisms **Module C** The Human Body **Unit 1** Human Body Systems **Unit 2** Human Health **Module D** Ecology and the Environment **Unit 1** Interactions of Living Things **Unit 2** Earth's Biomes and Ecosystems **Unit 3** Earth's Resources **Unit 4** Human Impact on the Environment

ScienceFusion Grade Levels and Units

	GRADE K	GRADE 1	GRADE 2	GRADE 3
Earth Science	**Unit 5** Day and Night **Unit 6** Earth's Resources **Unit 7** Weather and the Seasons	**Unit 6** Earth's Resources **Unit 7** Weather and Seasons **Unit 8** Objects in the Sky	**Unit 6** Earth and Its Resources **Unit 7** All About Weather **Unit 8** The Solar System	**Unit 5** Changes to Earth's Surface **Unit 6** People and Resources **Unit 7** Water and Weather **Unit 8** Earth and Its Moon
Physical Science	**Unit 8** Matter **Unit 9** Energy **Unit 10** Motion	**Unit 9** All About Matter **Unit 10** Forces and Energy	**Unit 9** Changes in Matter **Unit 10** Energy and Magnets	**Unit 9** Matter **Unit 10** Simple and Compound Machines

GRADE 4	GRADE 5	GRADES 6-8
Unit 5 Weather	**Unit 7** Natural Resources	**Module E** The Dynamic Earth
Unit 6 Earth and Space	**Unit 8** Changes to Earth's Surface	**Unit 1** Earth's Surface
	Unit 9 The Rock Cycle	**Unit 2** Earth's History
	Unit 10 Fossils	**Unit 3** Minerals and Rocks
	Unit 11 Earth's Oceans	**Unit 4** The Restless Earth
	Unit 12 The Solar System and the Universe	**Module F** Earth's Water and Atmosphere
		Unit 1 Earth's Water
		Unit 2 Oceanography
		Unit 3 Earth's Atmosphere
		Unit 4 Weather and Climate
		Module G Space Science
		Unit 1 The Universe
		Unit 2 The Solar System
		Unit 3 The Earth-Moon-Sun System
		Unit 4 Exploring Space
Unit 7 Properties of Matter	**Unit 13** Matter	**Module H** Matter and Energy
Unit 8 Changes in Matter	**Unit 14** Light and Sound	**Unit 1** Matter
Unit 9 Energy	**Unit 15** Forces and Motion	**Unit 2** Energy
Unit 10 Electricity		**Unit 3** Atoms and the Periodic Table
Unit 11 Motion		**Unit 4** Interactions of Matter
		Unit 5 Solutions, Acids, and Bases
		Module I Motion, Forces, and Energy
		Unit 1 Motion and Forces
		Unit 2 Work, Energy, and Machines
		Unit 3 Electricity and Magnetism
		Module J Sound and Light
		Unit 1 Introduction to Waves
		Unit 2 Sound
		Unit 3 Light

ScienceFusion

Video-Based Projects

Available in Online Resources

This video series, hosted by program authors Michael Heithaus and Michael DiSpezio, develops science learning through real-world science and engineering challenges.

Ecology

Leave your lab coat at home! Not all science research takes place in a lab. Host Michael Heithaus takes you around the globe to see ecology field research, including tagging sharks and tracking sea turtles. Students research, graph, and analyze results to complete the project worksheets.

S.T.E.M. Science, Technology, Engineering, and Math

Host Michael DiSpezio poses a series of design problems that challenge students' ingenuity. Each video follows the engineering process. Worksheets guide students through the process and help them document their results.

Module	Video Title
A	Photosynthesis
B	Expedition Evolution Animal Behavior
D	A Trip Down Shark River The Producers of Florida Bay
E	Transforming Earth
I	Animals in Motion
J	Animals and Sound
K	Invaders in the Everglades Data from Space

Module	Video Title
A	An Inside View**
C	Prosthetics Robotic Assist**
D	Got Water?
E	Seismic Monitoring
F	When the Wind Blows Tornado Warning
G	Soft Landing
H	Just Add Heat
I	Take the Long Way

** In partnership with Children's Hospital Of Boston

Enduring Understandings
Big Ideas, Essential Questions

It goes without saying that a primary goal for your students is to develop understandings of science concepts that endure well past the next test. The question is, what is the best way to achieve that goal?

by Marjorie Frank

Research and learning experts suggest that students learn most effectively through a constructivist approach in which they build concepts through active involvement in their own learning. While constructivism may lead to superior learning on a lesson-by-lesson basis, the approach does not address how to organize lessons into a program of instruction. Schema theory, from cognitive science, suggests that knowledge is organized into units and that information is stored in these units, much as files are stored in a digital or paper folder. Informed by our understanding of schema theory, we set about organizing *ScienceFusion*. We began by identifying the Big Ideas of science.

Big Ideas are generalizations—broad, powerful concepts that connect facts and events that may otherwise seem unrelated. Big Ideas are implicit understandings that help the world make sense. Big Ideas define the "folders," or units, of *ScienceFusion*. Each is a statement that articulates the overarching teaching and learning goals of a unit.

Essential Questions define the "files," or information, in a unit. Each Essential Question identifies the conceptual focus of a lesson that contributes to your students' growing understanding of the associated Big Idea. As such, Essential Questions give your students a sense of direction and purpose.

With *ScienceFusion*, our goal is to provide you with a tool that helps you help your students develop Enduring Understandings in science. Our strategy for achieving that goal has been to provide lesson plans with 5E-based learning experiences organized in a framework informed by schema theory.

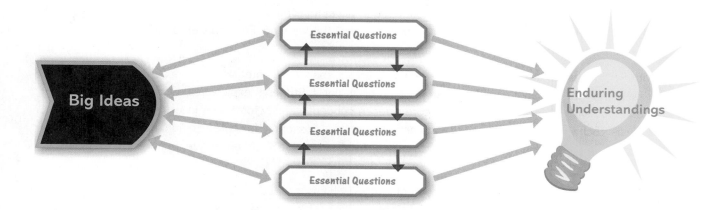

21st Century Skills/STEM

Skills Redefined

Our world has changed. Globalization and the digital revolution have redefined the skill set that is essential for student success in the classroom and beyond. Known collectively as 21st Century Skills, these areas of competence and aptitude go beyond the three Rs of reading, writing, and arithmetic. 21st Century Skills incorporate a battery of high-level thinking skills and technological capabilities.

by Michael A. DiSpezio

21st Century SKILLS A Sample List

Learning and Innovation Skills

- Creativity and Innovation
- Critical Thinking and Problem Solving
- Communication and Collaboration

Information, Media, and Technology Skills

- Information Literacy
- Media Literacy
- ICT (Information, Communications, and Technology) Literacy

Life and Career Skills

- Flexibility and Adaptability
- Initiative and Self-Direction
- Productivity and Accountability
- Leadership and Responsibility

S.T.E.M.

Curriculum that integrates Science, Technology, Engineering, and Mathematics

21st Century Skills are best taught in the context of the core subject areas. Science makes an ideal subject for integrating these important skills because it involves many skills, including inquiry, collaboration, and problem solving. An even deeper level of incorporating these skills can be found with Science, Technology, Engineering, and Mathematics (STEM) lessons and activities. Hands-on STEM lessons that provide students with engineering design challenges are ideal for developing Learning and Innovation Skills. Students develop creativity and innovation as they engineer novel solutions to posed problems. They communicate and collaborate as they engage higher-level thinking skills to help shape their inquiry experience. Students assume ownership of the learning. From this emerges increased self-motivation and personal accountability.

With STEM lessons and activities, related disciplines are seamlessly integrated into a rich experience that becomes far more than the sum of its parts. Students explore real-world scenarios using their understanding of core science concepts, ability for higher level analysis, technological know-how, and communication skills essential for collaboration. From this experience, the learner constructs not only a response to the STEM challenge, but the elements of 21st Century Skills.

ScienceFusion provides deep science content and STEM lessons, activities, and Video-Based Projects that incorporate and develop 21st Century Skills. This provides an effective learning landscape that will prepare students for success in the workplace—and in life.

Differentiated Instruction

Reaching All Learners

Your students learn in different ways, at different speeds, and through different means. Channeling the energy and richness of that diversity is part of the beauty of teaching. A classroom atmosphere that encourages academic risk-taking encourages learning. This is especially true in science, where learning involves making predictions (which could turn out to be inaccurate), offering explanations (which could turn out to be incomplete), and doing things (which could result in observable mistakes).

Like most people, students are more likely to take risks in a low-stress environment. Science, with its emphasis on exploring through hands-on activities and interactive reading, provides a natural vehicle for low-stress learning. Low stress, however, may mean different things to different people. For students with learning challenges, low stress may mean being encouraged to respond at the level they are able. Another factor in meeting the needs of diverse students is the instructional tools. Are they flexible? Inviting? *ScienceFusion* addresses the needs of diverse students at every step in the instructional process.

by Marjorie Frank

As You Plan

Select from these resources to meet individual needs.

- For each unit, the Differentiated Instruction page in the Teacher Edition identifies program resources specifically geared to diverse learners.

- Leveled activities in the Lesson Planning pages of the Teacher Edition provide additional learning opportunities for students with beginning, intermediate, or advanced proficiency.

- A bibliography contains notable trade books with in-depth information on content. Many of the books are recommendations of the National Science Teachers Association and the Children's Book Council.

- Online Resources: Alternative Assessment worksheets for each lesson provide varied strategies for learning content.

- Online Resources: Digital lessons, virtual labs, and video-based projects appeal to all students, especially struggling readers and visual learners.

- Student Edition with Audio is online as PDF files with audio readings for use with students who have vision impairments or learning difficulties.

- Student Edition reading strategies focus on vocabulary, concept development, and inquiry skills.

As You Teach

Take advantage of these point-of-use features.

- A mix of Directed Inquiry and Independent Inquiry prompts suitable for different kinds of learners

- Short-cut codes to specific interactive digital lessons

Take It Home

As you reach out to families, look for these school-home connections.

- Take It Home activities found at the beginning of many units in the Student Edition

- Additional Take It Home worksheets are available in the Online Resources

- School-Home Connection Letters for every unit, available online as files you can download and print as-is or customize

The 5E Model and Levels of Inquiry

How do students best learn science? Extensive research and data show that the most effective learning emerges from situations in which one builds understanding based upon personal experiences. Learning is not transmitted from instructor to passive receiver; instead, understanding is constructed through the experience.

by Michael A. DiSpezio

The 5E Model for Effective Science Lessons

In the 1960s, Robert Karplus and his colleagues developed a three-step instructional model that became known as the Learning Cycle. This model was expanded into what is today referred to as the 5E Model. To emulate the elements of how an actual scientist works, this model is broken down into five components for an effective lesson: Engage, Explore, Explain, Extend (or Elaborate), and Evaluate.

Engage—The engagement sets the scene for learning. It is a warm-up during which students are introduced to the learning experience. Prior knowledge is assessed and its analysis used to develop an effective plan to meet stated objectives. Typically, an essential question is then posed; the question leads the now motivated and engaged students into the exploration.

Explore—This is the stage where the students become actively involved in hands-on process. They communicate and collaborate to develop a strategy that addresses the posed problem. Emphasis is placed on inquiry and hands-on investigation. The hands-on experience may be highly prescribed or open-ended in nature.

Explain—Students answer the initial question by using their findings and information they may be reading about, discussing with classmates, or experiencing through digital media. Their experience and understanding of concepts, processes, and hands-on skills is strengthened at this point. New vocabulary may be introduced.

Extend (or Elaborate)—The explanation is now extended to other situations, questions, or problems. During this stage the learner more closely examines findings in terms of context and transferable application. In short, extension reveals the application and implication of the internalized explanation. Extension may involve connections to other curriculum areas.

Evaluate—Although evaluation is an ongoing process, this is the stage in which a final assessment is most often performed. The instructor evaluates lesson effectiveness by using a variety of formal and informal assessment tools to measure student performance.

The 5E lesson format is used in all the *ScienceFusion* Teacher Edition lessons.

Levels of Inquiry

It wasn't that long ago that science was taught mostly through demonstration and lecture. Today, however, most instructional strategies integrate an inquiry-based approach to learning science. This methodology is founded in higher-level thinking and facilitates the students' construction of understanding from experience. When offered opportunities to ask questions, design investigations, collect and analyze data, and communicate their findings, each student assumes the role of an active participant in shaping his or her own learning process.

The degree to which any activity engages the inquiry process is variable, from highly prescribed steps to a completely learner-generated design. Researchers have established three distinct levels of inquiry: directed (or structured) inquiry, guided inquiry, and independent (or open) inquiry. These levels are distinguished by the amount of guidance offered by the instructor.

DIRECTED inquiry

In this level of inquiry, the instructor poses a question or suggests an investigation, and students follow a prescribed set of instructions. The outcome may be unknown to the students, but it is known to the instructor. Students follow the structured outline to uncover an outcome that supports the construction of lesson concepts.

GUIDED inquiry

As in Directed Inquiry, the instructor poses to the students a question to investigate. While students are conducting the investigation, the instruction focuses on developing one or more inquiry skills. Focus may also be provided for students to learn to use methods or tools of science. In *ScienceFusion*, the Teacher Edition provides scaffolding for developing inquiry skills, science methods, or tools. Student pages accompany these lessons and provide prompts for writing hypotheses, recording data, and drawing conclusions.

INDEPENDENT inquiry

This is the most complex level of inquiry experience. A prompt is provided, but students must design their own investigation in response to the prompt. In some cases, students will write their own questions and then plan and perform scientific investigations that will answer those questions. This level of inquiry is often used for science fair projects. Independent Inquiry does not necessarily mean individual inquiry. Investigations can be conducted by individual students or by pairs or teams of students.

Response to Intervention

In a traditional model, assessment marks the end of an instructional cycle. Students work through a unit, take a test, and move on, regardless of their performance. However, current research suggests that assessment should be part of the instructional cycle, that it should be ongoing, and that it should be used to identify students needing intervention. This may sound like a tall order—who wants to give tests all the time?—but it may not be as difficult as it seems. In some ways, you are probably doing it already.

by Marjorie Frank

Assessment

Every student interaction has the potential to be an assessment. It all depends on how you perceive and use the interaction.

- Suppose you ask a question. You can just listen to your student's response, or you can assess it. Does the response indicate comprehension of the concept? If not, intervention may be needed.

- Suppose a student offers an explanation of a phenomenon depicted in a photo. You can assess the explanation. Does it show accurate factual knowledge? Does it reveal a misconception? If so, intervention may be needed.

- Suppose a student draws a diagram to illustrate a concept. You can assess the diagram. Is it accurate? If not, intervention may be needed.

As the examples indicate, assessing students' understandings can—and should—be an integral part of the instructional cycle and be used to make decisions about the next steps of instruction. For students making good progress, next steps might be exploring a related concept, a new lesson, or an additional challenge. For students who are not making adequate progress, intervention may be needed.

Assessment and intervention are tightly linked. Assessment leads to intervention—fresh approaches, different groupings, new materials—which, in turn, leads to assessment. Response to Intervention (RTI) gives shape and substance to this linkage.

RTI▶ Response to Intervention

Response to Intervention is a process for identifying and supporting students who are not making expected progress toward essential learning goals.

RTI is a three-tiered approach based on an ongoing cycle of superior instruction, frequent monitoring of students' learning (assessments), and appropriate interventions. Students who are found not to be making expected progress in one Tier move to the next higher Tier, where they receive more intense instruction.

- **Tier I:** Students receive whole-class, core instruction.
- **Tier II:** Students work in small groups that supplement and reinforce core instruction.
- **Tier III:** Students receive individualized instruction.

How RTI and *ScienceFusion* Work

ScienceFusion provides many opportunities to assess students' understanding and many components appropriate for students in all Tiers.

TIER III Intensive Intervention

Individualized instruction, with options for auditory, visual, and second language learners. Special education is a possibility.

Differentiated Instruction Strategies

🌐 **Online Student Edition**

ScienceFusion Components

🌐 **Online Student Edition lessons with audio recordings**

Differentiated Instruction strategies in the Teacher Edition for every lesson

Appropriate for:
- Auditory learners

Appropriate for:
- Struggling readers
- Second-language learners

Students achieving at a lower level than their peers in Tier II

TIER II Strategic Intervention

Small Group Instruction in addition to core instruction

Alternative Assessment Worksheets

Leveled TE Activities

ScienceFusion Components

Leveled activities in the Lesson Planning pages of the Teacher Edition

🌐 **Alternative Assessment Worksheets**

Appropriate for:
- Struggling readers
- Visual learners
- Second-language learners
- Screening tools to assess students' responses to Tier II instruction

Students achieving at a lower level than their peers in Tier I

TIER I Core Classroom Instruction

With the help of extensive point-of-use strategies that support superior teaching, students receive whole-class instruction and engage productively in small-group work as appropriate.

Teacher Edition

Student Edition

Assessment Guide

ScienceFusion Components

Student Edition

Differentiated Instruction strategies in the TE for every lesson

Teacher Edition

Assessment Guide

🌐 **Online Digital Curriculum**

Appropriate for:
- Screening tools to assess students' responses to Tier I instruction
- Tier I intervention for students unable to complete the activity independently

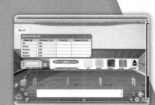

Digital Curriculum

Active Reading

Reading is a complex process in which readers use their knowledge and experience to make meaning from text. Though rarely accompanied by obvious large-muscle movement, reading is very much an active endeavor.

by Marjorie Frank

Think back to your days as a college student when you pored over your textbooks to prepare for class or for an exam—or, more recently, concentrated on an article or book with information you wanted to remember.

▶ You probably paid close attention to the text.

▶ Perhaps you paused to ask yourself questions.

▶ You might have broken off temporarily to look up an important, but unfamiliar, word.

▶ You may have stopped to reread a challenging passage or to "catch up" if your mind wandered for a moment.

If you owned the reading material, you also may have used a pencil or marker to interact with the text right there on the page (or in a digital file).

In short, you were having a conversation with yourself about the text. You were engaged. You were thinking critically.

These are the characteristics of active readers. This is precisely the kind of reader you want your students to be, because research suggests that active reading enables readers to understand and remember more information.

Active Reading involves interacting with text cognitively, metacognitively, and quite literally. You can actually see active readers at work. They are not sitting quietly as they read; they're underlining, marking, boxing, bracketing, drawing arrows, numbering, and writing comments. Here is what they may be noting:

▶ key terms and main ideas

▶ connections between ideas

▶ questions they have, opinions, agreements, and disagreements

▶ important facts and details

▶ sequences of events

▶ words, such as *because, before,* and *but,* that signal connections between ideas

▶ problems/solutions

▶ definitions and examples

▶ characteristics

The very process of interacting actively with text helps keep readers focused, thinking, comprehending, and remembering. But interacting in this way means readers are marking up the text. This is exactly why *ScienceFusion* Student Editions are consumable. They are meant to be marked up.

Active Reading and *ScienceFusion*

ScienceFusion includes Active Reading prompts throughout the Student Editions. The prompts appear as part of the lesson opener and on most two-page spreads.

Students are often given an Active Reading prompt before reading a section or paragraph. These prompts ask students to underline certain words or number the steps in a process. Marking the text in this way is called *annotating*, and the students' marks are called *annotations*. Annotating the text can help students identify important concepts while reading. Other ways of annotating the text include placing an asterisk by vocabulary terms, marking unfamiliar or confusing terms and information with a question mark, and underlining main ideas. Students can even invent their own systems for annotating the text. An example of an annotation prompt is shown at right.

> **Active Reading** 5 **Identify** As you read, underline sources of energy for living things.

In addition, there are Active Reading questions throughout each lesson. These questions have write-on lines accompanying them, so students can answer right on the page. Students will be asked to **describe** what they've just read about, **apply** concepts, **compare** concepts, **summarize** processes, and **identify cause-and-effect** relationships. By answering these Active Reading questions while reading the text, students will be strengthening those and other critical thinking skills that are used so often in science.

> **Active Reading** 16 **Compare** What is the difference between the pulmonary and systemic circulations?

Students' Responses to Active Reading Prompts

Active Reading has benefits for you as well as for your students. You can use students' responses to Active Reading prompts and the other interactive prompts in *ScienceFusion* as ongoing assessments. A quick review of students' responses provides a great deal of information about their learning.

- ▶ Are students comprehending the text?
- ▶ How deeply do they understand the concepts developed?
- ▶ Did they get the main idea? the cause? the order in which things happen?
- ▶ Which part of a lesson needs more attention? for whom?

Answers to these questions are available in students' responses to Active Learning prompts throughout a lesson—long before you might see poor results on an end-of-lesson or end-of-unit assessment. If you are following Response to Intervention (RTI) protocols, these frequent and regular assessments, no matter how informal, are integral parts of an effective intervention program.

The Active Reading prompts in *ScienceFusion* help make everyone a winner.

Project-Based Learning

For a list of the *ScienceFusion* Video-Based Projects, see page xxii.

by
Michael R. Heithaus

When asked why I decided to become a biologist, the answer is pretty simple. I was inspired by spending almost every day outdoors, exploring under every rock, getting muddy in creeks and streams, and fishing in farm ponds, rivers, and—when I was really lucky—the oceans. Combine that with the spectacular stories of amazing animals and adventure that I saw on TV and I was hooked. As I've progressed in my career as a biologist, that same excitement and curiosity that I had as a ten-year-old looking for a salamander is still driving me.

But today's kids live in a very different world. Cable and satellite TV, Twitter, MP3 players, cell phones, and video games all compete with the outdoors for kids' time and attention. Education budget cuts, legal issues, and the pressures of standardized testing have also limited the opportunities for students to explore outdoors with their teachers.

How do we overcome these challenges so as to inspire kids' curiosity, help them connect with the natural world, and get them to engage in science and math? This is a critical issue. Not only do we need to ensure our national competitiveness and the conservation of our natural resources by training the next generation of scientists, we also need to ensure that every kid grows up to understand how scientists work and why their work is important.

To overcome these challenges, there is no question that we need to grab students' attention and get them to actively engage in the learning process. Research shows that students who are active and engaged participants in their learning have greater gains in concept and skills development than students who are passive in the classroom.

Project-based learning is one way to engage students. And when the stimulus for the project is exciting video content, engaged and active learning is almost guaranteed. Nothing captures a student's attention faster than exciting video. I have noticed that when my university students have video to accompany a lesson, they learn and retain the material better. It's no different for younger students! Videos need to do more than just "talk at" students to have a real impact. Videos need to engage students and require participation.

Teachers and students who use *ScienceFusion* video-based projects have noticed the following:

- The videos use captivating imagery, dynamic scientists, and cool stories to inspire kids to be curious about the world around them.
- Students connect to the projects by having the videos present interesting problems for them to solve.
- The videos engage students with projects woven into the story of the video so students are doing the work of real scientists!

The start-to-finish nature of the video projects, where students do background research and develop their own hypotheses, should lead to students' personal investment in solving the challenges that are presented. By seeing real scientists who are excellent role models gather data that they have to graph and interpret, students will not only learn the science standards being addressed, they will see that they can apply the scientific method to their lives. One day, they too could be a scientist!

Based on my experiences teaching in the university classroom, leading field trips for middle school students, and taking the first project-based videos into the classroom, project-based learning has considerable benefits. The video-based projects generate enthusiasm and curiosity. They also help students develop a deeper understanding of science content as well as how to go about a scientific investigation. If we inspire students to ask questions and seek answers for themselves, we will go a long way toward closing achievement gaps in science and math and facilitate the development of the next generation of scientists and scientifically literate citizens.

Developing Visual Literacy

Science teachers can build the bridges between students' general literacy and their scientific literacy by focusing attention on the particular kinds of reading strategies students need to be successful. One such strategy is that of knowing how to read and interpret the various visual displays used in science.

by Donna M. Ogle

Many young readers receive little instruction in reading charts, tables, diagrams, photographs, or illustrations in their language arts/reading classes. Science is where these skills can and must be developed. Science provides a meaningful context where students can learn to read visually presented forms of information and to create their own visual representations. Research studies have shown that students take longer to read science materials containing combinations of visual displays and narrative texts than they do to read narrative text alone. The process of reading the combination materials is slower and more difficult because the reader must relate the visual displays to the narrative text and build a meaning that is based on information from both.

We also know that students benefit when teachers take time to explain how each visual form is constructed and to guide students in the thinking needed to make sense of these forms. Even the seemingly simple act of interpreting a photograph needs to be taught to most students. Here are some ways to help students develop the ability to think more critically about what they view:

▶ Model for students how to look carefully at a photograph and list what they notice.

▶ Divide the photograph into quadrants and have students think more deeply about what the photographer has used as the focus of the image and what context is provided.

▶ Have students use language such as *zoom, close-up, foreground, background,* or *panorama views* to describe photographs.

The ability to interpret a photograph is clearly a part of the scientific skill of engaging in careful observation. This skill helps students when they are using print materials, observing nature, and making their own photographs of aspects of their experiments.

Attention to the other forms of visual displays frequently used in science is also important to students' learning of scientific concepts and processes. For example, students in grades 4 through 8 need to learn to interpret and then construct each of the types of graphs, from circle graphs and bar graphs to more complex line graphs.

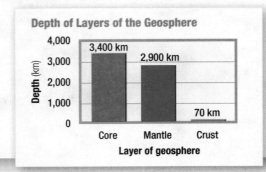

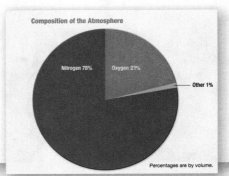

Students also need to be able to read diagrams and flow charts. Yet, in a recent study asking students to think aloud and point to how they visually scan tables and diagrams, we learned how inadequate many students were as readers of these visual forms. Because so much of the scientific information students will encounter is summarized in these visual formats, it is essential that students learn to interpret and construct visual displays.

A second aspect of interpreting visual displays is connecting the information in the visual formats with the narrative text information. Some students misinterpret what they see in visuals when even a few words differ between the text and the illustration. For example, in the excerpt below from a middle school Student Edition, the text says, "the arm of a human, the front leg of a cat, and the wing of a bat do not look alike . . . but they are similar in structure. "

The diagram labels (lower right) showing the bat wing and the cat's leg use *front limb*, not *wing* or *leg*. For students who struggle with English, the differing terms may cause confusion unless teachers show students how to use clues from later in the paragraph, where limb and wing/arm are connected, and how to connect this information to the two drawings. In some cases teachers have students draw lines showing where visual displays connect with the more extensive narrative text content. Developing students' awareness of how visual and narrative information support each other and yet provide different forms in which information can be shared is an important step in building scientific literacy.

Reading science requires students to use specific reading strategies. The more carefully science teachers across grade levels assess what students already know about reading scientific materials, the more easily they can focus instruction to build the scaffolds students need to gain independence and confidence in their reading and learning of science. Time spent explaining, modeling, and guiding students will yield the rewards of heightened student enjoyment, confidence, and engagement in the exciting world of scientific inquiry.

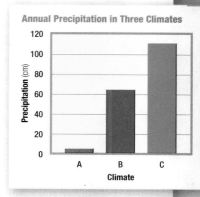

Annual Precipitation in Three Climates

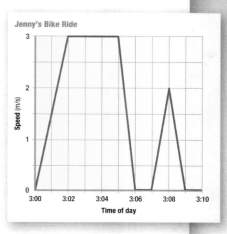

Jenny's Bike Ride

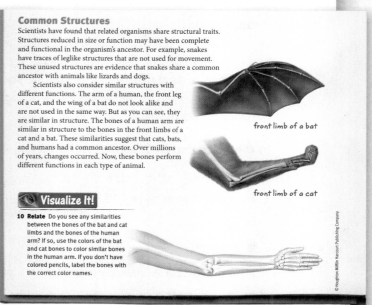

Common Structures

Scientists have found that related organisms share structural traits. Structures reduced in size or function may have been complete and functional in the organism's ancestor. For example, snakes have traces of leglike structures that are not used for movement. These unused structures are evidence that snakes share a common ancestor with animals like lizards and dogs.

Scientists also consider similar structures with different functions. The arm of a human, the front leg of a cat, and the wing of a bat do not look alike and are not used in the same way. But as you can see, they are similar in structure. The bones of a human arm are similar in structure to the bones in the front limbs of a cat and a bat. These similarities suggest that cats, bats, and humans had a common ancestor. Over millions of years, changes occurred. Now, these bones perform different functions in each type of animal.

front limb of a bat

front limb of a cat

Visualize It!

10 Relate Do you see any similarities between the bones of the bat and cat limbs and the bones of the human arm? If so, use the colors of the bat and cat bones to color similar bones in the human arm. If you don't have colored pencils, label the bones with the correct color names.

Science Notebooking

Science Notebooks are powerful classroom tools. They lead your students deep into the learning process, and they provide you with a window into that process as well as a means to communicate about it. Most middle-school students will have had some experience using a Science Notebook during their elementary years.

Notebook ▶ Why Use a Science Notebook?

A Science Notebook contains the writer's ideas, observations, and perceptions of events and endeavors. A Science Notebook also contains ideas and observations of scientific processes, data, conclusions, conjectures, and generalizations.

Inquiry Skills A Science Notebook is especially important when students do inquiry-based activities. It offers students a single place to record their observations, consider possibilities, and organize their thoughts. As such, it is a learner's version of the logs that professional scientists keep.

In their Science Notebooks, students can

▶ sketch their ideas and observations from experiments and field trips

▶ make predictions about what will happen in an experiment

▶ reflect on their work and the meaning they derived from experiments

▶ make inferences based on the data they have gathered

▶ propose additional experiments to test new hypotheses

▶ pose new questions based on the results of an activity or experiment

Process Skills A Science Notebook is an excellent extension of the textbook, allowing students to further practice and hone process skills. Students will not only apply these skills in relation to the specific science content they are learning, they will be gaining a deeper insight into scientific habits of mind.

In their Science Notebooks, students can

▶ record and analyze data

▶ create graphs and charts

▶ infer outcomes

▶ draw conclusions

▶ collect data from multiple experimental trials

▶ develop 21st Century organizational skills

A student's Science Notebook entry for a *ScienceFusion* Quick Lab ▼

Quick Lab: Balancing Act

Partner: Evan

Answers

2. Me: 12 adjustments
Evan: 10 adjustments

3. No, I was not aware of my muscles making adjustments the first time. I think I didn't notice because I was concentrating more on just staying on one leg.

4. Yes, I was aware of my muscles making adjustments the second time. I think my muscles worked harder the second time because my leg was getting tired.

5. 12 times

6. Your body is always having to make adjustments to maintain a balanced internal environment. Most of these adjustments aren't even noticed by a person, just like I didn't notice my leg muscles adjusting during the first balancing test.

Notebook ▸ Science Notebooks and *ScienceFusion*

In many ways, the *ScienceFusion* worktexts are Science Notebooks in themselves. Students are encouraged to write answers directly in the text and to annotate the text for better understanding. However, a separate Science Notebook can still be an invaluable part of your student's learning experience with *ScienceFusion*. Student uses for a Science Notebook along with the worktext include:

▶ writing answers for the Unit Review

▶ writing responses to the Think Outside the Book features in each lesson

▶ planning for and writing answers to the Citizen Science feature in each unit

▶ working through answers before writing them in the worktext

▶ writing all answers if you choose not to have students work directly in the worktext

▶ taking notes on additional materials you present outside of the worktext

▶ making observations and recording data from Daily Demos and additional activities provided in the Teacher Edition

▶ collecting data and writing notes for labs performed from the Lab Manual

▶ making notes and writing answers for Digital Lessons and Virtual Labs

▶ collecting data and writing answers for the Project-Based Videos

Notebook ▸ The Benefits (for You and Your Students) of Science Notebooking

No doubt, it takes time and effort to help students set up and maintain Science Notebooks, not to mention the time it takes you to review them and provide meaningful feedback. The payoff is well worth it. Here's why:

Keeping a Science Notebook:

▶ leads each learner to engage with ideas

▶ engages students in writing—an active, thinking, analytical process

▶ causes students to organize their thinking

▶ provides students with multiple opportunities and modes to process new information

▶ makes learning experiences more personal

▶ provides students with a record of their own progress and accomplishments

▶ doubles as a study guide for formal assessments

▶ creates an additional vehicle for students to improve their reading and writing skills

As you and your students embrace Science Notebooking, you will surely find it to be an engaging, enriching, and very valuable endeavor.

Using the *ScienceFusion* Worktext

Research shows that an interactive text teaches students how to relate to content in a personal, meaningful way. They learn how to be attentive, energetic readers who reach a deep level of comprehension. Still, the worktext format may be new to you and your students. Below are some answers to questions—both pedagogical and practical—you may have about *ScienceFusion's* worktext format.

How does the worktext format help my students learn?

▶ In this format, your students will interact with the text and visuals on every page. This will teach them to read expertly, to think critically, and to communicate effectively—all skills that are crucial for success in the 21st century.

▶ The use of images and text on every page of the *ScienceFusion* worktext accommodates both visual and verbal learners. Students are engaged by the less formal, magazine-like presentation of the content.

▶ By the end of the school year, the worktexts become a record of the knowledge and skills your students learned in class. Students can use their books as a study guide to prepare for tests.

What are some features that make the *ScienceFusion* worktext different from a regular textbook?

Some of the special features of the *ScienceFusion* worktext include these prompts for writing directly in the worktext:

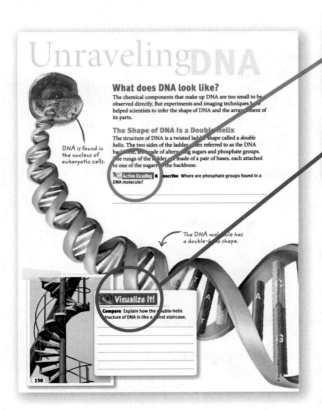

Active Reading
Annotation prompts and questions throughout the worktext teach students how to analyze and interact with content as they read.

Visualize It!
Questions and completion prompts that accompany images help develop visual literacy.

Engage Your Brain
Math problems, with on-page guidance, allow students to understand the relationships between math and science and to practice their math skills.

Do the Math
Interesting questions and activities on the lesson opener pages help prepare students for the lesson content.

Are my students really supposed to write directly in the book?

Yes! Write-on lines are provided for students to answer questions on-page, while the student is reading. Additional prompts are given for students to annotate the pages. You can even encourage your students to experiment with their own systems of annotation. More information can be found in "A How-To Manual for Active Reading" in the Look It Up! Section at the end of the Student Edition and Teacher Edition.

You might wish to encourage your students to write in the worktexts using pencils so that they can more easily revise their answers and notes as needed.

We will have to use the same set of worktexts for several years. How can students use the worktexts if they can't write in them?

Though *ScienceFusion* is set up in a worktext format, the books can still be used in a more traditional fashion. Simply tell your students that they cannot write in the textbooks but should instead use their Science Notebooks for taking notes and answering questions. (See the article titled "Science Notebooking" for more information about using Notebooks with *ScienceFusion*.)

How do I grade my students' answers in the worktext?

The pages in the worktext are conveniently perforated so that your students can turn in their work. Or you may wish for your students to leave the pages in the book, but turn in the books to you on a daily or weekly basis for you to grade them.

The Lesson Reviews and Unit Reviews are designed so students can turn in the pages but still keep their annotated pages for reference when moving on to the next lesson or unit or for review before a lesson or unit test.

- Tour the classroom while students are writing in their worktexts. Address any issues you see immediately or make note of items that need to be addressed with students later.

- Have students do 'self checks' and 'partner checks.' Choose a question in the worktext, and have all students check their responses. Or, have students trade their worktext with a partner to check each other's responses.

- Once a week, have students copy five questions and their responses from the worktext onto a sheet of notebook paper. You can review student answers to ensure they're using the worktext correctly without having students turn in worktext pages or the books themselves.

- Use a document camera to show students correct worktext answers.

- Every two weeks, review and grade one class's worth of student worktext answers per day. Or, grade a class's worktexts while the students are taking a test.

Pacing Guide

You have options for covering the lesson materials: you may choose to follow the digital path, the print path, or a combination of the two. Customize your Pacing Guide to plan print, inquiry, digital, and assessment mini-blocks based on your teaching style and classroom needs.

Pressed for Time? Follow the faster-paced compressed schedule.

| | Total Days | | | Customize Your Pacing Guide | | | |
	Traditional 1 = 45 min	Block 1 = 90 min	Compressed (T/B)	Print Path	Inquiry Labs & Activities	Digital Path	Review & Assess
UNIT 1 Cells							
Unit Project	3	1.5	3 (1.5)				
Lesson 1 The Characteristics of Cells	4	2	3 (1.5)				
Lesson 2 Chemistry of Life	4	2	3 (1.5)				
Lesson 3 Cell Structure and Function	5	2.5	4 (2)				
Lesson 4 Levels of Cellular Organization	5	2.5	4 (2)				
Lesson 5 Homeostasis and Cell Processes	5	2.5	4 (2)				
Lesson 6 Photosynthesis and Cellular Respiration	5	2.5	4 (2)				
Unit Review	2	2.5	1 (0.5)				
Total Days for Unit 1	33	18	26 (13)				
UNIT 2 Reproduction and Heredity							
Unit Project	3	1.5	3 (1.5)				
Lesson 1 Mitosis	4	2	3 (1.5)				
Lesson 2 Meiosis	4	2	3 (1.5)				
Lesson 3 Sexual and Asexual Reproduction	4	2	3 (1.5)				
Lesson 4 Heredity	5	2.5	4 (2)				
Lesson 5 Punnett Squares and Pedigrees	4	2	3 (1.5)				
Lesson 6 DNA Structure and Function	5	2.5	4 (2)				
Lesson 7 Biotechnology	4	2	3 (1.5)				
Unit Review	2	1	1 (0.5)				
Total Days for Unit 2	35	17.5	27 (13.5)				

The Big Idea and Essential Questions

This Unit was designed to focus on this Big Idea and Essential Questions.

Big Idea **All organisms are made up of one or more cells.**

Lesson	ESSENTIAL QUESTION	Student Mastery	PD Professional Development	Lesson Overview
LESSON 1 The Characteristics of Cells	What are living things made of?	To explain the components of the scientific theory of cells	Content Refresher, TE p. 8	TE p. 16
LESSON 2 Chemistry of Life	What are the building blocks of organisms?	To discuss the chemical makeup of living things	Content Refresher, TE p. 9	TE p. 30
LESSON 3 Cell Structure and Function	What are the different parts that make up a cell?	To compare the structure and function of cell parts in plant and animal cells	Content Refresher, TE p. 10	TE p. 44
LESSON 4 Levels of Cellular Organization	How are living things organized?	To describe the different levels of organization in living things	Content Refresher, TE p. 11	TE p. 60
LESSON 5 Homeostasis and Cell Processes	How do organisms maintain homeostasis?	To explain the important processes that organisms undergo to maintain stable internal conditions	Content Refresher, TE p. 12	TE p. 74
LESSON 6 Photosynthesis and Cellular Respiration	How do cells get and use energy?	To explain how cells capture and release energy	Content Refresher, TE p. 13	TE p. 92

©Quest/Photo Researchers, Inc.

 **Professional Development**   Science Background

Use the key words at right to access

- Professional Development from **The NSTA Learning Center**
- **SciLinks** for additional online content appropriate for students and teachers

Keywords
cells
cellular respiration
homeostasis
photosynthesis

National Science Teachers Association

SciLINKS®
THE WORLD'S A CLICK AWAY

Options for Instruction

Two parallel paths provide coverage of the Essential Questions, with a strong **Inquiry** strand woven into each. Follow the **Print Path,** the **Digital Path,** or your customized combination of print, digital, and inquiry.

	LESSON 1 The Characteristics of Cells	LESSON 2 Chemistry of Life	LESSON 3 Cell Structure and Function
Essential Questions	What are living things made of?	What are the building blocks of organisms?	What are the different parts that make up a cell?
Key Topics	• The Cell • The Cell Theory • Two Types of Cells	• Atoms and Molecules • Molecules for Life Processes	• Eukaryotic Cells • Parts of Eukaryotic Cells • Plant and Animal Cells
Print Path	Teacher Edition pp. 14–29 Student Edition pp. 4–13	Teacher Edition pp. 30–43 Student Edition pp. 14–23	Teacher Edition pp. 44–57 Student Edition pp. 24–35
Inquiry Labs	Lab Manual **Exploration Lab** Using a Microscope to Explore Cells **Quick Lab** How Do Tools that Magnify Help Us Study Cells? **Quick Lab** Investigating Cell Size	Lab Manual **Quick Lab** Analyzing Cell Components **Quick Lab** Molecules for Life Processes	Lab Manual **Quick Lab** Comparing Cells **Quick Lab** Making a 3-D Cell Model ■ Virtual Lab Analyzing Cells
Digital Path	Digital Path TS663070	Digital Path TS663000	Digital Path TS663160

LESSON 4	LESSON 5	LESSON 6 and
Levels of Cellular Organization	Homeostasis and Cell Processes	UNIT 1 Unit Projects
How are living things organized?	*How do organisms maintain homeostasis?*	*See the next page*
• Cells to Organisms • Cellular Structure and Function • Systems Work Together	• Homeostasis in Cells • Homeostasis in Organisms	

		Unit Assessment
Teacher Edition pp. 60–73 Student Edition pp. 38–49	Teacher Edition pp. 74–87 Student Edition pp. 50–61	*See the next page*

Lab Manual **Exploration Lab** The Organization of Organisms **Quick Lab** Eval. Specialization **Quick Lab** Observing Plant Organs	Lab Manual **Exploration Lab** Diffusion **Quick Lab** Homeostasis and Adaptations **Quick Lab** Investigate Microorganisms
Digital Path TS663014	Digital Path TS663120

Options for Instruction

Two parallel paths provide coverage of the Essential Questions, with a strong **Inquiry** strand woven into each. Follow the **Print Path,** the **Digital Path,** or your customized combination of print, digital, and inquiry.

	LESSON 6 Photosynthesis and Cellular Respiration	**UNIT 1** Unit Projects
Essential Questions	*How do cells get and use energy?*	**Citizen Science Project** Seeing through Microscopes Teacher Edition p. 15 Student Edition pp. 2–3
Key Topics	• Cells Need Energy • Photosynthesis • Cellular Respiration	Photosynthesis

Print Path

Teacher Edition
pp. 92–105

Student Edition
pp. 66–77

Inquiry Labs

Lab Manual
S.T.E.M. Lab Investigate Rate of Photosynthesis

Quick Lab Plant Cell Structures

 Virtual Lab Observing Photosynthesis

Digital Path

Digital Path
TS693070

Unit Assessment
Formative Assessment
Strategies `RTI`
Throughout TE
Lesson Reviews SE
Unit PreTest
Summative Assessment
Alternative Assessment
(1 per lesson) `RTI`
Lesson Quizzes
Unit Tests A and B
Unit Review `RTI`
Practice Tests
(end of module)
Project-Based Assessment
See the Assessment Guide for quizzes and tests.

Go Online to edit and create quizzes and tests.

Response to Intervention

See RTI teacher support materials on p. PD6.

Teacher Notes

Differentiated Instruction

English Language Proficiency

Strategies for **English Language Learners (ELL)** are provided for each lesson, under the Explain tabs.

LESSON 1 *Making Connections,* TE p. 21

LESSON 2 *Picture Glossary,* TE p. 35

LESSON 3 *Guess My Parts,* TE p. 49

LESSON 4 *All-Encompassing Terms,* TE p. 65

LESSON 5 *Modeling Molecular Structures,* TE p. 79

LESSON 6 *Native Processes,* TE p. 97

Vocabulary strategies provided for all students can also be a particular help for ELL. Use different strategies for each lesson or choose one or two to use throughout the unit. Vocabulary strategies can be found under the Explain tab for each lesson (TE pp. 21, 35, 49, 65, 79, and 97).

Leveled Inquiry

Inquiry labs, activities, probing questions, and daily demos provide a range of inquiry levels. Preview them under the Engage and Explore tabs starting on TE pp. 16, 30, 44, 60, 74, and 92.

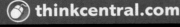

Levels of **Inquiry**	**DIRECTED** inquiry	**GUIDED** inquiry	**INDEPENDENT** inquiry
	introduces inquiry skills within a structured framework.	develops inquiry skills within a supportive environment.	deepens inquiry skills with student-driven questions or procedures.

Each long lab has two inquiry options:

LESSON 1 **Exploration Lab** *Using a Microscope to Explore Cells* Directed or Guided Inquiry

LESSON 4 **Exploration Lab** *The Organization of Organisms* Directed or Guided Inquiry

LESSON 5 **Exploration Lab** *Diffusion* Directed or Guided Inquiry

---

 Go Digital! 🌐 **thinkcentral.com**

Digital Path

The Unit 1 Resource Gateway is your guide to all of the digital resources for this unit. To access the Gateway, visit thinkcentral.com.

Digital Interactive Lessons

Lesson 1 The Characteristics of Cells TS663070

Lesson 2 Chemistry of Life TS663000

Lesson 3 Cell Structure and Function TS663160

Lesson 4 Levels of Cellular Organization TS663014

Lesson 5 Homeostasis and Cell Processes TS663120

Lesson 6 Photosynthesis and Cellular Respiration TS693070

More Digital Resources

In addition to digital lessons, you will find the following digital resources for Unit 1:

Video-Based Project: Photosynthesis (previewed on TE p. 15)

Virtual Labs: Analyzing Cells (previewed on TE p. 47)

Observing Photosynthesis (previewed on TE p. 95)

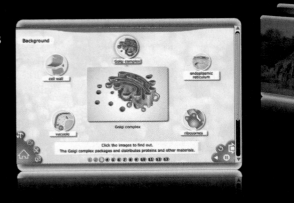

RTI ▶ Response to Intervention

Response to Intervention (RTI) is a process for identifying and supporting students who are not making expected progress toward essential learning goals. The following *ScienceFusion* components can be used to provide strategic and intensive intervention.

Component	Location	Strategies and Benefits
STUDENT EDITION Active Reading prompts, Visualize It!, Think Outside the Book	**Throughout each lesson**	Student responses can be used as screening tools to assess whether intervention is needed.
TEACHER EDITION Formative Assessment, Probing Questions, Learning Alerts	**Throughout each lesson**	Opportunities are provided to assess and remediate student understanding of lesson concepts.
TEACHER EDITION Extend Science Concepts	**Reinforce and Review, TE pp. 22, 36, 50, 66, 80, 98** **Going Further, TE pp. 22, 36, 50, 66, 80, 98**	Additional activities allow students to reinforce and extend their understanding of lesson concepts.
TEACHER EDITION Evaluate Student Mastery	**Formative Assessment, TE pp. 23, 37, 51, 67, 81, 99** **Alternative Assessment, TE pp. 23, 37, 51, 67, 81, 99**	These assessments allow for greater flexibility in assessing students with differing physical, mental, and language abilities as well as varying learning and communication modes.
TEACHER EDITION Unit Review Remediation	**Unit Review, TE pp. 106–109**	Includes reference back to Lesson Planning pages for remediation activities and assignments.
INTERACTIVE DIGITAL LESSONS and VIRTUAL LABS	**thinkcentral.com** **Unit 1 Gateway** **Lesson 1 TS663070** **Lesson 2 TS663000** **Lesson 3 TS663160** **Lesson 4 TS663014** **Lesson 5 TS663120** **Lesson 6 TS693070**	Lessons and labs make content accessible through simulations, animations, videos, audio, and integrated assessment. Useful for review and reteaching of lesson concepts.

Content Refresher

The Characteristics of Cells

ESSENTIAL QUESTION
What are living things made of?

1. The Cell

The Basic Unit of Life

Robert Hooke, an English scientist, used a microscope to observe slices of cork. In 1665, Hooke published a book of his observations. He pointed out that the woody parts of plants contained tiny rectangular chambers that he called cells. Hooke chose this name because the chambers reminded him of the tiny rooms in a monastery, which are also known as cells. Hooke believed that only plants were made of cells. This idea stood for almost 200 years!

Cell Size

Most cells are microscopic, because a cell must take in nutrients and remove wastes. Substances move into and out of a cell by passing through the cell membrane. This process limits the size to which a cell can grow, because cells need a large surface area-to-volume ratio.

2. The Cell Theory

The Development of the Cell Theory

During the 17th century, scientists were discovering the microscopic world. In 1838, Matthias Schleiden, a German scientist, used a microscope to study plant parts. He concluded that all plant parts are made up of cells. Just a year later, another German scientist, Theodor Schwann, found that some animal tissues closely resembled the cellular tissues of plants. As Schwann looked at animal tissues with better microscopes, he came to the conclusion that animals were also made up of cells. In the meantime, Robert Brown, a Scottish biologist, had discovered an object near the center of many cells, a structure now called the nucleus. Matthias Schleiden expanded on Brown's work and suggested that the cell's nucleus plays a part in reproduction. Rudolf Virchow further studied the cell and proposed that animal and plant cells are

produced only by the division of cells that already exist. The discoveries of these scientists are what make up the cell theory. This theory states that

- all organisms are made up of one or more cells;
- the cell is the basic unit of all organisms;
- all cells come from existing cells.

3. Two Types of Cells

Common Cell Structures

There are two basic types of cells: prokaryotes and eukaryotes. Nearly all cells have cell membranes, cytoplasm, organelles, and DNA. Eukaryotic cells also have a nucleus.

- The cell membrane is a protective layer that covers the cell's surface and acts as a barrier. The cell membrane is selectively permeable because it allows some substances to pass through it.
- Cytoplasm is a gel-like material that is inside the cell membrane.
- Organelles are structures that perform specific functions within the cell. The number and types of organelles vary in different cells.
- DNA is genetic material that transfers information from one generation to the next.
- A eukaryotic cell has a nucleus that contains the cell's DNA.

Prokaryotes

Cells that have no membrane around their DNA are prokaryotic cells. Most prokaryotes are small, single-celled organisms. All bacteria are prokaryotes. Recently, some examples of multicellular prokaryotes have been discovered, but these are uncommon.

Eukaryotes

A eukaryotic cell has a nucleus. Eukaryotes range from single-celled organisms to organisms composed of millions of cells. Animal and plant cells are eukaryotic cells. Eukaryotes are almost always significantly bigger than prokaryotes.

Teacher to Teacher

Angie Larson
Bernard Campbell Middle School
Lee's Summit, MO

Lesson 3 Cell Structure and Function Students may understand the functions of cell organelles better by comparing them with the functions of everyday items. Challenge students to name household or classroom items that can be considered analogous to cell organelles. Good examples include a battery, which has a similar function to the cell's mitochondria, and a door, which has a similar function to the cell membrane.

Lesson 2

Chemistry of Life

ESSENTIAL QUESTION
What are the building blocks of organisms?

1. Atoms and Molecules

Atoms

Atoms are very small, so small that 100 million atoms placed side by side would measure only 1 cm. In the center of every atom is the nucleus, not to be confused with the nucleus of a cell. The nucleus of an atom contains particles called protons and neutrons. Surrounding the nucleus is an electron cloud containing a third type of particle: electrons. A proton has a positive charge, an electron has a negative charge, and a neutron has no charge. There are over 100 known elements. The key difference between atoms of different elements is the number of protons they contain.

Molecules and Compounds

A molecule is composed of two or more atoms joined by covalent chemical bonds. Some molecules are compounds, meaning they contain atoms of two or more different elements. However, not all molecules are compounds. For example, an oxygen gas molecule (O_2) is made up of atoms of just one element.

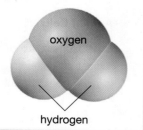

oxygen

hydrogen

2. Molecules for Life Processes

Four Major Classes of Molecules

The four major classes of molecules that organisms need are proteins, carbohydrates, lipids, and nucleic acids.

- A protein is a molecule made up of amino acids. Humans have 20 different amino acids in their bodies.
- Carbohydrates are sugars and starches. Carbohydrates are made of carbon, hydrogen, and oxygen.
- Lipids are waxy, fatty, oily compounds. They are also mostly made of carbon, hydrogen, and oxygen.
- Nucleic acids are information-carrying molecules. DNA is a nucleic acid that carries the hereditary information that parents pass to offspring.

Phospholipids

The cell membrane separates and protects the cell from its surroundings. The cell membrane is built around a core of lipid molecules, including phospholipids. A phospholipid has a hydrophilic head and a hydrophobic tail.

Water

When water moves by osmosis, it can produce a powerful pressure, enough to destroy a cell. The cytoplasm of a typical cell is filled with salts, sugars, and other dissolved substances. Therefore, if pure water should come in contact with a cell, water would rapidly enter the cell. The cell could burst. Cells protect themselves from this force in several ways.

- Plant cells have cell walls that prevent cells from bursting.
- Some cells pump out water.
- Many animal cells are bathed in blood or a bloodlike liquid to prevent direct contact with water.

   COMMON MISCONCEPTIONS **RTI**

Students sometimes confuse cells, molecules, and atoms. They may not realize that molecules contain atoms, and cells are made of molecules.

This misconception is addressed in the Basic Differentiated Instruction on p. 35 and on p. 39.

Content Refresher (continued)

Professional Development

Lesson 3

Cell Structure and Function

ESSENTIAL QUESTION

What are the different parts that make up a cell?

1. Eukaryotic Cells

Organisms made of cells that contain nuclei are called eukaryotes— *eu-* means "true" and *-karyon* means "nucleus." Organisms that do not contain nuclei are prokaryotes—*pro-* means "before."

Cell Membrane

Every cell has a cell membrane. Its principle job is to protect the cell from its surroundings. Cell membranes are composed predominantly of lipids, including phospholipids, and proteins. This lipid bilayer provides cell membranes with a tough yet flexible barrier. In general, substances that dissolve in lipids can easily pass through the cell membrane, but lipid-insoluble substances cannot.

Cytoskeleton

The cytoskeleton is a supporting framework for the cell. The cytoskeleton also helps move materials; in the case of single-celled organisms, the cytoskeleton helps the whole organism move. Proteins can attach to the cytoskeleton and move individual organelles along it.

Nucleus

The nucleus is important because it contains the cell's DNA. DNA is the molecule that contains coded instruction for making proteins. DNA is protected in the nucleus.

2. Parts of Eukaryotic Cells

Despite cell specialization, most eukaryotic cells contain the following organelles and structures:

- Mitochondria, in the presence of oxygen, help the cell convert glucose into a usable form of energy.
- Ribosomes are the places where proteins are assembled.
- The endoplasmic reticulum (ER) is a network of membranes within the cell. There are two types of ER. The surface of rough ER is studded with ribosomes, giving it a "rough" appearance. Smooth ER is not covered by ribosomes.
- The Golgi complex, a network of membranes, works with the ER to process and transport proteins and other molecules.

3. Plant and Animal Cells

Plant and animal cells have many of the same organelles, but some of their organelles are quite different.

Plant Cells

- Plant cells have a cell wall outside the cell membrane, which provides protection and support for the cell.
- In plants, a central vacuole stores water, waste, and dissolved salts. The pressure inside vacuoles helps plants support structures, such as leaves and flowers, and prevents wilting.
- Chloroplasts are organelles that convert energy from the sun to chemical energy.

Animal Cells

- Lysosomes, which are more common in animal cells than in plant cells, are small, ball-shaped organelles that help break down nonfunctioning organelles or foreign materials in the cell.

 COMMON MISCONCEPTIONS   RTI

PLANTS VS. ANIMALS Students might think they have little or nothing in common with plants. In fact, the cells of animals and plants have many characteristics in common, and plants and animals have many similar life processes as well.

This misconception is addressed in the Probing Question on p. 46 and the Learning Alert on p. 55.

Levels of Cellular Organization

ESSENTIAL QUESTION
How are living things organized?

1. Cells to Organism

Students will learn that organisms are unicellular or multicellular living things that carry out life processes, and that multicellular organisms have levels of organization.

Organisms are living things that carry out life processes by themselves. They can be either unicellular and made of only one cell, or they can be multicellular and made of more than one cell. Most cells in a multicellular organism are specialized. Cell specialization means that specific cells are uniquely suited to carry out specific functions. Some cells specialize in transporting materials, and others may specialize in sending messages. Still other cells may make products that the rest of the organism needs. One type of specialized cell is the macrophage. The macrophage travels through the body in the bloodstream and lymphatic system to attack invading organisms such as bacteria.

A tissue is a group of similar cells that perform a common function. For example, muscle cells are grouped into muscle tissue. These cells have filaments that contract and change the size of the cell. Muscle tissue forms part of some organs—for example, the heart, the stomach, and the intestines.

Each of these organs is part of an organ system. For example, the heart is part of the circulatory system. Organs combine more than one type of tissue in order to perform a specific function. For example, the heart contains muscle tissue, nerve tissue, epithelial tissue, and connective tissue. In most cases, a single organ is not capable of carrying out complex functions. For example, the organs in the circulatory system, including the heart, work together to pass nutrients, gases, and blood cells to and from the cells in your body. There are 11 major organ systems in the human body.

Animals contain four basic types of tissues: muscle, connective, epithelial, and nerve. Muscle tissue can be further grouped into smooth muscle, skeletal muscle, and cardiac muscle. Animals also contain connective tissue, which holds other tissues together; nerve tissue; and epithelial tissue. Epithelial tissue covers organ surfaces, such as the skin's surface and the lining of the digestive tract. The cells in epithelial tissue are tightly packed together.

Plant tissues include transport, protective, and ground tissue.

2. Cellular Structure and Function

Students will learn how the levels of organization work together.

The four levels of organization—cells, tissues, organs, and organ systems—are the same or similar for most multicellular organisms. Specialized cells that perform specialized functions make complex and diverse life forms possible. The relationship between structure and function is a remarkable characteristic of many living things.

3. Systems Work Together

Students will learn how organ systems work together.

Organ systems in both plants and animals work together to carry out the complex functions needed to maintain life. For example, when you eat an apple, your nervous system tells your salivary glands to make saliva. Saliva and chewing start the digestive process. As the apple moves through the digestive system and is broken down, nutrients in the apple pass into the bloodstream, and the circulatory system transports them to cells. The part of the apple that your body cannot use is eliminated through the excretory system. Because organ systems are interdependent, a malfunction in one system could create serious problems for an organism.

Content Refresher (continued)

 Professional Development

Homeostasis and Cell Processes

ESSENTIAL QUESTION
How do organisms maintain homeostasis?

1. Homeostasis in Cells

Maintaining Balance

The idea of homeostasis was first put forward by the French physiologist Claude Bernard (1813–1878). Homeostasis involves a huge range of activities. These include getting supplies, disposing of wastes, fighting off infections, maintaining a steady body temperature, reproducing, and obtaining energy.

Photosynthesis

In order to maintain homeostasis, living things must obtain energy. Photosynthesis is the process by which plants and other photosynthetic organisms use the energy of sunlight to produce carbohydrates. There are two types of reactions that take place in photosynthesis—light-dependent reactions and light-independent reactions.

Cellular Respiration

Respiration is the release of energy from the breakdown of food molecules in the presence of oxygen. In eukaryotic cells, respiration takes place inside the mitochondria. A mitochondrion is a cell organelle in which energy is released. In order to release the maximum amount of energy from glucose, animals need oxygen.

The Cell Cycle

In order for an organism to grow and replace dead or damaged cells, cells must also be able to reproduce. To reproduce, most eukaryotic cells increase in size, and then divide into two identical daughter cells. This period of time from the beginning of one cell division to the beginning of the next is known as the cell cycle. Two events in the cell cycle are so important that they are used as landmarks: the copying of the chromosomes that contain the cell's genetic information, and cell division, called mitosis in eukaryotic cells.

Active and Passive Transport

Cells must also be able to obtain materials and get rid of wastes across the cell membrane. In passive transport, materials are transported across the cell membrane without the use of energy. Some substances can diffuse directly across the lipid bilayer. Other substances can diffuse only through special protein channels, a process called facilitated diffusion. Although water is not lipid-soluble, it can pass through most membranes from areas of higher concentration to lower concentration. This process is known as osmosis. In active transport, materials move against a concentration differential. This process requires energy and is often compared to a pump.

3. Homeostasis in Organisms

Responding to Change

The cells of a multicellular organism must work together to maintain homeostasis for the entire organism. Disease and even death may result if homeostasis is not maintained.

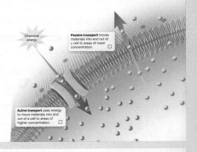

 COMMON MISCONCEPTIONS   **RTI**

PHOTOSYNTHESIS VS. CELLULAR RESPIRATION Some students may think that plants get their energy from photosynthesis and that animals get their energy from cellular respiration. Students should understand that both plants and animals undergo cellular respiration to provide cells with energy.

This misconception is addressed in the Activity *What Cell Am I?* on p. 80 and the Learning Alert on p. 84.

Photosynthesis and Cellular Respiration

Essential Question

How do cells get and use energy?

1. Cells Need Energy

Regardless of the type of food, or whether an organism makes its own food (producer) or obtains its own food by eating other organisms (consumer), food must be converted into an energy form that cells can use. The molecule ATP acts in this role. Cells need energy to perform all their functions, such as transporting materials or making new cells for growth or repair. It might be helpful to students if energy is compared to fuel or currency. Everything a cell does needs to be fueled or "paid for." Most often ATP is this fuel or currency.

2. Photosynthesis

Energy flows mainly from the sun through all organisms. Photosynthesis is the process that captures light energy from the sun and converts it into chemical energy that organisms can use. To do this, photosynthetic organisms combine light energy with carbon dioxide and water to make sugar. The chemical energy is stored in the bonds of sugar molecules. It is then converted into ATP, the energy carrier that cells use primarily to fuel their metabolic activities. Aside from some organisms capable of converting other chemicals into food, photosynthetic organisms provide the majority of available energy to living organisms on Earth.

Photosynthesis takes place in cellular organelles called chloroplasts. When chlorophyll, a green pigment in chloroplasts, catches light energy and combines it with carbon dioxide and water to make the sugar glucose, it produces oxygen. Molecular oxygen (O_2) allows aerobic organisms to live. The oxygen is used to break down the very molecules produced by photosynthesis. This cycle of building and breaking down molecules is how matter and energy flow in all ecosystems.

3. Cellular Respiration

Living organisms need large amounts of energy to carry out their many functions. When their cells need to use their food for energy, the food must be broken down and the energy carried in molecules of ATP. Cellular respiration is the process that breaks down food molecules, using oxygen, into energy cells can use. In prokaryotic cells, cellular respiration takes place in the cell membrane. In eukaryotic cells, it takes place in the organelles called mitochondria. In addition to energy, cell respiration also produces water and carbon dioxide.

The waste products of cellular respiration are the reactants of photosynthesis and vice versa. With the exception of the form of energy, photosynthesis and cellular respiration are nearly opposite reactions. Carbon dioxide, used in photosynthesis, is released as a waste product of cellular respiration. The same is true for water. Likewise, oxygen used in cellular respiration is released as a waste product of photosynthesis.

  COMMON MISCONCEPTIONS **RTI**

PHOTOSYNTHESIS AND CELLULAR RESPIRATION

1. Students often think that animals undergo cellular respiration and plants (and other photosynthetic organisms) undergo photosynthesis only.

This misconception is addressed in the Activity on p. 94 and in the Learning Alert on p. 104.

2. Students often think the components (water, oxygen, carbon dioxide) of photosynthesis and cellular respiration cycle only between these two processes.

This misconception is addressed in the Discussion on p. 94 and in the Learning Alert on p. 100.

Advance Planning

These activities may take extended time or special conditions.

Unit 1

Video-Based Project Photosynthesis, p. 14
  multiple activities spanning several lessons

Project Seeing through Microscopes, p. 15
  research and writing time

Graphic Organizers and Vocabulary pp. 21, 22, 35, 36, 49, 50, 65, 66, 79, 80, 97, 98
  ongoing with reading

Lesson 1

Quick Lab Investigating Cell Size, p. 19
  prepare gelatin one day in advance

Exploration Lab Using a Microscope to Explore Cells, p. 19
  collect pond water in advance; requires two 45-min periods

Lesson 3

Quick Lab Comparing Cells, p. 47
  prepared slides of plant and animal cells

Lesson 4

Exploration Lab The Organization of Organisms, p. 63
  prepared slides of plant and animal tissues

Lesson 5

Quick Lab Investigate Microorganisms, p. 77
  Daphnia and hydra cultures

Quick Lab Homeostasis and Adaptations, p. 77
  requires outdoor observations

Lesson 6

Quick Lab Investigate Carbon Dioxide, p. 95
  prepare limewater in advance

Quick Lab Plant Cell Structures, p. 95
  prepared slides of plant tissues

S.T.E.M. Lab Investigate Rate of Photosynthesis, p. 95
  requires observations over several days

What Do You Think?

Have students think about how microscopes are used in science.

Ask: What kinds of things might you look at under a microscope? Sample answers: cells; tissue samples; microorganisms

Ask: What are some questions you could answer with a microscope but not with your eyes alone? Sample answers: What are the parts of a cell? How many microorganisms are in a water sample?

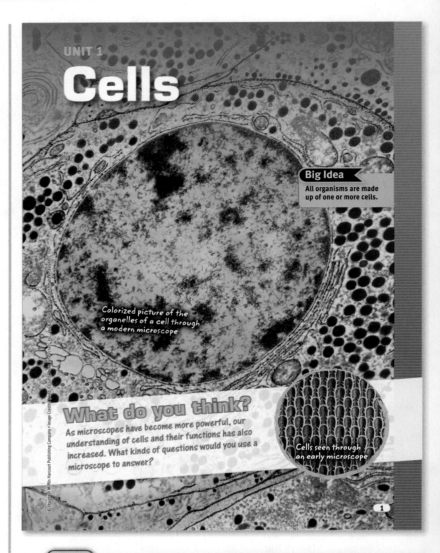

UNIT 1

Cells

Big Idea
All organisms are made up of one or more cells.

Colorized picture of the organelles of a cell through a modern microscope

What do you think?

As microscopes have become more powerful, our understanding of cells and their functions has also increased. What kinds of questions would you use a microscope to answer?

Cells seen through an early microscope

1

 Video-Based Project

Photosynthesis

Go Online to preview the videos, access teacher support pages, and print student activity worksheets.

Dr. Mike Heithaus and a colleague investigate the role of photosynthesis and some of the factors that affect the rates of photosynthesis within and between different ecosystems.

Activities

1 Photosynthesis and Respiration
2 Measuring Photosynthesis in the Rainforest
3 Photosynthesis Around the World

©Patrick Greene Productions

CITIZEN SCIENCE

Seeing through Microscopes

Microscopes have come a long way. Today, we can see the details of the surface of metals at the atomic level. Microscopes have allowed us to study our world at some of the smallest levels.

Circa 1000 CE
Although people may have used rock crystals to magnify things thousands of years ago, it wasn't until about 1000 CE that people were able to form and polish clear-glass partial spheres. Placing these reading stones on top of a page made it easier to read the words.

Reading stones magnify the words on a page.

Hooke's sketch of a flea

Hooke's microscope

1665
Robert Hooke was interested in many areas of science. In 1665, Hooke invented a light microscope to look at small creatures like fleas. Hooke's microscope was similar to a telescope, but it also had a way to shine light on the object.

1931
Ernst Ruska developed the electron microscope, which shows much greater detail than do light microscopes. The electron microscope uses an electron beam instead of light to show things as small as the structure of viruses. Ruska received the Nobel Prize in Physics in 1986 for his breakthrough.

Ruska with his electron microscope

Atoms at platinum's surface

1981
The scanning tunneling microscope changed again the way scientists look at things. Using this microscope, we can look at images of surfaces at the atomic level. The microscope uses a beam of electrons to map a surface. This information is collected and processed so that it can be viewed on a computer screen.

What's in a Microscope?

1 Think About It

A What characteristics do different microscopes have?

_____

_____

_____

B Why are microscopes used?

_____

_____

_____

2 Conduct Research

Choose a specific kind of microscope and research how it is used, whether it is used to view live or dead samples, and its range of magnification.

_____

_____

_____

_____

Take It Home
With an adult, prepare an oral presentation for your class on the microscope that you have researched.

CITIZEN SCIENCE

Unit Project Seeing through Microscopes

1. Think About It

A. Student answers may vary. Characteristics may include light source, electron beam, tube-like body, lenses, stage for specimen, and guides to hold specimen.

B. They are used to view things that are too small to be seen using only your eyes.

2. Conduct Research

Student answers will depend on the type of microscope they choose. Allow time for students to use library resources or the Internet for research. Students should be able to correctly answer each of the questions based on their research.

Take It Home

The oral presentation should include the type of microscope that the student decided to investigate; a description of the microscope, including its range of magnification and whether it is used to view live or dead samples; and the uses for this type of microscope. Encourage students to incorporate visuals into their presentations as necessary. As evidence of collaboration, you may also ask the student to provide a note from the adult with whom the student prepared this presentation.

Optional Online rubric: Oral Presentations

The Characteristics of Cells

Essential Question What are living things made of?

Professional Development

For more detailed information about the topics in this lesson, refer to the Content Refresher in the Unit Opener pages.

Opening Your Lesson

Begin the lesson by assessing students' prerequisite and prior knowledge.

Prerequisite Knowledge

- All organisms have basic needs and share the same life processes.
- All organisms have internal parts and external structures.

Accessing Prior Knowledge

Ask: What are some basic life processes of all organisms? Sample answers: reproducing; growing; using energy; getting rid of waste; responding to the environment

Ask: Brainstorm different ways organisms carry out the different life processes. Sample answers: A fish lays eggs; as a snake grows, it sheds its skin; an owl eats mice, and then gets rid of waste as pellets.

Customize Your Opening

- ☐ **Accessing Prior Knowledge,** above
- ☐ **Print Path** Engage Your Brain, SE p. 5
- ☐ **Print Path** Active Reading, SE p. 5
- ☐ **Digital Path** Lesson Opener

Key Topics/Learning Goals

The Cell

1 Describe the relationship between cells and organisms.
2 Explain why most cells are small in terms of their surface-area-to-volume ratio.

The Cell Theory

1 Summarize the cell theory.
2 Summarize the contributions to cell theory of Robert Hooke, Anton van Leeuwenhoek, Theodor Schwann, and Rudolf Virchow.
3 Compare unicellular and multicellular organisms.

Two Types of Cells

1 Identify the parts that all cells have in common.
2 Compare prokaryotes and eukaryotes.

Supporting Concepts

- A cell is the smallest functional and structural unit of all organisms.
- An organism is a living thing that is made up of one or more cells.
- Most cells are small, which means that there is more surface area per cell volume.

- The cell theory states that organisms are made up of one or more cells, that cells are the basic unit of life, and that all cells come from other cells.
- Robert Hooke and Anton van Leeuwenhoek observed cells using a microscope.
- Theodor Schwann proposed that all organisms are made of cells and that cells are the basic unit of life.
- Rudolf Virchow proposed that all cells come from other cells.
- Unicellular organisms are made up of a single cell; multicellular organisms are made up of multiple cells.

- All cells have a cell membrane, cytoplasm, organelles, and DNA.
- A prokaryote is single-celled with no nucleus or membrane-bound organelles, and is generally smaller than a eukaryote.
- A eukaryote is an organism made up of cells that contain their DNA in a nucleus and have membrane-bound organelles.
- Many eukaryotes are multicellular, and all multicellular organisms are eukaryotes.

Options for Instruction

Two parallel paths provide coverage of the Essential Questions, with a strong **Inquiry** strand woven into each. Follow the **Print Path,** the **Digital Path,** or your customized combination of print, digital, and inquiry.

 **Print Path**
Teaching support for the Print Path appears with the Student Pages.

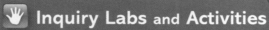 **Inquiry Labs and Activities**

Digital Path
Digital Path shortcut: TS663070

Print Path	Inquiry Labs and Activities	Digital Path
Cell-ebrate!, SE pp. 6–7 **What is a cell?** **Why are most cells small?**	**Quick Lab** **Investigating Cell Size**	**The Cell** **Interactive Image** **The Size of a Cell** **Animation**
Cell Hall of Fame!, SE pp. 8–9 **What is the cell theory?** • All Organisms are Made Up of One or More Cells • The Cell is the Basic Unit of All Organisms • All Cells Come From Existing Cells	**Activity** **Seeing and Understanding** **Activity** **Research a Scientist** **Quick Lab** **How Do Tools That Magnify Help Us Study Cells?** **Exploration Lab** **Using a Microscope to Explore Cells**	**Cell Theory** **Diagram** **The History of Cell Theory** **Interactive Image**
On the Cellular, SE pp. 10–11 **What structures do cells have in common?** • Cell Membrane • Cytoplasm • Organelles • DNA **What are two types of cells?** • Prokaryotes, Eukaryotes	**Daily Demo** **Modeling a Cell**	**Eukaryotic Cells** **Interactive Image** **Prokaryotic Cells** **Interactive Image**

Options for Assessment

See the Evaluate page for options, including Formative Assessment, Summative Assessment, and Unit Review.

Engage and Explore

Activities and Discussion

Discussion *Cells*

Introducing Key Topics　　 whole class
　　　　　　　　　　　　　　 15 min

Have students look at pictures of different types of cells. Include plant, animal, and single-cell organisms (paramecia and euglena). Also include human body cells with interesting shapes such as nerve and red blood cells. Have students list or describe ways the cells are similar. Prompt students to think about how a cell's shape might be related to its job, or function.

Activity *Seeing and Understanding*

The Cell Theory　　　　　 flexible
　　　　　　　　　　　　　　 20 min
　　　　　　　　　　　　　 Inquiry DIRECTED inquiry

First have students cut out a color photograph from a magazine and place it on a flat surface. Then provide students with a magnifying glass to look at the image. Direct students to start with the magnifying glass right on top of the image, and then slowly move the magnifying glass away. **Ask:** What happens as you move the magnifying glass away from the image? The image gets larger. **Ask:** How can the magnifying glass help you better understand how the image was formed? Sample answer: The magnifying glass shows that the image contains many ink dots, which blend together.

Probing Question *Is It Prokaryotic or Eukaryotic?*

Two Types of Cells　　　 individuals
　　　　　　　　　　　　　　 10 min
　　　　　　　　　　　　　 Inquiry GUIDED inquiry

Analyzing Ask students to imagine that they have a slide of an unknown cell. How could they tell whether the cell is prokaryotic or eukaryotic? **Prompt:** Check whether or not there is a nucleus.

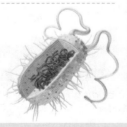

Discussion *Prokaryotes at Home*

Two Types of Cells　　　 whole class
　　　　　　　　　　　　　　 10 min
　　　　　　　　　　　　　 Inquiry DIRECTED inquiry

Remind students that all cells can be classified as prokaryotic or eukaryotic, and that the most important difference between the two cell types is in how they store their DNA. Tell students that there are many different kinds of prokaryotes and many different kinds of eukaryotes. Remind students that all bacteria are prokaryotes. Ask students to try to think of places in their homes where they might find bacteria. Encourage them to share their ideas with the class. Write students' ideas on the board. Sample answers: toilets, sinks, yogurt, kitchen counters, doorknobs

Activity *Research a Scientist*

The Cell Theory　　　　　 individuals
　　　　　　　　　　　　　　 30–40 min
　　　　　　　　　　　　　 Inquiry INDEPENDENT inquiry

Invite students to research one of the scientists responsible for the development of the cell theory: Matthias Schleiden, Theodor Schwann, or Rudolf Virchow. Each of these scientists played a huge part in the development of the cell theory. Encourage students to find out more about exactly how the scientist contributed to the cell theory, what his field of study was, and whether he had collaborators or other scientists he worked with. Encourage students to share their findings with the class.

Variation Interested students can research and explain how the cell theory forms the basis for life science.

Customize Your Labs

 See the Lab Manual for lab datasheets.

 Go Online for editable lab datasheets.

	DIRECTED inquiry	GUIDED inquiry	INDEPENDENT inquiry
	introduces inquiry skills within a structured framework.	develops inquiry skills within a supportive environment.	deepens inquiry skills with student-driven questions or procedures.

Labs and Demos

Daily Demo *Modeling a Cell*

Two Types of Cells

👥👥 whole class
🕐 10 min
Inquiry GUIDED inquiry

PURPOSE To model how organelles are suspended in cytoplasm

MATERIALS

- plain gelatin, premixed and partially gelled
- plastic bag, resealable
- small items (e.g., dry pasta, bottle caps, coins)
- spoon

Show students the plastic bag, and tell them that the plastic bag is going to represent the cell membrane. Using the spoon, fill the plastic bag two-thirds full with the partially gelled gelatin. Show students the variety of small objects you have collected, and encourage them to choose objects and place them in the bag. Seal the bag and squeeze it gently in order to distribute the objects throughout the gelatin. Show the filled bag to students. **Ask:** What do you think the gelatin inside the plastic bag represents? It represents the cytoplasm. **Ask:** What do you think the floating objects distributed throughout the gelatin represent? They represent the organelles, minus the nucleus.

Quick Lab *Investigating Cell Size*

PURPOSE To investigate how the surface-area-to-volume ratio of a cell would affect the diffusion of materials into the cell

See the Lab Manual or go Online for planning information.

Quick Lab *How do Tools that Magnify Help Us Study Cells?*

The Cell Theory

👥👥 individuals
🕐 30 min
Inquiry DIRECTED inquiry

Students use microscopes to observe samples and analyze how magnification helps them study cells.

PURPOSE To illustrate how microscopes magnify objects

MATERIALS

- coverslips (2)
- eyedropper
- microscope, compound
- lab apron
- microscope slides (2)
- samples, various
- water
- safety goggles

Exploration Lab *Using a Microscope to Explore Cells*

The Cell Theory

👥👥 pairs
🕐 two 45-min periods
Inquiry DIRECTED or GUIDED inquiry

Students use a microscope to examine various samples and describe what they observe.

PURPOSE To compare the types of cells from three different samples

MATERIALS

- cork
- coverslips (3)
- eyedropper
- iodine stain
- forceps
- microscope
- microscope slides (3)
- onion
- pond water

Activities and Discussion

- ☐ **Activity** Seeing and Understanding
- ☐ **Probing Question** Is it Prokaryotic or Eukaryotic?
- ☐ **Discussion** Prokaryotes at Home
- ☐ **Activity** Research a Scientist

Labs and Demos

- ☐ **Daily Demo** Modeling a Cell
- ☐ **Quick Lab** Investigating Cell Size
- ☐ **Quick Lab** How do Tools that Magnify Help Us Study Cells?
- ☐ **Exploration Lab** Using a Microscope

Your Resources

Explain Science Concepts

Key Topics	📖 **Print Path**	🖥 **Digital Path**
The Cell	☐ **Cell-ebrate!,** SE pp. 6–7 • Active Reading (Annotation strategy), #5 • Visualize It!, #6 • Do the Math, #7	☐ **The Cell** Learn about the relationship between a cell and an organism. ☐ **The Size of a Cell** Examine the surface area-to-volume ratio and its relationship to cell size.
The Cell Theory	☐ **Cell Hall of Fame,** SE pp. 8–9 • Visualize It!, #8 • Think Outside the Book, #9 • Active Reading, #10	☐ **Cell Theory** Learn about the three basic tenets of cell theory. ☐ **The History of Cell Theory** Learn about the scientists who contributed to the cell theory.
Two Types of Cells	☐ **On the Cellular,** SE pp. 10–11 • Active Reading, #11 • Active Reading (Annotation strategy), #12 • Visualize It!, #13	☐ **Eukaryotic Cells** Learn what structures are found in eukaryotic cells. ☐ **Prokaryotic Cells** Learn what structures are found in prokaryotic cells.

Basic *Comparing Two Types of Cells*

Two Types of Cells

 individuals

 15 min

Venn Diagram Students can create a Venn Diagram to organize and compare information about prokaryotic and eukaryotic cells. Students should include information about the structures these two types of cells have in common along with their differences.

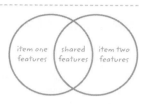

item one features | shared features | item two features

 Optional Online resource: Venn Diagram

Advanced *The Microscope*

The Cell Theory

 individuals

 ongoing

Diagram a Microscope After students have learned about microscopes, have them conduct research to compare different kinds of microscopes. Ask them to focus on the following: the history and design of various microscopes, including the light microscope, the electron microscope, and the scanning microscope. Ask them to choose one and create a diagram to show how it works. Display their diagrams in the classroom.

ELL *Making Connections*

Synthesizing Key Topics

pairs or small groups

20 min

Have EL learners focus on the words *cell, unicellular,* and *multicellular.* Encourage students to use words and pictures to define the word *cell.* Next, have students divide unicellular and multicellular into two parts (uni-cellular and multi-cellular). Again, have students use words and pictures to describe each part of these terms. English learners may not have prior knowledge of how English words can change with a prefix or a suffix. Other words to define using this method are *organelle* and *microscope.*

Lesson Vocabulary

cell   cytoplasm   prokaryote

organism   organelle   eukaryote

cell membrane   nucleus

Previewing Vocabulary

 whole class

 15 min

Word Origins Share the following to help students remember terms:
- **Cell** comes from the Latin word *cella* meaning "small room."
- **Prokaryote** comes from a Greek term that means "before a nucleus." *Pro* means "before" and *karyon* means "nut or kernel."
- **Eukaryote** comes from a Greek term that means "true nucleus." *Eu* in Greek means "true."

Reinforcing Vocabulary

 individuals

 ongoing

Four Square To help students remember the different terms introduced in the lesson, have them draw a matrix with a circle at the center. Students place a term in the circle, and then fill in the surrounding cells with the types of information shown.

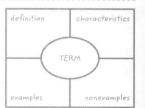

definition | characteristics
TERM
examples | nonexamples

 Optional Online resource: Four-Square Diagram

Customize Your Core Lesson

Core Instruction
- ☐ **Print Path** choices
- ☐ **Digital Path** choices

Vocabulary
- ☐ **Previewing Vocabulary** Word Origins
- ☐ **Reinforcing Vocabulary** Four Square

Your Resources

Differentiated Instruction
- ☐ **Basic** Comparing Two Types of Cells
- ☐ **Advanced** The Microscope
- ☐ **ELL** Making Connections

Extend Science Concepts

Reinforce and Review

Activity *Microscopic Jigsaw*

Synthesizing Key Topics small groups
20 min

Jigsaw Divide the class into six groups and assign each group a topic from the list below. Each group will work together until they become an expert in their area. Make sure groups stay together until each individual can teach what they have learned. After 5 to 10 min, reassign groups. Each new group should consist of one expert from each original group. The goal is for each new team to use their expert knowledge to compare a large living thing, such as a dog, with a microscopic, one-celled organism. Have groups make a list of traits for each organism.

Topics

1 Identify the common parts of cells.

2 Why are most cells small?

3 What are the three parts of the cell theory?

4 Summarize the differences between unicellular and multicellular organisms.

5 Distinguish between prokaryotic and eukaryotic cells.

⊙ *Optional Online resource: Jigsaw Activities*

Graphic Organizer

Two Types of Cells individuals
 ongoing

Two-Panel Flip Chart After students have studied the two types of cells they can create a Two-Panel Flip Chart that includes a panel for a prokaryotic cell and a panel for a eukaryotic cell. Students should illustrate each type of cell and label the structures. Ask students to write a sentence about each type of cell that will help them compare and contrast the two types of cells.

⊙ *Online resource: Two-Panel Flip Chart*

Going Further

Social Studies Connection

Two Types of Cells whole class
20 min

Discussion The organization of a cell can be compared to the organization of a city or town. In both, there is a boundary inside of which activities take place. Smaller parts act as city hall, power plants, and storage facilities. Have students discuss the different parts of the town or city in which they live. Identify some of the local municipal buildings that serve as the government center. Talk about the different local agencies that are responsible for the well being of the residents of their town, such as police and fire. Students might discuss current local issues affecting their municipality.

Health Connection

The Cell Theory individuals
varied

Research Project Two hundred years ago, people believed that life could be generated spontaneously from nonliving things; for example, people believed that the organisms that spoiled food arose from the food itself. This idea was called spontaneous generation. It meant that life could assemble itself from nonliving parts. French scientist Louis Pasteur argued that microorganisms came from their own kind, just like larger organisms. He conducted an experiment that proved the case against spontaneous generation. Have students conduct research to find out more about Pasteur's famous experiment and have them design a poster or a computer presentation to share with the class.

Customize Your Closing

⬙ *See the Assessment Guide for quizzes and tests.*

⊙ *Go Online to edit and create quizzes and tests.*

Reinforce and Review

☐ **Activity** Microscopic Jigsaw

☐ **Graphic Organizer** Two-Panel Flip Chart

☐ **Print Path** Visual Summary, SE p. 12

☐ **Digital Path** Lesson Closer

Evaluate Student Mastery

Formative Assessment

See the teacher support below the Student Pages for additional Formative Assessment questions.

Have students construct a diagram of a cell and discuss the common structures of a cell. **Ask:** How are the basic structures of unicellular organisms similar to the structures of a multicellular organism? What is the major difference? Sample answer: Both organisms have parts that are responsible for carrying out the basic life functions; however, the single cell of a unicellular organism must carry out all of the basic life functions of a living organism. **Ask:** Why is the cell theory important? Sample answer: The cell theory is important because it is the basis for the study of life science; it is also important to understanding the basic characteristics of all cells and organisms.

Reteach

Formative assessment may show that students need reinforcement for certain topics. The resources below are recommended for reteaching. If students were introduced to a topic through the Print Path, you can also use the Digital Path to reteach, and vice versa.

🎧 *Can be assigned to individual students*

The Cell
Discussion Cells

The Cell Theory
Activity Seeing and Understanding 🎧

Two Types of Cells
Probing Question Is It Prokaryotic or Eukaryotic?

Daily Demo Modeling a Cell

Summative Assessment

Alternative Assessment

The Basic Unit of Life

🌐 *Online resources: student worksheet, optional rubrics*

The Characteristics of Cells

Tic-Tac-Toe: *The Basic Unit of Life*

1. Work on your own, with a partner, or with a small group.

2. Choose three quick activities from the game. Check the boxes you plan to complete. They must form a straight line in any direction.

3. Have your teacher approve your plan.

4. Do each activity, and turn in your results.

__ Historical Cell Fiction	__ Something in Common	__ A Great Adventure
Research information on the scientists who contributed to the cell theory. Then, write a fictional story in which the scientists meet and discuss their ideas about cells.	Make a drawing of a eukaryotic cell and label its major parts. Make a drawing of a prokaryotic cell and label its major parts. Place the drawings side by side and use string or yarn to connect the common parts.	Pretend you are running an amusement park. All of the rides are built to resemble structures found within a eukaryotic cell. Write a guidebook describing each ride and what it does. Include a color-coded map of the amusement park.
__ A Simple Cell	__ How It Works	__ Time Capsule
Write a poem about being a prokaryotic cell. Select a type of bacteria or archaea. Include facts about this organism in the poem.	Write a persuasive essay about why it is a good thing to be small. Include information about why a cell must be small, and why it cannot survive if it is too large.	Write a journal entry from the point of view of Theodor Schwann. Describe his conclusions about cells.
__ A Model of a Cell	__ Public Service Announcement	__ A New Report
Make a 3-dimensional model of a eukaryotic cell using art supplies. Each organelle must be labeled and be a different color. Include a key that identifies each organelle.	Create an advertising campaign to tell people about the importance of the cell theory. Include a drawing to help convey your message.	Write a news report about a single-celled organism that lives inside your body. Include what this organism is, what it does, and where it can be found.

Going Further
☐ Social Studies Connection
☐ Health Connection

Formative Assessment
☐ Strategies Throughout TE
☐ Lesson Review SE

Summative Assessment
☐ Alternative Assessment The Basic Unit of Life
☐ Lesson Quiz
☐ Unit Tests A and B
☐ Unit Review SE End-of-Unit

Your Resources

_____

_____

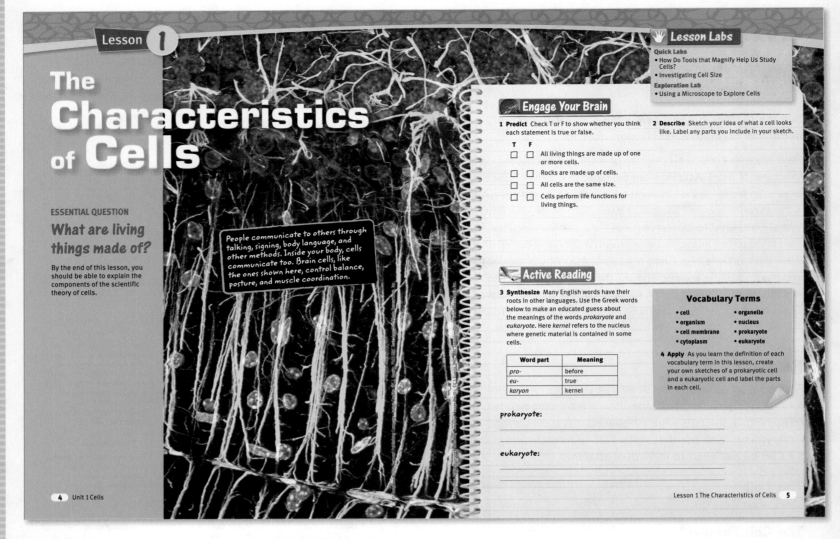

Answers

Answers for 1–3 should represent students' current thoughts, even if incorrect.

1. T; F; F; T

2. Students may draw a circle, oval, or square to represent the cell, and include different shapes inside it to represent cell parts. For example, squiggle lines may represent DNA. Students should include labels in their sketch.

3. Sample answer: before having a nucleus; having a true nucleus

4. Students should define or sketch each vocabulary term in the lesson.

Opening Your Lesson

Discuss students' drawings (item 2) to assess their prerequisite knowledge and to estimate what they already know about cells.

Preconceptions cells, atoms, and molecules are all about the same size; atoms and molecules are similar in structure to cells; chemicals associated with living things are made up of cells—for example, cells make up proteins.

Prerequisites Students should already know that all living things are made up of cells; that cells need to take in nutrients and release waste; and that cells need energy to sustain life.

Accessing Prior Knowledge To assess students' prior knowledge about cells, you may wish to have them conduct a Textbook DRTA. Begin by explaining to students that DRTA stands for **D**irected **R**eading/**T**hinking **A**ctivity. To complete the activity, students need to (1) preview the selection; (2) write what they know, what they think they know, and what they think they'll learn about cells; (3) read the selection; and (4) write what they learned. Discuss whether students' expectations were reasonable, and whether they learned additional information that they did not anticipate.

🌐 *Optional Online resource: Textbook DRTA*

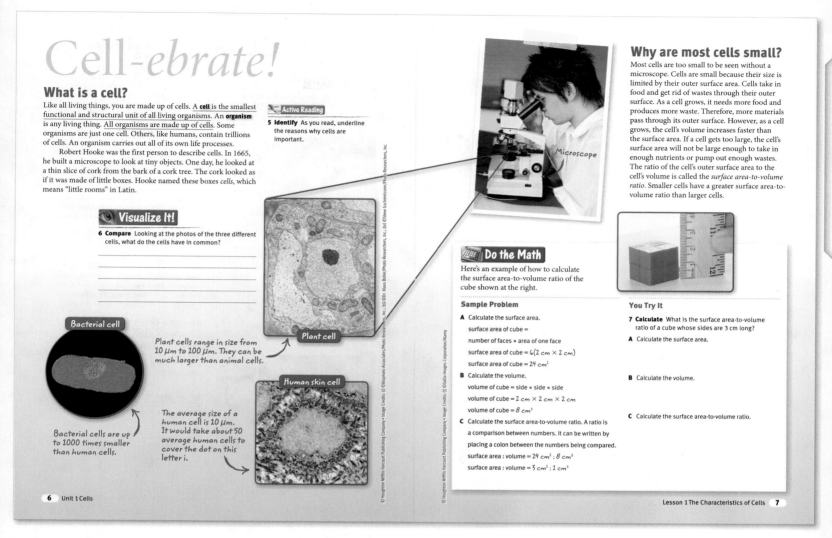

Cell-ebrate!

What is a cell?

Like all living things, you are made up of cells. A **cell** is the smallest functional and structural unit of all living organisms. An **organism** is any living thing. All organisms are made up of cells. Some organisms are just one cell. Others, like humans, contain trillions of cells. An organism carries out all of its own life processes.

Robert Hooke was the first person to describe cells. In 1665, he built a microscope to look at tiny objects. One day, he looked at a thin slice of cork from the bark of a cork tree. The cork looked as if it was made of little boxes. Hooke named these boxes *cells*, which means "little rooms" in Latin.

Active Reading

5 Identify As you read, underline the reasons why cells are important.

Visualize It!

6 Compare Looking at the photos of the three different cells, what do the cells have in common?

Bacterial cell

Plant cells range in size from 10 μm to 100 μm. They can be much larger than animal cells.

Plant cell

Bacterial cells are up to 1000 times smaller than human cells.

Human skin cell

The average size of a human cell is 10 μm. It would take about 50 average human cells to cover the dot on this letter i.

Why are most cells small?

Most cells are too small to be seen without a microscope. Cells are small because their size is limited by their outer surface area. Cells take in food and get rid of wastes through their outer surface. As a cell grows, it needs more food and produces more waste. Therefore, more materials pass through its outer surface. However, as a cell grows, the cell's volume increases faster than the surface area. If a cell gets too large, the cell's surface area will not be large enough to take in enough nutrients or pump out enough wastes. The ratio of the cell's outer surface area to the cell's volume is called the *surface area-to-volume ratio*. Smaller cells have a greater surface area-to-volume ratio than larger cells.

Microscope

Do the Math

Here's an example of how to calculate the surface area-to-volume ratio of the cube shown at the right.

Sample Problem

A Calculate the surface area.

surface area of cube =

number of faces × area of one face

surface area of cube = 6(2 cm × 2 cm)

surface area of cube = 24 cm²

B Calculate the volume.

volume of cube = side × side × side

volume of cube = 2 cm × 2 cm × 2 cm

volume of cube = 8 cm³

C Calculate the surface area-to-volume ratio. A ratio is a comparison between numbers. It can be written by placing a colon between the numbers being compared.

surface area : volume = 24 cm² : 8 cm³

surface area : volume = 3 cm² : 1 cm³

You Try It

7 Calculate What is the surface area-to-volume ratio of a cube whose sides are 3 cm long?

A Calculate the surface area.

B Calculate the volume.

C Calculate the surface area-to-volume ratio.

6 Unit 1 Cells

Lesson 1 The Characteristics of Cells 7

Answers

5. *See students' pages for annotations.*

6. Sample answer: All of these cells are microscopic, they have a membrane surrounding the cell, and they have parts inside the cell.

7. A: 54 cm²; B: 27 cm³;
   C: 54 cm² : 27 cm³ = 2 cm² : 1 cm³

Interpreting Visuals

Have students look at the cells in the photographs to identify some of the differences between the cells. Tell students that the cells have been stained to make them easier to study. Sample answer: The colors of the cells are different, the shapes of the cells are different, and the parts inside the cells are different.

Learning Alert

Cell as a Unit of Structure and Function Students easily understand that the cell is a structural unit but may not grasp that it is a functional unit.

Do the Math

Surface Area-to-Volume Ratio Remind students that first they must calculate the surface area. Point out that the 6 in the sample problem is the number of sides a cube has, and that they will need this number when they calculate the cube's surface area. After they have calculated surface area and volume and have come up with the ratio, ask them how this exercise relates to cells. Point out that the ratio in the sample problem is bigger than the ratio they calculated, showing that as the cube gets bigger, there is less surface area compared to volume.

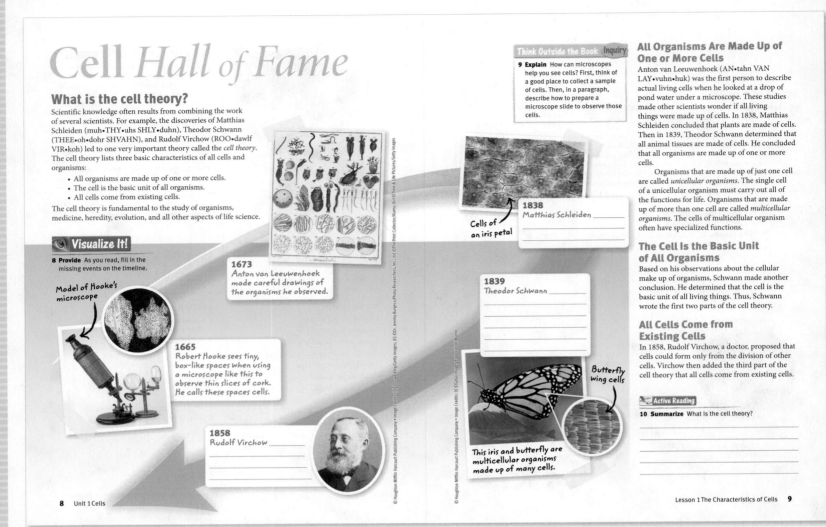

Cell *Hall of* Fame

What is the cell theory?

Scientific knowledge often results from combining the work of several scientists. For example, the discoveries of Matthias Schleiden (muh•THY•uhs SHLY•duhn), Theodor Schwann (THEE•oh•dohr SHVAHN), and Rudolf Virchow (ROO•dawlf VIR•koh) led to one very important theory called the *cell theory*. The cell theory lists three basic characteristics of all cells and organisms:

- All organisms are made up of one or more cells.
- The cell is the basic unit of all organisms.
- All cells come from existing cells.

The cell theory is fundamental to the study of organisms, medicine, heredity, evolution, and all other aspects of life science.

Visualize It!

8 Provide As you read, fill in the missing events on the timeline.

Model of Hooke's microscope

1673
Anton van Leeuwenhoek made careful drawings of the organisms he observed.

1665
Robert Hooke sees tiny, box-like spaces when using a microscope like this to observe thin slices of cork. He calls these spaces cells.

1858
Rudolf Virchow _____

Cells of an iris petal

1838
Matthias Schleiden _____

1839
Theodor Schwann _____

Butterfly wing cells

This iris and butterfly are multicellular organisms made up of many cells.

8 Unit 1 Cells

Think Outside the Book Inquiry

9 Explain How can microscopes help you see cells? First, think of a good place to collect a sample of cells. Then, in a paragraph, describe how to prepare a microscope slide to observe those cells.

All Organisms Are Made Up of One or More Cells

Anton van Leeuwenhoek (AN•tahn VAN LAY•vuhn•huk) was the first person to describe actual living cells when he looked at a drop of pond water under a microscope. These studies made other scientists wonder if all living things were made up of cells. In 1838, Matthias Schleiden concluded that plants are made of cells. Then in 1839, Theodor Schwann determined that all animal tissues are made of cells. He concluded that all organisms are made up of one or more cells.

Organisms that are made up of just one cell are called *unicellular organisms*. The single cell of a unicellular organism must carry out all of the functions for life. Organisms that are made up of more than one cell are called *multicellular organisms*. The cells of multicellular organism often have specialized functions.

The Cell Is the Basic Unit of All Organisms

Based on his observations about the cellular make-up of organisms, Schwann made another conclusion. He determined that the cell is the basic unit of all living things. Thus, Schwann wrote the first two parts of the cell theory.

All Cells Come from Existing Cells

In 1858, Rudolf Virchow, a doctor, proposed that cells could form only from the division of other cells. Virchow then added the third part of the cell theory that all cells come from existing cells.

Active Reading

10 Summarize What is the cell theory?

Lesson 1 The Characteristics of Cells 9

Answers

8. **Schleiden:** plants are made of cells

   Schwann: animal tissues are made of cells, organisms are made of one or more cells, cells are the basic unit of all organisms

   Virchow: cells come from existing cells

9. Answers should include the use of a clean slide and coverslip, and using a sterile swab to transfer the sample of cells to the microscope slide.

10. All organisms are made up of one or more cells, the cell is the basic unit of all living things, and all cells come from existing cells.

Probing Question GUIDED (Inquiry)

Synthesizing What do you think the development of the cell theory has in common with many other scientific discoveries? Sample answer: It was developed in stages, with contributions from multiple scientists over many years. **Prompt:** Think about the history and people behind the cell theory.

Interpreting Visuals

Have students trace the line on these pages. Ask them to explain what the line represents, and what each photograph along the way represents. Sample answer: The line represents the passage of time. Each photograph represents an important discovery in the history of the development of the cell theory.

Learning Alert

Cork Cells Robert Hooke was the scientist who first saw and named cells, but what he was actually seeing was cell walls, since the cork cells he was looking at were no longer alive. He did not describe any of the structures, or organelles, that we now know exist within cells.

On the Cellular

What parts do all cells have in common?

Different cells vary in size and shape. However, all cells have some parts in common, including cell membranes, cytoplasm, organelles, and DNA. These different parts help the cell to carry out all the tasks needed for life.

Active Reading

11 **Identify** As you read, underline the function of cell membranes, organelles, and DNA.

Cell Membrane

A **cell membrane** is a protective layer that covers a cell's surface and acts as a barrier between the inside of a cell and the cell's environment. It also controls materials, such as water and oxygen, that move into and out of a cell.

Cytoplasm

The region enclosed by the cell membrane that includes the fluid and all of the *organelles* of the cell is called the **cytoplasm** (SY•tuh•plaz•uhm).

Organelles

An **organelle** is a small body in a cell's cytoplasm that is specialized to perform a specific function. Cells can have one or more types of organelles. Most, but not all, organelles have a membrane.

DNA

Deoxyribonucleic acid, or DNA, is genetic material that provides instructions for all cell processes. Organisms inherit DNA from their parent or parents. In some cells, the DNA is contained in a membrane-bound organelle called the **nucleus**. In other types of cells, the DNA is not contained in a nucleus.

What are the two types of cells?

Although cells have some basic parts in common, there are some important differences. The way that cells store their DNA is the main difference between the two cell types.

Active Reading

12 **Define** As you read, underline the differences between prokaryotes and eukaryotes.

Prokaryotic

A **prokaryote** (proh•KAIR•ee•oht) is a single-celled organism that does not have a nucleus or membrane-bound organelles. Its DNA is located in the cytoplasm. Prokaryotic cells contain organelles called *ribosomes* that do not have a membrane. Some prokaryotic cells have hairlike structures called *flagella* that help them move. Prokaryotes, which include all bacteria and archaea, are smaller than eukaryotes.

Eukaryotic

A **eukaryote** (yoo•KAIR•ee•oht) is an organism made up of cells that contain their DNA in a nucleus. Eukaryotic cells contain membrane-bound organelles, as well as ribosomes. Not all eukaryotic cells are the same. Animals, plants, protists, and fungi are eukaryotes. All multicellular organisms are eukaryotes. Most eukaryotes are multicellular. Some eukaryotes, such as amoebas and yeasts, are unicellular.

Visualize It!

13 **Identify** Use the list of terms below to fill in the blanks with the matching cell parts in each cell. Some terms are used twice.

DNA in cytoplasm
DNA in nucleus
Cytoplasm
Cell membrane
Organelles

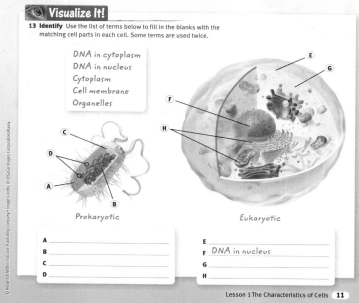

Prokaryotic

Eukaryotic

A	
B	
C	
D	

E	
F	DNA in nucleus
G	
H	

Answers

11. *See students' pages for annotations.*

12. *See students' pages for annotations.*

13. A: cell membrane; B: DNA in cytoplasm; C: cytoplasm; D: organelles; E: cell membrane; G: cytoplasm; H: organelles

Building Reading Skills: Compare/Contrast

Have students think about the ways prokaryotic and eukaryotic cells are the same. **Ask:** Which cells have a cell membrane and cytoplasm? both Which cells have genetic material? both Then have students find ways in which the two types of cells are different. **Ask:** Which cells have a nucleus? eukaryotic Which cells are smaller? prokaryotic

Learning Alert

Inside a Cell Students may think of cells as mostly empty with isolated structures inside. In fact, cells are full of cytoplasm, which is the region inside the cell wall that includes a thick fluid called cytosol, nutrients, wastes, and cell structures, and is full of activity.

Formative Assessment

Ask: Describe the main difference between prokaryotic and eukaryotic cells. A prokaryotic cell's DNA is not contained in a nucleus, and a eukaryotic cell has DNA in a nucleus.
Ask: What type of cell makes up all bacteria? prokaryotic What type of cells are plants and animals made of? eukaryotic

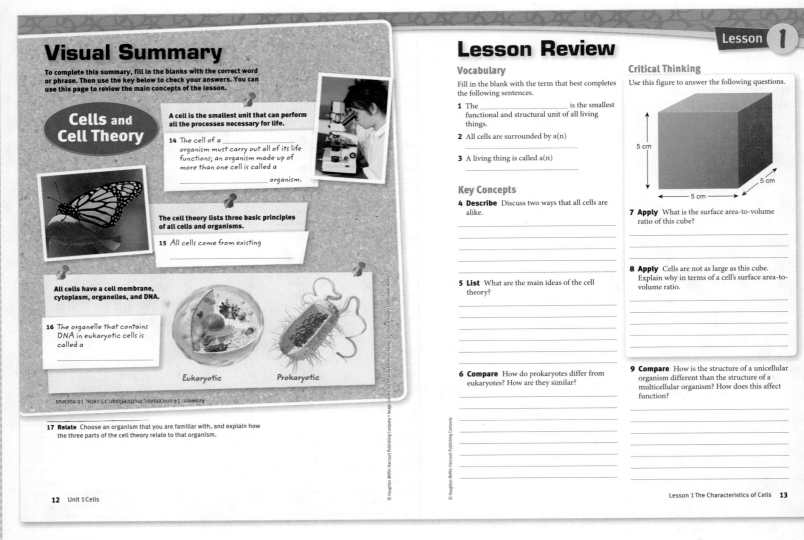

Visual Summary Answers

14. unicellular; multicellular

15. cells

16. nucleus

17. Student answers should relate the structure of the organism to the three parts of the cell theory. Students may discuss whether the organism is unicellular or multicellular, and that the cells of the organism must divide and carry out basic life processes in order for the organism to survive.

Lesson Review Answers

1. cell

2. cell membrane

3. organism

4. Sample answer: all cells have DNA, a cell membrane, cytoplasm, and organelles; all cells come from existing cells

5. All organisms are made up of one or more cells, the cell is the basic unit of all living things, and all cells come from existing cells.

6. The cells of both prokaryotes and eukaryotes contain DNA, a cell membrane, cytoplasm, and organelles. Eukaryotes' DNA is found in the nucleus, while prokaryotes' DNA is in the cytoplasm.

7. surface area = 6 × (5 cm × 5 cm) = 150 cm²
   volume = 5 cm × 5 cm × 5 cm = 125 cm³
   surface area-to-volume ratio = 150 cm² : 125 cm³ = 6 cm² : 5 cm³

8. If a cell were this large, it would have a small surface area-to-volume ratio. Cells need a proportionately larger surface area to efficiently move materials in and out of the cell.

9. A unicellular organism is made up of one cell. This cell must perform all of the life functions for the organism. A multicellular organism is made up of many cells, allowing these organisms to have specialized functions.

Chemistry of Life

Essential Question What are the building blocks of organisms?

 Professional Development

For more detailed information about the topics in this lesson, refer to the Content Refresher in the Unit Opener pages.

Opening Your Lesson

Begin the lesson by assessing students' prerequisite and prior knowledge.

Prerequisite Knowledge

- An atom is the smallest unit of an element that has the properties of that element.
- An element is made up of one or more of the same type of atom.

Accessing Prior Knowledge

Ask: Bread is made from several substances including sugar, water, and salt. Is bread an element? No, it contains many elements such as carbon, hydrogen, and oxygen.

Customize Your Opening

☐ **Accessing Prior Knowledge,** above

☐ **Print Path** Engage Your Brain, SE p. 15 #1–2

☐ **Print Path** Active Reading, SE p. 15 #3–4

☐ **Digital Path** Lesson Opener

Key Topics/Learning Goals

Atoms and Molecules

1 Explain that atoms join together to form the molecules found in living things.
2 List the six elements most commonly found in living things.
3 Define *compound*.

Molecules for Life Processes

1 Explain why nutrients are important to all organisms.
2 Identify the four main types of molecules in cells.
3 Illustrate the role of water in cells.

Supporting Concepts

- An atom is the smallest unit of an element that maintains the properties of that element.
- A molecule is a substance formed when two or more atoms are joined by chemical bonds.
- Most molecules in living things contain carbon, hydrogen, nitrogen, oxygen, phosphorus, and sulfur.
- A compound contains atoms of two or more different elements joined by chemical bonds.

- Organisms require certain nutrients for growth, repair, and other life processes.
- The four main types of molecules in cell are proteins, carbohydrates, lipids, and nucleic acids.
- Protein are molecules made of amino acids.
- Carbohydrates are molecules made of sugars.
- Lipids, such as fats and oils, are molecules that store energy and form cell membranes.
- DNA is a nucleic acid that stores information a cell needs to make certain molecules.
- Many cell processes require water. Nearly two-thirds of the mass of a cell is from water.
- Phospholipids form much of the cell membrane and regulate water in the cell.
- If water concentration inside a cell is less than outside a cell, the cell will take in water.
- If the water concentration outside a cell is lower than inside the cell, then water will move outside the cell.

Options for Instruction

Two parallel paths provide coverage of the Essential Questions, with a strong **Inquiry** strand woven into each.
Follow the **Print Path,** the **Digital Path,** or your customized combination of print, digital, and inquiry.

 Print Path
Teaching support for the Print Path appears with the Student Pages.

 Inquiry Labs and Activities

Digital Path
Digital Path shortcut: TS663000

Print Path	Inquiry Labs and Activities	Digital Path
It's Elementary, SE pp. 16–17 **What are atoms and molecules?** • Atoms are the Smallest Unit of Elements • Molecules are Made of Two or More Atoms	**Activity** Cell Circles	**Building Blocks** Interactive Image
Cell Fuel, SE pp. 18–19 **What are some important molecules in cells?** • Lipids • Proteins • Carbohydrates • Nucleic Acids **Waterworks,** SE pp. 20–21 **What are phospholipids?** **Why is water important?**	**Activity** Food Molecules **Activity** Menu Design **Activity** Spoonful of Sugar **Daily Demo** Oil and Water **Quick Lab** Molecules for Life Processes **Quick Lab** Analyzing Cell Components	**Polymers and Nutrients** Interactive Image **Phospholipids** Interactive Image

Options for Assessment

See the Evaluate page for options, including Formative Assessment, Summative Assessment, and Unit Review.

Engage and Explore

Activities and Discussion

Discussion *The Carbon Atom*

Atoms and Molecules

 whole class
 15 min

The carbon atom bonds easily with other atoms. Compounds that contain carbon and hydrogen atoms are known as organic compounds. Other compounds are inorganic. Organic compounds are vital to life, and there are almost an infinite number of them due to carbon's ability to form chains and rings. Show students this model of an organic compound. Have them name the elements in it (carbon, hydrogen, oxygen). Encourage students to count the number of each atom in the molecule.

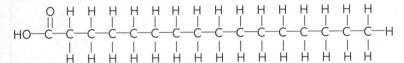

Activity *Food Molecules*

**Molecules for
Life Processes**

 flexible
 20 min
 GUIDED inquiry

Have students select ten packaged foods they eat regularly. Have them record the grams of carbohydrates, proteins, and fats (lipids) in a serving of each product. Then have them list the foods that contain the most proteins, carbohydrates, and fats in one column. In a second column, have them list the foods that contain the least nutrients. Which foods provide the most nutrients? Which provide the fewest? Have students use the data to analyze their findings and draw conclusions.

Activity *Menu Design*

**Molecules for
Life Processes**

 individuals
 10 min
 GUIDED inquiry

After discussing the role of lipids, proteins, and carbohydrates, have student pairs or individuals design a day's menu that features a well-balanced variety of foods that contain these molecules. Students can research foods online to find nutritional information. Have students write out their menu on posterboard, labeling each item as containing lipids, proteins, or carbohydrates. Encourage students to draw pictures or use images from magazines.

Activity *Spoonful of Sugar*

Engage

**Molecules for
Life Processes**

 individuals or small groups
 10 min
GUIDED inquiry

Direct students to half fill two cups with warm water. Next have students stir eight spoonfuls of sugar into one of the cups. Drop several raisins into each cup and wait for 6 hours. After 6 hours, have students compare the raisins. Prompt them to describe how the raisins are different. The raisins in the plain water are plumper. Have students discuss what they think caused the difference. Sample answer: More plain water than sugar water moved into the raisins because plain water and raisins contain very different concentrations of sugar. More plain water moved into the raisins to equalize the concentrations.

 **Levels of Inquiry**

DIRECTED inquiry introduces inquiry skills within a structured framework.

GUIDED inquiry develops inquiry skills within a supportive environment.

INDEPENDENT inquiry deepens inquiry skills with student-driven questions or procedures.

Labs and Demos

Daily Demo *Oil and Water*

Engage

Molecules for Life Processes

👥 whole class
🕐 10 min
 DIRECTED inquiry

Use this short demo after you have discussed phospholipids and water.

PURPOSE **To observe that fat is not water soluble**

MATERIALS

- beakers (3)
- food coloring
- juice
- stirring stick
- vegetable oil
- water

1 Put a small amount of oil into one beaker and an equal amount of juice into another.

2 Put water into a third beaker and add enough food coloring to make the water darkly colored.

3 Add equal amounts of the colored water to the beaker of oil and the beaker of juice. Stir the liquids to mix them.

4 **Observing** What did you see? Water and oil separate into distinct layers. Juice and water mix. Why does the mixture of oil and water behave differently than juice and water? Oil is made from lipids, juice is mostly water.

5 Cells are surrounded by fluid that contains water, and the insides of cells also contain water. Encourage students to discuss how the water-repelling nature of lipids can keep a cell's inside separated from its outside. Sample answer: Lipids act as a barrier.

Quick Lab *Molecules for Life Processes*

PURPOSE **To investigate the elements and chemical building blocks that make up proteins, carbohydrates, lipids, and nucleic acids**

See the Lab Manual or go Online for planning information.

Quick Lab *Analyzing Cell Components*

Molecules for Life Processes

👥 small groups
🕐 10 min
DIRECTED inquiry

Students observe how lipids, such as shortening, interact with water and soap.

PURPOSE **To explore and describe the nature of lipids**

MATERIALS

- shortening, vegetable
- soap, liquid dishwashing
- water supply or individual pans of water
- safety goggles
- cup, clear plastic
- lab aprons
- protective gloves

Customize Your Labs

📘 *See the Lab Manual for lab datasheets.*

🌐 *Go Online for editable lab datasheets.*

Activities and Discussion

☐ **Discussion** The Carbon Atom

☐ **Activity** Food Molecules

☐ **Activity** Menu Design

☐ **Activity** Spoonful of Sugar

Labs and Demos

☐ **Daily Demo** Oil and Water

☐ **Quick Lab** Molecules for Life Processes

☐ **Quick Lab** Analyzing Cell Components

Your Resources

Explain Science Concepts

	📖 Print Path	**🖥 Digital Path**
Key Topics		
Atoms and Molecules	☐ **It's Elementary,** SE pp. 16–17 • Active Reading, #5 • Pie Graph, #6 • Synthesize, #7	☐ **Building Blocks** Learn about the buildings blocks of life and the six elements most commonly found in living things.
Molecules for Life Processes	☐ **Cell Fuel,** SE pp. 18–19 • Active Reading, #8 • Describe, #9 • Summarize, #10	☐ **Polymers and Nutrients** Learn about the four main classes of molecules in cells. ☐ **Phospholipids** Learn about the relationship between water and phospholipids in a cell.

☐ **Waterworks,** SE pp. 20–21
• Active Reading, #11
• Visualize It! #12
• Apply, #13
• Think Outside the Book, #14

Differentiated Instruction

Basic *Cells, Atoms, and Molecules*

Atoms and Molecules

 individuals

15 min

Graphic Organizer To help students clarify misconceptions about the distinctions among cells, atoms, and molecules, have them devise their own graphic organizer that shows the relationships among these terms. Students might use a pyramid or concentric circles, or they might sketch each item to model the relationships. Their organizers should indicate a hierarchy with cells overarching molecules and molecules overarching atoms.

Advanced *Glucose Molecule*

Molecules for Life Processes

individuals

30 min

Quick Research One of the most familiar carbohydrate building blocks is glucose. Have students conduct research to find out what this molecule looks like. Ask them to use colored gumdrops and toothpicks to build a model of a glucose molecule. Guide students to assign a different color gumdrop to each type of atom. Have students provide a key that tells what type of atom each color represents.

ELL *Picture Glossary*

Molecules for Life Processes

 pairs or small groups

20 min

Picture Glossary ELL students can use index cards to create a picture glossary. Students should focus on the terms that describe the four main types of molecules found in cells: lipids, proteins, carbohydrates, and nucleic acids. Encourage students to draw a picture on one side to represent each molecule. Pictures could include foods that contain these molecules or diagrams that show what the molecules do. Have students use words to describe each picture. Have students write down their description under the picture.

Lesson Vocabulary

atom   molecule   lipid   protein

carbohydrate   nucleic acid   phospholipid

Previewing Vocabulary

 whole class

15 min

Word Origins Share the following to help students remember terms:
- **Atom** comes from a Greek word *atomos* meaning "indivisible."
- **Molecule** comes from the French word *molecule*, meaning "extremely minute particle."
- **Carbohydrate** comes from the word *carbo-*, which means "carbon" and the word *hydrate*, which denotes a compound containing hydrogen and oxygen.
- **Lipid** comes from the Greek word *lipos*, which referred to animal fat or vegetable oil.

Reinforcing Vocabulary

 individuals

ongoing

Four Square Have students draw a 2-by-2 matrix with a circle at the center. Students place a term in the circle and then fill in the surrounding cells with the types of information shown.

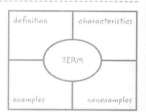

Customize Your Core Lesson

Core Instruction
- ☐ **Print Path** choices
- ☐ **Digital Path** choices

Vocabulary
- ☐ **Previewing Vocabulary** Word Origins
- ☐ **Reinforcing Vocabulary** Four Square

Your Resources

_____

_____

Differentiated Instruction
- ☐ **Basic** Cells, Atoms, and Molecules
- ☐ **Advanced** Glucose Molecule
- ☐ **ELL** Picture Glossary

Extend Science Concepts

Reinforce and Review

Activity *Cell Circles*

Synthesizing Key Topics whole class
 20 min

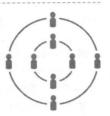

Inside/Outside Circles Give each student an index card with one of the questions listed below written on it. Students write their answers on the back of the index cards. Check that the students' answers are correct, and have students fix any incorrect answers. Next, have students pair up and form two circles. One partner is in an inside circle, and the other is in an outside circle. The student in the inside circle faces out of the circle, and the student on the outside faces in. Each student in the inside circle asks his or her partner the question on the index card. The partner answers. If the answer is incorrect, the student in the inside circle teaches the other student the correct answer. Repeat this step with the outside-circle student asking the questions. Next, each student on the outside circle rotates one person to the right. He or she faces a new partner and gets a new question. Students rotate after each pair of questions. Use the questions listed below, or make your own.

1 Define *element, atom, molecule,* and *compound.*

2 List the six common elements found in living things.

3 Why are nutrients important to all organisms?

4 What are the four main types of molecules in cells? What are their functions in a cell?

5 Why is water important for cells?

6 How do cell membranes regulate water moving into and out of a cell?

Optional Online resource: Inside/Outside Circles support

Graphic Organizer

Synthesizing Key Topics individuals
 ongoing

Mind Map After students have studied the lesson, ask them to create a mind map with the following terms: *atom, molecule, protein, carbohydrate, lipid, nucleic acids.*

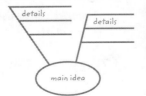

Optional Online resource: Mind Map support

Going Further

Health Connection

Molecules for Life Processes whole class
15 min

Discussion The U.S. government subsidizes corn crops; therefore, high fructose corn syrup is cheap and is used in many products Americans eat daily. Some studies indicate that corn syrup increases cholesterol in the blood and may play a role in obesity. The corn refiners state that high fructose corn syrup is made from corn and has the same calories as sugar. Have students discuss the debate on the health effects of high fructose corn syrup that is occurring in the media. Students may also want to compile a list of all the products they consume that contain the corn-based sweetener.

Real World Connection

Molecules for Life Processes individuals
varied

Research Project DNA fingerprinting uses a variety of techniques used for determining the genes that are present in a particular sample of DNA. Since DNA fingerprinting was introduced in 1984, it has been used for researching genetic diseases, solving crimes, and determining paternity. Have students conduct research to learn about different methods of DNA fingerprinting and how they are done. Have students prepare a brief presentation to share with the class.

 Optional Online rubric: Written Pieces

Customize Your Closing

See the Assessment Guide for quizzes and tests.

Go Online to edit and create quizzes and tests.

Reinforce and Review

☐ **Activity** Cell Circles

☐ **Graphic Organizer** Mind Map

☐ **Print Path** Visual Summary, SE p. 22

☐ **Digital Path** Lesson Closer

Evaluate Student Mastery

Formative Assessment

See the teacher support below the Student Pages for additional Formative Assessment questions.

Have students review four main types of molecules that are important for life processes. **Ask:** What are the four main types of molecules in cells made from, and what are their functions? Proteins are made of amino acids. They are used to build and repair body structures. Carbohydrates are made of sugars and are used as a source of energy. Lipids are fat molecules and have many jobs, including energy storage. Nucleic acids are molecules made up of smaller molecules called nucleotides. Nucleic acids carry information.

Reteach

Formative assessment may show that students need reinforcement for certain topics. The resources below are recommended for reteaching. If students were introduced to a topic through the Print Path, you can also use the Digital Path to reteach, and vice versa. 🎧 *Can be assigned to individual students.*

Atoms and Molecules
Discussion The Carbon Atom

Molecules for Life Processes
Activity Food Molecules 🎧

Activity Menu Design

Activity Spoonful of Sugar 🎧

Daily Demo Oil and Water

Summative Assessment

Alternative Assessment
Exploring Atoms and Molecules

🌐 *Online resources: student worksheet, optional rubrics*

Chemistry of Life

Points of View: *Exploring Atoms and Molecules*
Your class will work together to show what you've learned about the building blocks of organisms.

1. Work in groups as assigned by your teacher. Each group will be assigned to one or two viewpoints.

2. Complete your assignment, and present your perspective to the class.

 Vocabulary In your own words, define the terms *compound, nutrient, protein,* and *element.* Then write down a dictionary or textbook definition. Use each term in a sentence that describes how it relates to the cell.

 Details Describe how sugars and starches are related to carbohydrates. Then describe how amino acids are related to proteins. Finally, describe how DNA and nucleotides are related to nucleic acids.

 Illustrations Draw models of an atom and a water molecule. Finally, draw an illustration depicting how atoms and molecules relate to cells.

 Analysis Create a diagram that explains how the terms *molecule, atom, element,* and *compound* relate to each other.

Models Find a way to model the cell membrane. Make sure your model shows how the phospholipid molecules form this membrane.

Going Further
☐ Health Connection
☐ Real World Connection

Formative Assessment
☐ Strategies Throughout TE
☐ Lesson Review SE

Summative Assessment
☐ Alternative Assessment Exploring Atoms and Molecules
☐ Lesson Quiz
☐ Unit Tests A and B
☐ Unit Review SE End-of-Unit

Your Resources

_____

_____

_____

_____

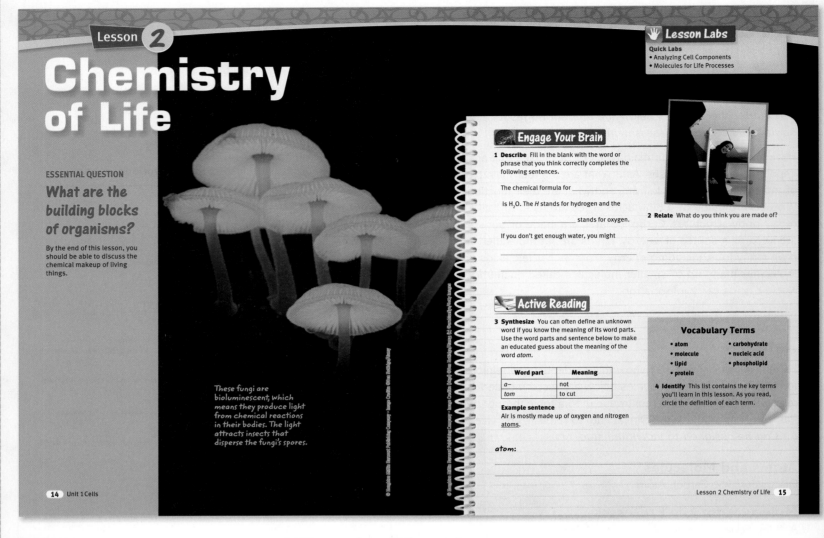

Answers

Answers for 1–3 should represent students' current thoughts, even if incorrect.

1. water; O; dehydrate, or lose more water than has been taken in

2. Sample answer: Humans are made up of cells, which are made up of atoms.

3. Sample answer: the smallest unit of an element

4. Students' annotations will vary.

Opening Your Lesson

Discuss student answers (item 3) to assess students' prerequisite knowledge and to estimate what they already know about the key topics.

Preconceptions Students often confuse atom, molecule, and cell, viewing them all as "microscopic things." Atoms are the basic building blocks of molecules. Millions of molecules make up a cell.

Prerequisites Students should already know that cells are the basic units of life and the building blocks for all living things; students should be familiar with the three characteristics of the cell theory, and should understand that all cells share certain common parts.

Learning Alert

Atoms and Cells Students are often confused about the difference between the nucleus of an atom and the nucleus of a cell, and may believe that an atom has DNA in its nucleus. The term *nucleus* refers generally to a central region or location. The nucleus of an atom is the central region made up of protons and neutrons. The nucleus of a cell contains DNA. DNA is a molecule made up of many atoms.

It's Elementary

What are atoms and molecules?

Think about where you live. The streets are lined with many types of buildings. But these buildings are made from a lot of the same materials, such as bricks, glass, wood, and steel. Similarly, all cells are made from the same materials. The materials in cells are made up of atoms that can join together to form molecules.

Atoms Are the Building Blocks of Matter

The matter that you encounter every day, both living and nonliving, is made up of basic particles called **atoms.** Not all atoms are the same. There are nearly one hundred types of atoms that occur naturally on Earth. These different types of atoms are known as *elements.* Each element has unique properties. For example, oxygen is a colorless gas made up of oxygen atoms. The element gold is a shiny metal made up of gold atoms. Just six elements make up most of the human body. These and other elements are important for cell processes in all living things.

Active Reading

5 Relate How do atoms relate to cells?

_____

_____

_____

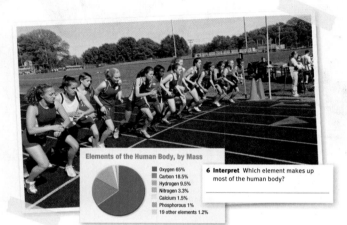

Elements of the Human Body, by Mass

- Oxygen 65%
- Carbon 18.5%
- Hydrogen 9.5%
- Nitrogen 3.3%
- Calcium 1.5%
- Phosphorous 1%
- 19 other elements 1.2%

6 Interpret Which element makes up most of the human body?

_____

Atoms and Molecules

The human body has trillions of cells made up of many different molecules.

Oxygen

Hydrogen

Water molecules are made of one oxygen atom joined to two hydrogen atoms.

Gold Gold
Gold Gold Gold
Gold Gold

If you could see the gold atoms that make up the outer coating of this medal, they would all look the same.

7 Synthesize How are the gold medal and the human cell similar? How do they differ?

_____

_____

_____

Molecules Are Made of Two or More Atoms

A **molecule** is a group of atoms that are held together by chemical bonds. For example, the molecule of water shown above is made of one oxygen atom bonded to two hydrogen atoms. If you separated the oxygen and hydrogen atoms, then you would no longer have a water molecule.

Some molecules are made up of only one type of atom. For example, a molecule of oxygen gas is made of two oxygen atoms. Other molecules contain different types of atoms. A substance made up of atoms of two or more elements joined by chemical bonds is called a *compound.* Most of the molecules found in cells are also compounds.

16 Unit 1 Cells

Lesson 2 Chemistry of Life 17

Answers

5. Sample answer: Cells and the materials in cells are made up of atoms.

6. oxygen

7. Sample answer: They are both made up of atoms. Also, gold is an element and the cell contains elements, such as oxygen and carbon. They differ because the human cell is living and the metal is not living.

Probing Questions   GUIDED Inquiry

Identifying Can you think of an example of an atom and an example of a molecule? Sample answers: atom: hydrogen or oxygen; molecule: water. **Prompt:** Look at the visuals on this page. Think about how an atom is different from a molecule.

Interpreting Visuals

Have students use the pie chart to identify the six major elements that make up the human body. What is the combined percentage for oxygen, carbon, and hydrogen? **93%**

Learning Alert ⚡ MISCONCEPTION ⚡

Cell, Atom, Molecule Have students rank the following by level of organization: cell, atom, molecule. If students order them incorrectly, they may be confused about what makes up cells and molecules. To correct this misconception, have students use a dictionary to find definitions of the three concepts. Ask them to draw what the three objects might look like. **Ask:** What is water? a molecule What atoms make up water? hydrogen and oxygen Describe how water is related to cells. All cells contain water.

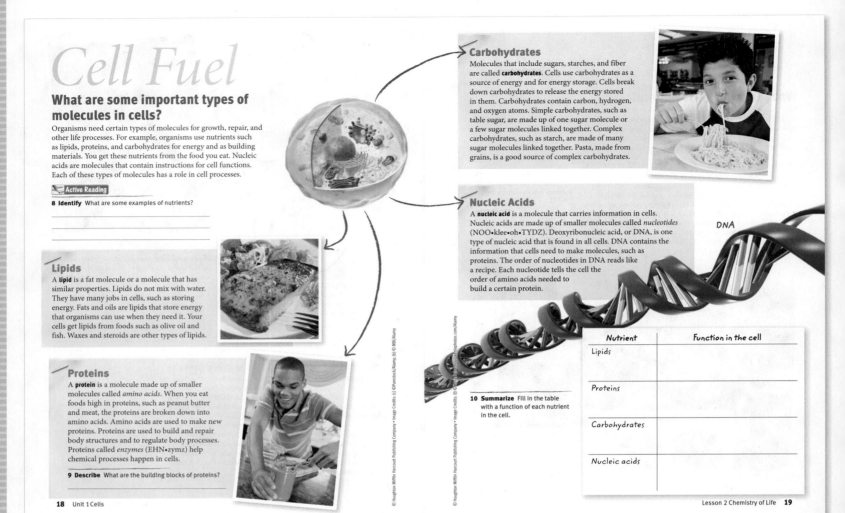

Cell Fuel

What are some important types of molecules in cells?

Organisms need certain types of molecules for growth, repair, and other life processes. For example, organisms use nutrients such as lipids, proteins, and carbohydrates for energy and as building materials. You get these nutrients from the food you eat. Nucleic acids are molecules that contain instructions for cell functions. Each of these types of molecules has a role in cell processes.

Active Reading

8 Identify What are some examples of nutrients?

Lipids

A **lipid** is a fat molecule or a molecule that has similar properties. Lipids do not mix with water. They have many jobs in cells, such as storing energy. Fats and oils are lipids that store energy that organisms can use when they need it. Your cells get lipids from foods such as olive oil and fish. Waxes and steroids are other types of lipids.

Proteins

A **protein** is a molecule made up of smaller molecules called *amino acids*. When you eat foods high in proteins, such as peanut butter and meat, the proteins are broken down into amino acids. Amino acids are used to make new proteins. Proteins are used to build and repair body structures and to regulate body processes. Proteins called *enzymes* (EHN•zymz) help chemical processes happen in cells.

9 Describe What are the building blocks of proteins?

Carbohydrates

Molecules that include sugars, starches, and fiber are called **carbohydrates**. Cells use carbohydrates as a source of energy and for energy storage. Cells break down carbohydrates to release the energy stored in them. Carbohydrates contain carbon, hydrogen, and oxygen atoms. Simple carbohydrates, such as table sugar, are made up of one sugar molecule or a few sugar molecules linked together. Complex carbohydrates, such as starch, are made of many sugar molecules linked together. Pasta, made from grains, is a good source of complex carbohydrates.

Nucleic Acids

A **nucleic acid** is a molecule that carries information in cells. Nucleic acids are made up of smaller molecules called *nucleotides* (NOO•klee•oh•TYDZ). Deoxyribonucleic acid, or DNA, is one type of nucleic acid that is found in all cells. DNA contains the information that cells need to make molecules, such as proteins. The order of nucleotides in DNA reads like a recipe. Each nucleotide tells the cell the order of amino acids needed to build a certain protein.

DNA

10 Summarize Fill in the table with a function of each nutrient in the cell.

Nutrient	Function in the cell
Lipids	
Proteins	
Carbohydrates	
Nucleic acids	

Answers

8. proteins, carbohydrates, lipids

9. amino acids

10. Students should fill in the table with the phrases: *store energy* (lipids); *used to build and repair body structures and regulate life processes* (proteins); *store and release energy* (carbohydrates); *carry information for cell processes* (nucleic acids).

Learning Alert

Building Blocks of Proteins Students may think that cells are the building blocks of proteins. Explain to students that proteins are built of molecules, and that cells make, store, and transport proteins. Remind them that cells grow and reproduce.

Formative Assessment

Ask: Describe the functions of the four main types of molecules in the cell. Proteins are used to build and repair body structures. They also regulate life processes. Carbohydrates are a source of energy. Lipids have many functions. Some store energy and some make up cell membranes. Nucleic acids carry the information a cell needs to make almost all of the other types of molecules that it needs.

Have students compile a list of foods that are available in the cafeteria. Remind them to also include liquids such as milk, juice, and water. Have them look up the nutritional information of each item online and then list which items contain the most protein, fat, or carbohydrates.

For greater depth, have students create visual models of each type of molecule.

Waterworks

What are phospholipids?

All cells are surrounded by a cell membrane. The cell membrane helps protect the cell and keep the internal conditions of the cell stable. A lipid that contains phosphorus is called a **phospholipid** (FOSS•foh•LIH•pyd). Phospholipids form much of the cell membrane. The head of a phospholipid molecule is attracted to water. The tail repels water, or pushes it away. Because there is water inside and outside the cell, the phospholipids form a double layer. One layer lines up so that the heads face the outside of the cell. A second layer of phospholipids line up so the heads face the inside of the cell. The tails from both layers face each other, forming the middle of the cell membrane. Molecules, such as water, are regulated into and out of a cell through the cell membrane.

Active Reading **11 Explain** Describe how phospholipids form a barrier between water inside the cell and water outside the cell.

_____

_____

_____

_____

Visualize It!

12 Identify Write *attracts* next to the end of the phospholipid that attracts water. Write *repels* next to the end that repels water.

Phospholipid molecule

Head

Tail

Cell membrane

Water

Water

20

Why is water important?

Many cell processes require water, which makes up nearly two-thirds of the mass of the cell. Thus, water is an important nutrient for life. Water moves through the cell membrane by a process called *osmosis*. Osmosis depends on the concentration of the water inside and outside of the cell. Pure water has the highest concentration of water molecules. If the water concentration inside the cell is lower than the water concentration outside the cell, then water will move into the cell. If the environment outside a cell has a low concentration of water, such as in a salty solution, water will move out of the cell.

14 Associate Think of an object that could be an analogy to the cell membrane. Draw a picture of the object and explain how it is similar to and different from a cell membrane.

Losing too much water can cause a cell to shrivel and die.

The right balance of water allows a cell to function normally.

If too much water enters a cell, it may swell up and burst.

These gates control the people who enter and exit a sports stadium.

13 Apply How do these gates function in a similar way to the cell membrane?

_____

_____

_____

21

Answers

11. The phospholipids form a double layer with the heads facing the inside and the outside of the cell. This structure allows the heads, which attract water, to regulate the water moving in and out.

12. Student should write *attracts water* next to the head, *repels water* next to the tail.

13. The gates control how people enter and exit much like a cell membrane controls the materials that enter and exit the cell.

14. Student should draw an object that is an analogy of a cell membrane. For example, they may draw a water faucet filter and explain that, like a cell membrane, the filter controls what comes out of the faucet, but it differs because it mainly filters out solids and generally works in only one direction.

Interpreting Visuals

Have students look at the diagram of the cell membrane to identify what the cell membrane is made of. phospholipids **Ask:** How are phospholipids structured to form two layers in the cell membrane? Each phospholipid has a head and a tail. The tails of the two layers are together, and there are two rows of heads, one facing inside the cell, the other facing outside the cell.

Probing Question

Examining Why are lipids good for making cell membranes? The head of the phospholipid molecule is attracted to water, while the tail is not. There is water inside the cell and outside the cell. **Prompt:** Think about the two different parts of the phospholipid molecule.

Building Reading Skills

Supporting Main Ideas The text states that water is important. Have students identify details from the passage that support the main idea. **Prompt:** What do many cell processes require?

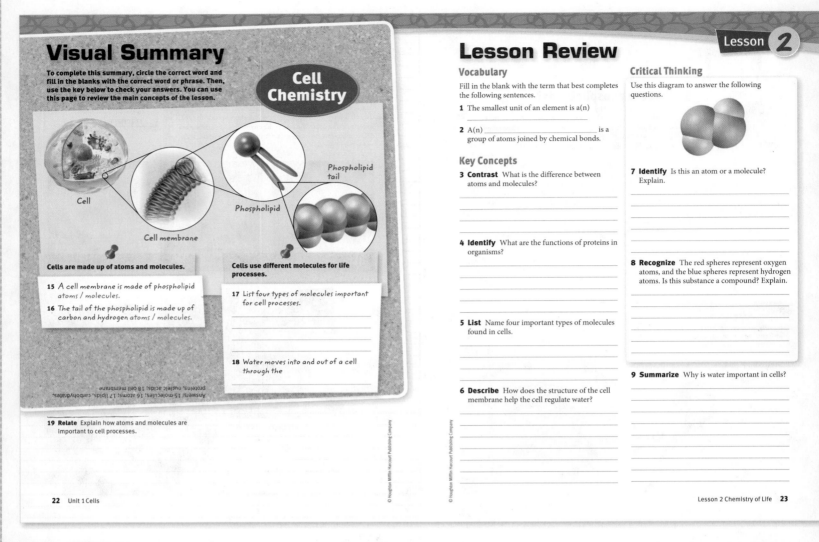

Visual Summary

To complete this summary, circle the correct word and fill in the blanks with the correct word or phrase. Then, use the key below to check your answers. You can use this page to review the main concepts of the lesson.

Cell Chemistry

Cell

Cell membrane

Phospholipid tail

Phospholipid

Cells are made up of atoms and molecules.

15 A cell membrane is made of phospholipid atoms / molecules.

16 The tail of the phospholipid is made up of carbon and hydrogen atoms / molecules.

Cells use different molecules for life processes.

17 List four types of molecules important for cell processes.

18 Water moves into and out of a cell through the

Answers: 15 molecules; 16 atoms; 17 lipids, carbohydrates, proteins, nucleic acids; 18 cell membrane

19 **Relate** Explain how atoms and molecules are important to cell processes.

© Houghton Mifflin Harcourt Publishing Company

Lesson Review

Lesson 2

Vocabulary

Fill in the blank with the term that best completes the following sentences.

1 The smallest unit of an element is a(n) _____

2 A(n) _____ is a group of atoms joined by chemical bonds.

Key Concepts

3 **Contrast** What is the difference between atoms and molecules?

4 **Identify** What are the functions of proteins in organisms?

5 **List** Name four important types of molecules found in cells.

6 **Describe** How does the structure of the cell membrane help the cell regulate water?

Critical Thinking

Use this diagram to answer the following questions.

7 **Identify** Is this an atom or a molecule? Explain.

8 **Recognize** The red spheres represent oxygen atoms, and the blue spheres represent hydrogen atoms. Is this substance a compound? Explain.

9 **Summarize** Why is water important in cells?

© Houghton Mifflin Harcourt Publishing Company

Visual Summary Answers

15. molecules
16. atoms
17. lipids, carbohydrates, proteins, nucleic acids
18. cell membrane
19. Sample answer: Atoms make up elements, molecules, and compounds, which cells use to carry out cell processes. For example, a water molecule is made up of hydrogen and oxygen atoms. Water is a compound that cells regulate and transport across the cell membrane.

Lesson Review Answers

1. atom
2. molecule
3. Atoms are the smallest unit of an element. Molecules are made up of atoms.
4. Cells use proteins to make new proteins, build and repair body structures, and regulate life processes.
5. lipids, proteins, carbohydrates, nucleic acids
6. Phospholipid molecules form the double layer of the cell membrane. The heads of one layer face outside the cell. The heads of the other layer face inside the cell. The heads attract water. The tails face each other and repel water. Water is regulated into and out of the cell membrane by osmosis.
7. This is a molecule because it is made up of a group of atoms held together by chemical bonds.
8. Yes, this is a compound because it is made up of atoms of two or more elements, oxygen and hydrogen, bonded together.
9. Water is important for many of the life processes that take place in cells. Water also helps cells keep their size and shape.

Cell Structure and Function

Essential Question What are the different parts that make up a cell?

Professional Development

For more detailed information about the topics in this lesson, refer to the Content Refresher in the Unit Opener pages.

Opening Your Lesson

Begin the lesson by assessing students' prerequisite and prior knowledge.

Prerequisite Knowledge

- There are four main parts of a cell: cell membrane, cytoplasm, DNA, and organelles.
- There are two types of cells: prokaryotes and eukaryotes.

Accessing Prior Knowledge

Ask: What structures do all cells have in common? Sample answer: cell membrane, cytoplasm, organelles, and DNA

Ask: How are prokaryotic cells and eukaryotic cells different? Sample answer: Eukaryotic cells have a nucleus, while prokaryotic cells do not.

Customize Your Opening

- ☐ **Accessing Prior Knowledge,** above
- ☐ **Print Path** Engage Your Brain, SE p. 25 #1–2
- ☐ **Print Path** Active Reading, SE p. 25 #3–4
- ☐ **Digital Path** Lesson Opener

Key Topics/Learning Goals	Supporting Concepts
Eukaryotic Cells 1 Identify general characteristics of eukaryotic cells. 2 Recognize how prokaryotes differ from eukaryotes.	• All eukaryotic cells have cell membranes; cytoplasm, which includes membrane-bound organelles; and genetic material contained in the nucleus. Prokaryotic cells also have a cell membrane, cytoplasm, and genetic material, but no nucleus. • Eukaryotic cells can differ from each other in the quantity and types of their organelles.
Parts of Eukaryotic Cells 1 Describe the cell membrane, cytoskeleton, and nucleus. 2 Describe the structure and function of organelles found in eukaryotic cells, including mitochondria, ribosomes, endoplasmic reticulum, and Golgi complex.	• All eukaryotes (and prokaryotes) have a cell membrane that separates their cytoplasm from surrounding material. Both also have a cytoskeleton that gives shape and support. • Eukaryotic cells have DNA within a nucleus. • Mitochondria produce energy for the cell. Ribosomes make proteins. The endoplasmic reticulum is a system of folded membranes in which proteins, lipids, and other materials are made. The Golgi complex packages and distributes proteins.
Plant and Animal Cells 1 Compare and contrast organelles found in plant and animal cells.	• Plant cells have cell walls, central vacuoles, and chloroplasts. Cell walls provide structure and protection. The large central vacuole in a plant cell stores water, waste, and dissolved salts. Chloroplasts are organelles in which photosynthesis takes place. • Animal cells contain lysosomes. Plant cells usually do not contain lysosomes. Lysosomes are responsible for digestion inside a cell.

Options for Instruction

Two parallel paths provide coverage of the Essential Questions, with a strong **Inquiry** strand woven into each. Follow the **Print Path**, the **Digital Path**, or your customized combination of print, digital, and inquiry.

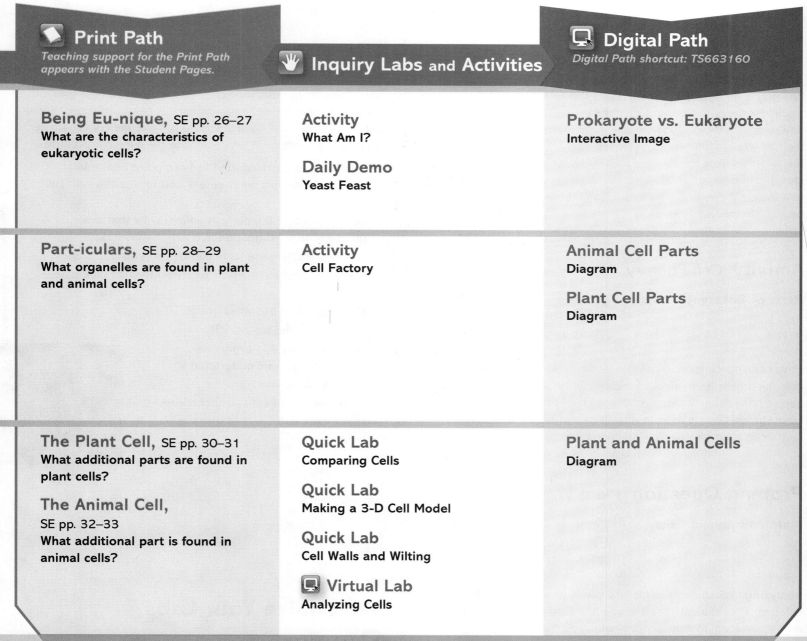

Print Path
Teaching support for the Print Path appears with the Student Pages.

Inquiry Labs and Activities

Digital Path
Digital Path shortcut: TS663160

Being Eu-nique, SE pp. 26–27
What are the characteristics of eukaryotic cells?

Activity
What Am I?

Daily Demo
Yeast Feast

Prokaryote vs. Eukaryote
Interactive Image

Part-iculars, SE pp. 28–29
What organelles are found in plant and animal cells?

Activity
Cell Factory

Animal Cell Parts
Diagram

Plant Cell Parts
Diagram

The Plant Cell, SE pp. 30–31
What additional parts are found in plant cells?

The Animal Cell,
SE pp. 32–33
What additional part is found in animal cells?

Quick Lab
Comparing Cells

Quick Lab
Making a 3-D Cell Model

Quick Lab
Cell Walls and Wilting

Virtual Lab
Analyzing Cells

Plant and Animal Cells
Diagram

Options for Assessment

See the Evaluate page for options, including Formative Assessment, Summative Assessment, and Unit Review.

Engage and Explore

Activities and Discussion

Discussion *Systems*

Eukaryotic Cells

 whole class
 10 min

The cell can be thought of as a system. A system usually consists of many parts that work together. A system will not function as well if one part is not working properly. Have students discuss some of the systems they use every day, such as a bicycle. Some of the parts in their bicycle are the gears, the brakes, and the materials used to make the frame. Ask students to think about what would happen to a bicycle if one of the parts, such as the brakes, stopped working.

Activity *Cell Factory*

Parts of Eukaryotic Cells

 flexible
 20 min
 GUIDED inquiry

Have students compare a cell to a factory. Ask students to list the different organelles in a eukaryotic cell. Tell students that in a factory, people have different jobs that all contribute to producing something. Have students create a poster that illustrates how cell organelles function in a similar way to the different jobs in a factory.

Probing Question *Plant Versus Animal*

Plant and Animal Cells

 individuals
 10 min
 GUIDED inquiry

Analyzing Ask students to discuss how a water lily and a frog are different. After students say that one is a plant and the other is an animal, ask them to think about what makes them the same.

 DIRECTED inquiry variation Work with students so they see that both plants and animals are made of eukaryotic cells that contain many of the same organelles.

Activity *What Am I?*

Introducing Key Topics

 whole class
10 min
GUIDED inquiry

Think Fast Read the following descriptions of organelles and characteristics of eukaryotic cells. Ask students to raise their hands when they think they know what is being described. If you call on a student and he or she does not give the correct answer, keep calling on students until someone gives the correct answer.

- A protective barrier found in both plant and animal cells that controls what enters and leaves the cell: cell membrane
- Organelles found mainly in animal cells that are responsible for digestion in a cell: lysosomes
- The smallest organelle; maker of proteins: ribosomes
- Green organelles in which photosynthesis takes place: chloroplasts
- Covered with ribosomes: rough ER
- Maker of lipids: smooth ER
- You won't find this organelle containing genetic material in a prokaryote: nucleus
- Powerhouses of cells: mitochondria
- These cells have no cell walls: animal cells

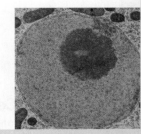

(r) ©Biophoto Associates/Photo Researchers, Inc.

Customize Your Labs

 See the Lab Manual for lab datasheets.

 Go Online for editable lab datasheets.

Levels of Inquiry

DIRECTED inquiry — introduces inquiry skills within a structured framework.

GUIDED inquiry — develops inquiry skills within a supportive environment.

INDEPENDENT inquiry — deepens inquiry skills with student-driven questions or procedures.

Labs and Demos

Daily Demo *Yeast Feast*

`Engage`

Eukaryotic Cells

👥 whole class

🕐 10 min, observation during the next day

`Inquiry` **DIRECTED** inquiry

Use this short demo so students can observe yeast, a unicellular eukaryotic organism, involved in one of its life processes.

PURPOSE **To observe a unicellular eukaryotic organism**

MATERIALS

- bowl
- paper towels
- plastic zip-top bags (2)
- sugar, 15 g
- water, warm, 200 mL
- yeast, 10 g

1 Pour half the water, half the yeast, and all the sugar into a bowl and stir until the yeast and sugar dissolve. Pour the mixture into a bag. Squeeze out as much air as you can. Seal the bag.

2 Repeat step 1 using a second bag and omitting the sugar.

3 Place both bags on a table under a lit lamp.

4 **Observing** Check the bags at regular intervals over the next day. What did you see? The yeast with the sugar grew in size; the bag inflated. Nothing happened to the sugarless bag.

5 What do you think caused the effects you observed? The yeast fed on the sugar. The yeast without sugar had no food. When yeast feeds on sugar, it breaks down the sugar for energy. The process gives off carbon dioxide, which inflates the bag.

Quick Lab *Comparing Cells*

PURPOSE **To compare and contrast plant and animal cells**

See the Lab Manual or go Online for planning information.

Quick Lab *Making a 3-D Cell Model*

Plant and Animal Cells

👥 individuals

🕐 30 min

`Inquiry` **GUIDED** inquiry

PURPOSE **To model an animal cell and analyze the organelles that make it function**

See the Lab Manual or go Online for planning information.

Quick Lab *Cell Walls and Wilting*

PURPOSE **To describe the functions of the cell wall and vacuole in plant cells**

See the Lab Manual or go Online for planning information.

Virtual Lab *Analyzing Cells*

Plant and Animal Cells

👥 flexible

🕐 45 min

`Inquiry` **GUIDED** inquiry

Students use a virtual light microscope to examine differences between cells.

PURPOSE **To observe prokaryotic, animal, and plant cells**

Activities and Discussion

- ☐ **Discussion** Systems
- ☐ **Activity** Cell Factory
- ☐ **Probing Question** Plant Versus Animal
- ☐ **Activity** What Am I?

Labs and Demos

- ☐ **Daily Demo** Yeast Feast
- ☐ **Quick Lab** Comparing Cells
- ☐ **Quick Lab** Making a 3-D Cell Model
- ☐ **Quick Lab** Cell Walls and Wilting
- ☐ **Virtual Lab** Analyzing Cells

Your Resources

Explain Science Concepts

	📖 **Print Path**	💻 **Digital Path**
Key Topics		
Eukaryotic Cells	☐ **Being Eu-nique,** SE pp. 26–27 • Active Reading (annotation strategy), #5 • Visualize It! #6 • Describe, #7 	☐ **Prokaryote vs. Eukaryote** Learn about the differences between prokaryotes and eukaryotes. 
Parts of Eukaryotic Cells	☐ **Part-iculars,** SE pp. 28–29 • Explain, #8 • Describe, #9 • Compare, #10 • Describe, #11 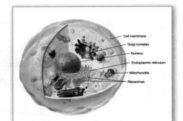	☐ **Animal Cell Parts** Explore the different organelles that make up an animal cell. ☐ **Plant Cell Parts** Explore the different organelles that make up a plant cell. 
Plant and Animal Cells	☐ **The Plant Cell,** SE pp. 30–31 • Active Reading, #12 • Compare, #13 • Visualize It! #14 • Describe, #15 • Think Outside the Book, #16 ☐ **The Animal Cell,** SE pp. 32–33 • Active Reading, #17 • Describe, #18 • Compare, #19 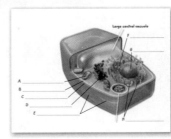	☐ **Plant and Animal Cells** Explore the differences between plant and animal cells.

Basic *Casting All Cells*

Parts of Eukaryotic Cells

 small groups

 15 min

Role-Playing After students have learned about the parts of a cell, ask them to develop a skit about how cell parts work together. Have each student play the role of a different part of a cell. Students may want to record their skit on video to be shared with the class.

Basic *Travel Brochure*

Plant and Animal Cells

 pairs or small groups

varied

Making Connections Have students design a travel brochure that attracts visitors to a plant or an animal cell. Have students think of their cell as an amusement park or other travel destination. Students should describe some of the organelles found in their cell. Encourage students to use drawings, magazine pictures, and computer images in their brochure.

Advanced *Where Did Eukaryotic Cells Come From?*

Eukaryotic Cells

individuals or pairs

30 min

Presentation Students probably know that eukaryotic cells have a nucleus and prokaryotic cells do not. However, that is only the beginning of the differences between these two types of cells. Prompt students to think about why these cells are so different. Lynn Margulis, a scientist from the University of Massachusetts, has an interesting hypothesis. Ask a group of students to research her hypothesis, and then prepare a short presentation about it.

ELL *Guess My Part*

Plant and Animal Cells

  individuals, then pairs

varied

Build Background To review lesson vocabulary, have students create unlabeled diagrams of the parts of the cell. Photocopy their diagrams and have them label the organelles on a master copy. Pair students for peer review, using the unlabeled diagrams to test knowledge and the master copy to check it.

Lesson Vocabulary

cytoskeleton	mitochondrion	ribosome
endoplasmic reticulum	Golgi complex	cell wall
vacuole	chloroplast	lysosome

Previewing Vocabulary

 whole class

15 min

Word Origins Share the following to help students remember terms:
- **Cytoskeleton** means "cell skeleton." *Cyto-* in this term means "cell" as in cytoplasm.
- **Golgi complex** is named after Camillo Golgi, the Italian scientist who first identified the organelle.
- **Vacuole** in French means "small vacuum"; it comes from the Latin *vacuum*.

Reinforcing Vocabulary

 individuals

ongoing

Four Square To help students remember the different terms introduced in the lesson, have them draw a 2-by-2 matrix with a circle at the center. Students place a term in the circle and then fill in the surrounding cells with the types of information shown.

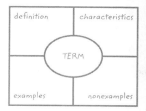

Customize Your Core Lesson

Core Instruction
- ☐ **Print Path** choices
- ☐ **Digital Path** choices

Vocabulary
- ☐ **Previewing Vocabulary** Word Origins
- ☐ **Reinforcing Vocabulary** Four Square

Your Resources

Differentiated Instruction
- ☐ **Basic** Casting All Cells
- ☐ **Basic** Travel Brochure
- ☐ **Advanced** Where Did Eukaryotic Cells Come From?
- ☐ **ELL** Guess My Part

Extend Science Concepts

Reinforce and Review

Activity *Which Cell Am I?*

Synthesizing Key Topics whole class   15 min

Four Corners Pick corners of the classroom and label them with the following: *eukaryotic cells, plant cells only, animal cells only, none of these*. Read the following descriptions to students. After each one, ask students to stand in the corner that they think the description refers to. Give each student in the correct corner a point. You can continue the game with additional examples provided by student volunteers.

1 Cells that have a double membrane-bounded organelle in which photosynthesis takes place. Photosynthesis is the process by which cells use sunlight, carbon dioxide, and water to make sugar and oxygen. plant cells only

2 Cells that have a cell membrane, cytoplasm, and a nucleus. This cell also has a cytoskeleton that is used to help the entire organism move. eukaryotic cells

3 Small single-celled organisms that do not contain DNA in a nucleus. Many bacteria are examples of this cell type. none of these

4 Cells that always contain an organelle that is responsible for digestion in the cell. This organelle engulfs damaged organelles, waste materials, and foreign invaders and breaks them down with digestive enzymes. animal cells only

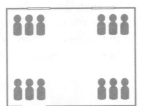

Graphic Organizer

Synthesizing Key Topics individuals   ongoing

Mind Map After students have studied the lesson, ask them to create a Mind Map with the following terms: *eukaryotic cells, plant cells, animal cells, cell membrane, cytoplasm, mitochondria, ribosome, endoplasmic reticulum, Golgi complex, vacuole, cell wall, chloroplast, lysosome.*

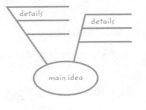

⊙ *Optional Online resource: Mind Map support*

Going Further

Technology Connection

Eukaryotic Cells whole class   15 min

Discussion The first electron microscope was built in the 1930s by German engineers Ernst Ruska and Max Knoll. They knew that a light microscope is limited by the wavelength of light. They also knew that electrons have the properties of waves that are thousands of times shorter than those of light. Putting these pieces of information together, Ruska and Knoll developed an electron lens that could focus electrons on an object, just as light could be focused. They built the first electron microscope by putting several of these lenses together in a series. Students may want to research how advanced electron micrography is aiding the study of the DNA in our cells.

Art Connection

Plant and Animal Cells individuals   varied

Design Project The abstract and geometric forms of cells and organelles have inspired contemporary painters and sculptors. Have students create designs for a stained-glass window that incorporate motifs from cell structures. Students can cut colored acetate to execute their designs. They can piece their "windows" together using clear tape and a cardboard frame. Display these works on a class window.

Customize Your Closing

▣ *See the Assessment Guide for quizzes and tests.*

⊙ *Go Online to edit and create quizzes and tests.*

Reinforce and Review

☐ **Activity** Which Cell Am I?

☐ **Graphic Organizer** Mind Map

☐ **Print Path** Visual Summary, SE p. 34

☐ **Digital Path** Lesson Closer

Evaluate Student Mastery

Formative Assessment

See the teacher support below the Student Pages for additional Formative Assessment questions.

Ask: What are some of the characteristics of eukaryotic cells? Eukaryotic cells have cell membranes, cytoplasm, and genetic material contained in a nucleus. Eukaryotic cells have mitochondria, ribosomes, endoplasmic reticulum, and a Golgi complex. **Ask:** How are plant and animal cells alike and different? Both have organelles that process and transport materials. Plant cells have chloroplasts, cell walls, and central vacuoles. Animal cells have lysosomes that break down nutrients. Plant cells usually do not.

Reteach

Formative assessment may show that students need reinforcement for certain topics. The resources below are recommended for reteaching. If students were introduced to a topic through the Print Path, you can also use the Digital Path to reteach, and vice versa.

🎧 *Can be assigned to individual students*

Eukaryotic Cells
Discussion Systems

Daily Demo Yeast Feast

Parts of Eukaryotic Cells
Activity Cell Factory 🎧

Plant and Animal Cells
Quick Lab Making a 3-D Cell Model 🎧

Probing Question Plant Versus Animal

Summative Assessment

Alternative Assessment
Structure and Function of Cell Organelles

🌐 *Online resources: student worksheet, optional rubrics*

Cell Structure and Function

Mix and Match: *Structure and Function of Cell Organelles*
Mix and match ideas to show what you've learned about the structure and function of cells.

1. Work on your own, with a partner, or with a small group.

2. Choose one information source from Column A, two topics from Column B, and one option from Column C. Check your choices.

3. Have your teacher approve your plan.

4. Submit or present your results.

A. Choose One Information Source	B. Choose Two Things to Analyze	C. Choose One Way to Communicate Analysis
___ observations of cells with a microscope	___ the difference between prokaryotes and eukaryotes	___ diagram or illustration
___ photographs of prokaryotic and eukaryotic cells	___ the general characteristics of the eukaryotic cell	___ colors, symbols, and/or arrows marked on a visual, with a key
___ photographs of cell organelles	___ how mitochondria function	___ model, such as drawings or descriptions showing differences or relationships
___ illustrations of cells and the types of organelles	___ how the ribosomes, ER, and the Golgi complex work together	___ field guide describing structures found in eukaryotic cells
___ video that includes the structure and function of various cell organelles engaged in life processes	___ Differences and similarities between the cell wall and the large central vacuole of plants	___ game
___ print or audio description that includes the life processes of a cell	___ the differences between chloroplasts found in plant cells and the lysosomes found in animal cells	___ story, song, or poem, with supporting details
___ digital simulation of cell organelles and their life processes		___ skit, chant, or dance, with supporting details
		___ multimedia presentation
		___ _____

Going Further

☐ **Technology Connection**

☐ **Art Connection**

Formative Assessment

☐ **Strategies** Throughout TE

☐ **Lesson Review** SE

Summative Assessment

☐ **Alternative Assessment** Structure and Function of Cell Organelles

☐ **Lesson Quiz**

☐ **Unit Tests A and B**

☐ **Unit Review** SE End-of-Unit

Your Resources

_____

_____

_____

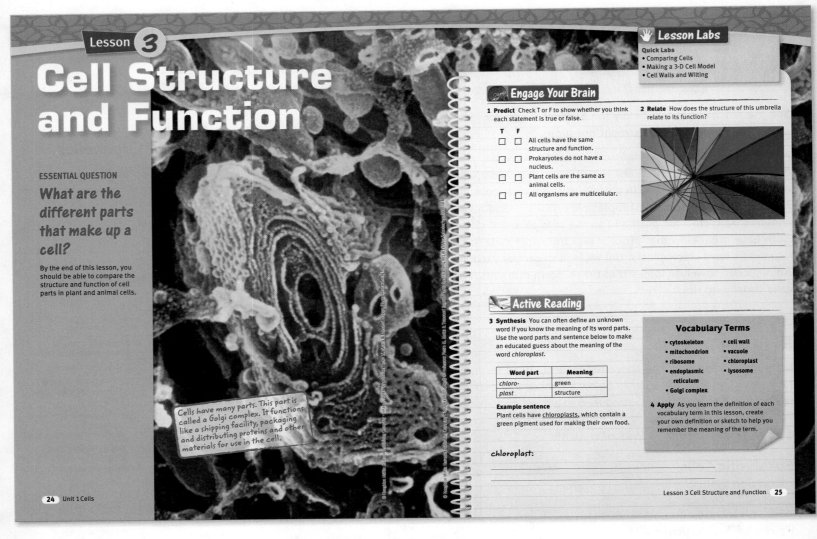

Lesson ③

Cell Structure and Function

ESSENTIAL QUESTION

What are the different parts that make up a cell?

By the end of this lesson, you should be able to compare the structure and function of cell parts in plant and animal cells.

Cells have many parts. This part is called a Golgi complex. It functions like a shipping facility, packaging and distributing proteins and other materials for use in the cell.

24 Unit 1 Cells

Lesson Labs

Quick Labs
• Comparing Cells
• Making a 3-D Cell Model
• Cell Walls and Wilting

Engage Your Brain

1 Predict Check T or F to show whether you think each statement is true or false.

T   F
☐   ☐ All cells have the same structure and function.
☐   ☐ Prokaryotes do not have a nucleus.
☐   ☐ Plant cells are the same as animal cells.
☐   ☐ All organisms are multicellular.

2 Relate How does the structure of this umbrella relate to its function?

Active Reading

3 Synthesis You can often define an unknown word if you know the meaning of its word parts. Use the word parts and sentence below to make an educated guess about the meaning of the word *chloroplast*.

Word part	Meaning
chloro-	green
plast	structure

Example sentence
Plant cells have chloroplasts, which contain a green pigment used for making their own food.

chloroplast:

Vocabulary Terms

• cytoskeleton   • cell wall
• mitochondrion   • vacuole
• ribosome   • chloroplast
• endoplasmic   • lysosome
  reticulum
• Golgi complex

4 Apply As you learn the definition of each vocabulary term in this lesson, create your own definition or sketch to help you remember the meaning of the term.

Lesson 3 Cell Structure and Function 25

Answers

Answers for 1–3 should represent students' current thoughts, even if incorrect.

1. F; T; F; F

2. Sample answer: An umbrella is made of flexible fabric that repels water and easily folds. The rods of the umbrella are sturdy to hold the fabric open, but can collapse to save space when not in use.

3. Sample answer: a cell part where plants make food or where photosynthesis takes place

4. Students should define or sketch each vocabulary term in the lesson.

Opening Your Lesson

Discuss student answers to item 1 to assess students' prerequisite knowledge and to estimate what they already know about the key topics.

Preconceptions Students often think in terms of two types of cells, animal and plant, rather than prokaryotes and eukaryotes.

Prerequisites Students should already have a basic understanding of the four parts of a cell (cell membrane, cytoplasm, DNA, and organelles). Students should also know the two basic types of cells (prokaryotes and eukaryotes).

Learning Alert

Cells Are Diverse Students should be aware that almost all multicellular organisms are eukaryotic and that most unicellular organisms are prokaryotic. However, students should understand that there are exceptions. For example, chlamydomonas are unicellular organisms that are composed of one eukaryotic cell.

Being Eu-nique

What are the characteristics of eukaryotic cells?

5 Identify As you read, underline the characteristics of eukaryotic cells.

All organisms are made up of one or more cells, but what kinds of cells? There are two types of organisms: prokaryotes and eukaryotes. Prokaryotes are made up of a single prokaryotic cell. Eukaryotes are made up of one or more eukaryotic cells. Prokaryotic cells do not have a nucleus or membrane-bound organelles. Eukaryotic cells have membrane-bound organelles, including a nucleus.

Eukaryotic cells can differ from each other depending on their *structure* and *function*. A cell's structure is the arrangement of its parts. A cell's function is the activity the parts carry out. For example, plant cells and animal cells have different parts that have different functions for the organism. This is what make plants and animals so different from each other. Even cells within the same organism can differ from each other depending on their function. Most of the cells in multicellular organisms are specialized to perform a specific function. However, all eukaryotic cells share some characteristics. They all have a nucleus, membrane-bound organelles, and parts that protect and support the cell.

Visualize It!

6 Apply A euglena is a unicellular organism. Why is it a eukaryote like the plant and animal cells shown here?

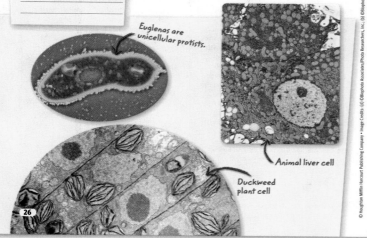

Euglenas are unicellular protists.

Animal liver cell

Duckweed plant cell

26

Parts that Protect and Support the Cell

Every cell is surrounded by a cell membrane. The cell membrane acts as a barrier between the inside of a cell and the cell's environment. The cell membrane protects the cell and regulates what enters and leaves the cell.

The cytoplasm is the region between the cell membrane and the nucleus that includes fluid and all of the organelles. Throughout the cytoplasm of eukaryotic cells is a **cytoskeleton**. The cytoskeleton is a network of protein filaments that gives shape and support to cells. The cytoskeleton is also involved in cell division and in movement. It may help parts within the cell to move. Or it may form structures that help the whole organism to move.

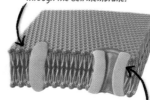

The cell membrane is a double layer of phospholipids. Water molecules and some gas molecules can pass through the cell membrane.

Other larger materials must pass through protein channels in the membrane.

Genetic Material in the Nucleus

The nucleus is an organelle in eukaryotic cells that contains the cell's genetic material. Deoxyribonucleic acid, or DNA, is stored in the nucleus. DNA is genetic material that contains information needed for cell processes, such as making proteins. Proteins perform most actions of a cell. Although DNA is found in the nucleus, proteins are not made there. Instead, instructions for how to make proteins are stored in DNA. These instructions are sent out of the nucleus through pores in the nuclear membrane. The nuclear membrane is a double layer. Each layer is similar in structure to the cell membrane.

7 Describe What are two functions of the cell membrane?

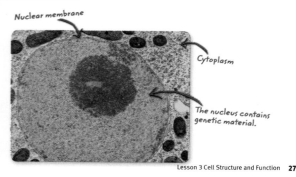

Nuclear membrane

Cytoplasm

The nucleus contains genetic material.

Answers

5. *See students' pages for annotations.*

6. A euglena is a eukaryote because it has a nucleus.

7. The cell membrane protects the inside of the cell from the environment around the cell and regulates what enters and leaves the cell.

Probing Questions GUIDED Inquiry

Examining How is a unicellular organism similar to a multicellular organism? Sample answer: Both types of organisms have a nucleus. **Prompt:** Look at the visuals of the different eukaryotic cells on this page. Think about how they are the same.

Interpreting Visuals

Have students use the pictures of the cells to find similarities and differences between eukaryotic cells. Sample answers: Similarities: cell membrane, cytoplasm, nucleus, and organelles; Differences: The euglena is a unicellular organism; the plant cell is shaped like a box; the animal cell is rounder.

Learning Alert

Eukaryotic Cells Many students will think that all eukaryotic cells contain the same structures. This is not true. While eukaryotic cells share many of the same structures, including a nucleus, they also have different structures. Different structures or different numbers of structures allow the cells to specialize, or have a specific function. For example, muscle cells contain more mitochondria because work is done there; plant root cells do not contain chloroplasts.

Part-iculars

What organelles are found in plant and animal cells?

Even though plant and animal cells are microscopic, they are very complex. They have many parts that function to keep the cell alive. Many of these parts are membrane-bound organelles that perform a specific function.

Cell membrane
Golgi complex
Nucleus
Endoplasmic reticulum
Mitochondria
Ribosomes

Golgi complex

Mitochondria

Organisms need energy for life processes. Cells carry out such processes for growth and repair, movement of materials into and out of the cell, and chemical processes. Cells get energy by breaking down food using a process called *cellular respiration.* Cellular respiration occurs in an organelle called the **mitochondrion** (my•TOH•kahn•dree•ahn). In cellular respiration, cells use oxygen to release energy stored in food. For example, cells break down the sugar glucose to release the energy stored in the sugar. The mitochondria then transfer the energy released from the sugar to a molecule called adenosine triphosphate, or ATP. Cells use ATP to carry out cell processes.

Mitochondria have their own DNA and they have two membranes. The outer membrane is smooth. The inner membrane has many folds. Folds increase the surface area inside the mitochondria where cellular respiration occurs.

8 Explain Why are mitochondria called the powerhouses of cells?

Ribosomes

Ribosomes

Proteins control most chemical reactions of cells and provide structural support for cells and tissues. Some proteins are even exported out of the cell for other functions throughout the body. Making, packaging, and transporting proteins requires many organelles. The **ribosome** is the organelle that makes proteins by putting together chains of amino acids using instructions encoded in the cell's DNA. An amino acid is any of about 20 different carbon-based molecules that are used to make proteins. Almost all cells have ribosomes, which are the smallest organelles.

Ribosomes are not enclosed in a membrane. In prokaryotes, the ribosomes are suspended freely in the cytoplasm. In eukaryotes, some ribosomes are free, and others are attached to another organelle called the *endoplasmic reticulum.*

9 Describe How do ribosomes make proteins?

Endoplasmic Reticulum

In the cytoplasm is a system of membranes near the nucleus called the **endoplasmic reticulum** (ehn•doh•PLAHZ•mick rhett•ICK•yoo•luhm), or ER. The ER assists in the production, processing, and transport of proteins and in the production of lipids. The ER is either smooth or rough. Rough ER has ribosomes attached to its membrane, while smooth ER does not. Ribosomes on the rough ER make many of the cell's proteins. Some of these proteins move through the ER to different places in the cell. The smooth ER makes lipids and breaks down toxic materials that could damage the cell.

10 Compare How does rough ER differ from smooth ER in structure and function?

Golgi Complex

The membrane-bound organelle that packages and distributes materials, such as proteins, is called the **Golgi complex** (GOHL•ghee COHM•plehkz). It is named after Camillo Golgi, the Italian scientist who first identified the organelle.

The Golgi complex is a system of flattened membrane sacs. Lipids and proteins from the ER are delivered to the Golgi complex where they may be modified to do different jobs. The final products are enclosed in a piece of the Golgi complex's membrane. This membrane pinches off to form a small bubble, or vesicle. The vesicle transports its contents to other parts of the cell or out of the cell.

11 Describe What is the function of the Golgi complex?

Answers

8. Mitochondria process sugars through cellular respiration and supply energy for the cell to use.

9. Ribosomes make proteins by assembling chains of amino acids using instructions encoded in the DNA.

10. Rough ER has ribosomes on its surface that make proteins. Smooth ER does not have ribosomes, and makes lipids and breaks down toxic materials in the cell.

11. The Golgi complex modifies and transports lipids and proteins delivered from the ER to do different jobs in the cell or outside of the cell.

Building Reading Skills

Main Idea/Details Remind students that the main idea is the most important point. Help students identify the main idea and the supporting details in the text about the mitochondria. Show students that the main idea is located near the bottom of the second paragraph. Have students write the main idea on a separate piece of paper and then identify at least three supporting details from the text. Students may want to practice identifying the main idea/details in the text about ribosomes, Golgi complex, and the endoplasmic reticulum.

Formative Assessment

Ask: What organelles do all eukaryotes have in common? Sample answer: nucleus, mitochondria, ribosomes, Golgi complex, and endoplasmic reticulum What is the function of each organelle? Sample answer: nucleus: contains genetic material; mitochondria: powerhouses of the cell that release energy; ribosomes: structures that make proteins; Golgi complex: organelle that packages and distributes proteins; and endoplasmic reticulum (ER): smooth ER makes lipids and breaks down toxic materials, and rough ER transports proteins.

Now Showing:
The Plant Cell

What additional parts are found in plant cells?

Think about some ways that plants are different from animals. Plants don't move around, and some have flowers. Plant cells do have a cell membrane, cytoskeleton, nucleus, mitochondria, ribosomes, ER, and a Golgi complex just like animal cells do. In addition, plant cells have a cell wall, large central vacuole, and chloroplasts.

Active Reading

12 Identify As you read, underline the functions of the cell wall, large central vacuole, and the chloroplasts.

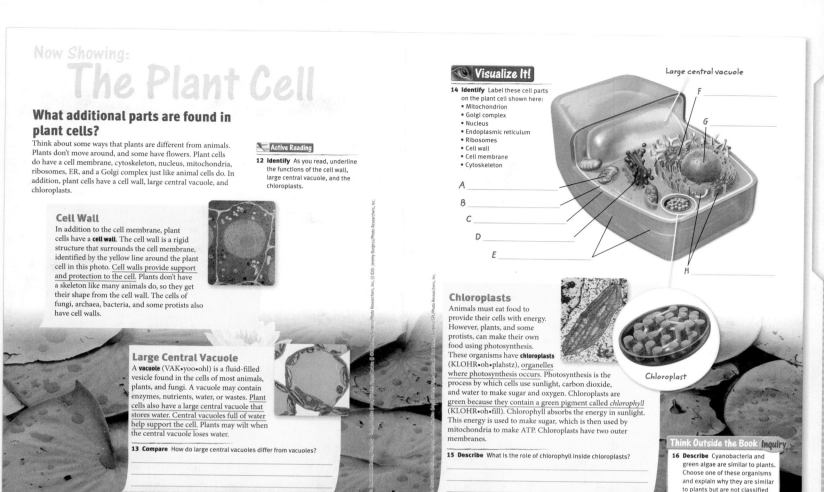

Large central vacuole

Visualize It!

14 Identify Label these cell parts on the plant cell shown here:
• Mitochondrion
• Golgi complex
• Nucleus
• Endoplasmic reticulum
• Ribosomes
• Cell wall
• Cell membrane
• Cytoskeleton

A _____
B _____
C _____
D _____
E _____
F _____
G _____
H _____

Cell Wall

In addition to the cell membrane, plant cells have a **cell wall**. The cell wall is a rigid structure that surrounds the cell membrane, identified by the yellow line around the plant cell in this photo. Cell walls provide support and protection to the cell. Plants don't have a skeleton like many animals do, so they get their shape from the cell wall. The cells of fungi, archaea, bacteria, and some protists also have cell walls.

Large Central Vacuole

A **vacuole** (VAK•yoo•ohl) is a fluid-filled vesicle found in the cells of most animals, plants, and fungi. A vacuole may contain enzymes, nutrients, water, or wastes. Plant cells also have a large central vacuole that stores water. Central vacuoles full of water help support the cell. Plants may wilt when the central vacuole loses water.

13 Compare How do large central vacuoles differ from vacuoles?

Chloroplasts

Animals must eat food to provide their cells with energy. However, plants, and some protists, can make their own food using photosynthesis. These organisms have **chloroplasts** (KLOHR•oh•plahstz), organelles where photosynthesis occurs. Photosynthesis is the process by which cells use sunlight, carbon dioxide, and water to make sugar and oxygen. Chloroplasts are green because they contain a green pigment called *chlorophyll* (KLOHR•oh•fill). Chlorophyll absorbs the energy in sunlight. This energy is used to make sugar, which is then used by mitochondria to make ATP. Chloroplasts have two outer membranes.

Chloroplast

15 Describe What is the role of chlorophyll inside chloroplasts?

Think Outside the Book Inquiry

16 Describe Cyanobacteria and green algae are similar to plants. Choose one of these organisms and explain why they are similar to plants but are not classified as plants.

30

31

Answers

12. *See students' pages for annotations.*

13. The large central vacuole stores water in a plant cell. The vacuole contains enzymes, nutrients, water, or wastes.

14. A, mitochondria; B, cell membrane (blue); C, cell wall (green); D, Golgi complex; E, cytoskeleton; F, endoplasmic reticulum; G, nucleus; H, ribosomes (red dots)

15. Chlorophyll is a green pigment used in photosynthesis. It absorbs the energy in sunlight, which is used to make sugar.

16. Cyanobacteria are similar to plants because they use photosynthesis to make food. They are not classified as plants because they are prokaryotes and do not have a nucleus.

Interpreting Visuals

Have students look at the diagram of the parts of a plant cell to identify the different parts found only in plant cells. **Ask:** How does the plant benefit from having a cell wall around the cell membrane? Cell walls provide structure and protection to the plant.

Probing Question

Comparing and Contrasting Plant and animal cells are different because they each need different things. What are some of the ways that plants and animals are different that might explain some of their cellular characteristics? Sample answers: Plants make their own food; animals eat food; animals breathe oxygen; plants breathe carbon dioxide.

Learning Alert ⚡ MISCONCEPTION ⚡

Plants vs. Animals Students may think that plants have nothing in common with animals. **Ask:** What do you have in common with celery? If students say "nothing," they may hold the misconception that plants are totally different from animals. **Prompt:** Talk about the criteria for life. Ask whether celery meets the criteria, and how that makes it similar to humans.

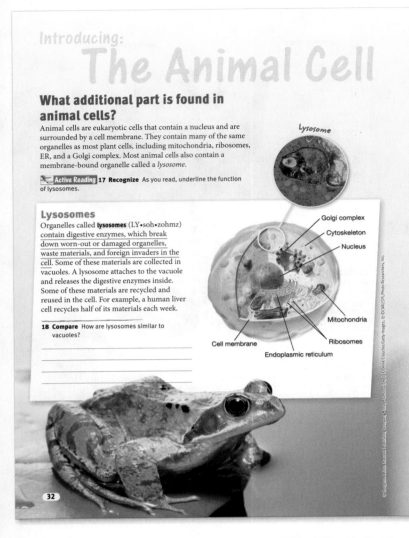

Introducing: The Animal Cell

What additional part is found in animal cells?

Animal cells are eukaryotic cells that contain a nucleus and are surrounded by a cell membrane. They contain many of the same organelles as most plant cells, including mitochondria, ribosomes, ER, and a Golgi complex. Most animal cells also contain a membrane-bound organelle called a *lysosome*.

Active Reading **17 Recognize** As you read, underline the function of lysosomes.

Lysosomes

Organelles called **lysosomes** (LY•soh•zohmz) contain digestive enzymes, which break down worn-out or damaged organelles, waste materials, and foreign invaders in the cell. Some of these materials are collected in vacuoles. A lysosome attaches to the vacuole and releases the digestive enzymes inside. Some of these materials are recycled and reused in the cell. For example, a human liver cell recycles half of its materials each week.

18 Compare How are lysosomes similar to vacuoles?

Lysosome

Golgi complex
Cytoskeleton
Nucleus

Mitochondria
Ribosomes

Cell membrane
Endoplasmic reticulum

19 Compare Draw a sketch for each organelle identified in the *Structure* column. Put check marks in the last two columns to identify whether the cell structure can usually be found in plant cells, animal cells, or both.

Structure	Function	In plant cell?	In animal cell?
Nucleus	Contains the genetic material		
Endoplasmic reticulum	Processes and transports proteins and makes lipids		
Golgi complex	Packages and distributes materials within or out of the cell		
Ribosome	Makes proteins		
Chloroplast	Uses sunlight, carbon dioxide, and water to make food by photosynthesis		
Mitochondrion	Breaks down food molecules to release energy by cellular respiration		
Large central vacuole	Stores water and helps give shape to the cell		
Lysosome	Produces enzymes that digest wastes, cell parts, and foreign invaders		

32

33

Answers

17. *See students' pages for annotations.*

18. Lysosomes are similar to vacuoles because they both process waste materials.

19. Students should draw structures of the cell parts similar to the images provided in this lesson. Students should check the following boxes.

In plant cell?: nucleus, endoplasmic reticulum, Golgi complex, ribosome, chloroplast, mitochondrion, large central vacuole

In animal cell?: nucleus, endoplasmic reticulum, Golgi complex, ribosome, mitochondrion, lysosome

Probing Question

Drawing Conclusions Why can't animal cells make food? Sample answer: Animal cells cannot make food because they do not contain chloroplasts. Chloroplasts are the organelles in which photosynthesis takes place.

Formative Assessment

Compare plant and animal cells. **Ask:** How are plant and animal cells alike and different? Sample answer: Both have organelles that process and transport. Only plant cells have chloroplasts to capture energy from sunlight. Only plant cells have cell walls and central vacuoles, which store water, wastes, and dissolved salts. Animal cells cannot make their own food. Animal cells have lysosomes, which digest wastes and store and break down nutrients.

For greater depth, have students create diagrams of plant and animal cells.

Learning Alert

Lysosomes Current evidence shows that some plant cells may contain lysosomes. This issue is currently being debated among plant biologists.

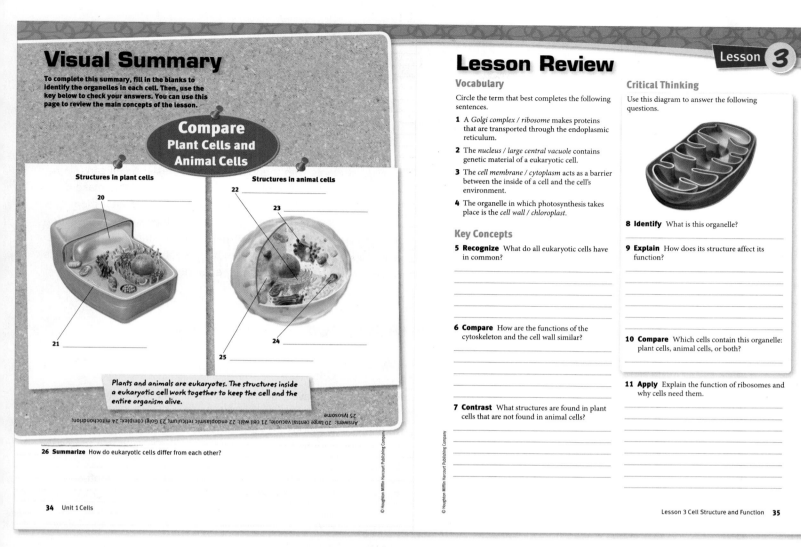

Visual Summary

To complete this summary, fill in the blanks to identify the organelles in each cell. Then, use the key below to check your answers. You can use this page to review the main concepts of the lesson.

Compare Plant Cells and Animal Cells

Structures in plant cells

20 _____

21 _____

Structures in animal cells

22 _____

23 _____

24 _____

25 _____

Plants and animals are eukaryotes. The structures inside a eukaryotic cell work together to keep the cell and the entire organism alive.

Answers: 20 large central vacuole; 21 cell wall; 22 endoplasmic reticulum; 23 Golgi complex; 24 mitochondrion; 25 lysosome

26 **Summarize** How do eukaryotic cells differ from each other?

© Houghton Mifflin Harcourt Publishing Company

Lesson Review

Vocabulary

Circle the term that best completes the following sentences.

1 A *Golgi complex / ribosome* makes proteins that are transported through the endoplasmic reticulum.

2 The *nucleus / large central vacuole* contains genetic material of a eukaryotic cell.

3 The *cell membrane / cytoplasm* acts as a barrier between the inside of a cell and the cell's environment.

4 The organelle in which photosynthesis takes place is the *cell wall / chloroplast*.

Key Concepts

5 **Recognize** What do all eukaryotic cells have in common?

6 **Compare** How are the functions of the cytoskeleton and the cell wall similar?

7 **Contrast** What structures are found in plant cells that are not found in animal cells?

Critical Thinking

Use this diagram to answer the following questions.

8 **Identify** What is this organelle?

9 **Explain** How does its structure affect its function?

10 **Compare** Which cells contain this organelle: plant cells, animal cells, or both?

11 **Apply** Explain the function of ribosomes and why cells need them.

© Houghton Mifflin Harcourt Publishing Company

Visual Summary Answers

20. large central vacuole

21. cell wall

22. endoplasmic reticulum

23. Golgi complex

24. mitochondrion

25. lysosome

26. Sample answer: Eukaryotic cells can have different structures and, therefore, perform different functions. For example, animal cells have lysosomes. Plant cells have a large central vacuole, a cell wall, and chloroplasts. These differences in structure and function are what make animals and plants so different from each other.

Lesson Review Answers

1. ribosome

2. nucleus

3. cell membrane

4. chloroplast

5. All eukaryotic cells have a nucleus, cell membrane, and membrane-bound organelles.

6. Both the cytoskeleton and the cell wall support the cell's structure and maintain its shape.

7. Plant cells have a cell wall, a large central vacuole, and chloroplasts. Animal cells do not have these parts.

8. mitochondrion

9. The structure includes a folded inner membrane. Folding increases the surface area on which cellular respiration can take place.

10. both

11. Sample answer: Ribosomes make proteins. All cells need proteins because proteins control most chemical reactions of cells and provide structural support for cells and tissues.

Think Science

Making Predictions

Purpose To learn about how scientists make predictions based on their hypotheses

Learning Goals
- Predict outcomes based on evidence for scientific investigations.

Informal Vocabulary
hypothesis, inhibited, bias, culture

Prerequisite Knowledge
- The characteristics of cells
- Cell structure and function
- Acids, bases, and pH

Discussion *Everyday Predictions*

 whole class | 15 min
 GUIDED inquiry

Talk to the class about making predictions. Point out that people make predictions all the time in their everyday lives. For example, **ask:** If the sky becomes cloudy and it gets windy out, what prediction might you make? Sample answer: It is going to rain. **Ask:** If you don't study for a big test, what might happen? Sample answer: You will get a bad grade. Encourage students to come up with their own scenarios and challenge the class to make predictions. Then explain that scientists make predictions all the time. Their predictions are more complicated than the predictions we make every day, but just like everyday predictions they require making observations and thinking critically about cause-and-effect relationships.

 Optional Online resource: Class Discussion rubric

Differentiated Instruction

Basic *pH Predictions*

 pairs | 🕐 10 min

Provide students with the following hypothesis: A cell can only function at certain pH levels. Then have students make a prediction based on the hypothesis in the form of an if-then statement. Have them use the example in the tutorial as a guide. If necessary, explain that the if part of each statement describes a scenario or idea that could test the hypothesis. The then part is a prediction of what would happen under that scenario.

Advanced *Design a Study*

 pairs | 🕐 15 min

Role Playing Have student pairs recall what they have already learned about the structure and function of cells. Then tell them to think of questions they still have about cells. Have them take the role of scientists and design a study they could use to answer one of their questions. First, they should develop a hypothesis. Next, they should make predictions based on their hypothesis. Finally, they should describe how they will test their predictions.

ELL *If-Then*

 individuals | 🕐 10 min

Provide students with the following hypothesis: In mice, different cells do different jobs. Then have students fill in *if-then* sentence frames that they can use to make predictions about the hypothesis. Use frames such as the following: If we look at cells from different parts of a mouse under a microscope, then we predict _____. If we move cells from one part of a mouse to another, then we predict _____.

Customize Your Feature

☐ **Discussion** Everyday Predictions

☐ **Basic** pH Predictions

☐ **Advanced** Design a Study

☐ **ELL** If-Then

☐ **Learning Alert**

☐ **Take It Home**

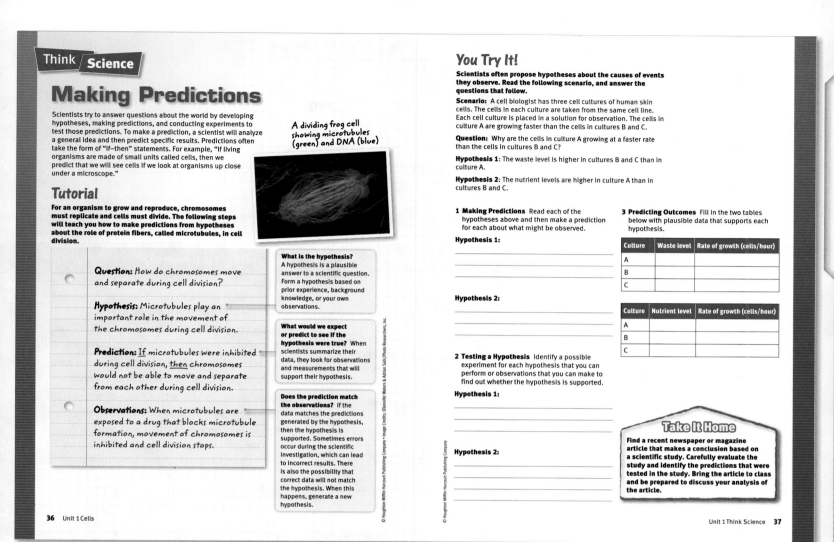

Think Science

Making Predictions

Scientists try to answer questions about the world by developing hypotheses, making predictions, and conducting experiments to test those predictions. To make a prediction, a scientist will analyze a general idea and then predict specific results. Predictions often take the form of "if–then" statements. For example, "If living organisms are made of small units called cells, then we predict that we will see cells if we look at organisms up close under a microscope."

A dividing frog cell showing microtubules (green) and DNA (blue)

Tutorial

For an organism to grow and reproduce, chromosomes must replicate and cells must divide. The following steps will teach you how to make predictions from hypotheses about the role of protein fibers, called microtubules, in cell division.

Question: How do chromosomes move and separate during cell division?

Hypothesis: Microtubules play an important role in the movement of the chromosomes during cell division.

Prediction: If microtubules were inhibited during cell division, then chromosomes would not be able to move and separate from each other during cell division.

Observations: When microtubules are exposed to a drug that blocks microtubule formation, movement of chromosomes is inhibited and cell division stops.

What is the hypothesis? A hypothesis is a plausible answer to a scientific question. Form a hypothesis based on prior experience, background knowledge, or your own observations.

What would we expect or predict to see if the hypothesis were true? When scientists summarize their data, they look for observations and measurements that will support their hypothesis.

Does the prediction match the observations? If the data matches the predictions generated by the hypothesis, then the hypothesis is supported. Sometimes errors occur during the scientific investigation, which can lead to incorrect results. There is also the possibility that correct data will not match the hypothesis. When this happens, generate a new hypothesis.

You Try It!

Scientists often propose hypotheses about the causes of events they observe. Read the following scenario, and answer the questions that follow.

Scenario: A cell biologist has three cell cultures of human skin cells. The cells in each culture are taken from the same cell line. Each cell culture is placed in a solution for observation. The cells in culture A are growing faster than the cells in cultures B and C.

Question: Why are the cells in culture A growing at a faster rate than the cells in cultures B and C?

Hypothesis 1: The waste level is higher in cultures B and C than in culture A.

Hypothesis 2: The nutrient levels are higher in culture A than in cultures B and C.

1 Making Predictions Read each of the hypotheses above and then make a prediction for each about what might be observed.

Hypothesis 1:

_____

_____

_____

Hypothesis 2:

_____

_____

_____

2 Testing a Hypothesis Identify a possible experiment for each hypothesis that you can perform or observations that you can make to find out whether the hypothesis is supported.

Hypothesis 1:

_____

_____

_____

Hypothesis 2:

_____

_____

_____

3 Predicting Outcomes Fill in the two tables below with plausible data that supports each hypothesis.

Culture	Waste level	Rate of growth (cells/hour)
A		
B		
C		

Culture	Nutrient level	Rate of growth (cells/hour)
A		
B		
C		

Take It Home

Find a recent newspaper or magazine article that makes a conclusion based on a scientific study. Carefully evaluate the study and identify the predictions that were tested in the study. Bring the article to class and be prepared to discuss your analysis of the article.

36 Unit 1 Cells

Unit 1 Think Science 37

Answers

1. Students should come up with one prediction for each hypothesis. The predictions should follow the "if–then" statement concept and should be related to the hypotheses which they are based upon.

2. Students should talk about one experiment per hypothesis, each testing a variable such as pH level or temperature, and evaluating the effect of changing this variable on the rate of growth of cells in culture.

Learning Alert

Remind students that pH is a measure of how acidic or basic a solution is. Solutions with a pH of less than 7 are acidic, while solutions with a pH of more than 7 are basic. A solution with a pH of 7 is neutral.

Take It Home

Remind students to reference the steps in the tutorial when analyzing their articles. Point out that the hypothesis and predictions made by the scientists in the study may not be directly stated, so they may have to infer them based on the description of the study and its results.

Levels of Cellular Organization

Essential Question How are living things organized?

Professional Development

For more detailed information about the topics in this lesson, refer to the Content Refresher in the Unit Opener pages.

Opening Your Lesson

Begin the lesson by assessing students' prerequisite and prior knowledge.

Prerequisite Knowledge

- Cells are the basic units of life; cells perform all of the processes necessary for life.
- Some organisms are made up of just one cell, while other organisms, such as humans, are made up of many cells.

Accessing Prior Knowledge

Ask: Why are cells important? Sample answer: Cells are the basic units of life.

Ask: How are multicellular organisms different from unicellular organisms? Sample answer: Multicellular organisms have groups of specialized cells that work together; unicellular organisms do not.

Customize Your Opening

☐ **Accessing Prior Knowledge**, above

☐ **Print Path** Engage Your Brain, SE p. 39

☐ **Print Path** Active Reading, SE p. 39

☐ **Digital Path** Lesson Opener

Key Topics/Learning Goals

Cells to Organisms

1 Define *organism*.
2 Identify that living things are unicellular and multicellular, and list characteristics of multicellular organisms.
3 List levels of structural organization.
4 Define specialization.
5 Define *tissue, organ,* and *organ system*.
6 Compare types of animal and plant tissues, organs, and organ systems.

Cellular Structure and Function

1 Define *structure* and *function*.
2 Explain the basic relationship between the structure and function of tissues, organs, and organ systems.

Systems Work Together

1 Describe how various organs and tissues serve the needs of cells for nutrient and oxygen delivery and waste removal.

Supporting Concepts

- An organism is made up of one or more cells and carries out its own life functions.
- Unicellular organisms are a single cell. Multicellular organisms are more than one cell.
- The levels of structural organization are cell, tissue, organ, organ system, and organism.
- Specialization is the adaptation of a cell, tissue, or organ for a specific function.
- A tissue is a group of cells that work together; an organ is a structure made up of two or more tissues; and an organ system is a group of organs working together.
- Animal tissues are nerve, muscle, connective, and epithelial tissue. Plant tissues are protective, transport, and ground tissue.

- Structure is the arrangement of parts in an organism.
- Function is the activity of an organ or part.
- The structure and function of tissues, organs, and organ systems allow organisms to carry out life processes.

- Body systems in multicellular organisms work together to maintain healthy cells.
- Xylem and phloem are tissues that make up a plant's vascular system, which transports water and nutrients to and from cells.
- The circulatory system works with the respiratory, excretory, and digestive systems in supplying oxygen and nutrients to the body and removing wastes from the body.

Options for Instruction

Two parallel paths provide coverage of the Essential Questions, with a strong Inquiry strand woven into each. Follow the **Print Path,** the **Digital Path,** or your customized combination of print, digital, and inquiry.

 Print Path
Teaching support for the Print Path appears with the Student Pages.

 Inquiry Labs and Activities

 Digital Path
Digital Path shortcut: TS663014

Body Building, SE pp. 40–43
How are living things organized?
- Into Cells
- Into Tissues
- Into Organs
- Into Organ Systems

Exploration Lab
The Organization of Organisms

Quick Lab
Evaluating Specialization

Daily Demo
From Leaf to Cell

Activity
Organ and Tissue Donation

Unicellular and Multicellular Organisms
Interactive Graphics

What's Your Function?,
SE p. 44
What is the connection between structure and function?
- Structure Determines Function

Activity
An Organized Review

Tissues
Interactive Graphics

Organs
Interactive Graphics

Systems at Work,
SE pp. 46–47
What tasks do systems perform to meet the needs of cells?
- Delivering Nutrients
- Delivering Oxygen
- Removing Waste

Activity
Roots and Leaves

Quick Lab
Observing Plant Organs

Organ Systems
Interactive Graphics

Keeping Cells Healthy
Video

Options for Assessment

See the Evaluate page for options, including Formative Assessment, Summative Assessment, and Unit Review.

Engage and Explore

Activities and Discussion

Discussion *Stem Cells*

Cellular Structure and Function

 whole class
 10 min
 DIRECTED inquiry

Specialized cells often cannot reproduce. Instead, the body gets new specialized cells from stem cells. Stem cells are not specialized. Every single cell in the human body "stems" or originates from stem cells. Stem cells can self-replicate, each time producing one new specialized cell and one new stem cell. Scientists are looking at how stem cells might be used to restore damaged tissues. Invite students to discuss ways stem cells might be used to help patients. Interested students may want to research stem cells.

Probing Question *How Is an Organism Similar to a City?*

Cells to Organisms

 individuals
 10 min
 GUIDED inquiry

Comparing Ask students to talk about how an organism could be compared to a city.

Work with students to help them understand that specialized cells do different jobs, just as people do. Organisms have tissues, while cities have roads, fences, and greenways.

Take It Home *Unusual Specialized Cells!*

Cellular Structure and Function

 adult-student pairs
 10–20 min
INDEPENDENT inquiry

With an adult, students brainstorm organisms that might have unusual specialized cells. For example, the electric eel has specialized cells that are capable of storing electricity. Pairs record ideas and conduct research about why these organisms might have specialized cells.

⟳ *Online resource: student worksheet*

Activity *Roots and Leaves*

Systems Work Together

 pairs or small groups, then whole class
 20 min
 DIRECTED inquiry

Have students compare the roots and leaves of a grass plant. First, students should soak a grass plant in a cup of water to clean away any dirt. Next, direct students' attention to the roots and leaves of the plant. Encourage them to compare these two plant organs and think about how the roots and leaves work together to supply nutrients and get rid of wastes. After students have written down their observations, discuss what they noticed.

Activity *Organ and Tissue Donation*

> Engage

Cellular Structure and Function

 small groups
 15 min
 GUIDED inquiry

Think, Pair, Share Tell students that organ and tissue transplants save many lives each year. Some donations can come from living donors; others must come from deceased donors. Give students the following list of tissues and organs that can be donated by someone living: lung, liver, kidneys, bone marrow, and blood. Direct students to think about why these can come from a living donor. Have students pair up and discuss their ideas, and then ask for volunteers to share their conclusions with the class. Sample answer: the structure of lungs and kidneys (paired sets) and the function of blood, bone marrow, and liver (they regenerate)

⟳ *Optional Online resource: Think, Pair, Share support*

Customize Your Labs

 See the Lab Manual for lab datasheets.

 Go Online for editable lab datasheets.

 Levels of **Inquiry**

| **DIRECTED** inquiry | **GUIDED** inquiry | **INDEPENDENT** inquiry |
| introduces inquiry skills within a structured framework. | develops inquiry skills within a supportive environment. | deepens inquiry skills with student-driven questions or procedures. |

Labs and Demos

Daily Demo *From Leaf to Cell*

Engage

Cells to Organisms

 whole class or small groups
🕐 10 min
Inquiry **DIRECTED** inquiry

PURPOSE To observe the sequence of cell to tissue to organ

MATERIALS

- lettuce leaf, preferably with large stems
- microscope, preferably digital
- slide and cover slip
- tweezers

1 Show students a leaf of the lettuce plant. Explain that the leaf is an organ that provides the plant with energy and materials.

2 Locate a rib in the leaf and bend it back against the curve until it snaps. You should be able to see the edges of a thin layer of tissue. Use tweezers to gently peel the tissue off the lettuce for students to see. Explain that this is a tissue and that it is one cell thick. Tell students that the leaf of a plant contains different types of tissue: tissue that brings in water and nutrients, tissue that uses the sun's energy to make sugar, and tissue that moves sugar to other parts of the plant.

3 After preparing the slide, use the microscope to show students the leaf cells from the lettuce plant. Demonstrate that similar cells make up a tissue.

Quick Lab *Evaluating Specialization*

PURPOSE To investigate how specialization affects efficiency

See the Lab Manual or go Online for planning information.

Quick Lab *Observing Plant Organs*

Synthesizing Key Topics

 individuals
🕐 40 min
Inquiry **DIRECTED** inquiry

Students observe the taproot system of a carrot and then describe a similar organ system in an animal.

PURPOSE To compare the structure and function of a plant and animal organ system

MATERIALS

- carrot
- colored pencils
- hand lens
- knife
- reference materials
- prepared carrot slide
- microscope
- safety goggles

Exploration Lab *The Organization of Organisms*

Cells to Organisms

👥 pairs
🕐 45 min
Inquiry **DIRECTED** or **GUIDED** inquiry

Students use drawings and images to create diagrams.

PURPOSE To observe the hierarchical organization of organisms

MATERIALS

- colored pencils
- paper, white
- light microscope
- posterboard, white
- prepared microscope slide
- ruler

Activities and Discussion

- ☐ **Discussion** Stem Cells
- ☐ **Probing Question** How is an...City?
- ☐ **Take it Home** Specialized Cells!
- ☐ **Activity** Roots and Leaves
- ☐ **Activity** Organ and Tissue Donation

Labs and Demos

- ☐ **Daily Demo** From Leaf to Cell
- ☐ **Quick Lab** Evaluating Specialization
- ☐ **Quick Lab** Observing Plant Organs
- ☐ **Exploration Lab** The Organization of Organisms

Your Resources

_____

_____

_____

Explain Science Concepts

	📖 Print Path	💻 Digital Path
Key Topics		

Cells to Organisms

☐ **Body Building,** SE pp. 40–43
- Active Reading (Annotation strategy), #5
- Venn Diagram, #6
- Visualize It!, #7
- Active Reading, #8
- Visualize It!, #9
- Infer, #10
- Think Outside the Book, #11

🌐 *Optional Online resource: Venn Diagram support*

☐ **Unicellular and Multicellular Organisms**
Learn about unicellular and multicellular organisms and identify the levels of organization.

Cellular Structure and Function

☐ **What's Your Function?,** SE p. 44
- Active Reading (Annotation strategy), #12
- Visualize It!, #13

☐ **Tissues**
Learn about different types of animal and plant tissues.

☐ **Organs**
Learn about different organs in plants and animals.

☐ **Cell Structure and Function**
Discover how cellular structure and function are related.

Systems Work Together

☐ **Systems at Work,** SE pp. 46–47
- Active Reading, #17
- Visualize It!, #18
- Visualize It!, #19

☐ **Organ Systems**
Learn about different systems in plants and animals.

☐ **Keeping Cells Healthy**
Explore how various organs and tissues serve the needs of cells for nutrient and oxygen delivery and waste removal.

Differentiated Instruction

Basic *"Super" Cells*

Cellular Structure and Function

 individuals or pairs

🕐 varies

After students have learned about cellular structure and function, ask them to design three superheroes, each with different special powers. One superhero will be a red blood cell, one will be a nerve cell (neuron), and one will be a muscle cell. These superheroes are on a mission inside the human body. Illustrations of the characters should relate the structure to its function. Check students' work to make sure they understand the structure and function of these cells. Make corrections as necessary.

Advanced *Artificial Blood*

Cells to Organisms

 individuals or pairs

🕐 30 min

Quick Research Invite students to investigate artificial blood. Artificial blood, or oxygen therapeutics, cannot replace blood, but it has big advantages in some situations. Students can use the following questions to guide their research: *What can blood do that artificial blood cannot? What do artificial blood and real blood have in common? In what situations might artificial blood be useful?* As a prompt to get students thinking about situations in which artificial blood might even be preferable, tell them that although our blood supply in the United States is safe, blood supplies in some other countries are not.

ELL *All-Encompassing Terms*

Synthesizing Key Topics

 individuals or pairs

🕐 10 min

Concentric Circles Struggling students or English language learners may confuse the terms *organ, organ system,* and *organism.* These words are key to understanding the hierarchical organization of organisms. Define these terms for students. Tell them to write *organ* in the center of a circle. Then, direct students to draw a larger circle around that circle and write *organ system* in it. Next, they should draw an even larger third circle around the second circle and write *organism* in it. Point out to students that organisms include organ systems and organs, and organ systems include organs. **To extend the activity,** ask students to begin their concentric circles with *cell* as the first circle and continue until you have five concentric circles, with *organism* encompassing the other four circles/levels.

Lesson Vocabulary

organism	tissue	organ
organ system	structure	function

Previewing Vocabulary

 whole class

🕐 15 min

Word Origins Share the following to help students remember terms:
- *Organ* comes from the Greek word *organon,* which means "tool." In science, this word refers to two or more tissues that work together to perform a specific function.
- *Structure* comes from the Latin word *structura,* which means "fitting together."
- *Function* comes from the Latin word *functio,* which means "performance."

Reinforcing Vocabulary

👥 individuals

🕐 20 min

Four Square To help students remember the different terms introduced in the lesson, have them draw a 2-by-2 matrix with a circle at the center. Students place a term in the circle and then fill in the surrounding cells with the types of information shown.

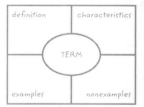

🌐 *Optional Online resource: Four Square support*

Customize Your Core Lesson

Core Instruction

☐ **Print Path** choices

☐ **Digital Path** choices

Vocabulary

☐ **Previewing Vocabulary** Word Origins

☐ **Reinforcing Vocabulary** Four Square

Your Resources

Differentiated Instruction

☐ **Basic** "Super" Cells

☐ **Advanced** Artificial Blood

☐ **ELL** All-Encompassing Terms

Extend Science Concepts

Reinforce and Review

Activity *An Organized Review*

Synthesizing Key Topics   small groups   20 min

Carousel Review Attach pieces of chart paper to the walls at different locations throughout the room. There should be one chart for cell, one for tissue, one for organ, and one for organ system. Include the following question on each chart: How does the structure of this part or system relate to its function? You may want to focus on one body system, such as the human digestive system, to tie the content together.

1 Divide the class into small groups and assign each group a chart. Provide each group with a different-colored marker.

2 Have groups review their question, discuss their answer, and write a response.

3 After about five minutes, have each group rotate to the next station. Groups place a check beside each answer they agree with, comment on answers they do not agree with, and add their own answers.

4 Repeat steps 2 and 3 until all groups have reviewed all charts.

5 Conclude the activity by reviewing the responses. Invite each group to share information about their responses with the class. Address any misconceptions or errors that arise.

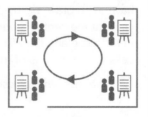

FoldNote

Cells to Organisms   individuals   15 min

Layered Book Have students create a Layered Book FoldNote that includes a page for each of the following: *Cells, Tissues, Organs,* and *Organ Systems.* Students should label each page and include a diagram and a description for that topic. Encourage students to also include key concepts from the text.

Optional Online resource: Layered Book support

Going Further

Health Connection

Systems Work Together   individuals   varied

Research Project Humans have 11 organ systems. Each organ system plays a particular role in the body in maintaining good health. The systems often affect one another, and some organs work as part of more than one system. If an organ fails, it will likely have a negative effect on the entire body. Have students research different diseases that affect specific organs; for example, heart disease and lung disease. Students should include the causes of the disease and possible treatments.

 Optional Online rubric: Written Pieces

Engineering Connection

Cellular Structure and Function   whole class   15 min

Discussion Science often uses ideas from nature to help solve problems. Space suits have specialized features that allow astronauts to live in harsh environments, similar to how unicellular organisms are specialized in ways that allow them to live in harsh environments. Ask students to compare a space suit with a unicellular organism. Features of a space suit that are similar include strong outer material, a special jet-propelled backpack, and tanks of compressed air. You can mention that one difference between a space suit and a unicellular organism is that a space suit carries its own oxygen, while a cell must get its oxygen from the environment.

Customize Your Closing

See the Assessment Guide for quizzes and tests.

Go Online to edit and create quizzes and tests.

Reinforce and Review

☐ **Activity** An Organized Review

☐ **FoldNote** Layered Book

☐ **Print Path** Visual Summary, SE p. 48

☐ **Print Path** Lesson Review, SE p. 49

☐ **Digital Path** Lesson Closer

Evaluate Student Mastery

See the teacher support below the Student Pages for additional Formative Assessment questions.

Have students review the hierarchical organization of organisms from the beginning of the lesson. **Ask:** Describe the levels of organization in an organism, such as a tree. Sample answer: A tree is an organism made of plant cells that form a tissue. Different tissues work together to form an organ, such as a leaf. Two organ systems in a tree are the shoot system (leaves and stems) and the root system. **Ask:** How does the structure of a cell relate to its function? Sample answer: The structure of a cell determines the type of job or function that the cell can perform. Follow this question by asking students to relate the structure of a particular cell, such as a red blood cell, to its function.

Reteach

Formative assessment may show that students need reinforcement for certain topics. The resources below are recommended for reteaching. If students were introduced to a topic through the Print Path, you can also use the Digital Path to reteach, and vice versa.

🎧 *Can be assigned to individual students*

Cells to Organisms
ELL All-Encompassing Terms 🎧
FoldNote Layered Book 🎧

Cellular Structure and Function
Basic "Super" Cells 🎧

Systems Work Together
Activity Roots and Leaves 🎧
Quick Lab Observing Plant Organs

Alternative Assessment
Design Artificial Organs

🌐 *Online resources: student worksheet, optional rubrics*

Levels of Cellular Organization

Tic-Tac-Toe: *Design Artificial Organs*
Imagine that you are on a committee that is considering whether or not to create artificial cells, tissues, or organs.

1. Work on your own, with a partner, or with a small group.

2. Choose three quick activities from the game. Check the boxes you plan to complete. They must form a straight line in any direction.

3. Have your teacher approve your plan.

4. Do each activity, and turn in your results.

__ Structure and Function	__ Diagram	__ Organ Journal
Every organ has a structure directly related to its function. Describe two organs and explain how each organ's structure helps it to function. Then, pick one of these organs and describe what type of artificial structure you think would be ideal for its function, and why.	Choose two or more organ systems and draw a diagram showing how they work together keep an organism healthy. You can choose either plant or animal systems.	Write a journal entry describing two artificial organs you would like to create. Include a diagram of these organs.
__ Human Cell Types	__ Building a System	__ Instruction Booklet
Look up different human cell types. There are more than 200! Briefly describe the function of 10 human body cells. Pick one type you would want to create and tell why, or discuss why this type of cell could never be created artificially.	The four levels of organization (cells, tissues, organs, and organ systems) are nearly the same for all multicellular organisms. Write a skit describing how these four levels make up an organism.	Pick an organ system. Research the names of the organs that make up this system. Design an instruction booklet on the use of this system.
__ Designer Cell	__ Life in a Pond	__ Which Tissue?
Design and sketch an imaginary specialized cell that could be part of an artificial life form. Describe the function of this cell that makes it unique.	Write a poem comparing a single-celled paramecium and a multicellular sunfish living in the same freshwater pond. Explore ways in which each organism is adapted for survival.	Describe the functions of the four types of tissues found in humans. Decide which type you think might be the most useful to manufacture, and compose a speech to convince others of the value of this type of tissue.

Going Further
☐ Health Connection
☐ Engineering Connection
☐ **Print Path** Why It Matters, SE p. 45

Formative Assessment
☐ **Strategies** Throughout TE
☐ **Lesson Review** SE

Summative Assessment
☐ Alternative Assessment Design Artificial Organs
☐ Lesson Quiz
☐ Unit Tests A and B
☐ Unit Review SE End-of-Unit

Your Resources

_____

_____

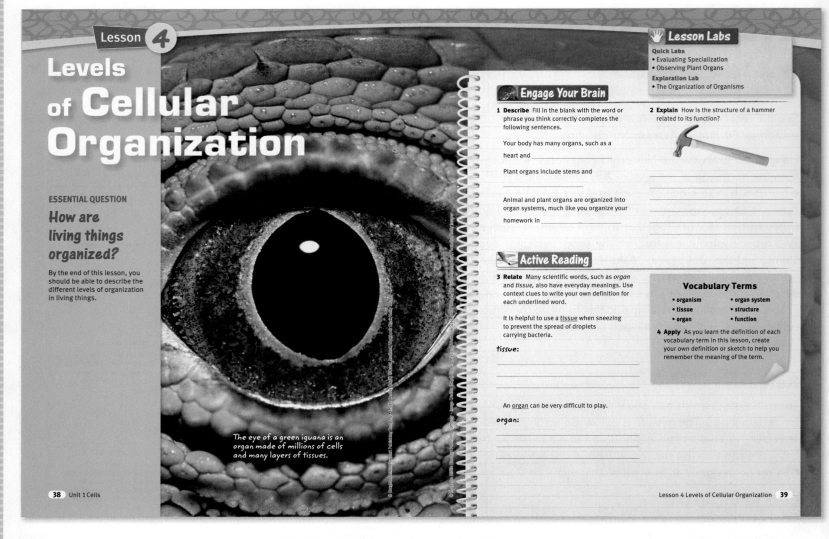

Lesson 4

Levels of Cellular Organization

ESSENTIAL QUESTION

How are living things organized?

By the end of this lesson, you should be able to describe the different levels of organization in living things.

The eye of a green iguana is an organ made of millions of cells and many layers of tissues.

Lesson Labs

Quick Labs
• Evaluating Specialization
• Observing Plant Organs

Exploration Lab
• The Organization of Organisms

Engage Your Brain

1 Describe Fill in the blank with the word or phrase you think correctly completes the following sentences.

Your body has many organs, such as a

heart and _____

Plant organs include stems and

_____

Animal and plant organs are organized into organ systems, much like you organize your

homework in _____

2 Explain How is the structure of a hammer related to its function?

_____
_____
_____
_____
_____

Active Reading

3 Relate Many scientific words, such as *organ* and *tissue*, also have everyday meanings. Use context clues to write your own definition for each underlined word.

It is helpful to use a <u>tissue</u> when sneezing to prevent the spread of droplets carrying bacteria.

tissue:
_____
_____
_____

An <u>organ</u> can be very difficult to play.

organ:
_____
_____
_____

Vocabulary Terms
• organism   • organ system
• tissue   • structure
• organ   • function

4 Apply As you learn the definition of each vocabulary term in this lesson, create your own definition or sketch to help you remember the meaning of the term.

Answers

Answers for 1–3 should represent students' current thoughts, even if incorrect.

1. Sample answers: stomach; roots; binders

2. Sample answer: The handle makes it easy to grip and swing back and forth. The end is heavy to push nails through some surfaces, and it has a V-shaped part to remove nails from surfaces.

3. **tissue:** a thin cloth or paper to cover or wipe the nose or mouth

   organ: an instrument made of many keys, foot pedals, and pipes

4. Students should define or sketch each vocabulary term in the lesson.

Opening Your Lesson

Discuss students' responses to the Engage Your Brain items to assess their prerequisite knowledge and to estimate what they already know about cellular organization.

Preconceptions All cells are flat and small. Remind students that cells come in various shapes and sizes depending on their function.

Prerequisites Students should already have a basic knowledge of cells and know that cells are the basic units of life. Students should also know that cells perform all of the processes necessary for life.

Learning Alert

Cells Students often think that cells are within the organisms, rather than understanding that the entire organism is composed of cells. This type of misconception often occurs when students are learning that red and white blood cells flow within arteries and veins. While this is correct, students may not realize that the arteries and veins themselves are composed of specialized cells. It is important to be aware of this misconception when discussing levels of cellular organization.

Body Building

How are living things organized?

Active Reading

5 Identify As you read, underline the characteristics of unicellular and multicellular organisms.

An **organism** is a living thing that can carry out life processes by itself. *Unicellular organisms* are made up of just one cell that performs all of the functions necessary for life. Unicellular organisms do not have levels of organization. Having only one cell has advantages and disadvantages. For example, unicellular organisms need fewer resources and some can live in harsh conditions, such as hot springs and very salty water. However, a disadvantage of being unicellular is that the entire organism dies if the single cell dies.

Into Cells

Multicellular organisms are made up of more than one cell. These cells are grouped into different levels of organization, including tissues, organs, and organ systems. The cells that make up a multicellular organism, such as humans and plants, are specialized to perform specific functions. Many multicellular organisms reproduce through sexual reproduction, during which a male sex cell fertilizes a female sex cell. The single cell that results from fertilization divides repeatedly. This cell division forms the basic tissues of an embryo, which further develop into all of the specialized tissues and organs within a multicellular organism. Other characteristics of multicellular organisms include a larger size and a longer lifespan than unicellular organisms.

There are some disadvantages to being multicellular. Multicellular organisms need more resources than do unicellular organisms. Also, the cells of multicellular organisms are specialized for certain jobs, which means that cells must depend on each other to perform all of the functions that an organism needs to live.

Diatoms are microscopic unicellular organisms that live in water.

Humpback whales are multicellular organisms.

Into Tissues

A **tissue** is a group of similar cells that perform a common function. Humans and many other animals are made up of four basic types of tissue: nervous, epithelial, connective, and muscle. Nervous tissue functions as a messaging system within the body. Epithelial tissue is protective and forms boundaries, such as skin. Connective tissue, including bones and blood, holds parts of the body together and provides support and nourishment to organs. Muscle tissue helps produce movement.

Plants have three types of tissue: transport, protective, and ground. Transport tissue moves water and nutrients through the plant. Protective tissue protects the outside of the plant. Ground tissue provides internal support and storage and absorbs light energy to make food in photosynthesis (foh•toh•SIN•thuh•sis).

Plant leaf tissue

Animal skin tissue

6 Compare Fill in the Venn diagram to compare the functions of animal tissues and plant tissues. What functions do they share?

Animal Tissues — Both — Plant Tissues

Visualize It!

7 Apply In which organism shown on the opposite page are cells organized into tissues? Explain your answer.

Answers

5. *See students' pages for annotations.*

6. **Animals:** nervous—messaging system; epithelial—barrier and protection; connective—support and nourishment; muscle—produces movement

   Plants: transport—moves food throughout plant; protective—barrier and protection; ground—support, storage, and photosynthesis

   Both: have tissues that provide protection, nourishment, and support

7. The humpback whale is a multicellular organism with tissues that provide protection, support, nourishment, response, and movement.

Probing Questions   GUIDED Inquiry

Examining What is one major difference between a specialized cell and a unicellular organism? Sample answer: A specialized cell is limited to its function in a multicellular organism. A unicellular organism can perform many functions and do everything it needs to live.

Applying How do you think the nervous, epithelial, connective, and muscle tissues in your stomach work together in the process of digestion? Sample answer: The nervous tissue carries messages from your stomach that it either needs food or is full. Muscle tissue contracts to help break down whatever food is in the stomach. Epithelial tissue lines the stomach and protects it from the process of digesting food. Connective tissue provides structural support for the stomach. **Prompt:** Think about the functions of the four types of tissues. **Prompt:** Epithelial tissue forms coverings on the inside and the outside of the body.

Learning Alert

Unicellular Organisms Students may think that all organisms have all levels of organization. Make sure students understand that some organisms consist of a single cell; some organisms are composed of specialized cells but do not have tissues (such as a sponge); and some organisms have cells, tissues, organs, and organ systems.

Into Organs

A structure made up of a collection of tissues that carries out a specialized function is called an **organ**. The stomach is an organ that breaks down food for digestion. Different types of tissues work together to accomplish this function. For example, nervous tissue sends messages to the stomach's muscle tissue to tell the muscle tissue to contract. When the muscle tissue contracts, food and stomach acids are mixed, and the food breaks down.

Plants also have organs that are made up of different tissues working together. For example, a leaf is an organ that contains protective tissue to reduce water loss, ground tissue for photosynthesis, and transport tissue to move nutrients from leaves to stems. Stems and roots are organs that function to transport and store water and nutrients in the plant. The trunk of most trees is a stem. Roots are usually below the ground.

Active Reading

8 Apply How do organs relate to cells and tissues?

_____

_____

_____

The digestive system is an organ system found in most animals, including humans.

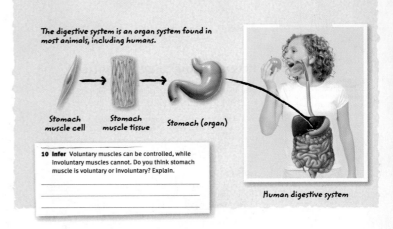

Stomach muscle cell → Stomach muscle tissue → Stomach (organ)

Human digestive system

10 Infer Voluntary muscles can be controlled, while involuntary muscles cannot. Do you think stomach muscle is voluntary or involuntary? Explain.

_____

_____

_____

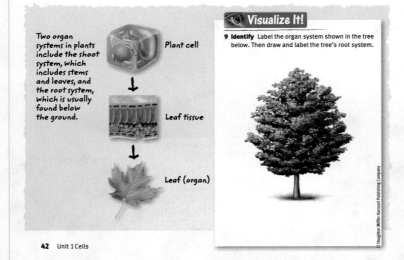

Two organ systems in plants include the shoot system, which includes stems and leaves, and the root system, which is usually found below the ground.

Plant cell

Leaf tissue

Leaf (organ)

Visualize It!

9 Identify Label the organ system shown in the tree below. Then draw and label the tree's root system.

Into Organ Systems

An **organ system** is a group of organs that work together to perform body functions. Each organ system has a specific job to do for the organism. For example, the stomach works with other organs of the digestive system to digest and absorb nutrients from food. Other organs included in the digestive system are the esophagus and the small and large intestines.

Humans are made up of many organ systems. All of the systems have specific functions to keep the body alive.

Think Outside the Book Inquiry

11 Illustrate Research an organ system of the human body other than the digestive system and draw a sketch of the organs included in that system.

42   Unit 1 Cells

43

Answers

8. Cells make up tissues, which make up organs.

9. Students should identify the leaves and stems, including the trunk, as the organ system and should draw and label the roots below ground as the root system.

10. Stomach muscle is involuntary. A person cannot control its contractions.

11. Students should draw a complete organ system. For example, a sketch of the lymphatic system should include the tonsil, thymus, spleen, lymph nodes, and lymph vessels.

Interpreting Visuals

Instruct students to look at the two diagrams on this page to compare the patterns in the hierarchical organization in a plant and an animal. **Ask:** What structures make up tissues? cells What structures make up organs? two or more tissues What are some examples of organs in animals? stomach, small and large intestines What are some examples of organs in plants? leaves, stems What is an example of a plant organ system? the root system What is an example of an animal organ system? the digestive system

Formative Assessment

Have students explain the hierarchical organization of organisms. **Ask:** What are the different levels of cellular organization in a living thing? The levels of cellular organization in a multicellular living thing are cells, tissues, organs, and organ systems. **Ask:** How are cells, tissues, and organs organized into an organ system? Specialized cells make up a tissue; tissues act together to form an organ; different organs work as part of an organ system to carry out life processes such as digestion. **Prompt:** Think about what makes up a tissue, an organ, and an organ system.

What's Your Function?

What is the connection between structure and function?

Cells, tissues, organs, and organ systems make up the structure of a multicellular organism. **Structure** is the arrangement of parts in an organism or an object. The structure of a cell, tissue, or organ determines its **function**, or the activity of each part in an organism. In fact, the structure of any object determines its function.

Active Reading

12 Recognize As you read, underline examples of multicellular structures.

Structure Determines Function

Cells, tissues, and organs vary in structure. For example, bone cells look different from plant leaf cells. A lung differs from a stomach because they have different functions. Cells, tissues, and organs are specialized to perform specific functions. For example, a lung is an organ made up of cells and tissues that work together to help you breathe. The lungs are made up of millions of tiny air sacs called *alveoli* (singular, *alveolus*). The large number of alveoli increases the surface area of the lungs to let enough oxygen and carbon dioxide move between the lungs and the blood.

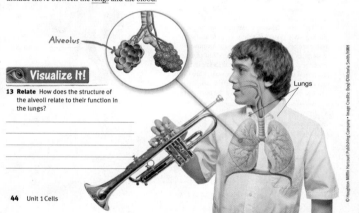

Alveolus

Lungs

Visualize It!

13 Relate How does the structure of the alveoli relate to their function in the lungs?

_____

_____

_____

44 Unit 1 Cells

Why It Matters

Odd Bodies

WEIRD SCIENCE

With millions of different organisms that exist on Earth, it's no wonder there are so many different body structures. Some organisms have special structures that can help them eat—or not be eaten!

Can't Touch This!
Named for its prickly body, the spiny katydid doesn't make much of a meal for its predator. Male katydids sing loudly at night to attract female katydids. The singing can also attract predators, such as bats, who hunt for food at night. Its spines provide the katydid with some protection from being eaten.

Blow on Your Food
The longhorn cowfish is a marine organism that lives on the sandy ocean bottom at depths up to 50 m. Its permanently puckered mouth helps the cowfish find food. The cowfish blows jets of water into the sand to find and feed on tiny organisms.

Night Vision
The tarsier's huge eyes provide excellent vision for hunting insects at night. Its eyes average 16 mm in diameter, but the tarsier's overall body size ranges from 85 mm to 165 mm. In comparison, your eyes would be the size of apples! When the tarsier spots its prey, it leaps through the air to pounce on it. The tarsier's long fingers help it grasp branches when it's on the move.

Extend

Inquiry

14 Relate How does the body structure of each of these organisms contribute to a particular function?

15 Contrast How do structures in living organisms compare with structures of nonliving things such as construction cranes, buildings, ships, airplanes, or bridges?

16 Imagine Describe an organism that might live in an extreme environment such as inside a volcano, deep in the ocean, or in an icy cave. What type of organism is it? What special structures would it have in order to survive in that environment?

45

Answers

12. *See students' pages for annotations.*

13. The lungs contain millions of alveoli. The alveoli provide a large surface area for gas exchange in the lungs.

14. Sample answer: The body structures of these organisms help them to get food or provide protection from being eaten.

15. Sample answer: Living and nonliving things have special structures for different functions. For example, a ship is structured to float and transport things. A longhorn cowfish has a mouth structured to uncover food in sand.

16. Answers should describe specific structures that function for the survival of the organism in the chosen environment.

Probing Questions GUIDED Inquiry

Applying How does the structure of your pencil relate to its function? Sample answer: A pencil is long and thin, so it is easy to hold in your hand. It contains a thin rod of graphite that is used for making marks. The graphite is covered with wood so it does not get your hands dirty.

Drawing Conclusions How does the structure of a specialized cell relate to its function? **Prompt:** Think about the functions of a red blood cell and a nerve cell. Sample answer: Cells vary in shape and size depending on the job they need to perform. Red blood cells are round and can flow easily so they can deliver oxygen, while nerve cells are long and spindly so they can transmit messages over long distances throughout the body.

Why It Matters

Tell students that they are likely familiar with some organisms that have unusual body structures. Ask students whether they can think of any unusual rodents. Tell students that although there are many species of porcupines, all porcupines have one thing in common: quills. Quills are modified hairs coated with keratin. Porcupines can raise their quills as a warning, and release quills when another organism comes in contact with them. Other rodents with unusual adaptations include beavers and naked mole rats.

Systems at Work

What tasks do systems perform to meet the needs of cells?

Complex organisms are made up of many systems. These systems work together to perform actions needed by cells to function properly. Whether it is a bone cell or a skin cell, each cell in the organism needs to receive nutrients, exchange carbon dioxide and oxygen, and have waste products taken away.

A unicellular organism must perform all functions necessary for life, such as getting nutrients, exchanging gases, and removing wastes. The functions must be performed by a single cell, because there is no opportunity for cell specialization.

Multicellular organisms face different challenges. Multicellular organisms have different cell types that can work together in groups to perform specific functions. Groups of cells that work together form tissues. Groups of tissues that work together form organs, and groups of organs that work together form systems. Systems work with other systems. In most animals, the digestive, respiratory, and excretory systems interact with the circulatory system to maintain healthy cells. A circulatory system delivers nutrients to body cells and carries away wastes. It carries oxygen to cells and removes carbon dioxide.

Some plants have a vascular system that transports water and nutrients to and from cells throughout the plant. Xylem and phloem are tissues that make up the vascular system. Xylem transports water from roots to cells. Phloem transports nutrients made in leaf cells to all parts of the plant.

📖 Active Reading

17 Compare How do unicellular organisms and multicellular organisms compare in meeting their needs to stay alive?

_____
_____
_____
_____

👁 Visualize It!

18 Analyze This diagram shows the xylem and phloem that make up the plant's vascular system. How does a vascular system serve the needs of plant cells?

_____
_____
_____

Leaf

Water Food

Stem

Xylem Phloem

Roots

© Houghton Mifflin Harcourt Publishing Company

46 Unit 1 Cells

Delivering Nutrients

The digestive system in most animals breaks down food mechanically and chemically. In most animals, the digestive system works with a circulatory system. In the small intestine, nutrients are absorbed through thousands of finger-like projections in the wall of the small intestine and then into the blood vessels of the circulatory system. Once in the blood, the nutrients are delivered to cells throughout the body.

Villus

Small intestine

Delivering Oxygen

In animals, taking in oxygen is a function of the respiratory system. Depending on the animal, oxygen enters a body through skin, gills, spiracles, or lungs. There, it comes in contact with the circulatory system. Oxygen enters the bloodstream and is carried to the cells of the body. Once in the cells, oxygen is used to release energy from nutrients from digestion.

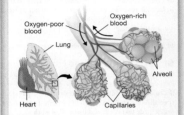

Oxygen-poor blood Oxygen-rich blood

Lung

Heart Alveoli Capillaries

Removing Wastes

Skin, lungs, the digestive system, and the kidneys all have processes for removing waste products from the body. Sweat evaporates from the skin. Solid wastes and some water move out as part of the digestive system. Carbon dioxide and some water are breathed out through the respiratory system. In humans, the largest amount of excess water and waste products from cells is carried by the blood to the kidneys. There, wastes are filtered out of the blood through a complex series of tubules in the kidneys and leave the body as urine.

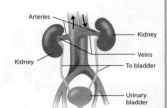

Arteries Kidney

Kidney Veins

To bladder

Urinary bladder

👁 Visualize It!

19 Synthesize Notice that oxygen-poor blood (blue) and oxygen-rich blood (red) are shown in all three diagrams. Describe the role of blood in the transportation of materials throughout the body.

_____
_____
_____
_____
_____

© Houghton Mifflin Harcourt Publishing Company

47

Answers

17. Structures within the single cell of a unicellular organism allow it to meet life's needs. Multicellular organisms have organs that work with other organs in systems to perform these tasks.

18. Xylem transports water from the roots throughout the plant. Phloem transports food made by the leaves throughout the plant.

19. Blood delivers nutrients and oxygen to cells and takes cellular wastes away from them.

Interpreting Visuals

Direct students to look at the at the yellow and blue arrows in the diagram of the plant. **Ask:** What do these arrows indicate? the movement of water and nutrients through the xylem and phloem Next, point out the text that says that phloem transports nutrients to all cells of the plant. Share with students that although the yellow arrows show movement in one direction, phloem can move nutrients in either direction to reach every cell. Xylem, on the other hand, can move water in only one direction.

Building Reading Skills

Context Clues Direct students' attention to the word _spiracles_ in the paragraph on delivering oxygen. Ask students to look for context clues to help them figure out the meaning of this word. Sample answer: Context clues include "oxygen enters a body," "gills," and "lungs." Invite students to guess what the word means. Tell students that spiracles are small gill slits behind the eye area of some fish, such as skates.

Formative Assessment

Ask: What are some ways body systems work together? Sample answer: The digestive system works with the circulatory system to take in and deliver nutrients to cells.

Visual Summary

To complete this summary, fill in the blanks with the correct word. Then, use the key below to check your answers. You can use this page to review the main concepts of the lesson.

Cellular Organization

All organisms are made up of one or more cells.

20 T ☐ F ☐ A plant is a unicellular organism.

The structures of cells, tissues, and organs determine their functions.

21 T ☐ F ☐ The protective tissue on a leaf has a structure that keeps the moisture in the leaf from drying out.

Multicellular organisms are organized into tissues, organs, and organ systems.

22 T ☐ F ☐ This leaf is an example of a plant organ.

Leaf
Water Food
Stem
Roots

23 T ☐ F ☐ A plant obtains water from its environment through the root system.

Answers: 20 False; 21 True; 22 True; 23 True

24 **Synthesize** How do cells, tissues, organs, and organ systems work together in a multicellular organism?

48   Unit 1 Cells

© Houghton Mifflin Harcourt Publishing Company

Lesson Review

Lesson 4

Vocabulary

Fill in the blank with the term that best completes the following sentences.

1 Animals have four basic types of _____: nervous, epithelial, muscle, and connective.

2 Together, the esophagus, stomach, and intestines are part of a(n) _____

Key Concepts

3 **Describe** What are the levels of organization in multicellular organisms?

4 **Analyze** Discuss two benefits of multicellular organisms' having some specialized cells rather than all the cells being the same.

5 **Relate** How do the structures in an organism relate to their functions?

Critical Thinking

Use the figure to answer the next two questions.

Human heart

6 **Apply** What level of organization is shown here?

7 **Relate** How does this level of organization relate to cells? To organ systems?

8 **Analyze** Explain why a circulatory system is important in meeting the needs of all cells throughout an animal's body.

© Houghton Mifflin Harcourt Publishing Company

Lesson 4 Levels of Cellular Organization   49

Visual Summary Answers

20. False
21. True
22. True
23. True
24. Sample answer: Cells make up tissues. Tissues make up organs. Organs are part of an organ system. All of these levels of organization help a multicellular organism to carry out life functions.

Lesson Review Answers

1. tissue
2. organ system
3. Cells that perform a common function form tissues. Tissues that carry out similar functions form organs, which have specialized functions in an organ system.
4. Sample answer: Specialization allows cells to do specific jobs, such as being part of the digestive system. Having different cells that perform different functions makes an organism more efficient. Also, the death of one cell does not mean the death of the organism because there are other cells to perform that function.
5. Structure is the arrangement of parts in an organism. Function is the activity the parts perform.
6. organ
7. Cells make up the heart tissues, which make up the heart. The heart is an organ that is part of the circulatory system, which is an organ system.
8. Sample answer: The circulatory system is found throughout the body in all organs. It picks up oxygen in the lungs and nutrients from the digestive system and removes wastes from all cells throughout the body.

Homeostasis and Cell Processes

Essential Question How do organisms maintain homeostasis?

 Professional Development

For more detailed information about the topics in this lesson, refer to the Content Refresher in the Unit Opener pages.

Opening Your Lesson

Begin the lesson by assessing students' prerequisite and prior knowledge.

Prerequisite Knowledge

- The structure and function of different cell parts
- The patterns in the hierarchical organization of organisms, from cells to tissues to organs to organ systems to organisms

Accessing Prior Knowledge

Ask: What structures do all eukaryotic cells have in common? Sample answer: mitochondria, ribosomes, endoplasmic reticulum, and the Golgi complex

Ask: What are the five levels of structural organization in a complex organism? Sample answer: cells, tissues, organs, organ systems, and organism

Customize Your Opening

- ☐ **Accessing Prior Knowledge,** above
- ☐ **Print Path** Engage Your Brain, SE p. 51
- ☐ **Print Path** Active Reading, SE p. 51
- ☐ **Digital Path** Lesson Opener

Key Topics/Learning Goals

Homeostasis in Cells

1 Explain why homeostasis is important for survival.
2 Identify the needs of cells.
3 Describe how cells can get energy by photosynthesis and cellular respiration.
4 Explain that homeostasis is maintained at the cellular level and at higher levels.
5 Explain why cells divide.
6 Describe the cell cycle.
7 Discuss why exchange is important for cells.
8 Compare passive transport and active transport.
9 Compare endocytosis and exocytosis.

Homeostasis in Organisms

1 Explain how organisms can respond to changes in their environment.

Supporting Concepts

- Homeostasis is the maintenance of a stable internal environment.
- Cells need to be able to use energy, eliminate wastes, reproduce, and grow in order to survive.
- In photosynthesis, the sun's energy is used to make food. In cellular respiration, food is broken down for energy.
- Cells in multicellular organisms work together to maintain homeostasis for the organism.
- Unicellular organisms divide to reproduce. The cells in a multicellular organism divide to grow and to replace dead or damaged cells.
- In cell division, DNA from an existing cell is copied and sorted into two new cells. In eukaryotes, this is called mitosis.
- Cells exchange materials with the environment to remove wastes and take in nutrients.
- Passive transport does not use energy. Active transport does use energy.
- In endocytosis, the cell surrounds materials and encloses them into the cell. In exocytosis, particles within a vesicle are transported outside of the cell.
- Organisms must respond to external environment changes in order to maintain homeostasis. For example, muscle cells contract to generate heat when a human is cold. Shivering is the body's way of creating warmth.

Options for Instruction

Two parallel paths provide coverage of the Essential Questions, with a strong Inquiry strand woven into each.
Follow the Print Path, the Digital Path, or your customized combination of print, digital, and inquiry.

 Print Path
Teaching support for the Print Path appears with the Student Pages.

 Inquiry Labs and Activities

Digital Path
Digital Path shortcut: TS663120

Stayin' Alive, SE pp. 52–53
What is homeostasis?
• Balance in Organisms

Get Growing!, SE pp. 54–55
How do cells get energy?
• Photosynthesis
• Cellular Respiration
How do cells divide?
• The Cell Cycle

Move It!, SE pp. 56–58
How do cells exchange materials?
• Passive Transport
• Active Transport
• Endocytosis
• Exocytosis
How do organisms respond to the environment?

Activity
Cell Division

Daily Demo
Diffusion

Exploration Lab
Diffusion

Cell Processes
Interactive Image

Photosynthesis
Diagram

Cellular Respiration
Interactive Image

Transport in and out of Cells
Interactive Image

Cell Division
Animation

Homeostasis and Cells
Interactive Image

Move It!, SE p. 59
How do organisms maintain homeostasis?

Quick Lab
Investigate Microorganisms

Activity
Balancing Act!

How Important Is Homeostasis?
Interactive Image

Options for Assessment

See the Evaluate page for options, including Formative Assessment, Summative Assessment, and Unit Review.

Engage and Explore

Activities and Discussion

Discussion *Maintaining Balance*

Homeostasis in Organisms

 whole class
 10 min

Homeostasis is a way that living things try to maintain balance. It is similar to the process of riding a bicycle. If you lose your balance and don't correct the imbalance, you will fall. Homeostasis is the process of correcting imbalances. As you become more proficient at riding a bicycle, you learn to make minor muscle adjustments to maintain balance. Have students discuss other physical activities that students participate in that require them to correct imbalances.

Activity *Balancing Act!*

Homeostasis in Organisms

 individuals or pairs
15 min

Have students find pictures in magazines that show plants, animals, and humans in the process of maintaining homeostasis. These could be pictures of animals eating food, rain falling on a plant, or a person exercising. Have students make a list of the different examples of homeostasis they find. Students can then share their examples with the class.

Take It Home *Photosynthesis*

Homeostasis in Cells

 adult-student pairs
 10–15 min
 GUIDED inquiry

Students work with an adult to observe plants and think about where in the plant photosynthesis mainly takes place. Encourage the pair to examine a plant, either outdoors or inside the home. After the pair decides in which part of the plant most photosynthesis takes place, they should discuss why they came to that conclusion.

⊘ *Optional Online resource: student worksheet*

Probing Question *How Does a Cell Cycle Compare to a Human Life Cycle?*

Homeostasis in Cells

 individuals
 10 min
GUIDED inquiry

Comparing Encourage students to discuss how a cell's life cycle compares with a human's life cycle. Tell students that the cell cycle is made up of two parts: a time of growth and a time of dividing. Most of the cell cycle is spent growing.

Inquiry **DIRECTED** inquiry Help students understand the steps in the cell cycle and in the human life cycle. Prompt them to make a graphic organizer of each cycle to use as a basis for comparison.

Activity *Cell Division*

Engage

Homeostasis in Cells

 groups of three
15 min

Have students model the separation of genetic material during mitosis by separating socks. Give groups of three students each one pile of paired socks, one pile of unpaired socks, and two blindfolds. Two students put on blindfolds. The third passes out the socks. One blindfolded student gets the paired group of socks, the other gets the unpaired group. Each student tries to separate his or her group of socks into two piles of single socks, one from each pair. The third student keeps time and stops the activity after 2 minutes. After the activity is over, students can discuss why it was easier to more accurately separate the paired set of socks into two identical groups.

(t) ©Wave Royalty Free/age Fotostock

Customize Your Labs

 See the Lab Manual for lab datasheets.

 Go Online for editable lab datasheets.

Levels of Inquiry

DIRECTED inquiry
introduces inquiry skills within a structured framework.

GUIDED inquiry
develops inquiry skills within a supportive environment.

INDEPENDENT inquiry
deepens inquiry skills with student-driven questions or procedures.

Labs and Demos

Daily Demo *Diffusion*

Engage

Homeostasis in Cells

- whole class
- 10 min
- **Inquiry** DIRECTED inquiry

PURPOSE **To observe how particles move by diffusion**

MATERIALS

- beaker
- water
- food coloring

1 Fill the beaker with tap water.

2 Add 3 drops of food coloring to the water.

3 For 10 minutes, observe what happens. Write down student observations on chart paper or on the board.

4 **Observing** What changes did you observe? The food coloring gradually colors all the water in the beaker.

5 What might have caused the changes? Sample answer: The food coloring diffused through the water.

Exploration Lab *Diffusion*

Homeostasis in Cells

- small groups
- 45 min
- **Inquiry** DIRECTED or GUIDED inquiry

Students use iodine, cornstarch, and plastic wrap to model the process of diffusion.

PURPOSE **To investigate how concentration and temperature affect diffusion across a membrane**

MATERIALS

- beaker, small
- plastic wrap
- cornstarch solutions
- iodine solution
- baby food jar, with lid

Quick Lab *Investigate Microorganisms*

Homeostasis in Organisms

- pairs
- 25 min
- **Inquiry** GUIDED inquiry

Students observe how microorganisms react to external stimuli such as light, temperature changes, and other organisms.

PURPOSE **To observe how microorganisms respond to changes in their environment**

MATERIALS

- *Daphnia* culture
- microscope
- eyedropper
- microscope slides
- hydra culture
- water, cold
- lamp or flashlight
- water, warm

Quick Lab *Homeostasis and Adaptations*

Homeostasis in Organisms

- small groups
- 30 min
- **Inquiry** INDEPENDENT inquiry

Students observe tree leaves and try to determine how the characteristics of a leaf relate to the needs of the plant to maintain homeostasis.

PURPOSE **To investigate how the physical characteristics of organisms relate to the environment in which they live**

MATERIALS

- camera (optional)
- pencil or pen
- journal

Activities and Discussion

- ☐ **Discussion** Maintaining Balance
- ☐ **Activity** Balancing Act!
- ☐ **Activity** Cell Division
- ☐ **Probing Question** Cell, Life Cycle
- ☐ **Take It Home** Photosynthesis

Labs and Demos

- ☐ **Daily Demo** Diffusion
- ☐ **Exploration Lab** Diffusion
- ☐ **Quick Lab** Investigate Microorganisms
- ☐ **Quick Lab** Homeostasis and Adaptations

Your Resources

_____

_____

_____

Explain Science Concepts

	Print Path	Digital Path

Key Topics

Print Path

☐ **Stayin' Alive,** SE pp. 52–53
- Active Reading, #5
- Think Outside the Book, #6
- Visualize It!, #7
- Active Reading (Annotation strategy), #8

☐ **Get Growing!,** SE pp. 54–55
- Four-column Chart, #9
- Visualize It!, #10
- Active Reading, #11

☐ **Move It!,** SE pp. 56–58
- Active Reading, #12
- Diffusion #13
- Visualize It!, #14
- Describing, #15
- Describing, #16

Digital Path

☐ **Cell Processes**
Learn how cells divide, obtain energy, and transport materials.

☐ **Photosynthesis**
Describe the process of photosynthesis.

☐ **Cellular Respiration**
Describe the process of cellular respiration.

☐ **Transport in and out of Cells**
Identify ways in which materials are exchanged between a cell and its environment.

☐ **Cell Division**
Observe a model of cell division.

☐ **Homeostasis and Cells**
Learn how cells work together to help an organism maintain homeostasis.

Homeostasis in Cells

Homeostasis in Organisms

☐ **Move It!,** SE p. 59
- Active Reading (Annotation strategy), #17
- Visualize It!, #18

☐ **How Important Is Homeostasis?**
Learn how organisms maintain homeostasis.

Differentiated Instruction

Basic *Moving Energy*

Homeostasis in Cells

 individuals or pairs
🕐 20 min

After students have learned about photosynthesis and cellular respiration, have them make a poster illustrating these two processes. Encourage students to illustrate the starting materials and end products with pictures cut from magazines that represent a graphic or vivid symbol of the concept. On their poster, they should include the information from the four-column chart shown in their textbook.

Basic *Flip Books*

Homeostasis in Cells

 individuals or pairs
🕐 15 min

Have students make flip books illustrating endocytosis and exocytosis. They can trace the diagrams from the textbook. They should use at least 12 sheets of 4" × 6" notepaper taped at the top. They should draw "in-betweens" to make the action appear smooth from step to step.

Advanced *What's That Smell?*

Homeostasis in Cells

 individuals or pairs
🕐 10 min, later, 20 min

Modeling Diffusion Have students use a dropper to put a drop or two of food extract, such as lemon extract, into a deflated balloon. Blow up the balloon, tie it, and place it inside a shoe box with the lid taped on. Later, students can remove the lid and smell the contents. Have students write an explanation of why the box smells like the extract when the extract was inside the balloon.

ELL *Modeling Molecular Structures*

Homeostasis in Cells

🧑 small groups
🕐 15 min

Demonstrations To review lesson vocabulary, have small groups of students model the following science words by acting as molecules and cellular membranes: *osmosis, diffusion, active transport,* and *passive transport.*

Lesson Vocabulary

homeostasis	diffusion	active transport
photosynthesis	osmosis	endocytosis
cellular respiration	passive transport	exocytosis
mitosis		

Previewing Vocabulary

 whole class
🕐 15 min

Word Origins Share the following to help students remember terms:

- **Homeostasis** comes from the Greek *homoios,* which means "of the same kind" and *stasis,* which means "standing still."
- **Mitosis** comes from the Greek *mitos,* which means "thread," and *osis,* which means "process." Chromosomes in the cell nucleus look like thick threads in the first stages of mitosis.
- **Endocytosis** comes from the Greek *endo,* which means "within," and *kytos,* which means "an empty vessel." *Exo* means "outside."

Reinforcing Vocabulary

 individuals
🕐 ongoing

Four Square To help students remember the terms introduced in the lesson, have them draw a 2-by-2 matrix with a circle at the center. Students place a term in the circle and then fill in the cells with definition, characteristics, examples, and nonexamples.

Customize Your Core Lesson

Core Instruction

☐ **Print Path** choices

☐ **Digital Path** choices

Vocabulary

☐ **Previewing Vocabulary** Word Origins

☐ **Reinforcing Vocabulary** Four Square

Your Resources

Differentiated Instruction

☐ **Basic** Moving Energy

☐ **Basic** Flip Books

☐ **Advanced** What's That Smell?

☐ **ELL** Modeling Molecular Structures

Extend Science Concepts

Reinforce and Review

Activity *What Cell Am I?*

Synthesizing Key Topics   small groups   15 min

Jigsaw Divide the class into six groups and assign each group a topic from the list below. Each group will work together until they become experts in their particular area. Make sure groups stay together until each individual can teach what they have learned to another group. After 5 to 10 minutes, reassign groups. Each new group should consist of one expert from each original group. The goal for each new team is to understand the different processes that organisms undergo to maintain homeostasis. Encourage groups to include visuals whenever possible to illustrate the different processes.

1 photosynthesis
2 cellular respiration
3 mitosis
4 passive transport, including diffusion and osmosis
5 active transport, including endocytosis and exocytosis
6 how organisms respond to the environment

Graphic Organizer

Synthesizing Key Topics   individuals ⏱ ongoing

Concept Map After students have studied the lesson, ask them to create a Concept Map with the following terms and phrases: *homeostasis, energy, take in materials, eliminate materials, photosynthesis, cellular respiration, mitosis, passive transport, diffusion, osmosis, active transport, endocytosis,* and *exocytosis.*

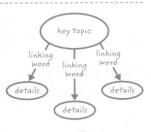

🌐 *Optional Online resource: Concept Map support*

Going Further

Physical Education Connection

Homeostasis in Cells   whole class ⏱ 15 min

Have students practice the tree pose in yoga to understand that the process of achieving balance is an active one. First, have students stand up straight with their feet together. They should visualize themselves as a tree rooted in the ground. Then, ask students to pick up their right foot and place the sole of this foot on the inside of the left thigh. If students feel stable here, challenge them to raise their arms above their head with their palms facing together. If students are having trouble, suggest that they focus on an object in the classroom to help them balance. Repeat, having them stand on the right foot and lifting the left. Afterward, have students discuss some of the challenges in maintaining balance.

Language Arts Connection

Synthesizing Key Topics 👥 individuals ⏱ varied

Encourage students to read Madeleine L'Engle's *A Wind in the Door.* Have students focus on the scene that occurs deep inside the mitochondria of one of the main characters. Interested students may want to try writing their own science-fiction story in which the main character is shrunken to molecular scale and is involved in several cellular processes, such as passive or active transport.

Customize Your Closing

💬 *See the Assessment Guide for quizzes and tests.*

🌐 *Go Online to edit and create quizzes and tests.*

Reinforce and Review

☐ **Activity** What Cell Am I?

☐ **Graphic Organizer** Concept Map

☐ **Print Path** Visual Summary, SE p. 60

☐ **Digital Path** Lesson Closer

Evaluate Student Mastery

See the teacher support below the Student Pages for additional Formative Assessment questions.

Ask: What life processes do cells undergo to maintain homeostasis? Sample answer: They need to be able to use energy, reproduce, get materials, and eliminate waste. **Ask:** How do plant and animal cells get energy? Sample answer: The sun provides energy for plants to make food. Both plants and animals use cellular respiration to get energy from food. **Ask:** How do eukaryotic cells produce new cells? Sample answer: The cell copies its DNA and divides to produce two identical new cells. **Ask:** How do cells take in materials and get rid of wastes? Sample answer: Cells move materials across the membrane using two processes: passive and active transport.

Reteach

Formative assessment may show that students need reinforcement for certain topics. The resources below are recommended for reteaching. If students were introduced to a topic through the Print Path, you can also use the Digital Path to reteach, and vice versa.
🎧 *Can be assigned to individual students.*

Homeostasis in Cells
Exploration Lab Diffusion

Activity Cell Division

Homeostasis in Organisms
Quick Lab Investigate Microorganisms

Quick Lab Homeostasis and Adaptations

Activity Balancing Act! 🎧

Alternative Assessment
Maintaining Homeostasis

⏱ *Online resources: student worksheet, optional rubrics*

Homeostasis and Cell Processes

Climb the Ladder: *Maintaining Homeostasis*
Select an idea from each rung of the ladder to show what you've learned about the different ways organisms maintain homeostasis.

1. Work on your own, with a partner, or with a small group.
2. Choose one item from each rung of the ladder. Check your choices.
3. Have your teacher approve your plan.
4. Submit or present your results.

__ **Illustrate a Poster**	__ **Build a Model**
Make a poster illustrating photosynthesis and cellular respiration. You can illustrate the starting materials and end products with drawings or photographs. Include an explanation of why these processes are essential for cells' survival. Give an oral explanation of how the two processes relate.	Make a 3-D model of photosynthesis and cellular respiration. Use materials such as clay, marshmallows, or pipe cleaners to represent the starting materials and end products. Label your model and give an oral explanation of photosynthesis, cellular respiration, and why they are essential to cells' survival.
__ **Write a Picture Book**	__ **Be a Broadcaster**
Write a picture book that shows the different stages of the eukaryotic cell cycle. Label the nucleus and chromosomes. Write one sentence to explain each stage of the cycle.	Look at the photographs of the plant and animal cell dividing. Imagine that you are a news broadcaster and these photographs are being shown behind you. Describe in detail what is happening as if it were breaking news. You can write or record your broadcast.
__ **Write a Skit**	__ **Create an Animation**
Write a skit that describes passive and active transport. Assign roles to the different type of materials that need to pass through a membrane. Include information on	Use a computer program to create an animation to demonstrate passive and active transport. Include a spoken description of both types of transport and how

Going Further
☐ **Physical Education Connection**
☐ **Language Arts Connection**

Formative Assessment
☐ **Strategies** Throughout TE
☐ **Lesson Review** SE

Summative Assessment
☐ **Alternative Assessment** Maintaining Homeostasis
☐ **Lesson Quiz**
☐ **Unit Tests A and B**
☐ **Unit Review** SE End-of-Unit

Your Resources

_____

_____

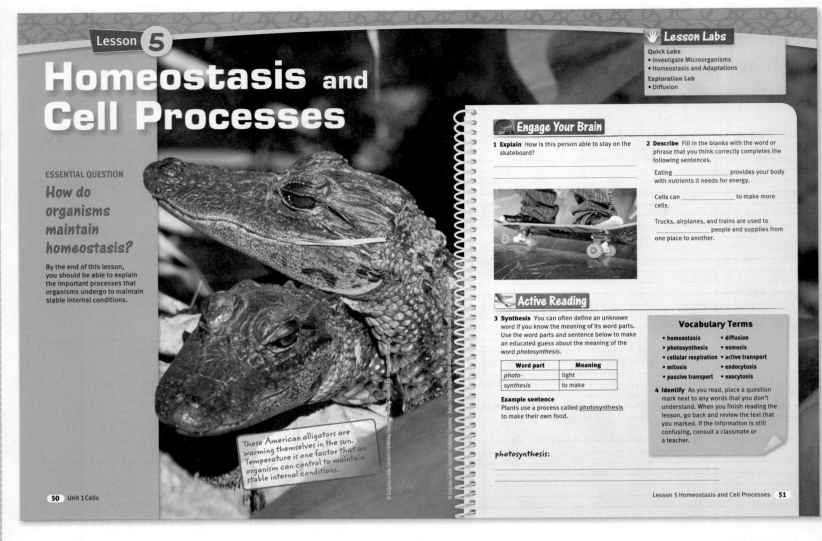

Answers

Answers for 1–3 should represent students' current thoughts, even if incorrect.

1. Sample answer: This person is using their body to balance in order to stay on the skateboard. Without balance, the person would be unstable and fall off of the skateboard.

2. food; divide; transport

3. using light (energy) to make food

4. *See students' pages for annotations.*

Opening Your Lesson

Discuss student answers to items 2 and 3 to assess students' prerequisite knowledge and to estimate what they already know about the key topics.

Preconceptions That homeostasis is a process that only happens on the cellular level. Homeostasis occurs both at the cellular level and at higher levels of organization. The organism as a whole maintains homeostasis.

Prerequisites Students should already have a basic understanding of the structure and function of the different cell parts. Students should also know the different levels of organization of multicellular organisms.

Interpreting Visuals

Look at the photograph of reptiles warming themselves in the sun. Why do reptiles need to use sunlight to regulate their temperature? Sample answer: They are ectotherms and therefore depend on their surroundings to stay warm. What do you think reptiles might do to regulate their temperature on a very hot day? Sample answer: lie in the shade

Stayin' Alive

What is homeostasis?

We all feel more comfortable when our surroundings are ideal—not too hot, not too cold, not too wet, and not too dry. Cells are the same way. However, a cell's environment is constantly changing. **Homeostasis** (hoh•mee•oh•STAY•sis) is the maintenance of a constant internal state in a changing environment. In order to survive, your cells need to be able to obtain and use energy, make new cells, exchange materials, and eliminate wastes. Homeostasis ensures that cells can carry out these tasks in a changing environment.

Active Reading 6 Summarize What are four things that cells can do to maintain homeostasis?

_____

_____

_____

> ### Think Outside the Book (Inquiry)
>
> **5 Select** Many mechanisms are used to regulate different things in our lives. Choose one of the following devices, and do some research to describe what it regulates and how it works:
> • thermostat
> • insulin pump
> • dam

> ### Visualize It!
>
> **7 Apply** Think about how this girl is feeling after she exercises. What things can you see that are helping to keep her body temperature stable?
>
> _____
>
> _____

Balance in Organisms

All cells need energy and materials in order to carry out life processes. A unicellular organism exchanges materials directly with its environment. The cell membrane and other parts of the cell regulate what materials get into and out of the cell. This is one way that unicellular organisms maintain homeostasis.

Cells in multicellular organisms must work together to maintain homeostasis for the entire organism. For example, multicellular organisms have systems that transport materials to cells from other places in the organism. The main transport system in your body is your cardiovascular system. The cardiovascular system includes the heart, blood vessels, and blood. The heart pumps blood through branched blood vessels that come close to every cell in the body. Blood carries materials to the cells and carries wastes away from the cells. Other multicellular organisms have transport systems, too. For example, many plants have two types of vascular tissues that work together as a transport system. *Xylem* is the tissue that transports water and minerals from the roots to the rest of the plant. Another tissue called *phloem* transports food made within plant cells.

> **Active Reading**
>
> **8 Compare** As you read, underline how unicellular organisms and multicellular organisms exchange materials.

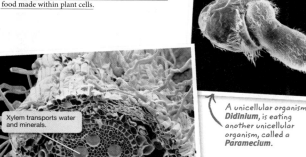

Xylem transports water and minerals.

Phloem transports food to different parts of the plant.

A unicellular organism, Didinium, is eating another unicellular organism, called a Paramecium.

Plants have two types of vascular tissue that they use to transport materials.

Answers

5. Sample answer: An insulin pump regulates the level of glucose in the body. It can pass insulin into the body continuously or in certain dosages. The dosages may occur between meals or at night. A larger dosage may be taken just before eating. The pump is programmed to deliver the correct dosages based on the person's diet and exercise schedule.

6. obtain and use energy, make new cells, exchange materials, eliminate wastes

7. She is sweating and drinking cold water.

8. *See students' pages for annotations.*

Probing Questions GUIDED (Inquiry)

Examining What are several things that you do each morning to maintain homeostasis? Sample answer: eat breakfast, drink juice, use the bathroom **Prompt:** Think about what cells need to do to maintain homeostasis.

Interpreting Visuals

Have students use the pictures on this page to compare the ways a unicellular organism and a multicellular organism obtain materials. Sample answers: A unicellular organism obtains or exchanges materials directly with its environment. The cell membrane helps to regulate what materials get in and out of the cell. A multicellular organism has systems that transport materials to cells from other places in the body.

Building Reading Skills

Compare/Contrast Have students use a Venn Diagram to compare the systems that mammals and plants use to transport materials.

⚙ *Optional Online resource: Venn Diagram support*

Get Growing!

How do cells get energy?

Cells need energy to perform cell functions. Cells get energy by breaking down materials, such as food, in which energy is stored. Breaking down food also provides raw materials the cell needs to make other materials for cell processes.

Photosynthesis

The sun provides the energy for plants to grow and make food. Plants use sunlight to change carbon dioxide and water into sugar and oxygen. This process by which plants, algae, and some bacteria make their own food is called **photosynthesis**. Inside plant and algal cells are special organelles, called chloroplasts, where photosynthesis takes place.

Cellular Respiration

All living things need food to produce energy for cell processes. The process by which cells use oxygen to produce energy from food is called **cellular respiration**. Plants, animals, and most other organisms use cellular respiration to get energy from food.

Nearly all the oxygen around us is made by photosynthesis. Animals and plants use oxygen during cellular respiration to break down food. Cellular respiration also produces carbon dioxide. Plants need carbon dioxide to make sugars. So, photosynthesis and respiration are linked, each one depending on the products of the other.

Plants provide the food for nearly all living thing on land. Some organisms eat plants for food. Other organisms eat animals that eat plants.

9 Synthesize Fill in the blanks with the materials that are involved in photosynthesis and cellular respiration.

Photosynthesis	_____ + carbon dioxide	sunlight →	_____ + oxygen
Cellular respiration	sugar + _____	→	water + _____ + energy

54

How do cells divide?

Cells grow, divide, and die. Some cells divide more often than others. For example, cells in the skin are constantly dividing to replace those that have died or are damaged. Some cells, such as nerve cells, cannot divide to produce new cells once they are fully formed. Multicellular organisms grow by adding more cells. These new cells are made when existing cells divide.

The Cell Cycle

Cell division in eukaryotes is a complex process. Before a cell can divide, its DNA is copied. Then, the DNA copies are sorted into what will become two new cells. In order to divide up the DNA evenly between the new cells, the DNA needs to be packaged. The packages are called *chromosomes* (croh•moh•SOHMS). Equal numbers of chromosomes are separated, and the nucleus splits to form two identical nuclei. This process is called **mitosis**. Then, the rest of the cell divides, resulting in two identical cells. Because the two new cells have DNA identical to that found in the original cell, all the cells in an organism have the same genetic material.

Active Reading

10 Explain Why is it important for DNA to be copied before cell division?

_____

_____

_____

Visualize It!

11 Compare How do new cells form in plants and animal?

_____

_____

_____

In animal cells, the cell membrane pinches inward through the cell to form two new cells.

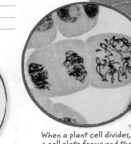

When a plant cell divides, a cell plate forms and the cell splits into two cells.

Lesson 5 Homeostasis and Cell Processes **55**

Answers

9. Students should fill in the table with the terms *water* (top left); *sugar* (top right); *oxygen* (bottom left); and *carbon dioxide* (bottom right).

10. DNA needs to be copied so that the two new nuclei have the same number of chromosomes as is found in the original cell.

11. In both plants and animals, the DNA is copied and separated into two new nuclei. In plants, a cell plate separates the two new cells. In animals, the cell membrane pinches through the middle of the cell to form two new cells.

Learning Alert ⚠ MISCONCEPTION ⚠

Photosynthesis vs. Cellular Respiration Some students may mistakenly conclude that plants get their energy from photosynthesis and animals get their energy from cellular respiration. Make sure students understand that both plants and animals undergo cellular respiration to provide cells with energy. The big difference is the source of the sugars that are used for cellular respiration. Plants make their own sugars by photosynthesis; animals get their sugars from food.

Probing Questions GUIDED Inquiry

Drawing Conclusions Where do you think plants get their energy from at night when the sun is not shining? They get energy from cellular respiration using stored sugars.

Interpreting Visuals

Have students use the photographs of the plant cell and the animal cell to discuss mitosis. **Ask:** What part of mitosis has already happened in the photographs? The DNA has already been copied. What is occurring in the photograph? The cells are in the process of dividing.

Move It!

How do cells exchange materials?

What would happen to a factory if its supply of raw materials never arrived or it couldn't get rid of its garbage? Like a factory, an organism must be able to obtain materials for energy, make new materials, and get rid of wastes. The exchange of materials between a cell and its environment takes place at the cell's membrane. Cell membranes are *semi-permeable* because they allow only certain particles to cross into or out of the cell.

Active Reading

12 Relate As you read, underline the similarity between diffusion and osmosis.

Passive Transport

The movement of particles across a cell membrane without the use of energy by the cell is called **passive transport**. For example, when a tea bag is added to a cup of water, the molecules in the tea will eventually spread throughout the water. **Diffusion** is the movement of molecules from high concentrations to low concentrations. Some nutrients move into a cell by diffusion. Some waste products move out of the cell by diffusion. **Osmosis** is the diffusion of water through a semi-permeable membrane. Many molecules are too large to diffuse through the cell membrane. Some of these molecules enter and exit cells through protein channels embedded in the cell membrane. When molecules move through these protein channels from areas of higher concentration to areas of lower concentration, the process usually requires no energy.

The tea has a higher concentration of molecules in the tea bag than in the rest of the mug.

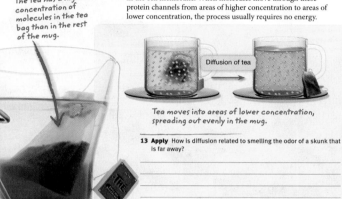

Diffusion of tea

Tea moves into areas of lower concentration, spreading out evenly in the mug.

13 Apply How is diffusion related to smelling the odor of a skunk that is far away?

Active Transport

Cells often need to move materials across the cell membrane from areas of low concentration into areas of higher concentration. This is the opposite direction of passive transport. **Active transport** is the movement of particles against a concentration gradient and requires the cell to use energy. Some large particles that do not fit through the protein channels may require active transport across the cell membrane by processes called *endocytosis* and *exocytosis*.

👁 Visualize It!

14 Identify Place a check mark next to the box that describes diffusion. Explain your answer.

Chemical energy

Passive transport moves materials into and out of a cell to areas of lower concentration. ☐

Active transport uses energy to move materials into and out of a cell to areas of higher concentration. ☐

56

57

Answers

12. *See students' pages for annotations.*

13. The molecules causing the odor from the skunk diffuse in the air. The molecules from the skunk are moving from a high concentration near the skunk to a lower concentration throughout the air.

14. Students should place a check mark next to passive transport. Diffusion is a type of passive transport because the molecules are moving from higher concentration to lower concentration.

Learning Alert

Active Transport Students might think that a cell can get all its nutrients through diffusion. However, only the smallest molecules, such as water, carbon dioxide, and oxygen, can diffuse freely into and out of cells. Larger molecules usually require active transport across the membrane.

Interpreting Visuals

To help students interpret the diagram of passive and active transport, have students focus on the yellow spheres first. **Ask:** Where are there more yellow spheres? inside the cell Where are they moving to? outside the cell What does this remind you of? Sample answer: the tea and hot water Explain that the yellow spheres are moving from an area of high concentration to an area of lower concentration. This is called *passive transport*. No energy is being used.

Now focus students' attention onto the green spheres. **Ask:** Where are there more green spheres? inside the cell Where are there fewer green spheres? outside the cell In which direction are they moving? They are moving into the cell. What is required of cells to move materials in this direction? energy This is called *active transport*. Active transport requires energy to move materials.

Endocytosis

The process by which a cell uses energy to surround a particle and enclose the particle in a vesicle to bring the particle into the cell is called **endocytosis** (en•doh•sye•TOH•sis). Vesicles are sacs formed from pieces of the cell membrane. Unicellular organisms, such as amoebas, use endocytosis to capture smaller organisms for food.

The cell comes into contact with a particle.

The cell membrane begins to wrap around the particle.

15 Describe What is happening in this step?

_____
_____
_____
_____
_____

Exocytosis

When particles are enclosed in a vesicle and released from a cell, the process is called **exocytosis** (ek•soh•sye•TOH•sis). Exocytosis is the reverse process of endocytosis. Exocytosis begins when a vesicle forms around particles within the cell. The vesicle fuses to the cell membrane and the particles are released outside of the cell. Exocytosis is an important process in multicellular organisms.

Large particles that must leave the cell are packaged in vesicles.

16 Describe What is happening in this step?

_____
_____
_____

The cell releases the particles to the outside of the cell.

How do organisms maintain homeostasis?

As you have read, cells can obtain energy, divide, and transport materials to maintain stable internal conditions. In multicellular organisms, the cells must work together to maintain homeostasis for the entire organism. For example, when some organisms become cold, the cells respond in order to maintain a normal internal temperature. Muscle cells will contract to generate heat, a process known as shivering.

Some animals adapt their behavior to control body temperature. For example, many reptiles bask in the sun or seek shade to regulate their internal temperatures. When temperatures become extremely cold, some animals hibernate. Animals such as ground squirrels are able to conserve their energy during the winter when food is scarce.

Some trees lose all their leaves around the same time each year. This is a seasonal response. Having bare branches during the winter reduces the amount of water loss. Leaves may also change color before they fall. As autumn approaches, chlorophyll, the green pigment used for photosynthesis, breaks down. As chlorophyll is lost, other yellow and orange pigments can be seen.

 Active Reading

17 Identify As you read, underline the different ways that organisms can respond to changes in the environment.

The leaves of some trees change colors when the season changes.

Visualize It!

18 Describe How is this boy's body responding to the cold weather?

_____
_____
_____

Answers

15. A vesicle forms around the particle to bring the particle into the cell.

16. The vesicle containing the particle fuses to the cell membrane before it is released.

17. *See students' pages for annotations.*

18. Sample answer: The boy is shivering to help warm his body.

Probing Question

Comparing What are the similarities between endocytosis and exocytosis? In both cases, the cell membrane folds to either take in or release a package of material. In both cases, material is moved across the cell membrane.

Formative Assessment

Ask: What are the three things all cells must do to maintain homeostasis? Sample answer: obtain and use energy, respond to the environment, move materials Next, have students explain some of the processes involved in maintaining homeostasis. **Ask:** How does a human being obtain energy? by eating food **Ask:** What process allows plants, animals, and humans to obtain energy from food? cellular respiration or the breaking down of food to obtain energy **Ask:** How do eukaryotic cells make more cells? **Prompt:** Think about the process that creates two new identical cells. Sample answer: First the DNA has to be copied and sorted. Then the cell can split. **Ask:** Describe the ways materials can move across cell membranes. **Prompt:** Think about passive and active transport. Sample answer: Cells can exchange materials by endocytosis or exocytosis, which requires the cell to use energy to move materials from areas of low concentrations to areas of high concentrations, or by diffusion, which does not require energy.

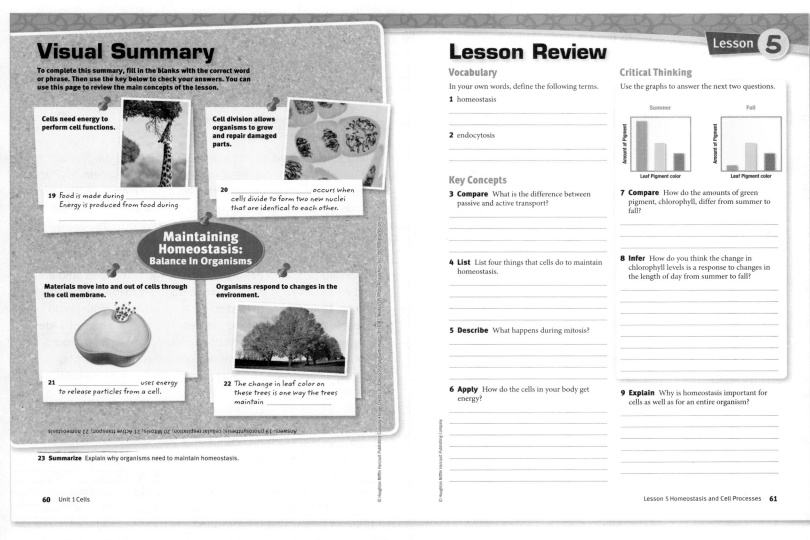

Visual Summary

To complete this summary, fill in the blanks with the correct word or phrase. Then use the key below to check your answers. You can use this page to review the main concepts of the lesson.

Cells need energy to perform cell functions.

Cell division allows organisms to grow and repair damaged parts.

19 Food is made during _____ Energy is produced from food during _____

20 _____ occurs when cells divide to form two new nuclei that are identical to each other.

Maintaining Homeostasis: Balance In Organisms

Materials move into and out of cells through the cell membrane.

Organisms respond to changes in the environment.

21 _____ uses energy to release particles from a cell.

22 The change in leaf color on these trees is one way the trees maintain _____

Answers: 19 photosynthesis; cellular respiration, 20 Mitosis, 21 Active transport, 22 homeostasis

23 Summarize Explain why organisms need to maintain homeostasis.

Lesson Review

Vocabulary

In your own words, define the following terms.

1 homeostasis

2 endocytosis

Key Concepts

3 Compare What is the difference between passive and active transport?

4 List List four things that cells do to maintain homeostasis.

5 Describe What happens during mitosis?

6 Apply How do the cells in your body get energy?

Critical Thinking

Use the graphs to answer the next two questions.

Summer — Amount of Pigment / Leaf Pigment color

Fall — Amount of Pigment / Leaf Pigment color

7 Compare How do the amounts of green pigment, chlorophyll, differ from summer to fall?

8 Infer How do you think the change in chlorophyll levels is a response to changes in the length of day from summer to fall?

9 Explain Why is homeostasis important for cells as well as for an entire organism?

Visual Summary Answers

19. photosynthesis; cellular respiration
20. Mitosis
21. Active transport
22. homeostasis
23. Organisms need to maintain homeostasis in order to survive. They must respond to the changing environment. Cells must be able to exchange materials, get rid of wastes, obtain and use energy, and reproduce to make new cells to repair or replace damaged or dead cells.

Lesson Review Answers

1. Sample answer: maintaining a stable internal environment
2. Sample answer: the process by which a cell uses energy to surround a particle and bring it into the cell
3. Passive transport does not require energy from the cell to move particles into or out of a cell. Active transport requires the cell to use energy to move particles.
4. exchange materials; get rid of wastes; obtain and use energy; reproduce new cells to repair or replace damaged or dead cells
5. During mitosis, a cell divides to make two new nuclei that are identical to each other.
6. Body cells get energy from food using cellular respiration, in which cells use oxygen to produce energy from food.
7. There is more chlorophyll in the plant during the summer than in the fall.
8. Chlorophyll is needed for photosynthesis. During summer the days are longer than during the fall, so there is more sunlight in the summer. As the days get shorter, there is less sunlight for photosynthesis, so the level of chlorophyll is reduced in the fall.
9. Cells must maintain homeostasis to survive and grow. If the cells in an organism cannot survive, then the organism will not function properly and could die.

Analyzing Nutrients

Purpose To compare nutritional information sources to learn about the nutritional value of common foods

Learning Goals
- Understand how to interpret nutritional information sources.
- Investigate nutritional values of common foods.
- Make a Pugh chart comparing nutritional values numerically.

Informal Vocabulary
nutrition, nutrient, Calorie, carbohydrate, protein, cholesterol

Prerequisite Knowledge
- Basic understanding of cells, nutrition, and fitness

Teacher Note To gather information on the nutritional values of foods, students will need access to Internet or supermarket resources. You may want to explain to students what resources are available to them at your school.

If students are unfamiliar with Pugh charts, demonstrate how to use one before students begin the activity. Explain that Pugh charts are tools for comparing items or options by ranking them numerically according to specific criteria.

Caution! All students should understand and follow school protocols for using the Internet.

Content Refresher

 Professional Development

MyPlate Background In 2011, the USDA unveiled the MyPlate icon. Like MyPyramid, the previous food guidance system, MyPlate does not provide recommendations about how many servings from each food group a person should eat every day. USDA research showed that many consumers consider a serving (a measured amount used for calculating nutrition information) to be the same thing as a portion (the amount one actually consumes). This confusion led people to eat more than the recommended amount of food while believing that they were correctly following the guidelines. MyPlate is intended to serve as a simple reminder to help people make healthy food choices. The MyPlate icon provides an easy way to visualize the relative amounts of five food groups that should be eaten to make up a healthy meal. For example, from the icon, one can quickly see that half of a person's meal should be made up of fruits and vegetables. More information on the different food groups, nutrition tips, sample meal plans, and healthy recipes can be found at the ChooseMyPlate.gov website. One can also find recommendations for daily food amounts based on an individual's age, gender, and activity level. The website also contains a daily food and activity tracker and a wide variety of tools to help people make healthy food and fitness choices. Although the MyPlate icon is not directly linked to physical fitness, the ChooseMyPlate.gov site does include recommendations about physical activity. According to ChooseMyPlate.gov, people should choose activities that they enjoy and do them a little at a time, slowly increasing their activity levels.

21st Century SKILLS   Theme: Health Literacy

Activities focusing on 21st Century Skills are included for this feature and can be found on the following pages.

These activities focus on the following skills:
- **Critical Thinking and Problem Solving**
- **Information Literacy**
- **Initiative and Self-direction**

You can learn more about the 21st Century Skills in the front matter of this Teacher Edition.

S.T.E.M. Engineering & Technology

Analyzing Technology

Skills	Objectives
✓ Identify risks ✓ Identify benefits Evaluate cost of technology Evaluate environmental impact Propose improvements Propose risk reduction Plan for technology failures ✓ Compare technology ✓ Communicate results	• Identify different resources for nutritional values. • Compare the nutritional value of common foods.

Analyzing Nutrients

Technology includes products, processes and systems developed to meet people's needs. Therefore, food is a kind of technology. Food supplies materials, called *nutrients*, that the body needs to perform its life functions. Your body gets nutrients from the food that you eat and the beverages that you drink. Each nutrient plays a role in keeping your body healthy. To make good decisions about what to eat, use nutrition guidelines such as the ChooseMyPlate.gov recommendations and the Nutrition Facts panels and ingredient labels on food packages.

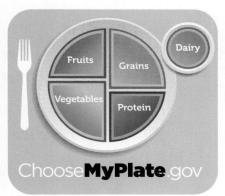

ChooseMyPlate.gov

The MyPlate image was designed to help people make healthy food choices. As shown on the MyPlate icon, a healthy meal should be made up primarily of fruits and vegetables. The rest should be made up of lean protein, whole grains, and low-fat dairy products.

1 Infer According to the MyPlate icon, what kinds of food should you eat to maintain a healthy body?

© Houghton Mifflin Harcourt Publishing Company • Image Credits: ©USDA

What's in Your Food?

Nutrients are listed on food labels by amounts and as percentages of Daily Values. The Daily Value (DV) of a nutrient is the recommended amount that a person should consume in a day. The percentage of the DV of a nutrient tells you what percentage of the recommended amount is provided by one serving of the food if your diet contains 2,000 Calories. A Calorie is a measurement of the amount of energy your body gets from a food. Your body gets energy from carbohydrates, proteins, and fats. So when is the amount of a nutrient in a food item low, and when is it high? If a food item has less than 5% of the DV of a nutrient, the Food and Drug Administration (FDA) says it's low in that nutrient. If the item has more than 20% of the DV of a nutrient, the FDA says it's high in that nutrient.

2 Calculate If a person consumes an entire can of this product, what percentage of his or her Daily Value of saturated fat would he or she consume?

© Houghton Mifflin Harcourt Publishing Company • Image Credits: ©Inti St Clair/Blend Images/Corbis

Fat Builds cell membranes, excess linked with heart disease

Sodium Needed for nerve function, excess linked with heart and kidney disease

Dietary Fiber Lowers risk of diabetes and heart disease

Protein Important for heart, brain, kidney, muscles

Vitamin A Important for eyes, skin

Calcium Important for bones, teeth, heart

Vitamin C Helps body absorb iron

Iron Vital for red blood cells

Nutrition Facts
Serving Size 8 ounces   Servings in can 2

Amount Per Serving	
Calories 155	Calories from Fat 93

	% Daily Value*
Total Fat 11g	**16%**
Saturated Fat 3g	**15%**
Trans Fat	
Polyunsaturated Fat 5g	
Monounsaturated Fat 3g	
Cholesterol 0mg	**0%**
Sodium 148mg	**6%**
Potassium 45mg	**1%**
Total Carbohydrate 14g	**5%**
Dietary Fiber 1g	**5%**
Sugars 1g	
Protein 2g	

Vitamin A	0%	Vitamin C	9%
Calcium	1%	Iron	3%

* Percent Daily Values are based on a 2,000 calorie diet. Your Daily Values may be higher or lower depending on your calorie needs.

✋ **You Try It!** →

Now it's your turn to compare the nutritional value of some food items.

Answers

1. grains, vegetables, and milk

2. This product contains 15% of the Daily Value of saturated fat per serving. The can contains 4 servings, so a person would consume 60% of their Daily Value of saturated fat by consuming the entire can.

You Try It! Answers

Sample answer: doughnuts, bacon, mayonnaise, broccoli, oatmeal, 2% milk

1.

Food item	Unhealthy nutrients	Other health risks
Doughnuts	sodium, fat	lots of sugar
Bacon	sodium, fat	lots of saturated fat, low in vitamins
Mayonnaise	sodium, fat	lots of calories from fat

2.

Food item	Healthy nutrients	Other health benefits
Broccoli	vitamin C, fiber	no sodium
Oatmeal	lots of soluble fiber	no saturated fat or cholesterol
2% milk	calcium, vitamin D	less fat than whole milk

Analyzing Technology

✋ You Try It!

Now it's your turn to use a Pugh chart and to compare the nutritional value of some common food items. You will analyze which foods are most likely to provide better nutrition, which allows you to make objective comparisons.

① Identify Risks

Using Nutrition Facts labels from Internet or supermarket resources, find out what nutrients are in each food on your list. Which foods are high in nutrients that are associated with health risks, such as saturated fat and cholesterol? Are there other health risks in these foods—for example, few healthy nutrients, or too many calories based on your recommended daily allowance? Use the information you find to fill in the table.

Food item	Unhealthy nutrients	Other health risks
1		
2		
3		
4		
5		

② Identify Benefits

Now use the same resources to identify which foods from your list are high in nutrients associated with health benefits. Are there other benefits you should consider for your foods? Use your information to fill in the table.

Food item	Healthy nutrients	Other health benefits
1		
2		
3		
4		
5		

S.T.E.M. Engineering & Technology

③ Compare Technologies

Now make a Pugh chart to compare nutritional values numerically. Write the names of the five foods you chose in the top row of the chart below. Fill in the boxes under each food item, ranking the food on a scale of 1–5, based on how it compares to the other foods for each nutrient.

Key for Ranking:
Each food is assigned 1 if it has the least of the listed nutrient and a 5 if it has the most.

1 = lowest
5 = highest

Fiber					
Protein					
Vitamin A					
Calcium					
Vitamin C					
Iron					
Total					

④ Communicate Results

Summarize your comparison of your food items, and interpret the information. Which of your foods has the highest total? Which has the lowest? What do your results tell you about the nutritional value of these foods?

You Try It Answers! (continued)

3. Sample answer:

	doughnuts	Bacon	Mayonnaise	Broccoli	Oatmeal	2% Milk
Fiber	2	1	1	4	4	1
Protein	1	5	1	1	1	2
Vitamin A	1	1	1	5	1	1
Calcium	1	1	1	2	1	4
Vitamin C	1	1	1	5	1	1
Iron	1	1	1	2	5	1
Total	7	10	6	19	13	10

4. Mayonnaise did the worst on my Pugh chart. I was a bit surprised by this because I thought that doughnuts would be the worst. However, doughnuts were only slightly better. Broccoli and oatmeal scored the highest. This seems reasonable because I would expect that unprocessed and wholegrain foods are healthier than processed foods.

21st Century SKILLS

Learning and Innovation Skills

 individuals   15 min

Critical Thinking and Problem Solving Based on the results of their Pugh charts, students should design a healthy, tasty meal plan for someone of their age and gender. Encourage students to not make the plan so restrictive that it would be unappealing to follow. Invite students to share their ideas with the class.

Information, Media, and Technology Skills

 small groups   20 min

Information Literacy Invite small groups of students to talk about and compare the resources they used to find nutritional information. What resources did they find especially helpful and reliable? What sources seemed least helpful and reliable? If students were to conduct this research again, what would they do differently? The same? Encourage students to list ways they could make their information searches more productive, efficient, and reliable.

Life and Career Skills

 individuals   ongoing

Initiative and Self-Direction Invite students to gather recipes to make a cookbook of healthy meals. Students may want to research cuisine from their heritage, certain food-cooking techniques, or styles of food they especially enjoy eating. Encourage students to examine their selected recipes and adapt them to make them as high in nutrients as possible. Have students copy or paste the recipes into a Booklet FoldNote.

🌐 *Online resource: Booklet FoldNote support*

Differentiated Instruction

Basic *Comparing Nutritional Values*

 individuals or pairs   20 min

Invite students to list other common food items that are similar to the ones on their Pugh charts. Encourage students to rank these foods from highest to lowest in nutritional value, based on what they learned while making the Pugh chart. Then have students conduct further research to see if their ideas are correct.

Advanced *Become a Food Scientist*

 individuals or pairs   20 min

Invite interested students to imagine they are food scientists working for a cereal, snack, or other food manufacturer. Challenge students to design a food product that would appeal to students their age, yet also contains ingredients with high nutrient values. Encourage students to share their food ideas with the class.

ELL *Nutritional Values of Favorite Foods*

 pairs or small groups   20 min

Have students choose a favorite healthy food from their culture or country (perhaps even a national dish). Encourage students to list the ingredients and quantities used to make the dish. Then have students adapt the recipe to make it as high in nutrients as possible, and as low in fat, cholesterol, and sodium as is reasonable.

Customize Your Feature

- [ ] **21st Century Skills** Learning and Innovation Skills
- [ ] **21st Century Skills** Information, Media, and Technology Skills
- [ ] **21st Century Skills** Life and Career Skills
- [ ] **Basic** Comparing Nutritional Values
- [ ] **Advanced** Become a Food Scientist
- [ ] **ELL** Nutritional Values of Favorite Foods

Photosynthesis and Cellular Respiration

Essential Question How do cells get and use energy?

 Professional Development

For more detailed information about the topics in this lesson, refer to the Content Refresher in the Unit Opener pages.

Opening Your Lesson

Begin the lesson by assessing students' prerequisite and prior knowledge.

Prerequisite Knowledge

- Examples of ecosystems
- General information about food chains

Accessing Prior Knowledge

Ask: How do plants get food? Sample answer: Plants use energy from the sun to make food.

Ask: How do animals get food? Sample answer: Animals get food by eating plants or other animals that eat plants.

Customize Your Opening

☐ **Accessing Prior Knowledge,** above

☐ **Print Path** Engage Your Brain, SE p. 67 #1–2

☐ **Print Path** Active Reading, SE p. 67 #3–4

☐ **Digital Path** Lesson Opener

Key Topics/Learning Goals	Supporting Concepts
Cells Need Energy 1 State that all organisms need energy. 2 Explain how organisms get energy.	• All organisms need energy. The cells of organisms use energy to carry out life activities. • Chemical energy is stored in food. Green plants and some other organisms make their own food using light energy from the sun. Animals get food by eating plants or other animals that eat plants.
Photosynthesis 1 Define and describe *photosynthesis*. 2 List the starting materials and the products of photosynthesis. 3 State the location where photosynthesis takes place.	• Photosynthesis is the process in which plants and other organisms use light energy, carbon dioxide, and water to make food that stores chemical energy. • The starting materials for photosynthesis are carbon dioxide, water, and light energy. The products are the simple sugar glucose and molecular oxygen. Glucose is a carbohydrate that stores energy in cells. • Photosynthesis takes place in the chloroplasts of plant cells.
Cellular Respiration 1 Define and describe *cellular respiration*. 2 List the starting materials and the products of cellular respiration. 3 State the location where cellular respiration takes place.	• Cellular respiration is the process in which cells use molecular oxygen to break down food and release stored energy. • The starting materials for cellular respiration are glucose and oxygen. The products are carbon dioxide, water, and energy in the form of ATP. • Cellular respiration takes place in the cell membrane of prokaryotic cells and in the mitochondria of eukaryotic cells.

Options for Instruction

Two parallel paths provide coverage of the Essential Questions, with a strong Inquiry strand woven into each.
Follow the Print Path, the Digital Path, or your customized combination of print, digital, and inquiry.

 Print Path
Teaching support for the Print Path appears with the Student Pages.

 Inquiry Labs and Activities

Digital Path
Digital Path shortcut: TS693070

Energize!, SE pp. 68–69
How do the cells in an organism function?
- Cells Need Energy
- Cells Get Energy from Food

Activity
Energy In, Stored, and Out

Activity
Why Is It Important?

Obtaining Energy
Interactive Graphics

Cooking with Chloroplasts,
SE pp. 70–71
How do plant cells make food?
- Capturing Light Energy
- Storing Chemical Energy

Merry-Go-Round!, SE p. 74
How are photosynthesis and cellular respiration connected?

Quick Lab
Plant Cell Structures

S.T.E.M. Lab
Investigate Rate of Photosynthesis

Activity
A Cellular Simulation

Virtual Lab
Observing Photosynthesis

Photosynthesis
Animation

Mighty Mitochondria,
SE pp. 72–73
How do cells get energy from food?
- Using Oxygen
- Releasing Energy

Merry-Go-Round!, SE p. 74
How are photosynthesis and cellular respiration connected?

Quick Lab
Investigate Carbon Dioxide

Activity
The Great Cycle

Activity
From Sugar to ATP

Cellular Respiration
Slideshow

Options for Assessment

See the Evaluate page for options, including Formative Assessment, Summative Assessment, and Unit Review.

Engage and Explore

Activity *Energy In, Stored, and Out*

Cells Need Energy

 flexible
 10–15 min
 DIRECTED inquiry

Collect a set of pictures or a list of organisms. For each one, ask the class to track its energy. Where does the organism get it? How is it stored? What is it used for? Sample answer: For the plants, the energy comes from the sun. The energy is stored as chemical energy in bonds found in the food it makes. The energy is used for anything a plant does, such as growth and reproduction. For animals, the energy comes from the food it eats. The energy is stored in the body as fat and in the chemical bonds of other molecules (animals also store energy as glycogen). The energy is used for anything an animal does, such as moving, breaking down food, and reproducing.

Discussion *Not the Only Ones*

Photosynthesis Cellular Respiration

 whole class
 10 min
 GUIDED inquiry

Discussion Photosynthesis and cellular respiration are major processes that move carbon, oxygen, and water through ecosystems, and between the atmosphere and ecosystems on land and water. However, these materials are involved in many other processes as well. Discuss in class other processes that they are familiar with that involve carbon, oxygen, and/or water. Some examples include:

- when gasoline is burned by cars, carbon dioxide is released into the atmosphere
- when water moves through the water cycle via evaporation, condensation (forming clouds), and precipitation (rain, snow, hail)
- oxygen reacts with iron to form rust, during a process called oxidation

Activity *From Sugar to ATP*

Cellular Respiration

 individuals
 15–20 min

Model Instruct students to draw a simple eukaryotic cell and label the cell membrane, cytoplasm, and mitochondria. Then complete a diagram of cellular respiration. They'll need to label the starting materials (*glucose, O_2*) and the products (CO_2, H_2O, *ATP*). It should include numbered steps and small descriptions of each part, along with arrows showing the flow of molecules in and out of the cell and mitochondria.

Variation While working in pairs, direct one student to draw a plant cell while the other draws an animal cell. This reinforces that plants undergo cellular respiration in addition to photosynthesis.

Activity *The Great Cycle*

Photosynthesis Cellular Respiration

 individuals
 15–20 min

Two-Panel Flipchart Students need to grasp the big picture connections between cellular respiration and photosynthesis. Have each student make a Two-Panel Flipchart showing photosynthesis on one side and cellular respiration on the other. Direct them to cut out molecules of glucose, CO_2, O_2, H_2O, and ATP. Then, tell students to use the pieces to simulate the flow of molecules back and forth between the two processes.

⊘ *Online resource: Two-Panel Flipchart support*

© Corbis

Customize Your Labs

◇ *See the Lab Manual for lab datasheets.*

⊘ *Go Online for editable lab datasheets.*

Labs and Demos

Quick Lab *Plant Cell Structures*

Photosynthesis

👥 pairs
🕐 15 min
Inquiry **DIRECTED** inquiry

Students observe samples of plant tissue using a microscope and compare the structures of different plant cells.

PURPOSE **To compare cellular structures of different plant specimens and relate cell structure to function**

MATERIALS

- colored pencils, assorted
- microscope, compound
- 2 prepared slides of plant tissue
- paper, blank
- safety goggles

Quick Lab *Investigate Carbon Dioxide*

Cellular Respiration

👥 pairs
🕐 20 min
Inquiry **DIRECTED** inquiry

Students take three samples of air and test each sample for the presence of carbon dioxide.

PURPOSE **To investigate the presence of carbon dioxide in various air samples**

MATERIALS

- bag, sealable plastic
- 3 jars of limewater, 15 mL each
- spoon, plastic
- sugar, granulated
- syringe, small plastic
- yeast, active dry
- water, distilled

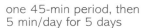 S.T.E.M. Lab *Investigate Rate of Photosynthesis*

Photosynthesis

👥 small groups
🕐 one 45-min period, then 5 min/day for 5 days
Inquiry **GUIDED or INDEPENDENT** inquiry

Students investigate how the amount of oxygen produced by an aquatic plant varies when they change one variable.

PURPOSE **To compare the amount of gas produced by a photosynthesizing plant as a single variable is changed**

MATERIALS

- balance
- baking soda and water solution, 5% (1L)
- 2 beakers (600 mL)
- 2 or 3 *Elodea* sprigs
- 2 funnels
- ruler, metric
- 2 test tubes

Virtual Lab *Observing Photosynthesis*

Photosynthesis

👥 flexible
🕐 45 min
Inquiry **GUIDED** inquiry

Students observe and analyze factors that affect the rates of photosynthesis and cellular respiration.

PURPOSE **To explore factors that affect biological processes**

Activities and Discussion

- ☐ **Activity** Energy In, Stored, and Out
- ☐ **Discussion** Not the Only Ones
- ☐ **Activity** From Sugar to ATP
- ☐ **Activity** The Great Cycle

Labs and Demos

- ☐ **Quick Lab** Plant Cell Structures
- ☐ **Quick Lab** Investigate Carbon Dioxide
- ☐ **S.T.E.M. Lab** Investigate Rate of Photosynthesis
- ☐ **Virtual Lab** Observing Photosynthesis

Your Resources

Explain Science Concepts

| | 📖 Print Path | 🖥 Digital Path |

Key Topics

Cells Need Energy

☐ **Energize!,** SE pp. 68–69
• Active Reading (Annotation strategy), #5
• Active Reading, #6
• Venn Diagram, #7

💿 *Optional Online resource:*
Venn Diagram
support

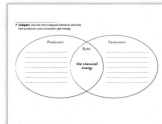

☐ **Obtaining Energy**
Explore how cells obtain and use energy.

Photosynthe-sis

☐ **Cooking with Chloroplasts,**
SE pp. 70–71
• Active Reading, #8
• Infer, #9

☐ **Merry-Go-Round!,** SE p. 74
• Visualize It!, #13
• Summarize, #14

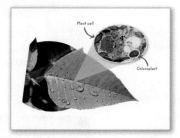

☐ **Photosynthesis**
Learn about the process of photosynthesis.

Cellular Respiration

☐ **Mighty Mitochondria,** SE pp. 72–73
• Active Reading (Annotation strategy), #10
• Think Outside the Book, #11
• Summarize, #12

☐ **Merry-Go-Round!,** SE p. 74
• Visualize It!, #13
• Summarize, #14

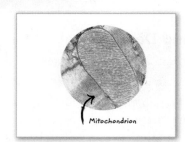

☐ **Cellular Respiration**
Learn about the process of cellular respiration.

Basic *Step by Step*

Synthesizing Key Topics

 individuals

🕐 20 min

Process Chart After students have learned about photosynthesis, ask them to summarize the process into steps. Repeat for cellular respiration. Then have them link the two charts into a cycle.

🌐 *Optional Online resource: Process Chart support*

Advanced *What If?*

Synthesizing Key Topics

 individuals or pairs

🕐 20–30 min

Assign each group a specific type of ecosystem (forest, coral reef). Instruct students to research and identify an example of that ecosystem (Jennings State Forest, Florida Reef). Within their ecosystem, require them to identify a simple food chain and predict what would happen if one of the organisms was removed from the ecosystem (remind students to include plants and microorganisms). For each organism, students should show how it connects to photosynthesis and demonstrate connections to other organisms.

ELL *Native Processes*

Synthesizing Key Topics

 individuals

🕐 20 min

Word Square Instruct students to make a Word Square for photosynthesis and cellular respiration. They should set it up as follows: box 1) the term and a translation of the term in their native language; box 2) the definition from the book and a definition in their native language; box 3) the products and the reactants (labeled as such); and box 4) a sentence using the terms in English and in their native language.

photosynthesis   chlorophyll   cellular respiration

Previewing Vocabulary

 whole class

🕐 10 min

Word Roots and Origins Share the following with the class:
- **Photosynthesis** is made of two parts, *photo* and *synthesis*. *Photo* means "light." *Synthesis* means "to put together."
- **Chlorophyll** comes from the Greek word *chloros*, meaning "green."
- **Cellular respiration** is composed of *cellular*, referring to cells, and *respiration* from the word *respire*, which means "to breathe."

Then ask students to use the meanings of the word roots to figure out the definitions of the words. For example, cellular respiration is cells exchanging and processing molecules (like breathing), because they take in oxygen and release carbon dioxide.

Reinforcing Vocabulary

 individuals or pairs

🕐 15–20 min

Sentence Sets Instruct students to write sentences that accurately relate sets of words from the lesson together. Each set should include at least one vocabulary word. An example word set is *chlorophyll, photosynthesis,* and *glucose; or photosynthesis, cellular respiration,* and *energy.*

Customize Your Core Lesson

Core Instruction
- ☐ **Print Path** choices
- ☐ **Digital Path** choices

Vocabulary
- ☐ **Previewing Vocabulary**
  Word Roots and Origins
- ☐ **Reinforcing Vocabulary**
  Sentence Sets

Your Resources

Differentiated Instruction
- ☐ **Basic** Step by Step
- ☐ **Advanced** What If?
- ☐ **ELL** Native Processes

Extend Science Concepts

Reinforce and Review

Activity *A Cellular Simulation*

Synthesizing Key Topics

 whole class
 15–20 min

Simulation Set up the class like the inside of a plant cell. Arrange certain desks as chloroplasts and others as mitochondria. Station students at each; there can be more than one of each. Require them to become familiar with the appropriate process (photosynthesis or cellular respiration). Assign other students into groups of reactants or products. Instruct each group of reactants or products to visit the chloroplasts and mitochondria. Then, have the students at the organelles and the reactants and products play out the appropriate process. Assign individual students to be "energy," some as "light" (energy) and some as ATP. When needed, each organelle group can call them over to complete the process.

Activity *Why Is It Important?*

Synthesizing Key Topics

 individuals
 15–20 min

Creative Writing Direct students to write a story, poem, or article about why photosynthesis and cellular respiration are important to their lives. Encourage them to be creative but to also fully explain the connections, including all of the products and reactants involved.

 Optional Online rubric: Written Pieces

Graphic Organizer

Synthesizing Key Topics

 individuals
 15 min

Mind Map After students have studied the lesson, ask them to design a Mind Map graphic organizer for photosynthesis and cellular respiration. Require them to include all reactants, products, and descriptions of the overall purposes of each.

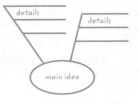

 Optional Online resource: Mind Map support

Going Further

Real World Connection

Synthesizing Key Topics

 whole class
 10 min

Discussion In the past 150 years, people have cleared most of the forests in the United States. In addition, burning fossil fuels to power cars and produce electricity has increased the amount of carbon emissions over many decades. Allow students to discuss how these two situations relate to photosynthesis and cellular respiration. Encourage students to discuss how reduced oxygen and increased carbon dioxide relate to and affect photosynthesis and cellular respiration. Then ask students to discuss choices they might make in their lives that are involved in the cycle.

Marine Biology Connection

Photosynthesis

 whole class
 10 min

Discussion One study has shown that sunscreen is polluting shallow ocean waters, causing harm to coral reefs and fish. The same chemicals that protect skin from sunlight may be awakening dormant viruses in symbiotic photosynthetic algae that live in coral polyps. Once these viruses reproduce, they cause their algae hosts to explode and are released into the ocean, where they spread to other coral reefs. The algae are important because they provide food for the corals. Without the algae, coral "bleaches" (turns white). Lead a discussion about the nature of science using this example. Point out that this is a singular study and further data are needed. To close the discussion, you can mention that coral-safe sunscreen is available.

Customize Your Closing

 See the Assessment Guide for quizzes and tests.

 Go Online to edit and create quizzes and tests.

Reinforce and Review

☐ **Activity** A Cellular Simulation

☐ **Activity** Why Is It Important?

☐ **Graphic Organizer** Mind Map

☐ **Print Path** Visual Summary, SE p. 76

☐ **Digital Path** Lesson Closer

Evaluate Student Mastery

Formative Assessment

See the teacher support below the Student Pages for additional Formative Assessment questions.

Provide students with a photo or picture of a complex ecosystem or area of high levels of human activity. Ask them to find as many instances of photosynthesis and cellular respiration as possible. Then ask them to find as many relationships and connections between organisms based on these processes. Have them write out their answers as a list.

Reteach

Formative assessment may show that students need reinforcement for certain topics. The resources below are recommended for reteaching. If students were introduced to a topic through the Print Path, you can also use the Digital Path to reteach, and vice versa.

🎧 *Can be assigned to individual students*

Cells Need Energy
Activity Energy In, Stored, and Out 🎧

Photosynthesis
Quick Lab Plant Cell Structures

Virtual Lab Observing Photosynthesis 🎧

Cellular Respiration
Activity From Sugar to ATP 🎧

Quick Lab Investigate Carbon Dioxide

Summative Assessment

Alternative Assessment
Energy Flows!

💿 *Online resources: student worksheet, optional rubrics*

Photosynthesis and Cellular Respiration

Points of View: *Energy Flows!*
Your class will work together to show what you've learned about how energy flows from several different viewpoints.

1. Work in groups as assigned by your teacher. Each group will be assigned to one or two viewpoints.

2. Complete your assignment, and present your perspective to the class.

 Vocabulary Define *photosynthesis* and *cellular respiration* in terms of how energy flows. Then write three sentences that use the words to show the sequence of events that occur during photosynthesis and cellular respiration.

 Examples Find two types of plants in your classroom or an outside area. Explain a possible pathway of flow of energy to and from each plant.

 Illustrations Make illustrations to compare photosynthesis with cellular respiration. How are they similar? How are they different? Can you think of an analogy for the relationship between photosynthesis and cellular respiration?

 Analysis Analyze the elements and compounds of photosynthesis and cellular respiration based on their chemical formulas. Make a chart to show how many atoms of each type are in the starting and end products. Then compare the four (the start and end for each of the two equations).

 Modeling Make a clay or other three-dimensional model of the flow of energy that includes photosynthesis and cellular respiration. Use your model to estimate how much photosynthesis is needed relative to a plant's cellular respiration.

Going Further
- [ ] **Real World Connection**
- [ ] **Marine Biology Connection**
- [ ] **Print Path** Why It Matters, SE p. 75

Formative Assessment
- [ ] **Strategies** Throughout TE
- [ ] **Lesson Review** SE

Summative Assessment
- [ ] **Alternative Assessment** Energy Flows!
- [ ] **Lesson Quiz**
- [ ] **Unit Tests A and B**
- [ ] **Unit Review** SE End-of-Unit

Your Resources

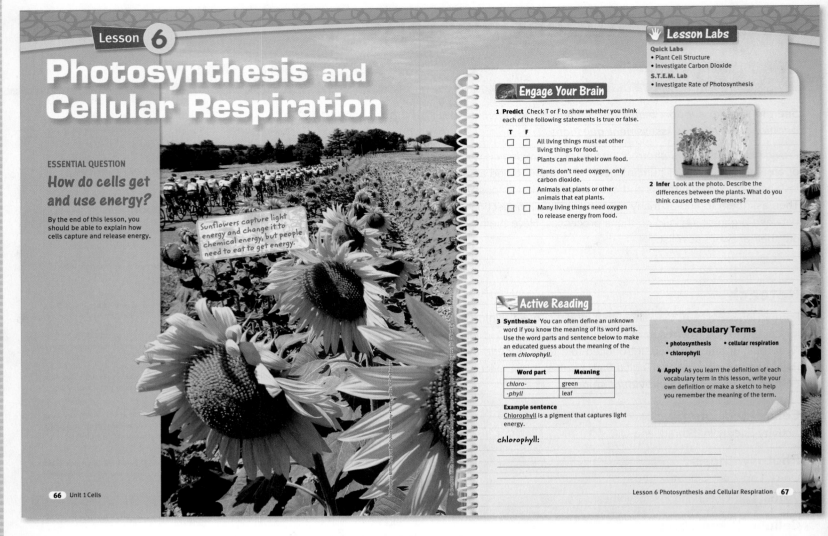

Lesson 6

Photosynthesis and Cellular Respiration

ESSENTIAL QUESTION

How do cells get and use energy?

By the end of this lesson, you should be able to explain how cells capture and release energy.

Sunflowers capture light energy and change it to chemical energy, but people need to eat to get energy.

66 Unit 1 Cells

Lesson Labs

Quick Labs
• Plant Cell Structure
• Investigate Carbon Dioxide

S.T.E.M. Lab
• Investigate Rate of Photosynthesis

Engage Your Brain

1 Predict Check T or F to show whether you think each of the following statements is true or false.

T	F	
☐	☐	All living things must eat other living things for food.
☐	☐	Plants can make their own food.
☐	☐	Plants don't need oxygen, only carbon dioxide.
☐	☐	Animals eat plants or other animals that eat plants.
☐	☐	Many living things need oxygen to release energy from food.

2 Infer Look at the photo. Describe the differences between the plants. What do you think caused these differences?

_____

_____

_____

_____

_____

Active Reading

3 Synthesize You can often define an unknown word if you know the meaning of its word parts. Use the word parts and sentence below to make an educated guess about the meaning of the term *chlorophyll*.

Word part	Meaning
chloro-	green
-phyll	leaf

Example sentence
Chlorophyll is a pigment that captures light energy.

chlorophyll: _____

_____

_____

Vocabulary Terms
• photosynthesis
• chlorophyll
• cellular respiration

4 Apply As you learn the definition of each vocabulary term in this lesson, write your own definition or make a sketch to help you remember the meaning of the term.

Lesson 6 Photosynthesis and Cellular Respiration 67

Answers

Answers for 1–3 should represent students' current thoughts, even if incorrect.

1. F; T; F; T; T

2. Sample answer: The plant on the left is green and shorter than the plant on the right. The plant on the right is yellow instead of green, and it is taller. The plant on the right probably didn't get any light.

3. Sample answer: Chlorophyll is a green pigment found in the leaves of plants.

4. Students should define or sketch each vocabulary term in the lesson.

Opening Your Lesson

Discuss true/false questions (item 1) to assess students' prerequisite knowledge and to estimate what they already know about the key topics.

Prerequisites Students should have a sense of the need for energy by living things. They should know that plants use sunlight to make food and that animals need to obtain food for energy.

Interpreting Visuals

Direct students to look at the image of the plant. **Ask:** What is the source of energy for the plant? Sample answer: the sun; the food it makes **Ask:** What do you think a plant uses energy for? Sample answer: to grow or reproduce **Ask:** How might plants pass this energy on to other organisms such as animals? Sample answer: Animals eat the plants.

Learning Alert ⚠ MISCONCEPTION ⚠

Photosynthesis and Cellular Respiration Cycle Even though these two processes can form a cycle, it does not mean that their components only cycle between them. Oxygen, carbon dioxide, and water are also part of other cycles and processes. Ask students to think about the water cycle. Help students trace the path of a water molecule through the cycle.

Energize!

How do the cells in an organism function?

Active Reading 5 **Identify** As you read, underline sources of energy for living things.

How do you get the energy to run around and play soccer or basketball? How does a tree get the energy to grow? All living things, from the tiniest single-celled bacterium to the largest tree, need energy. Cells must capture and use energy or they will die. Cells get energy from food. Some living things can make their own food. Many living things get their food by eating other living things.

Your cells use energy all the time, whether you are active or not.

Cells Need Energy

Growing, moving, and other cell functions use energy. Without energy, a living thing cannot replace cells, build body parts, or reproduce. Even when a living thing is not very active, it needs energy. Cells constantly use energy to move materials into and out of the cell. They need energy to make different chemicals. And they need energy to get rid of wastes. A cell could not survive for long if it did not have the energy for all of these functions.

Active Reading 6 **Relate** Why do living things need energy at all times?

_____

_____

Cells Get Energy from Food

The cells of all living things need chemical energy. Food contains chemical energy. Food gives living things the energy and raw materials needed to carry out life processes. When cells break down food, the energy of the chemical bonds in food is released. This energy can be used or stored by the cell. The atoms and molecules in food can be used as building blocks for the cell.

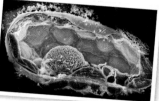

Plant cells make their own food using energy from the sun.

Living things get food in different ways. In fact, they can be grouped based on how they get food. Some living things, such as plants and many single-celled organisms, are called *producers* (proh•DOO•suhrz). Producers can make their own food. Most producers use energy from the sun. They capture and store light energy from the sun as chemical energy in food. A small number of producers, such as those that live in the deepest parts of the ocean, use chemicals to make their own food. Producers use most of the food they produce for energy. The unused food is stored in their bodies.

Many living things, such as people and other animals, are *consumers* (kun•SOO•muhrz). Consumers must eat, or consume, other living things to get food. Consumers may eat producers or other consumers. The cells of consumers break down food to release the energy it contains. A special group of consumers is made up of *decomposers* (dee•cum•POH•zhurhz). Decomposers break down dead organisms or the wastes of other organisms. Fungi and many bacteria are decomposers.

7 **Compare** Use the Venn diagram below to describe how producers and consumers get energy.

Producers — Both — Consumers

Both: Use chemical energy

Answers

5. *See student pages for annotations.*

6. Sample answer: Cells constantly use energy to move materials into and out of the cell. They make different chemicals and get rid of wastes. Because these functions always happen, cells need energy all the time.

7. Sample answer:

   Producers: Producers make their own food by capturing light energy and converting it to chemical energy that they can use.

   Consumers: Consumers get chemical energy by eating producers or other consumers.

Probing Question GUIDED Inquiry

Comparing Prompt: Sometimes a cell is compared to a city. **Ask:** How would the energy needs of a cell be compared to the energy needs of a city? Sample answer: A city needs energy for nearly everything it does. Buildings, homes, and businesses need electricity for lights and appliances, just as cell parts (such as the nucleus) need energy to do their jobs. Cities need energy or fuel for transportation (buses and subways) and communication (cell phones and computers), just as cells do.

Building Reading Skills

Text Structure: Main Idea/Details An important reading strategy for science is knowing how to identify the main idea and the supporting details in text passages. Ask the students to read the second paragraph. **Ask:** What is the main idea of this paragraph? Sample answers: Cells need energy to stay alive. Cells use energy for lots of things. Remind them that they can use headings as clues. Then direct students to draw a Main Idea Web to help them organize the supporting details around the main idea.

 Optional Online resources: Text Structure: Main Idea/Details, Main Idea Web support

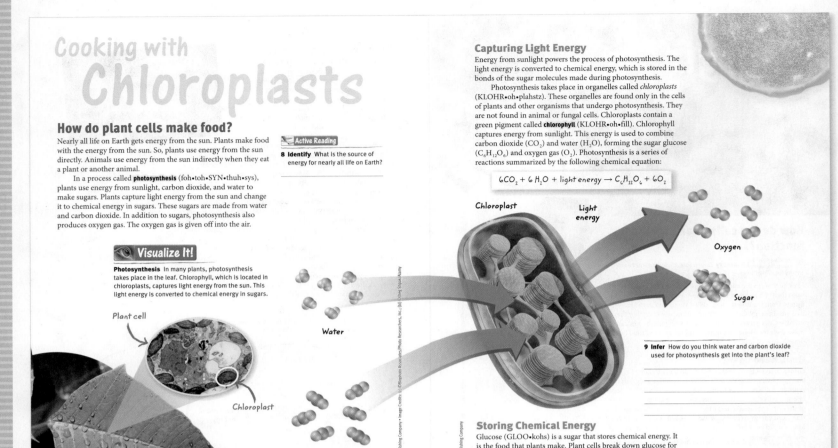

Cooking with Chloroplasts

How do plant cells make food?

Nearly all life on Earth gets energy from the sun. Plants make food with the energy from the sun. So, plants use energy from the sun directly. Animals use energy from the sun indirectly when they eat a plant or another animal.

In a process called **photosynthesis** (foh•toh•SYN•thuh•sys), plants use energy from sunlight, carbon dioxide, and water to make sugars. Plants capture light energy from the sun and change it to chemical energy in sugars. These sugars are made from water and carbon dioxide. In addition to sugars, photosynthesis also produces oxygen gas. The oxygen gas is given off into the air.

Active Reading

8 Identify What is the source of energy for nearly all life on Earth?

Visualize It!

Photosynthesis In many plants, photosynthesis takes place in the leaf. Chlorophyll, which is located in chloroplasts, captures light energy from the sun. This light energy is converted to chemical energy in sugars.

Plant cell

Chloroplast

Water

Carbon dioxide

Capturing Light Energy

Energy from sunlight powers the process of photosynthesis. The light energy is converted to chemical energy, which is stored in the bonds of the sugar molecules made during photosynthesis.

Photosynthesis takes place in organelles called *chloroplasts* (KLOHR•oh•plahstz). These organelles are found only in the cells of plants and other organisms that undergo photosynthesis. They are not found in animal or fungal cells. Chloroplasts contain a green pigment called **chlorophyll** (KLOHR•oh•fill). Chlorophyll captures energy from sunlight. This energy is used to combine carbon dioxide (CO_2) and water (H_2O), forming the sugar glucose ($C_6H_{12}O_6$) and oxygen gas (O_2). Photosynthesis is a series of reactions summarized by the following chemical equation:

$$6CO_2 + 6H_2O + light\ energy \rightarrow C_6H_{12}O_6 + 6O_2$$

Chloroplast

Light energy

Oxygen

Sugar

9 Infer How do you think water and carbon dioxide used for photosynthesis get into the plant's leaf?

Storing Chemical Energy

Glucose (GLOO•kohs) is a sugar that stores chemical energy. It is the food that plants make. Plant cells break down glucose for energy. Excess sugars are stored in the body of the plant. They are often stored as starch in the roots and stem of the plant. When another organism eats the plant, the organism can use these stored sugars for energy.

© Houghton Mifflin Harcourt Publishing Company • Image Credits: (c) ©Biophoto Associates/Photo Researchers, Inc.; (bl) ©Oleg Shpak/Alamy

© Houghton Mifflin Harcourt Publishing Company

Answers

8. the sun

9. Sample answer: Carbon dioxide comes from the air, and water comes from the soil. Carbon dioxide likely enters through openings in leaves. Water is pulled up from the roots.

Interpreting Visuals

Ask students to trace the path of carbon and oxygen atoms through photosynthesis. For each one, walk through the individual pathways of each element, showing how it changes form but is still conserved. Carbon enters the reaction as carbon dioxide and then becomes part of glucose. Oxygen enters the reaction in water or carbon dioxide and is released as oxygen molecules or as part of glucose.

Learning Alert

Forms of Energy It is important that students understand the big picture of energy flow and transfer. Be sure to emphasize the larger perspective that photosynthesis acts as a process that converts energy from one form into another, which can then be used by the plant and other living things.

Formative Assessment

Ask: How is a chloroplast like a solar panel on a house? Sample answer: Both solar panels and chloroplasts absorb energy from the sun. Both convert it into a different form of energy—solar panels into electrical energy, chloroplasts into chemical energy. Both new forms of energy can then be used as energy sources for accomplishing other things.

Mighty Mitochondria

How do cells get energy from food?

When sugar is broken down, energy is released. It is stored in a molecule called *adenosine triphosphate* (ATP). ATP powers many of the chemical reactions that enable cells to survive. The process of breaking down food to produce ATP is called **cellular respiration** (SELL•yoo•lahr ress•puh•RAY•shuhn).

Mitochondria are found in both plant cells and animal cells.

Active Reading

10 Identify As you read, underline the starting materials and products of cellular respiration.

Using Oxygen

Cellular respiration takes place in the cytoplasm and cell membranes of prokaryotic cells. In eukaryotic cells, cellular respiration takes place in organelles called *mitochondria* (singular, *mitochondrion*). Mitochondria are found in both plant and animal cells. The starting materials of cellular respiration are glucose and oxygen.

In eukaryotes, the first stage of cellular respiration takes place in the cytoplasm. Glucose is broken down into two 3-carbon molecules. This releases a small amount of energy. The next stage takes place in the mitochondria. This stage requires oxygen. Oxygen enters the cell and travels into the mitochondria. As the 3-carbon molecules are broken down, energy is captured and stored in ATP.

Mitochondrion

Visualize It!

Cellular Respiration During cellular respiration, cells use oxygen gas to break down sugars and release energy.

Oxygen

Sugar from photosynthesis

3-carbon molecules

72   Unit 1 Cells

Releasing Energy

The products of cellular respiration are chemical energy (ATP), carbon dioxide, and water. The carbon dioxide formed during cellular respiration is released by the cell. In many animals, the carbon dioxide is carried to the lungs and exhaled during breathing.

Some of the energy produced during cellular respiration is released as heat. However, much of the energy produced during cellular respiration is transferred to ATP. ATP can be carried throughout the body. When ATP is broken down, the energy released is used for cellular activities. The steps of cellular respiration can be summarized by the following equation:

$$C_6H_{12}O_6 + 6O_2 \rightarrow 6CO_2 + 6H_2O + \text{chemical energy (ATP)}$$

Think Outside the Book Inquiry

11 Identify With a partner, write a creative story or play that describes the process of cellular respiration.

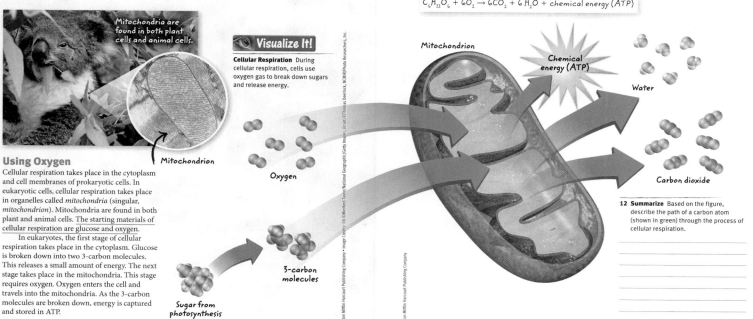

Mitochondrion

Chemical energy (ATP)

Water

Carbon dioxide

12 Summarize Based on the figure, describe the path of a carbon atom (shown in green) through the process of cellular respiration.

Lesson 6 Photosynthesis and Cellular Respiration   73

Answers

10. *See student pages for annotations.*

11. Students should accurately describe the process of cellular respiration in their stories and plays.

12. Sample answer: The carbon atom starts out as part of glucose. During cellular respiration, glucose is broken down into smaller carbon molecules. Eventually, the carbon atoms are released into the atmosphere in carbon dioxide.

Formative Assessment

Help students write a general equation that shows the process of cellular respiration. Then, help them write a second equation that shows the process of photosynthesis. They should put the materials that are used in the processes on the left of the arrow and the materials that are produced to the right of the arrow. cellular respiration: oxygen + glucose → carbon dioxide + water + energy; photosynthesis: energy from the sun + carbon dioxide + water → glucose (food) and oxygen **Ask:** What do you notice about these equations? Sample answer: The materials that are used in cellular respiration are the products of photosynthesis, and vice versa. Remind students that the energy used in photosynthesis is different from the energy produced in cellular respiration.

Probing Question   GUIDED Inquiry

Inferring Prompt: Scientists think mitochondria originated in ancient eukaryotes as engulfed bacteria that could break down sugars to release chemical energy stored in the chemical bonds of these molecules. **Ask:** Explain why this might make sense. Sample answer: Mitochondria can convert food into chemical energy. With energy, an organism has the fuel to do other things. Scientists actually base this theory on the DNA evidence that shows a relationship between mitochondria and bacteria. Similar DNA evidence suggests that chloroplasts originated as independent organisms too.

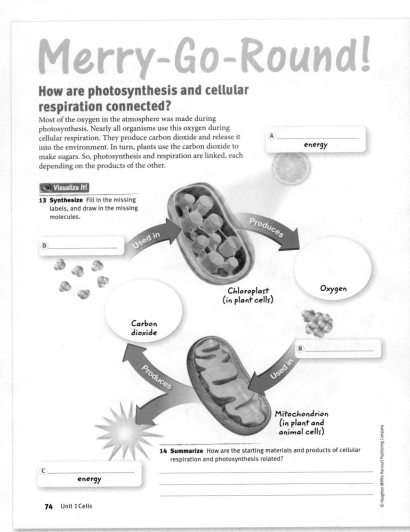

Merry-Go-Round!

How are photosynthesis and cellular respiration connected?

Most of the oxygen in the atmosphere was made during photosynthesis. Nearly all organisms use this oxygen during cellular respiration. They produce carbon dioxide and release it into the environment. In turn, plants use the carbon dioxide to make sugars. So, photosynthesis and respiration are linked, each depending on the products of the other.

Visualize It!

13 Synthesize Fill in the missing labels, and draw in the missing molecules.

A _____ energy

D _____

Used in | Produces

Chloroplast (in plant cells)

Oxygen

Carbon dioxide

B _____

Produces | Used in

Mitochondrion (in plant and animal cells)

C _____ energy

14 Summarize How are the starting materials and products of cellular respiration and photosynthesis related?

© Houghton Mifflin Harcourt Publishing Company

74 Unit 1 Cells

Why It Matters

Out of Air

When there isn't enough oxygen, living things can get energy by anaerobic respiration (AN•uh•roh•bick ress•puh•RAY•shuhn). *Anaerobic* means "without oxygen." Like cellular respiration, anaerobic respiration produces ATP. However, it does not produce as much ATP as cellular respiration.

WEIRD SCIENCE

Rising to the Top
Fermentation is a type of anaerobic respiration. Many yeasts rely on fermentation for energy. Carbon dioxide is a product of fermentation. Carbon dioxide causes bread to rise, and gives it air pockets.

Feel the Burn!
The body uses anaerobic respiration during hard exercise, such as sprinting. This produces lactic acid, which can cause muscles to ache after exercise.

196

Extend | Inquiry

15 Compare What products do both cellular and anaerobic respiration have in common?

16 Research Blood delivers oxygen to the body. If this is the case, why does the body rely on anaerobic respiration during hard exercise? Research the reasons why the body switches between cellular and anaerobic respiration.

17 Compare Research and compare cellular respiration and fermentation. How are they similar? How do they differ? Summarize your results by doing one of the following:
• make a poster   • write a brochure
• draw a comic strip • make a table

75

Answers

13. A. light; B. glucose or sugar; C. chemical; D. water; Students should draw 6 carbon dioxide molecules and 6 diatomic oxygen molecules.

14. Sample answer: The products of photosynthesis are the reactants of cellular respiration, and vice versa.

15. ATP and carbon dioxide

16. Students should note that the body does not deliver oxygen as efficiently during hard exercise, leading to the use of anaerobic respiration.

17. Students should note similarities such as common reactants (sugars) and products (carbon dioxide and energy). They should note that cellular respiration requires oxygen, while fermentation does not require it and is less efficient.

Learning Alert 📐 MISCONCEPTION 📐

Photosynthesis and Cellular Respiration Cycle Students often think that animals undergo cellular respiration and plants undergo photosynthesis only. Make an analogy to cooking. Preparing the meal (photosynthesis) is a different process from eating the meal (cellular respiration).

Why It Matters

Explain to students that cellular respiration produces much larger amounts of ATP than fermentation. **Ask:** How is it possible for some organisms to survive using only fermentation and not cellular respiration? Sample answer: Some organisms are not very large, and are quite simple. They do not need as much energy as larger, more complex organisms. **Ask:** Which process, fermentation or cellular respiration, probably developed first on Earth? Sample answer: Early Earth did not have oxygen. Therefore it is likely fermentation developed first, allowing life to begin before oxygen was available. **Ask:** Why did a much greater variety of life evolve after oxygen became abundant and useable through cellular respiration? Sample answer: By using oxygen, cellular respiration releases much more energy than fermentation. Over very long periods of geologic time, greater amounts of available energy helped allow for more diverse and complex organisms to evolve.

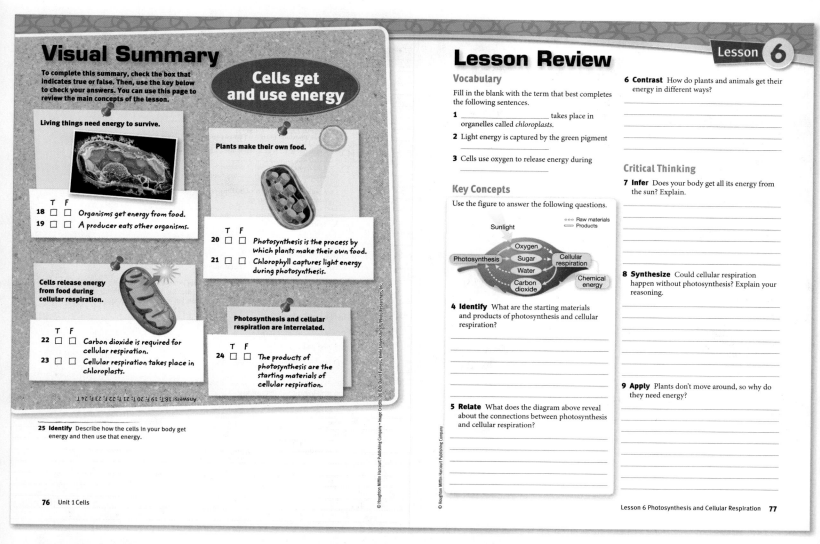

Visual Summary

To complete this summary, check the box that indicates true or false. Then, use the key below to check your answers. You can use this page to review the main concepts of the lesson.

Cells get and use energy

Living things need energy to survive.

T F
18 ☐ ☐ Organisms get energy from food.
19 ☐ ☐ A producer eats other organisms.

Plants make their own food.

T F
20 ☐ ☐ Photosynthesis is the process by which plants make their own food.
21 ☐ ☐ Chlorophyll captures light energy during photosynthesis.

Cells release energy from food during cellular respiration.

T F
22 ☐ ☐ Carbon dioxide is required for cellular respiration.
23 ☐ ☐ Cellular respiration takes place in chloroplasts.

Photosynthesis and cellular respiration are interrelated.

T F
24 ☐ ☐ The products of photosynthesis are the starting materials of cellular respiration.

Answers: 18 T, 19 F, 20 T, 21 T, 22 F, 23 F, 24 T

25 Identify Describe how the cells in your body get energy and then use that energy.

76 Unit 1 Cells

© Houghton Mifflin Harcourt Publishing Company • Image Credits: (t) ©Dr. David Furness, Keele University/SPL/Photo Researchers, Inc.

Lesson Review

Lesson 6

Vocabulary

Fill in the blank with the term that best completes the following sentences.

1 _____ takes place in organelles called *chloroplasts*.

2 Light energy is captured by the green pigment _____

3 Cells use oxygen to release energy during _____

Key Concepts

Use the figure to answer the following questions.

Sunlight
Photosynthesis
Oxygen
Sugar
Water
Carbon dioxide
Cellular respiration
Chemical energy
○○○ Raw materials
═══ Products

4 Identify What are the starting materials and products of photosynthesis and cellular respiration?

5 Relate What does the diagram above reveal about the connections between photosynthesis and cellular respiration?

6 Contrast How do plants and animals get their energy in different ways?

Critical Thinking

7 Infer Does your body get all its energy from the sun? Explain.

8 Synthesize Could cellular respiration happen without photosynthesis? Explain your reasoning.

9 Apply Plants don't move around, so why do they need energy?

Lesson 6 Photosynthesis and Cellular Respiration 77

© Houghton Mifflin Harcourt Publishing Company

Visual Summary Answers

18. T
19. F
20. T
21. T
22. F
23. F
24. T
25. Sample answer: I eat different kinds of food. The energy in this food is produced by photosynthesis directly or indirectly. The food is broken down to produce ATP, which powers cell functions. My cells use energy to move materials in and out, to make different chemicals, to grow, and to reproduce.

Lesson Review Answers

1. Photosynthesis
2. chlorophyll
3. cellular respiration
4. For photosynthesis, the starting materials are water and carbon dioxide, and the products are sugar and oxygen. For cellular respiration, the starting materials are oxygen and sugar, and the products are carbon dioxide and water.
5. The products of cellular respiration are the reactants of photosynthesis, and vice versa.
6. Sample answer: Plants get energy by making their own food. Animals get energy by eating plants or other animals.
7. Sample answer: Yes, all of the energy I get comes from the sun. I eat plants, which capture light energy from the sun to make food. The energy in the animals I eat comes from plants, which in turn get energy from the sun.
8. Sample answer: No. The starting materials of cellular respiration are the products of photosynthesis. Without photosynthesis, there wouldn't be any oxygen or glucose for cellular respiration.
9. Sample answer: Plants do not move around, but the cells of plants need to move materials into and out of the cells. They also need to make different chemicals, and they need to grow, develop, and reproduce. All of these functions require energy.

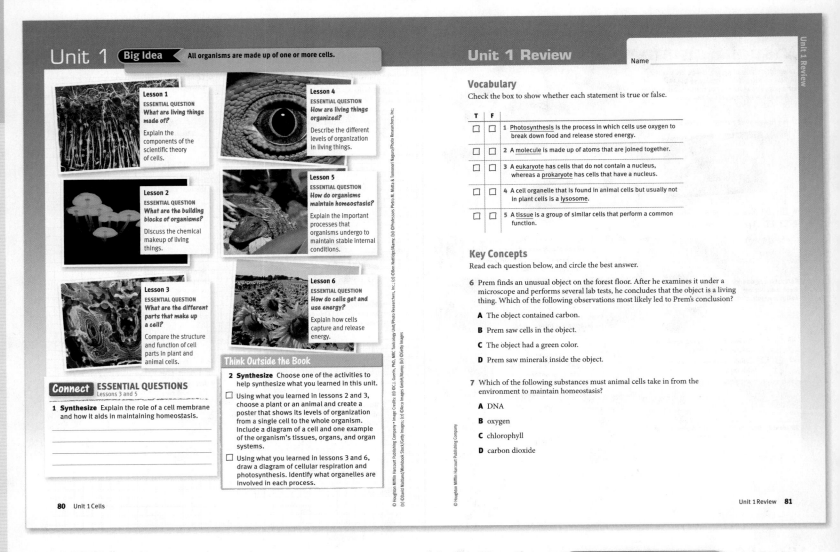

Unit Summary Answers

1. The cell membrane controls the exchange of materials in and out of a cell. By exchanging materials with the environment, it helps to ensure that needed materials enter the cell, and it also helps to prevent the buildup of waste materials inside the cell.

2. Option 1: Posters should correctly identify the structures found in a cell of their chosen organism and correctly identify at least one tissue, one organ, and one organ system found in their chosen organism.

   Option 2: Diagrams should indicate that cellular respiration takes place in the mitochondria of a plant or animal cell and that photosynthesis takes place in the chloroplasts of plant cells.

Unit Review   Response to Intervention

A Quick Grading Chart follows the Answers. See the Assessment Guide for more detail about correct and incorrect answer choices. Refer back to the Lesson Planning pages for activities and assignments that can be used as remediation for students who answer questions incorrectly.

Answers

1. False This statement is false because the food that is made during photosynthesis is broken down during cellular respiration. (Lesson 6)

2. True This statement is true because atoms join together with chemical bonds to form molecules. (Lesson 2)

3. False This statement is false because eukaryotic cells contain a nucleus and prokaryotic cells do not. (Lesson 1)

4. True This statement is true because only animal cells have lysosomes. (Lesson 3)

8 Juana made the following table.

Organelle	Function
Mitochondrion	Cellular respiration
Ribosome	DNA synthesis
Chloroplast	Photosynthesis
Endoplasmic reticulum	Makes proteins and lipids
Golgi complex	Packages proteins

Juana's table lists several cell organelles and their functions, but she made an error. Which of the organelles shown in the table is listed with the wrong function?

A mitochondrion   **C** cell membrane

B ribosome   **D** Golgi complex

9 Which molecule is a source of energy, a store of energy in the body, and can mix with water?

A lipid   **C** nucleic acid

B chlorophyll   **D** carbohydrate

10 Which method of material exchange uses up energy?

A osmosis   **C** active transport

B diffusion   **D** passive transport

11 The following diagram shows a common cell organelle.

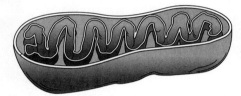

What process takes place in the organelle shown?

A photosynthesis   **C** cellular respiration

B protein synthesis   **D** packaging of proteins

12 Plants contain xylem and phloem tissue. What organ system in animals performs a similar function as the xylem and phloem of plants?

A digestive system

B excretory system

C respiratory system

D circulatory system

13 Which statement correctly tells why the cells of unicellular and multicellular organisms divide?

A The cells of unicellular organisms divide to reproduce; those of multicellular organisms divide to replace cells and to grow.

B The cells of unicellular organisms divide to replace cells and to grow; those of multicellular organisms divide to reproduce.

C The cells of both kinds of organisms divide to reproduce.

D The cells of both kinds of organisms divide to replace cells and to grow.

14 The following picture shows *Escherichia coli* cells, a species of bacterium.

Which of the following statements correctly compares the cells shown in the picture with a human cell?

A Both types of cells divide by mitosis.

B Human cells contain proteins but *E. coli* cells do not.

C Both cells contain ribosomes and a cell membrane.

D Human cells contain DNA but *E. coli* cells do not.

Answers *(continued)*

5. **True** This statement is true because each tissue contains similar cells that perform a common function. (Lesson 4)

6. **Answer B is correct** because only living things are made up of one or more cells. (Lesson 1)

7. **Answer B is correct** because animal cells need a constant supply of oxygen to convert food into energy. (Lesson 5)

8. **Answer B is correct** because protein synthesis, not DNA synthesis, takes place in the ribosomes. (Lesson 5)

9. **Answer D is correct** because many carbohydrates, such as sugars, are soluble in water and are the cells' main energy source. (Lesson 2)

10. **Answer C is correct** because energy is required to move materials against a concentration gradient. (Lesson 5)

11. **Answer C is correct** because the organelle shown is a mitochondrion, the site of cellular respiration. (Lesson 3)

12. **Answer D is correct** because the circulatory system transports nutrients to cells and removes wastes. This function is similar to that performed by the vascular tissue of plants. Xylem and phloem transport water and nutrients throughout a plant. (Lesson 4)

13. **Answer A is correct** because unicellular organisms have only one cell, so cell division is reproduction. Multicellular organisms grow larger by making more cells. (Lesson 1)

14. **Answer C is correct** because both prokaryotic and eukaryotic cells have ribosomes and cell membranes. (Lesson 1)

15. **Answer C is correct** because an organ is a collection of different tissues that each carry out a specialized function. (Lesson 4)

16. **Answer A is correct** because cell model A has the most cell membrane compared to its volume. Therefore it has the largest surface-area-to-volume ratio, allowing nutrients and water to be efficiently transported into the cell. (Lesson 5)

Unit 1 Review continued

Name _____

15 A plant leaf is an organ that traps light energy to make food. In what way is an animal stomach similar to a plant leaf?

A Both organs make food.

B Both organs are made up of only one kind of cell.

C Both organs are made up of several kinds of tissues.

D Both organs take in oxygen and release carbon dioxide.

16 The following table shows the surface area-to-volume ratio of four cube-shaped cell models.

Cell Model	Surface Area	Volume	Surface Area-to Volume Ratio
A	6 cm²	1 cm³	6 : 1 = 6
B	24 cm²	8 cm³	24 : 8 = 3
C	54 cm²	27 cm³	54 : 27 = 2
D	96 cm²	64 cm³	96 : 64 = 1.5

Cells are small, and their surface area is large in relation to their volume. This is an important feature for the proper transport of nutrients and water in to and out of the cell. Which of the four model cells do you think will be best able to supply nutrients and water to its cell parts?

A cell model A

B cell model B

C cell model C

D cell model D

17 Cells of a multicellular organism are specialized. What does this statement mean?

A Cells of a multicellular organism are adapted to perform specific functions.

B Cells of a multicellular organism perform all life functions but not at the same time.

C Cells of a multicellular organism are specialized because they have a complex structure.

D Cells of a multicellular organism can perform all the life functions the organism needs to survive.

Critical Thinking

Answer the following questions in the space provided.

18 The following diagram shows a cell that Dimitri saw on his microscope slide.

Dimitri's teacher gave him an unlabeled slide of some cells and asked him to identify whether the cells were plant cells or animal cells. Dimitri examined the slide under a microscope and concluded that the cells were plant cells. How did Dimitri reach his conclusion? Is his conclusion correct? What life process can these cells carry out that a cell from another kind of multicellular organism cannot?

_____
_____
_____
_____
_____
_____

19 Most animals can survive without food for a longer time than they can survive without water. Why is water so important to animals? Why can an animal survive without food for longer?

_____
_____
_____
_____
_____
_____
_____
_____
_____

Answers *(continued)*

17. **Answer A is correct** because each type of cell in a multicellular organism performs a specialized function but cannot perform all functions. (Lesson 4)

18. Key Elements:

   • *Dimitri likely identified the cell based on his observation of a cell wall, a central vacuole, and the presence of chloroplasts.*

   • *Dimitri is correct because none of these organelles are found in animal cells.*

   • *This cell contains chloroplasts, so can carry out photosynthesis. Animal cells cannot photosynthesize.* (Lesson 3)

19. Key Elements:

   • *Water is vital for life because most of the substances important to life are dissolved in water within cells and in the body, making them easier to transport across cell membranes. As a result, many life processes require water. Without water, life's processes will stop.*

   • *Extra energy from food can be stored in the body in the form of carbohydrates and fat, so an animal could continue to function for a while without taking food in. However animals cannot make water, and they cannot store it the way they can store food energy. They must take in water from an external source.* (Lesson 5)

20. Key Elements:

   • *Organisms must respond to environmental changes in order to maintain a stable internal environment. This process is called homeostasis.*

   • *A drop in environmental temperature is a change in the environment that an animal would have to respond to in order to maintain normal body temperature. An animal could move to a warmer spot, or a person could put on more clothes.*

   • *The animal may get sick because its body is no longer able to maintain homeostasis. If there is a large change in the external environment that the organism cannot adapt to, it may die.* (Lesson 5)

Unit 1 Review continued

20 One of the characteristics of living things is that they respond to external changes in their environment so that their internal environment stays as stable as possible. Why must an organism do this? Name an environmental change that an animal must respond to in order to keep a stable internal environment. What might happen to an organism if it could not adapt to an external change?

_____

_____

_____

Connect ESSENTIAL QUESTIONS
Lessons 2, 3, 4, 5, and 6

Answer the following question in the space provided.

21 The following picture shows the process of photosynthesis.

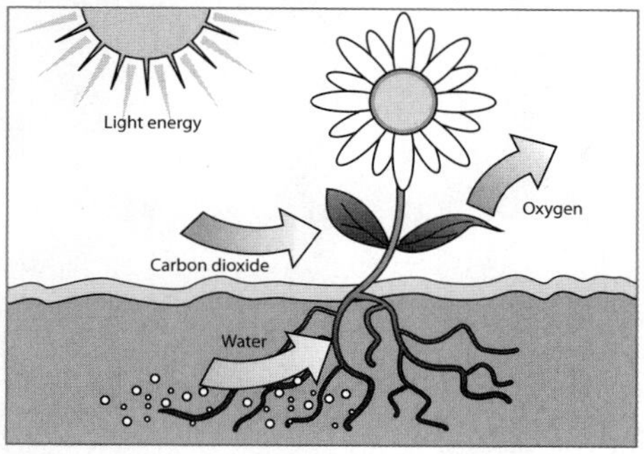

Light energy

Oxygen

Carbon dioxide

Water

In which plant organ and organelle does photosynthesis take place? One of the products of photosynthesis is missing from the diagram. What is this missing product? Describe the role of this substance in cells. How do animals get this substance?

_____

_____

_____

_____

86 Unit 1 Cells

Quick Grading Chart

Use the chart below for quick test grading. The lesson correlations can help you target reteaching for missed items.

Item	Answer	Cognitive Complexity	Lesson
1.	False	Low	6
2.	True	Low	2
3.	False	Low	1
4.	True	Low	3
5.	True	Low	4
6.	B	Moderate	1
7.	B	Moderate	5
8.	B	Moderate	5
9.	D	Moderate	2
10.	C	Low	5
11.	C	Moderate	3
12.	D	High	4
13.	A	Moderate	1
14.	C	Moderate	1
15.	C	Moderate	4
16.	A	High	5
17.	A	Low	4
18.	—	Moderate	3
19.	—	High	5
20.	—	Moderate	5
21.	—	Moderate	6

Cognitive Complexity refers to the demand on thinking associated with an item, and may vary with the answer choices, the number of steps required to arrive at an answer, and other factors, but not the ability level of the student.

Answers *(continued)*

21. Key Elements:

- *Photosynthesis takes place in leaves and within the chloroplasts of the leaf cells.*

- *The missing product in the photosynthesis diagram is glucose.*

- *Glucose is broken down during cellular respiration. The energy in the chemical bonds of glucose is transferred to ATP, which the cell uses to fuel its life functions.*

- *Animals cannot make their own food, so they must take it into their bodies. Non-photosynthesizing organisms do this by eating plants. Energy from plant food in the form of carbohydrates fuels life processes in animals.* (Lesson 6)

Teacher Notes

The Big Idea and Essential Questions

This Unit was designed to focus on this Big Idea and Essential Questions.

Big Idea | **Characteristics from parents are passed to offspring in predictable ways.**

Lesson	ESSENTIAL QUESTION	Student Mastery	PD Professional Development	Lesson Overview
LESSON 1 Mitosis	How do cells divide?	To relate the process of mitosis to its functions in single-celled and multicellular organisms	Content Refresher, TE p. 118	TE p. 128
LESSON 2 Meiosis	How do cells divide for sexual reproduction?	To describe the process of meiosis and its role in sexual reproduction	Content Refresher, TE p. 119	TE p. 142
LESSON 3 Sexual and Asexual Reproduction	How do organisms reproduce?	To describe asexual and sexual reproduction and list the advantages and disadvantages of each	Content Refresher, TE p. 120	TE p. 158
LESSON 4 Heredity	How are traits inherited?	To analyze the inheritance of traits in individuals	Content Refresher, TE p. 121	TE p. 172
LESSON 5 Punnett Squares and Pedigrees	How are patterns of inheritance studied?	To explain how patterns of heredity can be predicted by Punnett squares and pedigrees	Content Refresher, TE p. 122	TE p. 188
LESSON 6 DNA Structure and Function	What Is DNA?	To describe the structure and main functions of DNA	Content Refresher, TE p. 123	TE p. 202
LESSON 7 Biotechnology	How does biotechnology impact our world?	To explain how biotechnology impacts human life and the world around us	Content Refresher, TE p. 124	TE p. 218

©Rachel Weill/Botanica/Getty Images

 **Professional Development** **Science Background**

Use the key words at right to access

- Professional Development from **The NSTA Learning Center**
- **SciLinks** for additional online content appropriate for students and teachers

Keywords
DNA
heredity
mitosis and meiosis
reproduction

NSTA National Science Teachers Association

SciLINKS. THE WORLD'S A CLICK AWAY

Options for Instruction

Two parallel paths provide coverage of the Essential Questions, with a strong **Inquiry** strand woven into each. Follow the **Print Path,** the **Digital Path,** or your customized combination of print, digital, and inquiry.

	LESSON 1 Mitosis	LESSON 2 Meiosis	LESSON 3 Sexual and Asexual Reproduction
Essential Questions	*How do cells divide?*	*How do cells divide for sexual reproduction?*	*How do organisms reproduce?*
Key Topics	• Why Cells Divide • Genetic Material and Cell Division • Mitosis	• Sex Cells • Meiosis • Steps of Meiosis • Meiosis vs. Mitosis	• Asexual Reproduction • Sexual Reproduction • Comparing Asexual and Sexual Reproduction
Print Path	**Teacher Edition** pp. 128–141 **Student Edition** pp. 90–99	**Teacher Edition** pp. 142–155 **Student Edition** pp. 100–109	**Teacher Edition** pp. 158–171 **Student Edition** pp. 112–121
Inquiry Labs	**Lab Manual** **Exploration Lab** Stages of the Cell Cycle **Quick Lab** Modeling Mitosis **Quick Lab** Mitosis Flipbooks	**Lab Manual** **Quick Lab** Crossover and Meiosis 🖥 **Virtual Lab** Comparing Cell Division	**Lab Manual** **Field Lab** Investigate Asexual Reproduction **Quick Lab** Reproduction and Diversity **Quick Lab** Egg vs. Sperm
Digital Path	**Digital Path** TS673240	**Digital Path** TS673230	**Digital Path** TS673220

LESSON 4 Heredity	LESSON 5 Punnett Squares and Pedigrees	LESSONS 6, 7, and UNIT 2 Unit Projects
How are traits inherited?	How are patterns of inheritance studied?	See the next page
• Mendel's Work • DNA's Role in Inheritance • Genes, Traits, and Characteristics	• Punnett Squares • Pedigrees	

Teacher Edition pp. 172–185 **Student Edition** pp. 122–133	**Teacher Edition** pp. 188–201 **Student Edition** pp. 136–145	**Unit Assessment** *See the next page*
Lab Manual **Quick Lab** Dominant Alleles **Quick Lab** What's the Difference Between a Dominant Trait and a Recessive Trait?	**Lab Manual** **S.T.E.M. Lab** Matching Punnett Square Predictions ▣ Virtual Lab Crossing Pea Plants	
Digital Path TS673140	**Digital Path** TS673190	

Options for Instruction

Two parallel paths provide coverage of the Essential Questions, with a strong **Inquiry** strand woven into each. Follow the **Print Path,** the **Digital Path,** or your customized combination of print, digital, and inquiry.

	LESSON 6 DNA Structure and Function	LESSON 7 Biotechnology	UNIT 2 Unit Projects
Essential Questions	**What is DNA?**	**How does biotechnology impact our world?**	**Citizen Science Project** **Pass It On** Teacher's Edition p. 127 Student Edition pp. 88–89
Key Topics	• DNA Structure • DNA Replication • Mutations • DNA Transcription and Translation	• Applications of Biotechnology • Biotechnology and Society	**Video-Based Projects** An Inside View

Print Path

Teacher Edition pp. 202–215	Teacher Edition pp. 218–231
Student Edition pp. 146–157	Student Edition pp. 160–169

Inquiry Labs

Lab Manual **Exploration Lab** Extracting DNA **Quick Lab** Modeling DNA **Quick Lab** Mutations Cause Diversity	Lab Manual **Quick Lab** Observing Selective Breeding **Quick Lab** How Can a Simple Code Be Used to Make a Product?

Digital Path

Digital Path TS673120	Digital Path TS673280

Unit Assessment

Formative Assessment
> **Strategies** [RTI]
> Throughout TE
> **Lesson Reviews** SE
> **Unit PreTest**

Summative Assessment
> **Alternative Assessment** (1 per lesson) [RTI]
> **Lesson Quizzes**
> **Unit Tests A and B**
> **Unit Review** [RTI]
> **Practice Tests** (end of module)

Project-Based Assessment
- *See the Assessment Guide for quizzes and tests.*
- *Go Online to edit and create quizzes and tests.*

Response to Intervention

See RTI teacher support materials on p. PD6.

Teacher Notes

Differentiated Instruction

English Language Proficiency

Strategies for **English Language Learners (ELL)** are provided for each lesson, under the Explain tabs.

LESSON 1 *Phases of Mitosis Comic,* TE p. 133

LESSON 2 *Vocabulary; Meiosis by the Numbers,* TE p. 147

LESSON 3 *Fertilization Diagram; Vocabulary,* TE p. 163

LESSON 4 *Mendel Comic,* TE p. 177

LESSON 5 *Probability; Ratios and Percentages,* TE p. 193

LESSON 6 *Protein Performance,* TE p. 207

LESSON 7 *Biotechnology Terms,* TE p. 223

Vocabulary strategies provided for all students can also be a particular help for ELL. Use different strategies for each lesson or choose one or two to use throughout the unit. Vocabulary strategies can be found under the Explain tab for each lesson (TE pp. 133, 147, 163, 177, 193, 207, and 223).

Leveled Inquiry

Inquiry labs, activities, probing questions, and daily demos provide a range of inquiry levels. Preview them under the Engage and Explore tabs starting on TE pp. 130, 144, 160, 174, 190, 204, and 220.

 Levels of Inquiry

| **DIRECTED** inquiry introduces inquiry skills within a structured framework. | **GUIDED** inquiry develops inquiry skills within a supportive environment. | **INDEPENDENT** inquiry deepens inquiry skills with student-driven questions or procedures. |

Each long lab has two inquiry options:

LESSON 1 **Exploration Lab** *Stages of the Cell Cycle* Guided or Independent Inquiry

LESSON 3 **Field Lab** *Investigate Asexual Reproduction* Guided or Independent Inquiry

LESSON 6 **Exploration Lab** *Extracting DNA* Directed or Guided Inquiry

---

 Go Digital! 🔴 **thinkcentral.com**

Digital Path

The Unit 2 Resource Gateway is your guide to all of the digital resources for this unit. To access the Gateway, visit thinkcentral.com.

Digital Interactive Lessons

Lesson 1 Mitosis TS673240

Lesson 2 Meiosis TS673230

Lesson 3 Sexual and Asexual Reproduction TS673220

Lesson 4 Heredity TS673140

Lesson 5 Punnett Squares and Pedigrees TS673190

Lesson 6 DNA Structure and Function TS673120

Lesson 7 Biotechnology TS673280

More Digital Resources

In addition to digital lessons, you will find the following digital resources for Unit 2:

Video-Based Project: An Inside View (previewed on TE p. 127)

People in Science: Michael Coble

Virtual Labs: Comparing Cell Division (previewed on TE p. 131) Crossing Pea Plants (previewed on TE p. 191)

RTI ▶ Response to Intervention

Response to Intervention (RTI) is a process for identifying and supporting students who are not making expected progress toward essential learning goals. The following *ScienceFusion* components can be used to provide strategic and intensive intervention.

Component	Location	Strategies and Benefits
STUDENT EDITION Active Reading prompts, Visualize It!, Think Outside the Book	**Throughout each lesson**	Student responses can be used as screening tools to assess whether intervention is needed.
TEACHER EDITION Formative Assessment, Probing Questions, Learning Alerts	**Throughout each lesson**	Opportunities are provided to assess and remediate student understanding of lesson concepts.
TEACHER EDITION Extend Science Concepts	**Reinforce and Review, TE pp. 134, 148, 164, 178, 194, 208, 224** **Going Further, TE pp. 134, 148, 164, 178, 194, 208, 224**	Additional activities allow students to reinforce and extend their understanding of lesson concepts.
TEACHER EDITION Evaluate Student Mastery	**Formative Assessment, TE pp. 135, 149, 165, 179, 195, 209, 225** **Alternative Assessment, TE pp. 135, 149, 165, 179, 195, 209, 225**	These assessments allow for greater flexibility in assessing students with differing physical, mental, and language abilities as well as varying learning and communication modes.
TEACHER EDITION Unit Review Remediation	**Unit Review, TE pp. 232–235**	Includes reference back to Lesson Planning pages for remediation activities and assignments.
INTERACTIVE DIGITAL LESSONS and VIRTUAL LABS	**thinkcentral.com** **Unit 2 Gateway** **Lesson 1 TS673240** **Lesson 2 TS673230** **Lesson 3 TS673220** **Lesson 4 TS673140** **Lesson 5 TS673190** **Lesson 6 TS673120** **Lesson 7 TS673280**	Lessons and labs make content accessible through simulations, animations, videos, audio, and integrated assessment. Useful for review and reteaching of lesson concepts.

Content Refresher

Professional Development

Mitosis

ESSENTIAL QUESTION
How do cells divide?

1. Why Cells Divide

Students will learn how cell division forms new cells.

In a unicellular organism, cell division is a means of reproduction—the single-celled organism divides to form two new cells that are genetically identical to the parent cell. If the unicellular organism is a eukaryote, cell division includes mitosis, the process that divides the nucleus to form two new nuclei. Because prokaryotes lack a nucleus, mitosis does not occur in them.

In multicellular organisms, cell division takes place in body cells. A young organism grows because cell division increases the number of cells that make up the individual. As a multicellular organism develops and its cells divide, many of the cells become specialized, and most continue to divide. These healthy cells divide to replace injured and damaged cells.

DNA, or deoxyribonucleic acid, is the genetic material in all living cells. It contains the information that determines the traits an organism inherits and it controls cell activities. The DNA that determines inherited traits is packaged into structures called chromosomes that are found in the nucleus. Eukaryotic cells have many chromosomes in their nuclei. Before a cell divides, it duplicates its DNA. The DNA is then distributed evenly between the two cells formed from the original cell. Each new cell has the same amount of DNA and the same number of chromosomes as the original cell. The new cells also have the same information in their DNA, which is the same as that in the original parent cell.

2. Genetic Material and Cell Division

Students will learn about the cell cycle.

The three stages of the cell cycle in eukaryotic cells are *interphase, mitosis,* and *cytokinesis.* Cells spend most of their lives in interphase, a stage in which they carry out normal life activities, including growth. A cell also prepares for cell division during interphase by replicating its DNA and chromosomes. Correct copying of the chromosomes is very important, as it ensures that after cell division, each new cell has the same DNA as the original cell.

3. Mitosis

Students will learn that mitosis forms identical nuclei.

Mitosis is a four-stage process in which the chromosomes replicated during interphase are separated into two new nuclei. During the first stage, prophase, chromosomes condense and the nuclear membrane dissolves. In the second stage, metaphase, the duplicated chromosomes align in the center of the cell. During the third stage, anaphase, the duplicated chromosomes separate and are pulled to opposite sides of the cell. In the fourth and final stage of mitosis, telophase, a new nuclear membrane forms around each set of chromosomes, and the chromosomes return to their threadlike form.

After mitosis separates the nuclei, the process of cytokinesis separates the cytoplasm and the nuclei that resulted from mitosis into two new daughter cells that are genetically identical to the original parent cell.

 COMMON MISCONCEPTIONS   **RTI**

A common misconception is that interphase is the first stage of mitosis; however, prophase is actually the first stage.

This misconception is addressed in the Activity *Cell Cycle Sequence* on p. 130.

Teacher to Teacher

Matt Moller, M.Ed.
Carmel Middle School
Carmel, IN

Lesson 6 DNA Structure and Function   Provide your students with colored mini-marshmallows and toothpicks. On the board or projector, list the four nitrogenous bases of DNA, and assign a marshmallow color to each base. Have each student construct a 5-rung DNA "ladder" (gene) with 10 marsh-mallows. Be sure that students understand complementary base-pairing. Then, have students connect their "genes" to form a double-helix molecule.

Lesson 2

Meiosis

ESSENTIAL QUESTION
How do cells divide for sexual reproduction?

1. Sex Cells

Students will learn that a sex cell is a haploid cell.

Sex cells have one of each homologous chromosome, while body cells have pairs of homologous chromosomes. Homologous chromosomes are two chromosomes, one inherited from the mother and the other inherited from the father, that have the same sequence of genes and the same structure. Homologous chromosomes have copies of the same genes, but the forms of the genes may differ. Sex cells are found only in reproductive organs. Females produce egg cells; males produce sperm cells. In a cell, one pair of chromosomes is made up of sex chromosomes, which control the development of sex and other characteristics.

2. Meiosis

Students will learn that meiosis produces haploid cells through two divisions of the nucleus.

Taking place only in the reproductive structures of an organism, meiosis produces sex cells, each with one of each homologous chromosome. Human egg and sperm cells contain 23 chromosomes each. When the egg and sperm join during sexual reproduction, they form a fertilized egg cell, or zygote, with two copies of each chromosome. In humans, zygotes usually have 46 chromosomes.

Meiosis plays a critical role in spreading existing variants of genes around in a population. Two features of meiosis that accomplish this are crossing-over and independent assortment. Crossing-over occurs early in the first stage of meiosis, when pieces of the four chromatids (two chromatids times two homologs) of each homologous pair of chromosomes are exchanged. This results in genetic recombination within each pair of homologous chromosomes. Independent assortment is the random distribution of each homologous chromosome within a pair to the nuclei produced during the first stage of meiosis. As a result, the chromosomes that an individual got from its mother and those from its father are distributed randomly to the two nuclei.

3. Steps of Meiosis

Students will learn that meiosis includes two steps, each involving division.

Meiosis I is a series of steps in which a diploid cell (a cell with pairs of homologous chromosomes), is reduced to a haploid cell (a cell with one of each of the pairs of homologous chromosome). During meiosis I, chromosomes condense and crossing-over occurs between the chromatids of homologous chromosomes. Then, chromosome pairs line up at the cell's equator before each of the pair of homologous chromosomes moves to the cell's poles. The result of the random way in which homologous chromosomes are sorted is known as independent assortment. Each of the two resulting nuclei have copies of one of each of the pairs of homologous chromosomes, and the cytoplasm is divided, resulting in two cells. These cells then undergo meiosis II. In meiosis II, chromosomes line up at the cell's equator before the chromatids separate and move to the cell's poles. Nuclei re-form and the cytoplasm is divided again between two new cells. In this way, meiosis of a single diploid cell results in four new haploid cells.

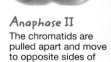

Anaphase II
The chromatids are pulled apart and move to opposite sides of the cell.

4. Meiosis vs. Mitosis

Students will learn how meiosis and mitosis differ.

Meiosis produces haploid sex cells with recombined genes and various combinations of maternal and paternal homologs. Mitosis produces diploid cells that are genetically identical to each other and to the parent cell. Meiosis takes place only in cells located in reproductive structures; all other body cells divide by mitosis. In meiosis a cell divides twice, but the chromosomes are copied only in meiosis I. In mitosis, one division occurs, and chromosomes are copied before division.

Content Refresher (continued)

Professional Development

Lesson 3

Sexual and Asexual Reproduction

ESSENTIAL QUESTION
How do organisms reproduce?

1. Asexual Reproduction

Students will learn about the four ways in which asexual reproduction commonly occurs.

Asexual reproduction requires only one parent and results in offspring that are genetically identical to the parent. It commonly occurs in one of four ways: binary fission, budding, spore formation, or vegetative reproduction.

- During binary fission, a single-celled organism divides equally to form two identical organisms.

- During budding, a new organism grows from the outside surface of the parent organism. Organisms such as hydras and sea anemones can reproduce by budding.

- Some bacteria can reproduce by forming specialized spores including endospores. The cells are not active, and they can survive harsh conditions. When environmental conditions improve, endospores can be activated to re-form bacterial cells.

- Vegetative reproduction takes place in plants. New plants develop from modified stems or roots or from plantlets, tiny plants that form along the leaves of some plants. Human action can lead to vegetative reproduction; a human may place a piece of root, stem, or leaf in soil or water until a new root system appears, or graft a branch from one tree onto another, often used with apple trees.

2. Sexual Reproduction

Students will learn that sexual reproduction results in offspring similar to, but not identical to, the parents.

Sexual reproduction involves two parents and results in offspring that have characteristics of both parents but that are not identical to either parent. During fertilization, the male gamete and female gamete, each of which is haploid, combine to form a zygote, a diploid cell that contains genetic material from both parents.

3. Comparing Asexual and Sexual Reproduction

Students will learn that both forms of reproduction have advantages for organisms.

Asexual reproduction involves one parent; sexual reproduction usually involves two parents (exceptions exist, such as when the flowers on some plants self-pollinate, sexual reproduction involving one parent). The offspring produced by asexual reproduction are identical to the parent; the offspring produced by sexual reproduction are not identical to either parent.

Asexual reproduction's major advantage for organisms is that it allows organisms to increase in number very quickly. Additionally, organisms that rely on asexual reproduction do not need to expend energy on attracting a mate.

The major advantage of sexual reproduction is that it fosters genetic diversity, which increases the chance that organisms will have traits that ensure their survival. Some organisms undergo both asexual and sexual reproduction. Many of these organisms reproduce asexually until a change in the environment or unfavorable environmental conditions cause the organism to undergo sexual reproduction.

 COMMON MISCONCEPTIONS   **RTI**

HOW PLANTS REPRODUCE Some students may hold the misconception that plants can reproduce only asexually. They may not understand that pollination is sexual reproduction, because pollen is a male sex cell with half the plant's genetic information.

The pollen combines with the female sex cell in a flower to form a cell that contains the complete set of genetic information.

This misconception is addressed in the Probing Question activity on p. 160.

Heredity

ESSENTIAL QUESTION

How are traits inherited?

1. Mendel's Work

Students will learn about the work of Gregor Mendel.

Gregor Mendel (1822–1884), an Austrian monk, studied seven characteristics of pea plants. He discovered that three principles controlled how these characteristics were passed down through generations. First, the cells of the plant could contain two different forms of the characteristic, called traits; second, the traits are inherited independently of one another; third, each characteristic is governed by two different forms of a "factor" of heredity, which we now call genes. Mendel noted that some traits were present in each generation, and he called these dominant traits. Other traits showed up sporadically, appearing in one generation and apparently vanishing in the next. Mendel referred to these as recessive traits. His theory explains the pattern of inheritance known as complete dominance.

2. DNA's Role in Inheritance

Students will learn that DNA specifies the traits of an organism.

Deoxyribonucleic acid (DNA) is a self-replicating molecule that serves as a set of instructions that determines an organism's traits. DNA contains sections called genes, which are sets of instructions for particular traits. Genes are located on the chromosomes of each cell.

An allele is one of the alternative forms of

a gene that governs a characteristic, such as hair color. An allele carries the specific information to produce one form of the characteristic, such as red hair. The expression of those genes—that is, the appearance they produce—is called a phenotype. A genotype is the entire genetic makeup of an organism. Genotype also refers to the combination of genes for one or more specific characteristics. When an organism has two alleles that are both either dominant or recessive, it is said to be homozygous for the characteristic; if it has one dominant and one recessive allele, it is called heterozygous.

3. Genes, Traits, and Characteristics

Students will learn about how traits are expressed.

In complete dominance, only the dominant allele contributes to the phenotype of the heterozygous individual. An example is the allele for brown eyes in humans.

Incomplete dominance is a condition in which both alleles of a gene contribute to the phenotype of a heterozygous individual, resulting in a phenotype that is an intermediate of the phenotypes of the two parents. An example is blossom color in the four-o'clock flower; when a red flowering plant is crossed with a white one, the offspring will have pink flowers.

When genes are codominant, both alleles contribute to the phenotype of a heterozygous individual. The phenotype that results is a combination of those of the two parents. For example, in some birds, crossing a parent with white feathers and a parent with black feathers will result in offspring with black and white feathers.

One gene can be responsible for many characteristics. For example, a single gene determines a tiger's fur color, but it also influences eye color. In this case, a single gene affects the expression of another gene. Many genes can contribute to a single characteristic; eye color is one example.

COMMON MISCONCEPTIONS RTI

ACQUIRED TRAITS ARE GENETIC Students may not understand which traits are passed on by genes. They may think that acquired traits, such as muscle mass or running speed, are genetic.

This misconception is addressed in the Probing Question *What's Your Inheritance?* on p. 174.

Content Refresher (continued)

 **Professional Development**

Punnett Squares and Pedigrees

ESSENTIAL QUESTION
How are patterns of inheritance studied?

1. Punnett Squares

Students will learn that Punnett squares show various combinations of alleles.

A Punnett square illustrates how the parents' alleles may be passed on to potential offspring. The top of the Punnett square shows one parent's alleles for a trait. The left side of the Punnett square shows the other parent's alleles for the same trait. Each box in the Punnett square shows a way the alleles from each parent could combine in potential offspring. When using Punnett squares, a ratio shows the probability of inheriting certain traits. (A ratio compares, or shows the relationship between, two quantities.) Probability is the likelihood, or chance, of a specific outcome in relation to the total number of possible outcomes. Punnett squares can be used to predict the genotypes of offspring that might result from a specific cross.

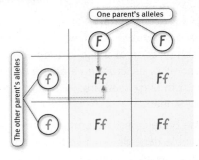

2. Pedigrees

Students will learn how pedigrees can trace inheritance through generations.

A pedigree is a diagram of family relationships that includes two or more generations. In a typical pedigree, boxes represent males and circles represent females. A shaded shape indicates that a person shows the trait. A white shape indicates that a person does not show the trait. A half-shaded shape indicates that a person is a carrier of the trait. In addition, lines connect a person with his or her mate and to their children.

A sex-linked gene is a gene that is located on a sex chromosome. Sex-linked traits can be either X-linked or Y-linked; most are X-linked. (The Y chromosome is smaller, so it has fewer genes on it.) If a trait is X-linked, it can be expressed in males or females. A Y-linked trait can be expressed in males only.

In general, sex-linked traits are recessively inherited. If an X-linked trait is recessively inherited, a female with one defective copy of the gene and one normal copy will not have the disease but will be a carrier. A female with two copies of the defective gene will have the disease. A male with one defective copy of the gene will have the disease. Males cannot be carriers. If the disease is fatal before reproductive age, affected males and females will not pass along their defective genes. If it is not fatal before reproductive age, then affected females and males could pass along their defective genes.

Sex-linked disorders include hemophilia, Duchenne muscular dystrophy, and red-green color blindness.

COMMON MISCONCEPTIONS ## **RTI**

ONE PARENT CONTRIBUTES MORE TRAITS THAN THE OTHER Students may think that if a child looks like one parent more than the other, the child has inherited more traits from one parent than the other. In humans, offspring receive half their chromosomes from each parent. In addition, students may think that acquired traits, such as scars or love of running, are genetic.

IF THE FIRST CHILD IS A GIRL, THE SECOND CHILD IS MORE LIKELY TO BE A BOY Students who have trouble with probability may think that if a human mother has a girl for a first child, the second child is more likely to be a boy. Explain that each event is independent, and prior occurrences have no effect on future events.

DNA Structure and Function

ESSENTIAL QUESTION
What is DNA?

1. DNA Structure

Students will learn that DNA is a double helix.

Many scientists have contributed to our understanding of DNA (deoxyribonucleic acid). The DNA molecule was first isolated in 1869, but it was not until the Hershey-Chase experiments in 1952 that the function of DNA as genetic material was conclusively demonstrated.

Building on previous research, in 1953, Francis Crick and James Watson determined the structure of DNA to be a double helix. The DNA double helix consists of two strands that look like a twisted ladder. The sides of the ladder are composed of the sugar deoxyribose and phosphates. Nitrogen bases make up the rungs of the ladder. Together, a base, a sugar, and a phosphate group form the basic unit of DNA known as a nucleotide. The nitrogen bases in DNA are adenine (A), thymine (T), guanine (G), and cytosine (C). The molecular conformation of the nucleotides ensures that A always pairs with T and that G always pairs with C. Each strand of DNA contains millions of nucleotide bases, which are in a set order based on genetic ancestry. This order determines numerous characteristics, such as height, skin tone, and eye color.

2. DNA Replication

Students will learn how DNA replicates.

When a cell divides, DNA replicates, or copies itself. The process begins as a DNA molecule unzips, or opens up along its base pairs, forming two new strands. These new strands serve as templates to which free nucleotides attach, allowing a complementary strand to be formed from each of the original strands. The product, unless mutations occur, is two exact copies of the original DNA molecule.

3. Mutations

Students will learn that mutations are changes in DNA.

The DNA sequence can change due to environmental factors, such as exposure to radiation, or by errors during replication. A change to the nucleotide sequence of DNA is called a mutation. Some mutations are harmful, such as those that result in genetic disorders. Other mutations can be beneficial and can improve an organism's ability to survive. Mutations can also have no apparent effect. Only mutations that occur in sex cells (sperm and egg) can be passed on to future generations.

4. DNA Transcription and Translation

Students will learn that DNA drives protein production.

DNA codons (sequences of three bases) are translated into amino acids. Each DNA codon codes for a specific amino acid. Strings of codons form genes. Some genes encode RNA molecules. Others encode proteins. The following text focuses on protein-coding genes.

RNA (ribonucleic acid) is needed to make proteins. RNA is a single-stranded nucleic acid made of the sugar ribose; phosphates; and the bases adenine (A), uracil (U), guanine (G), and cytosine (C). Since RNA does not contain the base thymine, uracil (U) pairs with adenine (A).

Protein synthesis begins with transcription. First, the two DNA strands in a gene for a given protein unzip. A complementary strand of RNA called messenger RNA (mRNA) is synthesized from one strand (the template strand) of the gene, using the DNA as a template.

Translation is the next part of the process of protein synthesis. In eukaryotes, the new mRNA leaves the nucleus and travels to the ribosomes in the cytoplasm. The mRNA moves through a ribosome one codon at a time. The mRNA code is translated by transfer RNA (tRNA) molecules. Specific amino acids from the cytoplasm attach to the tRNA molecules, which deliver the amino acids to the ribosome. Within the ribosome, the tRNA matches up with the bases on the mRNA, and then releases its amino acids. The amino acids become linked together in a growing polypeptide chain that, when complete, folds to form a new protein.

Content Refresher (continued)

Professional Development

Biotechnology

ESSENTIAL QUESTION
How does biotechnology impact our world?

1. Applications of Biotechnology

Students will learn biotechnology has many applications.

Biotechnology is the use and application of living things and biological processes. Humans have practiced a form of biotechnology called artificial selection, or selective breeding, for thousands of years. Although they were unaware of it, early farmers were actually selecting alleles, particular versions of a gene, that were already present in some members of the population. People were not changing DNA, but they were causing certain alleles to become more common in a particular animal or plant species.

Genetic engineering is the process by which a piece of DNA is modified for medical, scientific, or commercial use. The first genetically modified organisms were made in 1973, when scientists isolated the gene for ribosomal RNA from the DNA of an African clawed frog. They inserted the gene into the DNA of *Escherichia coli* bacteria, causing the bacteria to produce frog RNA! Genetic engineering is possible because the genetic code is universal. Thus, one organism's cells can transcribe and translate a gene containing DNA from another organism, making a protein not coded for by its own DNA but by the DNA of the other organism.

Cloning is the process in which a genetic duplicate is made. A clone is an organism, cell, or piece of genetic material that is genetically identical to one from which it was derived.

A scientist is gathering DNA from clothing found at a crime scene. Then many copies of the DNA sample will be made. This will allow the scientist to better study the DNA. Then the scientist might be able to confirm the identity of the person at the crime scene.

Most often, pieces of DNA of interest are cloned for certain applications or further study. Much less often, entire animals are cloned. In 1996, scientists produced the first clone of a mammal, a sheep named Dolly.

Biotechnology has many applications. For example, genes of microorganisms that produce natural pesticides have been successfully transferred into the DNA of crop plants. The cells of these plants then produce their own pesticide. Many human illnesses occur when the body fails to make critical proteins. Pharmaceutical companies are now making these medically important proteins using genetic engineering. Biotechnology is also used in law enforcement to determine if a suspect committed a crime or was at a crime scene.

2. Biotechnology and Society

Students will learn how biotechnology benefits society.

Genetic engineering offers potential benefits to society. It also carries potential risks. Some people are concerned that genetically modified crops might harm the environment in unusual ways, such as if introduced genes for herbicide resistance moved from a genetically modified crop to one of its wild relatives. Scientists and nonscientists are involved in identifying and addressing potential ethical, legal, social, and environmental issues that may arise from genetic engineering.

 COMMON MISCONCEPTIONS RTI

DINO DNA Due to portrayals in science fiction, students may think scientists can bring dinosaurs back from extinction using fragments of ancient dinosaur DNA and DNA from modern organisms. In fact, it is highly unlikely any dinosaur DNA could survive the millions of years since dinosaurs became extinct. Even if it could survive, a fragment of DNA is not enough information to make an entire organism.

This misconception is addressed in the Discussion *Ancient DNA* on p. 221.

Teacher Notes

Advance Planning

These activities may take extended time or special conditions.

Unit 2

Video-Based Project An Inside View, p. 126
  multiple activities spanning several lessons

Project Pass It On, p. 127
  planning and writing time

Graphic Organizers and Vocabulary pp. 133, 134, 147, 148, 163, 164, 177, 178, 193, 194, 207, 208, 223, 224
  ongoing with reading

Lesson 1

Exploration Lab Stages of the Cell Cycle, p. 131
  prepared slides of onion root tips

Lesson 3

Activity Growing Plants, p. 160
  activity will require several class periods

Quick Lab Egg vs. Sperm, p. 161
  human egg cell slide and human sperm cell slide

Field Lab Investigate Asexual Reproduction, p. 161
  requires three 45-min periods and outdoor sample collection

Lesson 6

Exploration Lab Extracting DNA, p. 205
  prepare lab materials in advance

UNIT 2

Reproduction and Heredity

Big Idea
Characteristics from parents are passed to offspring in predictable ways.

What do you think?
Every organism—including orange trees and dogs—shares traits with its offspring. How are qualities passed on from generation to generation?

87

What Do You Think?

Have students name traits that are passed on from human parents to their offspring. List ideas on the board.

Ask: What are some traits that are not passed on from parent to offspring? Sample answers: how many languages you speak, how strong you are, what you eat

Ask: Which parent has the most influence over the offspring's traits? Sample answer: Both parents contribute half of the offspring's genetic material, so each parent contributes equally.

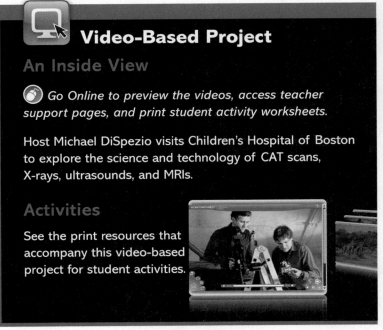

Video-Based Project

An Inside View

🖱 *Go Online to preview the videos, access teacher support pages, and print student activity worksheets.*

Host Michael DiSpezio visits Children's Hospital of Boston to explore the science and technology of CAT scans, X-rays, ultrasounds, and MRIs.

Activities

See the print resources that accompany this video-based project for student activities.

©Patrick Greene Productions

Unit 2
Reproduction and Heredity

CITIZEN SCIENCE
Pass It On

Heredity was a mystery that scientists worked to crack over hundreds of years. The modern field of genetics is vital to the understanding of hereditary diseases. The study of genetics can also predict which traits will be passed from parent to offspring.

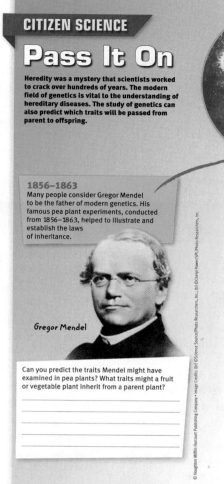

Gregor Mendel

1856–1863
Many people consider Gregor Mendel to be the father of modern genetics. His famous pea plant experiments, conducted from 1856–1863, helped to illustrate and establish the laws of inheritance.

Can you predict the traits Mendel might have examined in pea plants? What traits might a fruit or vegetable plant inherit from a parent plant?

_____
_____
_____
_____
_____

Pairs of chromosomes viewed under a microscope

Fruit fly

1882
Walther Flemming discovered chromosomes while observing the process of cell division. He didn't know it, but chromosomes pass characteristics from parents to offspring.

1908
Thomas Hunt Morgan was the first to actually realize that chromosomes carry traits. Morgan's fruit fly studies established that genes are located on chromosomes. Scientists still use fruitflies in research today.

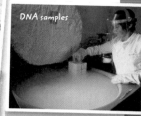

DNA samples

2003
Our DNA carries information about all of our traits. In fact, the human genome is made up of 20,000–25,000 genes! In 2003, the Human Genome Project successfully mapped the first human genome.

Take It Home | Making Trait Predictions

1 Think About It

Different factors influence appearance. Family members may look similar in some ways but different in others. What factors influence a person's appearance?

2 Ask Some Questions

Can you spot any physical traits, such as bent pinky fingers, that people in your family share?

_____
_____
_____

3 Make A Plan

A Consider the traits that are most distinctive in your family. How can you trace the way these traits have been passed through the family? Design an investigation of hereditary characteristics in your family.

_____
_____
_____

B Describe how these characteristics might be the same or different as they are passed on to offspring. What factors might influence this? Make notes here, and illustrate your descriptions on a separate sheet of paper.

_____
_____
_____

CITIZEN SCIENCE

Unit Project **Pass It On**

Students' answers will vary. Answers should include traits such as plant height and color of flowers.

Take It Home

1. Think About It

Students' answers will vary. Sample answers include the genetic traits of biological parents as well as environmental factors such as diet and exposure to sun.

2. Ask Some Questions

Students' answers will vary. Common traits include hair on knuckles of fingers or toes, cleft in the chin, bent pinky fingers, free or joined earlobes, and dimples, as well as more obvious traits such as skin color and tone, hair color and texture, and eye color.

3. Make a Plan

Students' answers will vary. Students may wish to create a questionnaire for family members, or investigate family photos. Factors that will affect whether traits change or stay the same include whether family members produce offspring with people who share the same traits.

Mitosis

Essential Question How do cells divide?

Professional Development

For more detailed information about the topics in this lesson, refer to the Content Refresher in the Unit Opener pages.

Opening Your Lesson

Begin the lesson by assessing students' prerequisite and prior knowledge.

Prerequisite Knowledge

- Basic structure of a cell
- Structure and function of various cellular organelles

Accessing Prior Knowledge

Ask: What is reproduction? a characteristic of living things whereby they produce new organisms similar to themselves

Ask: In a eukaryotic cell, which organelle contains the genetic information of the cell? the nucleus

Customize Your Opening

☐ **Accessing Prior Knowledge,** above

☐ **Print Path** Engage Your Brain, SE p. 91, #1–2

☐ **Print Path** Active Reading, SE p. 91, #3–4

☐ **Digital Path** Lesson Opener

Key Topics/Learning Goals	Supporting Concepts
Why Cells Divide 1 Describe the function of cell division in unicellular organisms. 2 Describe the function of cell division in multicellular organisms.	• Unicellular organisms reproduce through cell division. • Mitosis takes place in all body cells of multicellular organisms. • A multicellular organism grows as cell division increases its number of cells. It also replaces damaged cells with new cells formed through cell division.
Genetic Material and Cell Division 1 Explain how cell division results in two new cells, each with a full set of genetic material that is identical to the parent cell's. 2 Define *DNA*. 3 Define *chromosome*.	• DNA contains the information that determines the traits of a living thing. • DNA is packaged into structures called chromosomes. Eukaryotic cells have multiple chromosomes in the nucleus. • Before a cell divides, it duplicates its DNA, which is distributed evenly in the two resulting cells. Each new cell has the same amount of DNA and the same number of chromosomes with the same information as that in the original cell.
Mitosis 1 Define *cell cycle and* identify its three stages. 2 Describe *interphase*. 3 Define *mitosis*. 4 Name the four phases of mitosis. 5 Define *cytokinesis*.	• The cell cycle is the life cycle of a cell. Its three stages are interphase, mitosis, and cytokinesis. • During interphase, the cell carries out normal activities and duplicates chromosomes. • Mitosis is the process that forms two new nuclei, each with complete copies of DNA. • The phases of mitosis are prophase, metaphase, anaphase, and telophase. • Cytokinesis is the separation of the cytoplasm to form two new cells.

Options for Instruction

Two parallel paths provide coverage of the Essential Questions, with a strong **Inquiry** strand woven into each.
Follow the **Print Path,** the **Digital Path,** or your customized combination of print, digital, and inquiry.

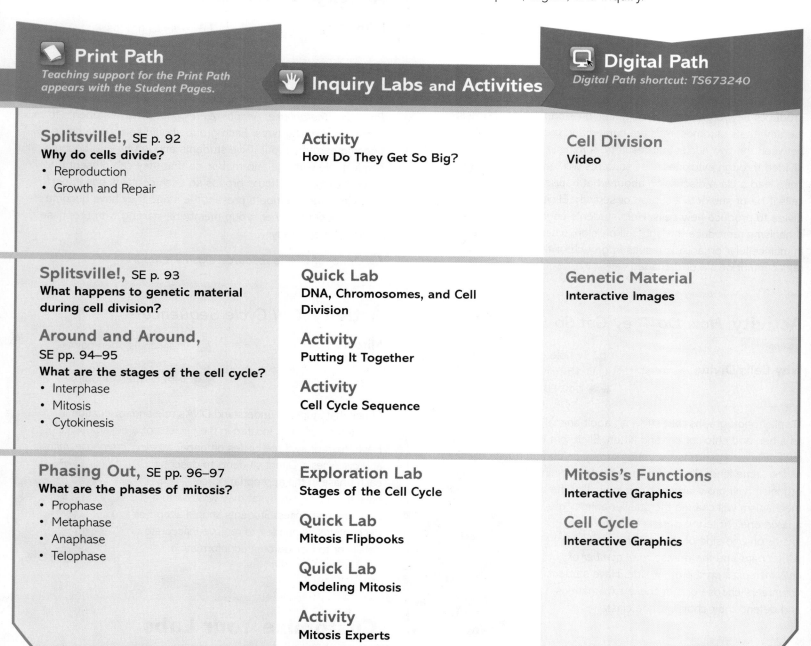

Print Path
Teaching support for the Print Path appears with the Student Pages.

Inquiry Labs and Activities

Digital Path
Digital Path shortcut: TS673240

Splitsville!, SE p. 92
Why do cells divide?
- Reproduction
- Growth and Repair

Activity
How Do They Get So Big?

Cell Division
Video

Splitsville!, SE p. 93
What happens to genetic material during cell division?

Around and Around,
SE pp. 94–95
What are the stages of the cell cycle?
- Interphase
- Mitosis
- Cytokinesis

Quick Lab
DNA, Chromosomes, and Cell Division

Activity
Putting It Together

Activity
Cell Cycle Sequence

Genetic Material
Interactive Images

Phasing Out, SE pp. 96–97
What are the phases of mitosis?
- Prophase
- Metaphase
- Anaphase
- Telophase

Exploration Lab
Stages of the Cell Cycle

Quick Lab
Mitosis Flipbooks

Quick Lab
Modeling Mitosis

Activity
Mitosis Experts

Mitosis's Functions
Interactive Graphics

Cell Cycle
Interactive Graphics

Options for Assessment

See the Evaluate page for options, including Formative Assessment, Summative Assessment, and Unit Review.

Engage and Explore

Activities and Discussion

Discussion *Out with the Old*

Introducing Key Topics

 whole class
🕐 20 min

Display a sequence of photos that shows an amoeba reproducing. Have students discuss the fact that an amoeba reproduces, or produces new organisms, through cell division. (In this process, the amoeba's chromosomes are copied and then distributed evenly between the two nuclei that result from mitosis. The cytoplasm is then divided through cytokinesis, as students will learn later in the lesson.) Then lead a class discussion about what happens to a person's skin cells if he or she gets a scrape or scratch. Elicit that healthy cells divide to produce new cells. Help students conclude that unicellular organisms reproduce through cell division, whereas cell division in multicellular organisms results in growth of the organism or the replacement of old or damaged cells.

Activity *How Do They Get So Big?*

> Engage

Why Cells Divide

 whole class
🕐 15 min
Inquiry **GUIDED** inquiry

Display photographs that show an adult animal with its young, such as a hen and chick or cat and kitten. Elicit that each photo shows two multicellular organisms—a young organism and an adult organism of the same kind. Challenge students to explain how the younger organism will grow larger until it looks like the adult, that is, what mechanism will change the smaller animal into a large one. Write the phrase *cells increase in size* on one side of the chalkboard or whiteboard and the phrase *total number of cells increases* on the other side. Have student volunteers choose one of these explanations and defend their choice to the class.

Activity *Mitosis Experts*

Mitosis

 4 small groups
🕐 30 min
Inquiry **GUIDED** inquiry

Jigsaw List the phases of mitosis on a chalkboard or whiteboard: *Prophase, Metaphase, Anaphase, Telophase*. Have students form four equal-sized groups. Each group should select one stage to become experts about. Give students enough time to become comfortable with the information so that they can present it to others. Then, reconfigure groups so each contains one expert on each stage. Members present the stage they have become experts about to other group members, starting with prophase. Monitor for accuracy.

🌐 *Optional Online resource: Jigsaw support*

Activity *Cell Cycle Sequence*

Mitosis

 individuals, then pairs
🕐 20 min
Inquiry **INDEPENDENT** inquiry

Check that students understand DNA's role and its location in cells (chromosomes located in the nucleus of a eukaryotic cell). Have them draw three circles on paper, labeled *interphase, mitosis,* and *cytokinesis*. Direct students to describe each phase in the appropriate circle. Then, have them compare what they wrote with a partner's responses. Students should alter their descriptions as needed to remove inaccurate details or to include omitted information.

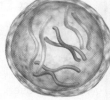

Customize Your Labs

🗎 *See the Lab Manual for lab datasheets.*

🌐 *Go Online for editable lab datasheets.*

Levels of **Inquiry**

DIRECTED inquiry
introduces inquiry skills within a structured framework.

GUIDED inquiry
develops inquiry skills within a supportive environment.

INDEPENDENT inquiry
deepens inquiry skills with student-driven questions or procedures.

Labs and Demos

  ### Exploration Lab *Stages of the Cell Cycle*

Mitosis

 pairs
🕐 45 min
Inquiry **GUIDED/INDEPENDENT** inquiry

Students observe a microscope slide of actively dividing cells from an onion root tip.

PURPOSE **To identify cells that represent different stages of the cell cycle and to count the number of cells at each stage**

MATERIALS

* microscope
* microscope slide, prepared onion root tip
* paper, graphing

  ### Quick Lab *Modeling Mitosis*

Mitosis

👥 small groups
🕐 30 min
Inquiry **INDEPENDENT** inquiry

Students model the phases of mitosis using physical movement.

PURPOSE **To model the phases of mitosis**

MATERIALS

* adhesive tape
* index cards (10–15)
* markers
* materials for modeling cell structures involved in mitosis
* paper (optional)
* self-stick notes

Quick Lab *Mitosis Flipbooks*

PURPOSE **To review and illustrate the cell changes that occur during the phases of mitosis**

See the Lab Manual or go Online for planning information.

Quick Lab *DNA, Chromosomes, and Cell Division*

PURPOSE **To investigate the relationship between DNA and chromosomes using models**

See the Lab Manual or go Online for planning information.

   ### Virtual Lab *Comparing Cell Division*

Mitosis

👥 flexible
🕐 45 min
Inquiry **GUIDED** inquiry

Students observe the steps of meiosis and compare it to mitosis.

PURPOSE **To study the process of meiosis**

Activities and Discussion

☐ **Discussion** Out with the Old
☐ **Activity** How Do They Get So Big?
☐ **Activity** Mitosis Experts
☐ **Activity** Cell Cycle Sequence

Labs and Demos

☐ **Exploration Lab** Stages of the Cell Cycle
☐ **Quick Lab** Mitosis Flipbooks
☐ **Quick Lab** DNA, Chromosomes…
☐ **Quick Lab** Modeling Mitosis
☐ **Virtual Lab** Comparing Cell Division

Your Resources

_____

_____

Explain Science Concepts

Key Topics	📖 **Print Path**	🖥 **Digital Path**
Why Cells Divide	☐ **Splitsville!,** SE p. 92 • Visualize It!, #5 Paramecium	☐ **Cell Division** Learn about the process of mitosis.
Genetic Material and Cell Division	☐ **Splitsville!,** SE p. 93 • Active Reading, #6 • Visualize It!, #7 ☐ **Around and Around,** SE pp. 94–95 • Active Reading (Annotation strategy), #8 • Active Reading, #9 • Visualize It!, #10 	☐ **Genetic Material** Learn about the role of genetic material in a cell.
Mitosis	☐ **Phasing Out,** SE pp. 96–97 • Active Reading (Annotation strategy) #11 • Think Outside the Book, #12 • Apply, #13 Telophase	☐ **Mitosis's Functions** Learn about the different functions provided by cell division. ☐ **Cell Cycle** Explore the different steps of the cell cycle, including the process of mitosis.

Differentiated Instruction

Basic *Mitosis Chart*

Mitosis
- 👥 individuals
- 🕐 20 min

Two-column Chart Have students create a Two-column Chart. On the left, they should write *prophase, metaphase, anaphase,* and *telophase*. On the right, they should describe what happens to the cell during that phase.

🌐 *Optional Online resource: Two-column Chart support*

Advanced *Order Matters*

Mitosis
- 👥 individuals, then pairs
- 🕐 15 min

Card Scramble Have students write a brief explanation of why mitosis might fail if metaphase did not occur between prophase and anaphase. Explanations should include the idea that the two sets of chromosomes might not separate properly. Then have these students partner with a classmate who would benefit from a review of mitosis. Provide both students with a scrambled set of simple mitosis diagrams on index cards. Allow the mentoring student to assist the partner in properly unscrambling the cards.

ELL *Phases of Mitosis Comic*

Mitosis
- 👥 individuals
- 🕐 25 min

Comic Strip Remind English language learners or struggling readers that mitosis is the part of the cell cycle where the nucleus divides to form two new nuclei that each have the same amount of DNA, the same number of chromosomes, and the same information in their DNA as the original cell. These students may be challenged by the names of the stages of mitosis: *prophase, metaphase, anaphase, telophase.* To help students associate what happens during each phase with the name of the phase, have them make a *Phases of Mitosis* cartoon. Students who are comfortable with drawing can work with students who are better with words to create a panel comic strip illustrating mitosis.

Lesson Vocabulary

DNA	chromosomes	cell cycle
interphase	mitosis	cytokinesis

Previewing Vocabulary

- 👥 whole class
- 🕐 15 min

Word Roots and Origins Share the following to help students remember terms.
- **Interphase** contains the roots *inter-,* which means "between," and *-phase,* which means "appearance."
- **Mitosis** comes from the Greek word *mitos,* meaning "thread," and the word part *osis,* meaning "act" or "process."
- **Cytokinesis** comes from Greek word parts *kyto,* meaning "hollow receptacle," and *kinesis,* meaning "movement."

Reinforcing Vocabulary

- 👥 individuals or groups
- 🕐 ongoing

Word Triangle Have students make Word Triangle diagrams for the vocabulary words. They should write the definition in the bottom, write a sentence using the term in the middle section, and illustrate the term in the top section.

Customize Your Core Lesson

Core Instruction
- ☐ **Print Path** choices
- ☐ **Digital Path** choices

Vocabulary
- ☐ **Previewing Vocabulary** Word Roots and Origins
- ☐ **Reinforcing Vocabulary** Word Triangle

Your Resources

Differentiated Instruction
- ☐ **Basic** Mitosis Chart
- ☐ **Advanced** Order Matters
- ☐ **ELL** Phases of Mitosis Comic

Extend Science Concepts

Reinforce and Review

Activity *Putting It Together*

Synthesizing Key Topics

 small groups

 40–45 min

Jigsaw Divide the class into three groups. Assign each group a key topic from the lesson. Have members of each group work together to become an expert on their topic as it relates to the Essential Question, "How do cells divide?" Have students work together in their groups until all students are confident that they can teach what they have learned to the members of another group, or team. Reassign students to three new mixed groups that include experts for each topic. Have individuals in each mixed group share their expertise with other students in the group until all students are able to explain how each key topic relates to the essential question for the lesson.

 Optional Online resource: Jigsaw support

Graphic Organizer

Synthesizing Key Topics

 large groups, then partners

 25 min

Process Chart After students have completed the lesson, divide the class into two equal groups. Have students in one group complete a Process Chart to show the stages in the cell cycle. Direct the other group to complete a Process Chart to show all the phases in mitosis. Then have students share the information on their diagram with a partner from the other group.

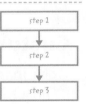

 Optional Online resource: Process Chart support

Going Further

Language Arts Connection

Synthesizing Key Topics

 whole class, then groups

 45 min

Write and Perform a Play Have students work together as a class to write a script for a radio play titled "A Day in the Life of a Cell." Students should divide the play into three acts. Act 1 is Interphase; Act 2 is Mitosis; and Act 3 is Cytokinesis. Different roles should be identified, such as the parts of the nucleus, chromosomes, and cell membrane. After a general discussion, divide students into small groups, each to work on a different act. Encourage students to be creative and even humorous in their writing and presentation, while maintaining scientific accuracy.

Math Connection

Mitosis

 individuals

 15 min

Compute the Number of Cells Pose the following problem. Suppose a scientist needs to know about how many cells are produced by mitosis in 1 second in a laboratory animal. Tell students to assume the rate of mitosis in the animal is about 25 million cells (2.5×10^7) per second. Have them use that rate to find the approximate number of cells produced by mitosis in 5 minutes. Have students record all their calculations. Calculate the number of cells produced in 5 min by first finding the number of seconds in 5 min: 60 s/min × 5 min = 300 s. Then multiply the rate of mitosis by the number of seconds in 5 min: 2.5×10^7 cells/s × 300 s = 7.5×10^9 (7,500,000,000 cells).

Customize Your Closing

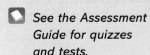 *See the Assessment Guide for quizzes and tests.*

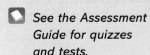 *Go Online to edit and create quizzes and tests.*

Reinforce and Review

☐ **Activity** Jigsaw

☐ **Graphic Organizer** Process Chart

☐ **Print Path** Visual Summary, SE p. 98

☐ **Digital Path** Lesson Closer

Evaluate Student Mastery

See the teacher support below the Student Pages for additional Formative Assessment questions.

Ask: What is the difference in the function of cell division in unicellular and multicellular organisms? In unicellular organisms, cell division is the means of reproduction; in multicellular organisms, it is a way to grow and replace damaged cells. Have students use labeled drawings and captions to describe the life cycle of a cell and to show how cell division results in two new cells with the same DNA as the parent cell. Cell cycle drawings should show interphase (normal life activities and copying of DNA), mitosis (duplicate chromosomes separate, move to opposite sides of the cell; nuclear membrane forms around each set), and cytokinesis (the cell separates into two cells).

Reteach

Formative assessment may show that students need reinforcement for certain topics. The resources below are recommended for reteaching. If students were introduced to a topic through the Print Path, you can also use the Digital Path to reteach, and vice versa.
🎧 *Can be assigned to individual students.*

Why Cells Divide
Discussion Out with the Old

Genetic Material and Cell Division
Quick Lab DNA, Chromosomes, and Cell Division

Mitosis
Exploration Lab Stages of the Cell Cycle

Activity Cell Cycle Sequence 🎧

Alternative Assessment

Mitosis

🌐 *Online resources: student worksheet; optional rubrics*

Mitosis

Climb the Ladder: *Mitosis*
Complete the activities to show what you've learned about mitosi~~s and cell division.~~

1. Work on your own, with a partner, or with a small group.
2. Choose one item from each rung of the ladder. Check your choices.
3. Have your teacher approve your plan.
4. Submit or present your results.

__ **Understanding the Cycle**	__ **An Ode to Mitosis**
Make a scrapbook that shows the three stages of the cell cycle. Include at least one illustration of each stage and describe what occurs during each stage.	Write a poem about the ways that a multicellular organism appreciates mitosis.
__ **Tracking Mitosis**	__ **This Just In!**
Using the Internet, find two video simulations of mitosis. Take notes about and make sketches of the process as your watch. Then compare the strengths and weaknesses of the two simulations.	Present a news report about a new cell that has just formed. Explain how the cell formed, including the three stages of the cell cycle. Also, identify the cell as a unicellular organism or part of a multicellular organism.
__ **To Be DNA**	__ **Why, Oh Why?**
Imagine that you are the DNA in a cell that is about to go through mitosis. Present a monologue in which you describe the changes you'll go through before and during mitosis.	Create a video in which you describe the reasons that unicellular organisms go through cell division and the reasons that multicellular organism go through cell division. Include examples in your video.

Going Further
☐ **Language Arts Connection**
☐ **Math Connection**

Your Resources

Formative Assessment
☐ **TE Questions** Throughout TE
☐ **Lesson Quiz** SE

Summative Assessment
☐ **Alternative Assessment** Mitosis
☐ **Lesson Quiz**
☐ **Unit Tests A and B**
☐ **Unit Review** SE End-of-Unit

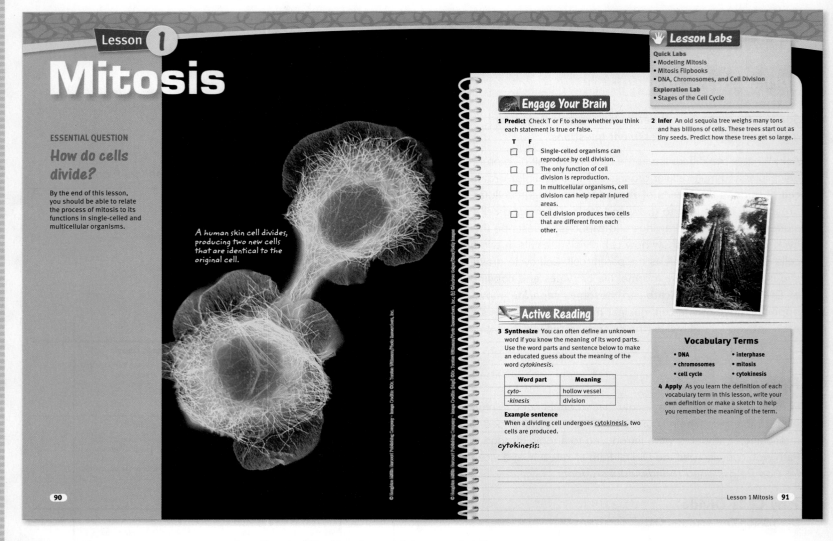

Answers

Answers 1–3 should represent students' current thoughts, even if incorrect.

1. T; F; T; F

2. Sample answer: The trees get bigger because of cell division. Cells divide, and as the number of cells gets bigger, the tree gets bigger.

3. Sample answer: Cytokinesis is the process of cell division during which two new cells are made.

4. Students should define or sketch each vocabulary term in the lesson.

Opening Your Lesson

Have students write down what they already know about reproduction and cell division. Then ask them what they still need to know, or still have questions about.

Preconceptions: Many students equate cell division exclusively with reproduction of single-celled organisms and do not associate cell division with growth and body maintenance of multicellular organisms.

Prerequisites: Students should be familiar with the basic structure of the cell and with the functions of various organelles, including the cell nucleus.

Learning Alert

Single-Cell or Multicellular Help students distinguish between the role of cell division in single and multicellular organisms. Draw a Venn diagram on the board. Write the term *single-celled organism* in one circle and the term *multicellular organism* in the other. Write the term *cell division* in the overlap section. Then have students discuss in which part of the diagram they think you should write the word *reproduction* and in which part they think you should write the terms *growth* and *replacement cells*. Have students defend their choices. Reproduction belongs with single-celled organism; growth and replacement cells belong with multicellular organism.

Splitsville!

Why do cells divide?

Cell division happens in all organisms. Cell division takes place for different reasons. For example, single-celled organisms reproduce through cell division. In multicellular organisms, cell division is involved in growth, development, and repair, as well as reproduction.

Reproduction

Cell division is important for asexual reproduction, which involves only one parent organism. In single-celled organisms, the parent divides in two, producing two identical offspring. In single-celled and some multicellular organisms, offspring result when a parent organism buds, producing offspring. In multicellular organisms, reproduction by cell division can include plant structures such as runners and plantlets.

Growth and Repair

One characteristic of all living things is that they grow. You are probably bigger this year than you were last year. Your body is made up of cells. Although cells themselves grow, most growth in multicellular organisms happens because cell division produces new cells.

Cell division also produces cells for repair. If you cut your hand or break a bone, the damaged cells are replaced by new cells that form during cell division.

 Visualize It!

5 Apply Take a look at the photos below. Underneath each photo, describe the role of cell division in what is taking place.

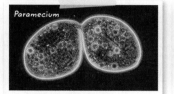
Paramecium

Role of cell division:
_____
_____

Starfish

Role of cell division:
_____
_____

What happens to genetic material during cell division?

The genetic material in cells is called DNA (deoxyribonucleic acid). A **DNA** molecule contains the information that determines the traits that a living thing inherits and needs to live. It contains instructions for an organism's growth, development, and activities. In eukaryotes, DNA is found in the nucleus.

During most of a cell's life cycle, DNA, along with proteins, exists in a complex material called *chromatin* (KROH•muh•tin). Before cell division, DNA is duplicated, or copied. Then, in an early stage of cell division, the chromatin is compacted into visible structures called **chromosomes** (KROH•muh•sohmz). A duplicated chromosome consists of two identical structures called *chromatids* (KROH•muh•tidz). The chromatids are held together by a *centromere* (SEN•truh•mir).

Active Reading

6 Describe What happens to DNA before cell division?
_____
_____
_____

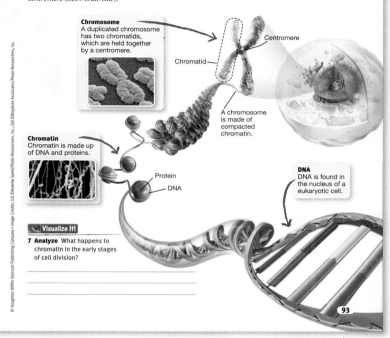

Chromosome
A duplicated chromosome has two chromatids, which are held together by a centromere.

Chromatid

Centromere

A chromosome is made of compacted chromatin.

Chromatin
Chromatin is made up of DNA and proteins.

Protein

DNA

DNA
DNA is found in the nucleus of a eukaryotic cell.

Visualize It!

7 Analyze What happens to chromatin in the early stages of cell division?
_____
_____

93

Answers

5. Sample answer: *Paramecium*: Cell division is used for reproduction; Starfish: Cell division repairs arms that have been removed. It can also be used for growth or reproduction.

6. Sample answer: DNA is duplicated, or copied.

7. Sample answer: Chromatin condenses. Chromosomes have two chromatids connected by a centromere.

Learning Alert

Reproduction Find out if students are confused about the difference between sexual and asexual reproduction. **Ask:** How do you know if a cell is reproducing asexually when it divides? If students cannot answer, they are likely confused about the distinction. Explain that cell division is a part of both asexual and sexual reproduction. In sexual reproduction, cell division(meiosis) produces cells with half the number of chromosomes as other body cells. One of these cells, called a sex cell, combines with a sex cell usually from another individual and produces a new organism. In asexual reproduction, one organism alone can produce another entire organism using cell division. **Ask:** What role does mitosis play in asexual reproduction? Mitosis produces two new nuclei that are genetically identical to the original nucleus from which they formed and to each other. Each nucleus becomes part of a new cell (or organism in single-celled eukaryotes) formed through cell division.

Probing Questions   GUIDED Inquiry

Identifying What occurs in a cell when it is not undergoing cell division? Sample answer: It obtains food and breaks down food, uses energy, grows, excretes waste products; before cell division, it duplicates its DNA in preparation for division. **Prompt:** Think about life processes. **Ask:** How do chromosomes change before cell division? Chromosomes condense, becoming visible under a microscope.

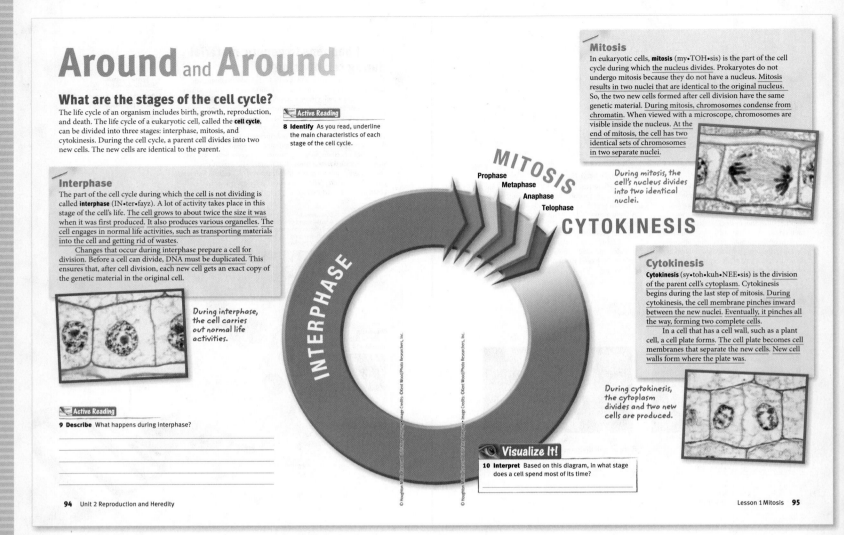

Around and Around

What are the stages of the cell cycle?

The life cycle of an organism includes birth, growth, reproduction, and death. The life cycle of a eukaryotic cell, called the **cell cycle**, can be divided into three stages: interphase, mitosis, and cytokinesis. During the cell cycle, a parent cell divides into two new cells. The new cells are identical to the parent.

Active Reading

8 Identify As you read, underline the main characteristics of each stage of the cell cycle.

Interphase

The part of the cell cycle during which the cell is not dividing is called **interphase** (IN•ter•fayz). A lot of activity takes place in this stage of the cell's life. The cell grows to about twice the size it was when it was first produced. It also produces various organelles. The cell engages in normal life activities, such as transporting materials into the cell and getting rid of wastes.

Changes that occur during interphase prepare a cell for division. Before a cell can divide, DNA must be duplicated. This ensures that, after cell division, each new cell gets an exact copy of the genetic material in the original cell.

During interphase, the cell carries out normal life activities.

Active Reading

9 Describe What happens during interphase?

_____

_____

_____

_____

Mitosis

In eukaryotic cells, **mitosis** (my•TOH•sis) is the part of the cell cycle during which the nucleus divides. Prokaryotes do not undergo mitosis because they do not have a nucleus. Mitosis results in two nuclei that are identical to the original nucleus. So, the two new cells formed after cell division have the same genetic material. During mitosis, chromosomes condense from chromatin. When viewed with a microscope, chromosomes are visible inside the nucleus. At the end of mitosis, the cell has two identical sets of chromosomes in two separate nuclei.

During mitosis, the cell's nucleus divides into two identical nuclei.

MITOSIS
Prophase
Metaphase
Anaphase
Telophase

CYTOKINESIS

Cytokinesis

Cytokinesis (sy•toh•kuh•NEE•sis) is the division of the parent cell's cytoplasm. Cytokinesis begins during the last step of mitosis. During cytokinesis, the cell membrane pinches inward between the new nuclei. Eventually, it pinches all the way, forming two complete cells.

In a cell that has a cell wall, such as a plant cell, a cell plate forms. The cell plate becomes cell membranes that separate the new cells. New cell walls form where the plate was.

During cytokinesis, the cytoplasm divides and two new cells are produced.

INTERPHASE

Visualize It!

10 Interpret Based on this diagram, in what stage does a cell spend most of its time?

Answers

8. *See students' pages for annotations.*

9. Sample answer: The cell grows and engages in normal life activities such as moving materials into the cell and getting rid of wastes.

10. interphase

Interpreting Visuals

Direct students to study the diagram of the cell cycle. Have them identify the number of stages shown and the name of each stage. three stages: interphase, mitosis, cytokinesis Ask students which is the longest stage of the cell cycle and how they know this. interphase; because interphase makes up the largest part of the diagram

Learning Alert

Preparing for Mitosis Students should be able to identify the events that occur in preparation for a cell's carrying out mitosis. Have students compare cell size prior to mitosis with cell size when that cell was first produced. The cell has gotten larger.

Formative Assessment

Ask: What is mitosis? the division of a nucleus into two nuclei that contain identical genetic material **Ask:** Why doesn't mitosis occur in prokaryotes? They do not have a nucleus. **Ask:** What would happen if DNA did not duplicate during interphase? The new cells formed through cell division would not both get a complete set of DNA. **Ask:** What is cytokinesis? division of the cytoplasm of the parent cell

Phasing Out

What are the phases of mitosis?

Mitosis has four phases: prophase (PROH•fayz), metaphase (MET•uh•fayz), anaphase (AN•uh•fayz), and telophase (TEE•luh•fayz). By the end of these phases, the cell will have two identical nuclei and cytokinesis will begin.

Active Reading

11 Identify As you read, underline the major events that take place in each phase of mitosis.

Prophase

During prophase, the chromatin in the nucleus of a cell condenses and becomes visible under a microscope. Each chromosome consists of two chromatids held together by a centromere. The membrane around the nucleus breaks down.

Metaphase

During metaphase, chromosomes line up in the middle of the cell. Centromeres of the chromosomes are the same distance from each side of the cell.

Anaphase

During anaphase, the chromatids separate. They are pulled to opposite sides of the cell. Each side of the cell ends up with a complete set of chromosomes.

Telophase

The last phase of mitosis is telophase. A new nuclear membrane forms around each group of chromosomes. So, the cell now has two identical nuclei. The chromosomes become less condensed. Cytokinesis begins during this phase.

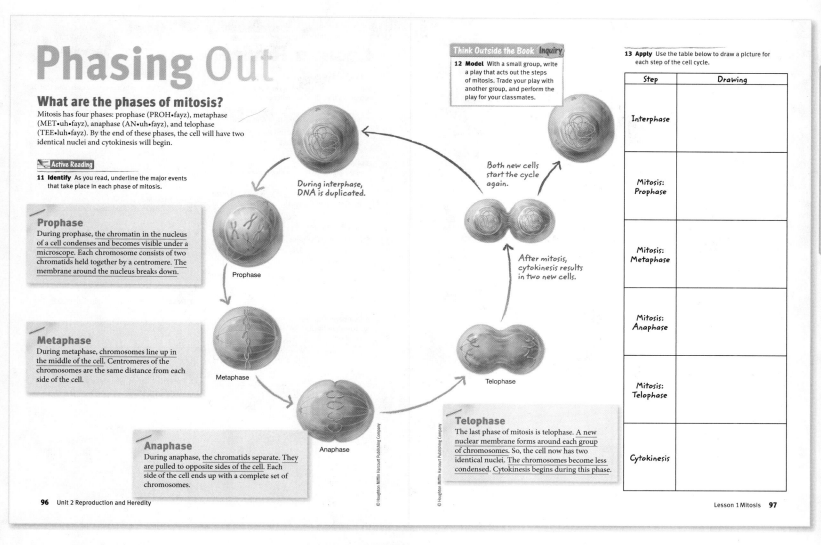

During interphase, DNA is duplicated.

Prophase

Metaphase

Anaphase

Telophase

After mitosis, cytokinesis results in two new cells.

Both new cells start the cycle again.

Think Outside the Book — Inquiry

12 Model With a small group, write a play that acts out the steps of mitosis. Trade your play with another group, and perform the play for your classmates.

13 Apply Use the table below to draw a picture for each step of the cell cycle.

Step	Drawing
Interphase	
Mitosis: Prophase	
Mitosis: Metaphase	
Mitosis: Anaphase	
Mitosis: Telophase	
Cytokinesis	

© Houghton Mifflin Harcourt Publishing Company

Answers

11. *See student pages for annotations.*

12. Students should write plays that accurately describe prophase, metaphase, anaphase, and telophase. Some students may include interphase and cytokinesis in their plays.

13. Students should accurately draw cells in interphase, prophase, metaphase, anaphase, telophase, and cytokinesis.

Interpreting Visuals

To help students interpret the diagram, ask questions out of sequence about the phases of cell division. **Ask:** During what phase do chromosomes line up? metaphase During what phase do they separate? anaphase When do the chromosomes condense and become visible under a microscope? prophase What happens to the chromosomes during anaphase? The chromatids separate into two identical chromosomes, which move to opposite sides of the cell. In what phase does the cell's nuclear membrane break down? prophase

Building Reading Skills

Knowing how to identify the sequence of events in text is an important reading strategy. Help students with this concept by writing the following words on the board: *first, next, then,* and *finally.* Tell students that words such as these indicate the order in which events occur. Have students use these words as they describe the phases of mitosis in order.

Probing Questions — INDEPENDENT Inquiry

Infer Sometimes a cell inaccurately duplicates its DNA, and the resulting cells are not identical. **Ask:** What effects might such results have? Sample answer: Daughter cells may have differences that are beneficial or harmful, or that have no apparent effect.

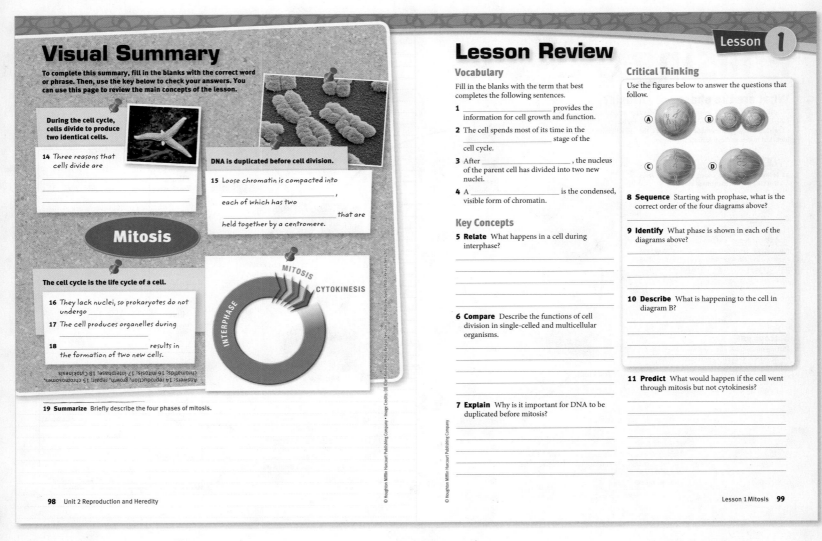

Visual Summary

Lesson 1

To complete this summary, fill in the blanks with the correct word or phrase. Then, use the key below to check your answers. You can use this page to review the main concepts of the lesson.

During the cell cycle, cells divide to produce two identical cells.

14 Three reasons that cells divide are _____

DNA is duplicated before cell division.

15 Loose chromatin is compacted into _____, each of which has two _____ that are held together by a centromere.

Mitosis

The cell cycle is the life cycle of a cell.

16 They lack nuclei, so prokaryotes do not undergo _____

17 The cell produces organelles during _____

18 _____ results in the formation of two new cells.

MITOSIS
CYTOKINESIS
INTERPHASE

Answers: 14 reproduction, growth, repair; 15 chromosomes, chromatids; 16 mitosis; 17 interphase; 18 Cytokinesis

19 Summarize Briefly describe the four phases of mitosis.

98 Unit 2 Reproduction and Heredity

Lesson Review

Vocabulary

Fill in the blanks with the term that best completes the following sentences.

1 _____ provides the information for cell growth and function.

2 The cell spends most of its time in the _____ stage of the cell cycle.

3 After _____, the nucleus of the parent cell has divided into two new nuclei.

4 A _____ is the condensed, visible form of chromatin.

Key Concepts

5 Relate What happens in a cell during interphase?

6 Compare Describe the functions of cell division in single-celled and multicellular organisms.

7 Explain Why is it important for DNA to be duplicated before mitosis?

Critical Thinking

Use the figures below to answer the questions that follow.

Ⓐ Ⓑ
Ⓒ Ⓓ

8 Sequence Starting with prophase, what is the correct order of the four diagrams above?

9 Identify What phase is shown in each of the diagrams above?

10 Describe What is happening to the cell in diagram B?

11 Predict What would happen if the cell went through mitosis but not cytokinesis?

Lesson 1 Mitosis 99

Visual Summary Answers

14. reproduction; growth; repair

15. chromosomes; chromatids

16. mitosis

17. interphase

18. Cytokinesis

19. Sample answer: During prophase, chromosomes condense and the nuclear membrane breaks down. During metaphase, the chromosomes line up in the middle of the cell. During anaphase, the chromosomes separate and are pulled to opposite sides of the cell. During telophase, the nuclear membrane re-forms and the chromosomes unwind back into chromatin.

Lesson Review Answers

1. DNA

2. interphase

3. mitosis

4. chromosome

5. Sample answer: During interphase, the cell undergoes normal life functions. Cell size increases, and various organelles are produced. DNA is duplicated in preparation for cell division.

6. Sample answer: In single-celled organisms, cell division is used for reproduction. In multicellular organisms, cell division is used for reproduction, growth, and repair.

7. Sample answer: DNA must replicate before mitosis so new cells can have a full set of genetic material.

8. A, C, D, B

9. A: prophase; B: cytokinesis; C: metaphase; D: anaphase

10. Sample answer: The cell has undergone mitosis and is now undergoing cytokinesis. Cytokinesis results in two new cells that are identical to the original cell.

11. Sample answer: The cells that result would have too many nuclei. The nucleus of the original cell would continue to divide, but there would only be one cell because cytokinesis is the process that produces new cells.

Meiosis

Essential Question **How do cells divide for sexual reproduction?**

Professional Development

For more detailed information about the topics in this lesson, refer to the Content Refresher in the Unit Opener pages.

Opening Your Lesson

Begin the lesson by assessing students' prerequisite and prior knowledge.

Prerequisite Knowledge

- Cell structure
- How cells can divide by mitosis to produce two new cells identical to the parent cell

Accessing Prior Knowledge

Ask: How is genetic material organized in a cell? DNA and proteins form chromatin, which condenses into visible chromosomes before cell division.

Ask: What happens to the genetic material before a cell divides by mitosis? The DNA is duplicated, or copied.

Customize Your Opening

- ☐ **Accessing Prior Knowledge,** above
- ☐ **Print Path** Engage Your Brain, SE p. 101, #1–2
- ☐ **Print Path** Active Reading, SE p. 101, #3–4
- ☐ **Digital Path** Lesson Opener

Key Topics/Learning Goals	Supporting Concepts
Sex Cells 1 Define *sex cell*. 2 Explain how sex cells differ from body cells. 3 Define *homologous chromosome*.	• Unlike body cells, sex cells, or gametes, are haploid and contain one of each homologous chromosome. Females produce eggs and males produce sperm. • Homologous chromosomes have the same genes in the same sequences and have the same structure, but the alleles may differ. • Sex chromosomes control the development of sex and some other characteristics.
Meiosis 1 Define *meiosis*. 2 Identify the relationship between meiosis and sexual reproduction.	• Meiosis is the type of cell division that produces cells for sexual reproduction. When an egg and a sperm join, they form a diploid cell called a *zygote*. • During meiosis, one diploid cell undergoes two cycles of division to produce four haploid sex cells.
Steps of Meiosis 1 Describe the steps of meiosis. 2 Identify the results of meiosis I and meiosis II.	• During meiosis I, chromosomes condense and pairs line up, then separate randomly and are distributed to one of the two new nuclei. The two new cells each have one duplicated homologous chromosome from each pair. • During meiosis II, duplicated chromosomes separate, resulting in four haploid cells.
Meiosis vs. Mitosis 1 Compare meiosis and mitosis.	• Mitosis produces two cells that are genetically identical to the parent cell. Meiosis produces haploid sex cells. • Mitosis is used for growth, repair, or asexual reproduction. Meiosis produces sex cells for sexual reproduction.

Options for Instruction

Two parallel paths provide coverage of the Essential Questions, with a strong **Inquiry** strand woven into each. Follow the **Print Path,** the **Digital Path,** or your customized combination of print, digital, and inquiry.

📖 **Print Path**	✋ **Inquiry Labs and Activities**	🖥️ **Digital Path**
Teaching support for the Print Path appears with the Student Pages.		Digital Path shortcut: TS673230
Number Off!, SE pp. 102–103 **How do sex cells differ from body cells?** • Chromosome Number **Why do organisms need sex cells?** **How are sex cells made?** • Meiosis	**Activity** **Modeling Chromosomes**	**Sex Cells** **Slideshow**
One Step at a Time, SE pp. 104–106 **What are the stages of meiosis?** • Meiosis I • Meiosis II **How does meiosis compare to mitosis?**	**Quick Lab** **Crossover and Meiosis** **Daily Demo** **Modeling Meiosis** **Activity** **Meiosis Skit**	**Meiosis Process** **Interactive Graphics**
One Step at a Time, SE pp. 104–106 **What are the stages of meiosis?** • Meiosis I • Meiosis II **How does meiosis compare to mitosis?**	**Quick Lab** **Meiosis Flipbooks** **Activity** **Meiosis Posters**	**Meiosis Process** **Interactive Graphics**
One Step at a Time, SE pp. 104–106 **What are the stages of meiosis?** • Meiosis I • Meiosis II **How does meiosis compare to mitosis?**	**Activity** **Tracking Sequence**	**Mitosis and Meiosis** **Interactive Graphics**

Options for Assessment

See the Evaluate page for options, including Formative Assessment, Summative Assessment, and Unit Review.

Engage and Explore

Activities and Discussion

Activity *Meiosis Skit*

Engage

Meiosis

👥 small groups
🕐 20 min
Inquiry **INDEPENDENT** inquiry

Invite students to write and perform a skit that shows the phases of meiosis. Students will need to think about and assign roles for the skit, make necessary props for the skit, and run through the skit a few times. Then encourage students to present their polished skit to the rest of the class.

Activity *Meiosis Posters*

Steps of Meiosis

👥 individuals or pairs
🕐 20 min
Inquiry **GUIDED** inquiry

Invite students to make posters that show the steps of meiosis. Students may want to make their posters three-dimensional by using yarn, beads, string, macaroni noodles, and so on, to represent chromosomes, cell walls, spindle fibers, organelles, and other cellular features. Have students label each illustration with the name of the step it depicts and with the parts of the cell. Students should also include a brief description of what occurs at that step.

Activity *Tracking Sequence*

Meiosis vs. Mitosis

👥 individuals or pairs
🕐 20 min
Inquiry **GUIDED** inquiry

Provide students with blank sequence diagram graphic organizers or have them draw their own. They should fill in the boxes on one organizer with the steps of meiosis and then complete the other organizer with the steps of mitosis. They should include descriptions of what happens to chromosomes at each step in the process. The last box should state what type of cell results from the process. Students will need one organizer for mitosis, and two for meiosis, because they will need to make sequences for meiosis I and meiosis II.

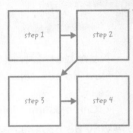

Activity *Modeling Chromosomes*

Sex Cells

👥 individuals or small groups
🕐 20 min
Inquiry **GUIDED** inquiry

Invite students to use dry beans or jelly beans to model chromosome pairs in body cells and in sex cells. Give students index cards to label their models. Students should include these terms: *homologous chromosomes*, *diploid body cells*, *sex cells*, *haploid cells*, *chromosomes*, *egg cell*, *sperm cell*, *zygote*.

Customize Your Labs

📄 *See the Lab Manual for lab datasheets.*

🌐 *Go Online for editable lab datasheets.*

 Levels of **Inquiry**

DIRECTED inquiry
introduces inquiry skills within a structured framework.

GUIDED inquiry
develops inquiry skills within a supportive environment.

INDEPENDENT inquiry
deepens inquiry skills with student-driven questions or procedures.

Labs and Demos

Daily Demo *Modeling Meiosis*

Engage

Meiosis

👥 whole class
🕐 10 min
Inquiry **GUIDED** inquiry

Use this short demo after students have read about meiosis. After completing the demo, review the diagram in the lesson that shows the stages of meiosis I and II, and make connections between the diagram and the demo.

PURPOSE **To show the stages of meiosis**

MATERIALS

- colored ribbons or construction paper (4 of each color)
- string large enough to circle the perimeter of the group

To help students better understand the concept of meiosis, have them act as chromosomes by holding colored ribbons or colored sheets of construction paper. There should be four of each color, so students can pair up to become homologous pairs. Have other students position a long piece of string to represent the cell membrane. Walk students through the stages of meiosis I and II, until they end up with four cells with half the number of chromosomes that were in the original cell.

Quick Lab *Crossover and Meiosis*

Meiosis

👥 pairs
🕐 15 min
Inquiry **DIRECTED** inquiry

Advanced students may use clay to demonstrate the crossing over of chromosomes during meiosis.

PURPOSE **To model crossing over, meiosis, and fertilization**

MATERIALS

- clay, red, yellow, blue, and green (2 balls of each)
- plastic knife
- lab apron
- safety goggles

Quick Lab *Meiosis Flipbooks*

Steps of Meiosis

👥 small groups
🕐 20 min
Inquiry **DIRECTED** inquiry

Students model the gradual transitions throughout meiosis by making a flipbook.

PURPOSE **To show the steps and intermediate stages of meiosis**

MATERIALS

- colored pencils, 2 shades of 1 color
- 22 index cards
- 2 paper brads
- hole punch
- safety goggles

Activities and Discussion

☐ **Activity** Meiosis Skit
☐ **Activity** Meiosis Posters
☐ **Activity** Tracking Sequence
☐ **Activity** Modeling Chromosomes

Labs and Demos

☐ **Daily Demo** Modeling Meiosis
☐ **Quick Lab** Crossover and Meiosis
☐ **Quick Lab** Meiosis Flipbooks

Your Resources

_____

_____

_____

_____

_____

Explain Science Concepts

	📖 Print Path	💻 Digital Path

Key Topics

Sex Cells

☐ **Number Off!,** SE pp. 102–103
- Active Reading, #5
- Visualize It!, #6
- Summarize, #7

Visualize It! Inquiry

6 Predict The cell shown is a body cell that has two pairs of homologous chromosomes. Use the space to the right to draw a sex cell for the same organism.

Body cell

☐ **Sex Cells**

Learn about the difference between sex cells and body cells.

Meiosis

☐ **One Step at a Time,** SE pp. 104–106
- Active Reading, #8
- Visualize It!, #9
- Think Outside the Book, #10
- Identify, #11
- Summarize, #12

Active Reading

8 Sequence As you read, underline what happens to chromosomes during meiosis.

☐ **Meiosis Process**

Explore the different steps that make up the process of meiosis.

Steps of Meiosis

☐ **One Step at a Time,** SE pp. 104–106
- Active Reading, #8
- Visualize It!, #9
- Think Outside the Book, #10
- Identify, #11
- Summarize, #12

11 Identify At the end of meiosis II, how many cells have formed?

☐ **Meiosis Process**

Explore the different steps that make up the process of meiosis.

Meiosis vs. Mitosis

☐ **One Step at a Time,** SE pp. 104–106
- Active Reading, #8
- Visualize It!, #9
- Think Outside the Book, #10
- Identify, #11
- Summarize, #12

12 Summarize Using the table below, compare meiosis and mitosis.

Characteristic	Meiosis	Mitosis
Number of nuclear divisions		
Number of cells produced		
Number of chromosomes in new cells (diploid or haploid)		
Type of cell produced (body cell or sex cell)		
Steps of the process		

☐ **Mitosis and Meiosis**

Compare the processes of mitosis and meiosis.

Differentiated Instruction

Basic *Sequence Cards*

Steps of Meiosis

 individuals
⏱ 10 min

Have students make sequence cards showing the steps in the process of meiosis. Let students put drawings on one side of each card and written explanations on the other. Encourage students to practice rearranging their sequence cards after they have been scrambled.

Advanced *Clay Models*

Meiosis

 individuals
⏱ ongoing

Have students use colored clay to model the stages of meiosis. Suggest they use dark/light pairs (such as 2 red and 2 pink or 2 navy and 2 light blue) to represent homologous pairs. If students are especially intrepid, they can film and move their models to make a claymation video showing the entire process of meiosis.

ELL *Vocabulary*

Sex Cells

 pairs
⏱ 20 min

Have pairs of students work together to write the terms *homologous chromosomes*, *haploid*, *diploid*, *zygote*, and *meiosis* on index cards. Underneath each term, have students write a brief definition. Then encourage students to draw an illustration to help them remember each word on the back of the card.

ELL *Meiosis By the Numbers*

Meiosis

 individuals or pairs
⏱ 10 min

Discuss meiosis with numbers. Start with a number representing the chromosomes in a cell; for example, 4. First, the DNA doubles. **Ask:** What do we get when we double 4? 8 These 8 chromosomes divide into two cells. **Ask:** What is half of 8? 4 **Ask:** How many chromosomes are in each cell? 4 Next, the two cells divide into four cells. **Ask:** How many chromosomes are in each cell? 2 **Ask:** What has happened to the number of chromosomes in each cell? The number per cell is half of what it was to start.

Lesson Vocabulary

homologous chromosome   **meiosis**

Previewing Vocabulary

 whole class   ⏱ 10 min

Word Origins Explain to students that learning word origins can help them understand and recall the meanings of new words.
- Explain to students that *homo* is a Greek word meaning "same," and that *logos* is a Greek word meaning "word, structure" So two things that are *homologous* are the same in structure or function. In genetics, *homologous* means that two chromosomes have the same sequence of genes.
- *Meiosis* comes from a Greek word meaning "to diminish." In genetics, meiosis is the process of cell division that reduces the number of chromosomes in reproductive cells.

Reinforcing Vocabulary

individuals   ⏱ ongoing

Four Square To help students remember the vocabulary terms and any other terms from the lesson that they find difficult, provide them with a Four Square graphic organizer. Students place the term in the circle and then fill in the surrounding cells with the types of information shown.

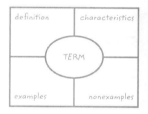

Customize Your Core Lesson

Core Instruction
☐ **Print Path** choices
☐ **Digital Path** choices

Vocabulary
☐ **Previewing Vocabulary** Word Origins
☐ **Reinforcing Vocabulary** Four Square

Your Resources

Differentiated Instruction
☐ **Basic** Sequence Cards
☐ **Advanced** Clay Models
☐ **ELL** Vocabulary
☐ **ELL** Meiosis By the Numbers

_____

_____

Extend Science Concepts

Reinforce and Review

Activity *Modeling Meiosis*

Synthesizing Key Topics   small groups or whole class
🕐 15 min

Have students think about a way that they can model the process of meiosis.

- They might want to have people represent chromosomes and role-play the process.
- They might want to use clay or other craft items to show the stages of meiosis.
- They might want to make a large poster showing all the steps in the process of meiosis in the proper sequence.
- They might want to make a video explaining the process of meiosis. The video should include visuals to make the process clear.
- Students might want to create an interactive model with pieces they can move to show the process of meiosis.

When groups have finished, let them share their models with the class.

Graphic Organizer

Sex Cells   individuals
🕐 15 min

Venn Diagram Have students make a Venn diagram that compares and contrasts haploid and diploid cells.

🎧 *Optional Online support: Venn Diagram*

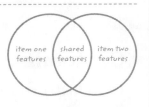

Going Further

Life Science Connection

Meiosis   individuals
🕐 ongoing

Research Plant Meiosis Have students conduct research to find out more about meiosis in plants. Have students explain how meiosis in plant cells is different from and similar to meiosis in animal cells.

Music Connection

Meiosis 👥 individuals or pairs
🕐 ongoing

Ask students, individually or in pairs, to write a poem or song that describes the process of meiosis. Encourage students to perform or play a recording of their song for the class. Students may even want to perform the song for other classes or the entire school.

Customize Your Closing

📓 *See the Assessment Guide for quizzes and tests.*

⏱ *Go Online to edit and create quizzes and tests.*

Reinforce and Review

- ☐ **Activity** Modeling Meiosis
- ☐ **Graphic Organizer** Venn Diagram
- ☐ **Print Path** Visual Summary, SE p. 108
- ☐ **Digital Path** Lesson Closer

Evaluate Student Mastery

Formative Assessment

See the teacher support below the Student Pages for additional Formative Assessment questions.

Have students describe in their own words how cells and chromosomes divide during meiosis. **Ask:** What happens to cells and chromosomes during meiosis? Sample answer: The DNA in the chromosomes is copied, but the cell goes through two divisions. In meiosis I, the pair of homologous chromosomes splits up. In meiosis II, the two copies of each homolog separate, so that each new cell gets one copy. This results in four cells with a single set of homologs.

Reteach

Formative assessment may show that students need reinforcement for certain topics. The resources below are recommended for reteaching. If students were introduced to a topic through the Print path, you can also use the Digital Path to reteach, or vice versa.

🎧 *Can be assigned to individual students*

Sex Cells
Activity Modeling Chromosomes 🎧

Meiosis
Basic Sequence Cards 🎧

Quick Lab Crossover and Meiosis

Steps of Meiosis
Quick Lab Meiosis Flipbooks 🎧

Meiosis vs. Mitosis
Activity Tracking Sequence 🎧

Summative Assessment

Alternative Assessment
Meiosis

⏱ *Online resources: student worksheet, optional rubrics*

Meiosis

Points of View: *Meiosis*
Your class will work together to show what you've learned about meiosis from several different viewpoints.

1. Work in groups as assigned by your teacher. Each group will be assigned to one or two viewpoints.

2. Complete your assignment and present your perspective to the class.

 Vocabulary Define *spindle, cell, chromosome,* and *duplicate* in your own words. Then find a dictionary or textbook definition. Finally, write a short paragraph using the terms that shows what you know about meiosis.

 Calculations A diploid cell from a squirrel contains 40 chromosomes. A diploid cell from corn contains 20 chromosomes. Calculate how many chromosomes are present in a haploid cell from a squirrel and corn. Then, calculate how many chromosomes are present in a diploid cell from an alligator if one of its haploid cells contains 16 chromosomes.

 Details Use a Venn diagram or other graphic organizer to show how meiosis and mitosis are alike and different.

 Illustrations Draw a sketch that illustrates the differences between the final stages of meiosis I and meiosis II.

 Analysis Explain why meiosis is important for many living things.

 Models Make a model of one of the phases in meiosis. You might use string for cell walls, macaroni noodles for chromosomes, chenille sticks/pipe cleaners for spindle fibers, and other items as needed.

Going Further
- ☐ Life Science Connection
- ☐ Music Connection
- ☐ Print Path Why It Matters, SE p. 107

Formative Assessment
- ☐ Strategies Throughout TE
- ☐ Lesson Review SE

Summative Assessment
- ☐ Alternative Assessment Meiosis
- ☐ Lesson Quiz
- ☐ Unit Tests A and B
- ☐ Unit Review SE End-of-Unit

Your Resources

_____

_____

_____

_____

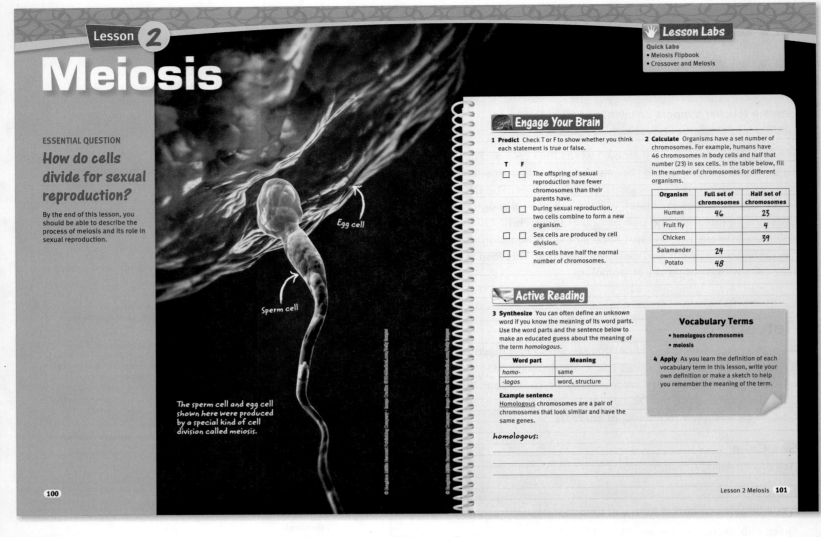

Meiosis

ESSENTIAL QUESTION

How do cells divide for sexual reproduction?

By the end of this lesson, you should be able to describe the process of meiosis and its role in sexual reproduction.

Egg cell

Sperm cell

The sperm cell and egg cell shown here were produced by a special kind of cell division called meiosis.

100

Lesson Labs

Quick Labs
• Meiosis Flipbook
• Crossover and Meiosis

Engage Your Brain

1 Predict Check T or F to show whether you think each statement is true or false.

T   F

☐   ☐   The offspring of sexual reproduction have fewer chromosomes than their parents have.

☐   ☐   During sexual reproduction, two cells combine to form a new organism.

☐   ☐   Sex cells are produced by cell division.

☐   ☐   Sex cells have half the normal number of chromosomes.

2 Calculate Organisms have a set number of chromosomes. For example, humans have 46 chromosomes in body cells and half that number (23) in sex cells. In the table below, fill in the number of chromosomes for different organisms.

Organism	Full set of chromosomes	Half set of chromosomes
Human	46	23
Fruit fly		4
Chicken		39
Salamander	24	
Potato	48	

Active Reading

3 Synthesize You can often define an unknown word if you know the meaning of its word parts. Use the word parts and the sentence below to make an educated guess about the meaning of the term *homologous*.

Word part	Meaning
homo-	same
-logos	word, structure

Example sentence

Homologous chromosomes are a pair of chromosomes that look similar and have the same genes.

homologous:

_____

_____

_____

Vocabulary Terms

• homologous chromosomes
• meiosis

4 Apply As you learn the definition of each vocabulary term in this lesson, write your own definition or make a sketch to help you remember the meaning of the term.

Lesson 2 Meiosis 101

Answers

Answers for 1–3 should represent students' current thoughts, even if incorrect.

1. F; T; T; T

2. 8; 78; 12; 24

3. Sample answer: Homologous means having the same structure.

4. Students should define or sketch each vocabulary term in the lesson.

Opening Your Lesson

Discuss students' answers to item 1 to assess their understanding of sexual reproduction and where they might have misconceptions. Explain that some organisms get half their genetic material from their mother and half from their father. So each parent contributes a sex cell with half the amount of genetic information found in a body cell.

Prerequisites Students should already understand how asexual reproduction through mitosis works.

Learning Alert

Meiosis vs. Mitosis Students may have difficulty differentiating between the terms meiosis and mitosis. Explain that meiosis comes from a Greek word that means "less." As they learn about meiosis, encourage them to keep this word origin in mind. Then discuss how it applies when they finish the lesson.

Number Off!

How do sex cells differ from body cells?

Before sexual reproduction can take place, each parent produces sex cells. *Sex cells* have half of the genetic information that body cells have. Thus, when the genetic information from two parents combines, the offspring have a full set of genetic information. The offspring will have the same total number of chromosomes as each of its parents.

Active Reading 5 **Relate** Describe sex cells.

_____

Chromosome Number

In body cells, most chromosomes are found in pairs that have the same structure and size. These **homologous chromosomes** (huh•MAHL•uh•guhs KROH•muh•sohmz) carry the same genes. A homologous chromosome pair may have different versions of the genes they carry. One chromosome pair is made up of *sex chromosomes*. Sex chromosomes control the development of sexual characteristics. In humans, these chromosomes are called X and Y chromosomes. Cells with a pair of every chromosome are called *diploid* (DIP•loyd). Many organisms, including humans, have diploid body cells.

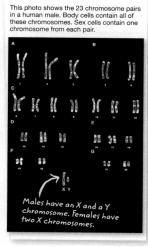

This photo shows the 23 chromosome pairs in a human male. Body cells contain all of these chromosomes. Sex cells contain one chromosome from each pair.

Males have an X and a Y chromosome. Females have two X chromosomes.

Visualize It! (Inquiry)

6 **Predict** The cell shown is a body cell that has two pairs of homologous chromosomes. Use the space to the right to draw a sex cell for the same organism.

Body cell   Sex cell

102 Unit 2 Reproduction and Heredity

Why do organisms need sex cells?

Most human body cells contain 46 chromosomes. Think about what would happen if two body cells were to combine. The resulting cell would have twice the normal number of chromosomes. A sex cell is needed to keep this from happening.

Sex cells are also known as *gametes* (GAM•eetz). Gametes contain half the usual number of chromosomes—one chromosome from each homologous pair and one sex chromosome. Cells that contain half the usual number of chromosomes are known as *haploid* (HAP•loyd).

Gametes are found in the reproductive organs of plants and animals. An egg is a gamete that forms in female reproductive organs. The gamete that forms in male reproductive organs is called a sperm cell.

How are sex cells made?

You know that body cells divide by the process of mitosis. Mitosis produces two new cells, each containing exact copies of the chromosomes in the parent cell. Each new cell has a full set of chromosomes. But to produce sex cells, a different kind of cell division is needed.

Meiosis

A human egg and a human sperm cell each have 23 chromosomes. When an egg is joined with, or *fertilized* by, a sperm cell, a new diploid cell is formed. This new cell has 46 chromosomes, or 23 pairs of chromosomes. One set is from the mother, and the other set is from the father. The newly formed diploid cell may develop into an offspring. **Meiosis** (my•OH•sis) is the type of cell division that produces haploid sex cells such as eggs and sperm cells.

Visualize It!

For the example of fertilization shown, the egg and sperm cells each have one chromosome.

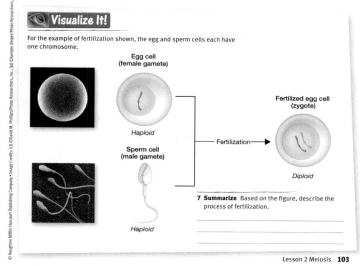

Egg cell (female gamete)
Haploid

Sperm cell (male gamete)
Haploid

Fertilization →

Fertilized egg cell (zygote)
Diploid

7 **Summarize** Based on the figure, describe the process of fertilization.

_____

Lesson 2 Meiosis 103

Answers

5. Sample answer: Sex cells have half the genetic information that body cells have.

6. Students should draw a cell that has two chromosomes, one long and one short. If done in color, the long chromosome should be red or pink and the short chromosome should be a shade of blue.

7. Sample answer: During fertilization, two sex cells combine. Each sex cell provides one-half of the full set of chromosomes in the offspring.

Probing Questions

Inferring Discuss the process of meiosis. **Ask:** Why do you think sexual reproduction requires meiosis? If meiosis did not occur, a fertilized cell would end up with twice as many chromosomes as it needs. **Ask:** Why do you think getting genetic information from each parent might be good for the offspring? It mixes up the genes, which helps make the offspring more diverse.

Interpreting Visuals

Have students look at the image of the male human's chromosomes. **Ask:** How are the chromosomes in most pairs alike? Both have the same structure and are about the same size. **Ask:** How are the chromosomes in the last pair in the image different? The chromosomes are different sizes.

Learning Alert

Sex Cells Help students to understand that after sex cells join, they have a full complement of chromosomes. They are no longer sex cells but rather are body cells.

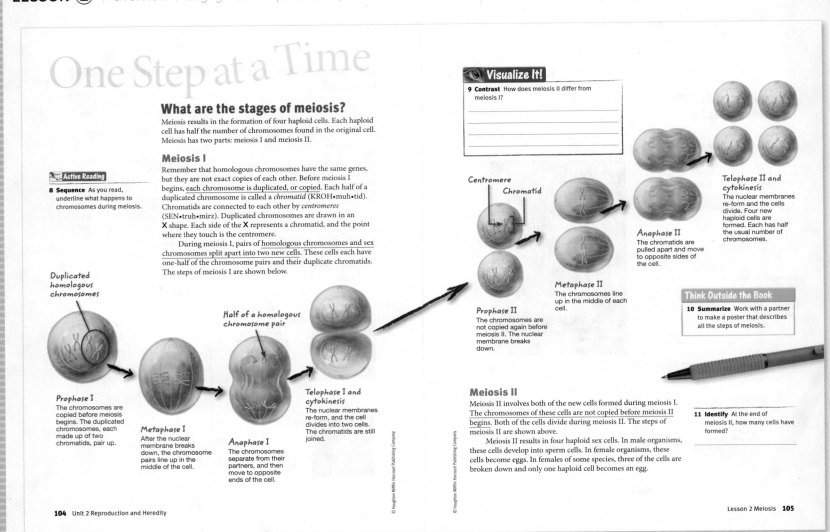

One Step at a Time

What are the stages of meiosis?

Meiosis results in the formation of four haploid cells. Each haploid cell has half the number of chromosomes found in the original cell. Meiosis has two parts: meiosis I and meiosis II.

Meiosis I

Remember that homologous chromosomes have the same genes, but they are not exact copies of each other. Before meiosis I begins, each chromosome is duplicated, or copied. Each half of a duplicated chromosome is called a *chromatid* (KROH•muh•tid). Chromatids are connected to each other by *centromeres* (SEN•truh•mirz). Duplicated chromosomes are drawn in an **X** shape. Each side of the **X** represents a chromatid, and the point where they touch is the centromere.

During meiosis I, pairs of homologous chromosomes and sex chromosomes split apart into two new cells. These cells each have one-half of the chromosome pairs and their duplicate chromatids. The steps of meiosis I are shown below.

Active Reading

8 Sequence As you read, underline what happens to chromosomes during meiosis.

Duplicated homologous chromosomes

Half of a homologous chromosome pair

Prophase I
The chromosomes are copied before meiosis begins. The duplicated chromosomes, each made up of two chromatids, pair up.

Metaphase I
After the nuclear membrane breaks down, the chromosome pairs line up in the middle of the cell.

Anaphase I
The chromosomes separate from their partners, and then move to opposite ends of the cell.

Telophase I and cytokinesis
The nuclear membranes re-form, and the cell divides into two cells. The chromatids are still joined.

Visualize It!

9 Contrast How does meiosis II differ from meiosis I?

Centromere
Chromatid

Prophase II
The chromosomes are not copied again before meiosis II. The nuclear membrane breaks down.

Metaphase II
The chromosomes line up in the middle of each cell.

Anaphase II
The chromatids are pulled apart and move to opposite sides of the cell.

Telophase II and cytokinesis
The nuclear membranes re-form and the cells divide. Four new haploid cells are formed. Each has half the usual number of chromosomes.

Think Outside the Book

10 Summarize Work with a partner to make a poster that describes all the steps of meiosis.

Meiosis II

Meiosis II involves both of the new cells formed during meiosis I. The chromosomes of these cells are not copied before meiosis II begins. Both of the cells divide during meiosis II. The steps of meiosis II are shown above.

Meiosis II results in four haploid sex cells. In male organisms, these cells develop into sperm cells. In female organisms, these cells become eggs. In females of some species, three of the cells are broken down and only one haploid cell becomes an egg.

11 Identify At the end of meiosis II, how many cells have formed?

© Houghton Mifflin Harcourt Publishing Company

104 Unit 2 Reproduction and Heredity

Lesson 2 Meiosis **105**

Answers

8. *See students' pages for annotations.*

9. Sample answer: Chromosomes are copied before meiosis I, but they are not copied before meiosis II.

10. Students should illustrate all of the steps of meiosis, including both meiosis I and meiosis II.

11. four cells

12. Nuclear divisions: 2; 1; cells produced: 4; 2; chromosomes in new cells: haploid; diploid; cell produced: sex cell; body cell. Steps: prophase I, metaphase I, anaphase I, telophase I and cytokinesis, prophase II, metaphase II, anaphase II, telophase II and cytokinesis; prophase, metaphase, anaphase, telophase, and cytokinesis

Interpreting Visuals

Help students interpret the diagrams of meiosis. **Ask:** What must happen in metaphase I before the chromosomes can move? The nuclear membrane must break down. **Ask:** What happens to each homolog in the chromosome pairs during anaphase I? The pairs split, and the homologs go to opposite ends of the cell. **Ask:** What does each homolog look like in telophase I? It still has two chromatids. **Ask:** When do the chromatids in a single homolog split? during anaphase II

Probing Questions

Compare and Contrast Have students look at the diagram showing the stages of meiosis. **Ask:** How are meiosis I and meiosis II similar? In both meiosis I and meiosis II, the cells divide. **Ask:** How are meiosis I and meiosis II different? Before meiosis II, the chromosomes are NOT copied. So when the cells divide, there are only half the usual number of chromosomes in each cell. **Ask:** Why are there only half as many chromosomes as usual? So each sex cell can combine with another sex cell to make a cell with a complete set of chromosomes. For advanced students, explain that crossing over is an important part of meiosis, as it is a source of genetic variation. **Ask:** At what stage of meiosis would you expect crossing over to happen? During prophase I, after the chromosomes are duplicated.

How does meiosis compare to mitosis?

The processes of meiosis and mitosis are similar in many ways. However, they also have several very important differences.

- Only cells that will become sex cells go through meiosis. All other cells divide by mitosis.
- During meiosis, chromosomes are copied once, and then the nucleus divides twice. During mitosis, the chromosomes are copied once, and then the nucleus divides once.
- The cells produced by meiosis contain only half of the genetic material of the parent cell—one chromosome from each homologous pair and one sex chromosome. The cells produced by mitosis contain exactly the same genetic material as the parent—a full set of homologous chromosomes and a pair of sex chromosomes.

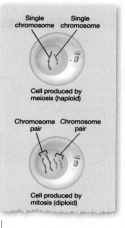

Single chromosome Single chromosome

Cell produced by meiosis (haploid)

Chromosome pair Chromosome pair

Cell produced by mitosis (diploid)

12 Summarize Using the table below, compare meiosis and mitosis.

Characteristic	Meiosis	Mitosis
Number of nuclear divisions		
Number of cells produced		
Number of chromosomes in new cells (diploid or haploid)		
Type of cell produced (body cell or sex cell)		
Steps of the process		

106   Unit 2 Reproduction and Heredity

© Houghton Mifflin Harcourt Publishing Company

Why It Matters   HEALTH WATCH

Down Syndrome

Down syndrome is a genetic disease. It is usually caused by an error during meiosis. During meiosis, the chromatids of chromosome 21 do not separate. So, a sex cell gets two copies of chromosome 21 instead of one copy. When this sex cell joins with a normal egg or sperm, the fertilized egg has three copies of chromosome 21 instead of two copies.

Beating the Odds
Down syndrome causes a number of health problems and learning difficulties, but many people with Down syndrome have fulfilling lives.

One Too Many
Someone who has Down syndrome has three copies of chromosome 21 instead of two copies.

Extend   Inquiry

13 Identify What type of error in meiosis causes Down syndrome?

14 Investigate Research the characteristics of Down syndrome. How can some of the difficulties caused by the disorder be overcome?

15 Recommend Research the Special Olympics. Then make an informative brochure, poster, or oral presentation that describes how the Special Olympics gives people with Down syndrome and other disabilities the chance to compete in sports.

107

Answers

13. The chromatids of chromosome 21 do not separate, so a sex cell gets two copies of chromosome 21 instead of one. When the sex cell joins a normal sex cell, the zygote has three copies of chromosome 21 instead of two.

14. Accept all reasonable answers. Students should recognize that the symptoms of Down syndrome vary and that some people have greater success than others overcoming the difficulties of the disease. Students may discuss special therapies, learning programs, and mainstreaming.

15. Accept all reasonable answers. Students should accurately relate the history of the Special Olympics and provide sources for their reports.

Formative Assessment

Ask: What happens to cells and chromosomes during meiosis? The DNA in the chromosomes is copied, and the cell goes through two divisions. The DNA is divided twice, resulting in four cells, each having half as much DNA as the original cell. In meiosis I, each pair of homologs splits up. In meiosis II, the two copies of each homolog separate. This results in four cells with a single set of homologs.

Probing Questions

Analyze Describe the cells that are produced following mitosis and meiosis. Mitosis forms two diploid cells that are genetically identical to the parent. Meiosis produces four haploid cells that each have just one chromosome from each homologous chromosome pair.

Why It Matters

Have students identify chromosome 21. Explain that *trisomy* is the word used to describe three chromosomes in a somatic (body) cell. Invite students to identify the word parts in *trisomy* and look up their meanings.

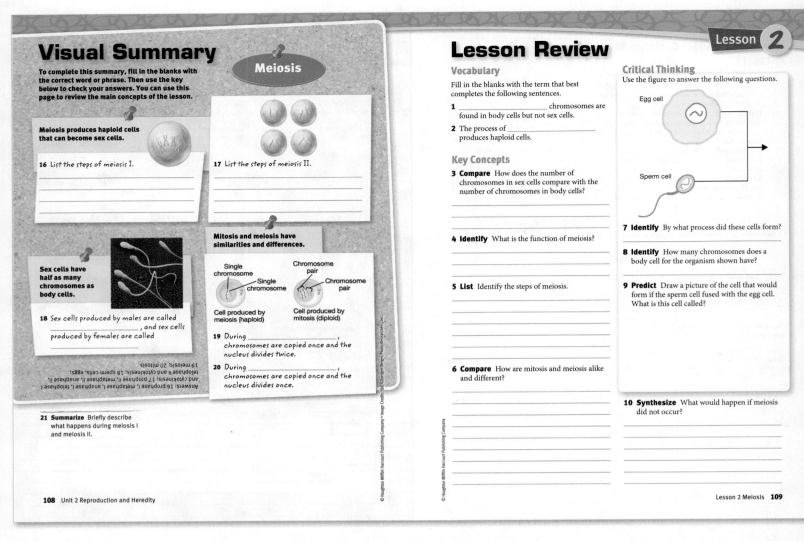

Visual Summary Answers

16. prophase I, metaphase I, anaphase I, telophase I and cytokinesis

17. prophase II, metaphase II, anaphase II, telophase II and cytokinesis

18. sperm cells; eggs

19. meiosis

20. mitosis

21. Sample answers: During meiosis I, chromosomes are copied and the chromosome pairs are separated into two new cells. In meiosis II, the chromosomes are not copied. Instead, the chromatids are separated into new cells, resulting in four haploid cells.

Lesson Review Answers

1. Homologous

2. meiosis

3. Sample answer: Sex cells have half the number of chromosomes found in body cells.

4. Sample answer: The function of meiosis is to produce haploid cells that will become sex cells for sexual reproduction.

5. prophase I, metaphase I, anaphase I, telophase I and cytokinesis, prophase II, metaphase II, anaphase II, telophase II and cytokinesis

6. Sample answer: Meiosis and mitosis are part of cell division. They both involve one instance where chromosomes are copied. However,

meiosis involves two nuclear divisions, while mitosis involves one. Meiosis produces four haploid cells while mitosis produces two diploid cells. Mitosis produces cells exactly like the parent cell, while meiosis produces cells with half the genetic information found in a body cell.

7. meiosis

8. two chromosomes

9. Students should draw a cell that has two chromosomes, or one homologous pair of chromosomes. The cell is a fertilized egg or zygote.

10. Without meiosis, offspring would have too many chromosomes. This number would increase with each generation. So, sexual reproduction likely would not be possible without meiosis.

People in Science

Michael Coble: Geneticist

Purpose To learn about the work of Michael Coble and other geneticists

Learning Goals
- Identify contributions made by a scientist.
- Recognize that scientists come from different backgrounds.
- Identify jobs in science fields.

Academic Vocabulary
dominant genes, recessive genes, fertility

Prerequisite Knowledge
- Basic knowledge of reproduction
- Basic knowledge that genes pass from parents to offspring

Probing Question *Controversial Genetics*

 whole class   15 min
 GUIDED inquiry

Point out to students that new research in genetics has allowed scientists to test people to see if they carry genes for diseases, such as Alzheimer's disease and Huntington's disease, both of which have no cure. Some people feel that having this knowledge would be beneficial, while others feel there would be no benefit to knowing that their risk of developing these diseases is high. **Ask:** What are some of the pros and cons with this type of testing? Sample answer: pros: being able to prepare for the disease, avoiding behaviors that increase the risk of developing the disease; cons: worrying that you might get sick, others judging you

 Optional Online rubric: Class Discussion

Differentiated Instruction

Basic *Career Timeline*

 individuals   🕐 15 min

Timeline Have students make timelines to organize what they learned about Michael Coble's career in science. Tell them to include in their timelines all the important events in Michael Coble's life mentioned in the article. Remind them to pay close attention to the sequence of events and to note that articles do not always present information in chronological order.

Advanced *DNA Detective*

 pairs   🕐 30 min

DNA evidence was not understood in the time of the Romanov royal family, but it is frequently used today to help solve mysteries. Have interested students look up and read about another mystery that was solved with the help of geneticists. Students should summarize what they learned on a poster that identifies the mystery and tells how the geneticists helped uncover the truth.

ELL *Interview a Geneticist*

👥 pairs   🕐 20 min

Have students brainstorm questions they would like to ask Michael Coble or another geneticist. Encourage students to think of a range of questions, from specific questions about what type of work they do and what instruments they use to do it, to more personal questions about what they enjoy about genetics. Pairs should then take turns asking each other the questions they brainstormed and making up answers based on the profile of Michael Coble.

Customize Your Feature

☐ **Probing Question** Controversial Genetics

☐ **People in Science** Online

☐ **Basic** Career Timeline

☐ **Advanced** DNA Detective

☐ **ELL** Interview a Geneticist

People in Science

Michael Coble
GENETICIST

Michael Coble's interest in genetics began when, as young child, he learned about Gregor Mendel's discoveries. While Coble was in college, his interest increased due to a science project in which he had to find dominant and recessive genes in fruit flies. Little did Coble know at the time that his work in genetics would lead him to solve one of history's greatest mysteries: What happened to Russia's royal family, the Romanovs, during the Russian revolution?

The whole family had supposedly been executed in 1918. However, many people believed there was a chance that at least one of the children had escaped.

Coble says that "since 1918, over 200 individuals have claimed to be one of the five 'surviving' Romanov children." Fueling the mystery was the fact that there were no remains in the Romanov's grave for two of the children.

However, in 2007, a grave with the remains of two people was found. Coble and his team used the DNA evidence to identify the remains as the missing Romanov children.

Coble continues his work in genetics today. He says, "It is very rewarding to know that something you were involved with will be used for finding criminals, exonerating the innocent, or helping to identify missing persons."

If the bands of DNA on the film line up correctly, you have a match.

Dr. Coble solved the mystery of Princess Anastasia and the other Romanov children.

Social Studies Connection

Research Find out more about what happened to the Romanovs, including the mystery around Princess Anastasia. Put together a slideshow or a video to report your findings.

110

JOB BOARD

Genetic Counselor

What You'll Do: Analyze a family's risk factors for inherited conditions and disorders

Where You Might Work: At a doctor's office, a health clinic, or a hospital

Education: A graduate degree in genetic counseling

Other Job Requirements: Certification from the American Board of Genetic Counseling

Plant Nursery Manager

What You'll Do: Grow plants from seeds, cuttings, or by other methods. Manage a plant-related business or organization.

Where You Might Work: At a botanical garden, a garden center, or a plant nursery

Education: A degree in plant science and/or business management

Other Job Requirements: A green thumb!

PEOPLE IN SCIENCE NEWS

MULTIPLE Births

Not so rare anymore

Dr. Brian Kirshon and his medical team made history in December 1998. They delivered the world's first known set of surviving octuplets. Octuplets are a very rare type of multiple birth in which the mother carries eight fetuses in her uterus at once. There have been only 19 recorded instances of octuplets. Only two of those sets survived past birth—the first in 1998, and another in 2009. Considering how rare octuplets are, how is it possible that two pairs were born so recently?

The birth rate for twins increased by 70% from 1980 to 2004. In 2006, the birth rate for twins was up to 32 for every 1,000 births. The birth rate in 2006 for having triplets or a larger birth was 153 for every 100,000 births.

What's going on? Doctors point to modern fertility drugs and treatments. In addition, many women are now waiting until later in life to have children. This increases the chance of having a multiple birth.

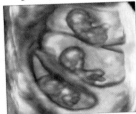

3D ultrasound image of triplets

Unit 2 People in Science **111**

Answers

Social Studies Connection

Encourage students to find images, anecdotes, and historical documents to learn more about the story of the Romanovs, including the mystery around Princess Anastasia. Slideshows or videos should explain what social and political events contributed to the events that unfolded in Russia during this time.

Building Math Skills

Point out to students that the data about twins and triplets could be confusing to some readers because the information is presented in two different ways—the rate for twins is 32 out of every 1,000 births, but the rate for triplets and more is 153 out of every 100,000 births. **Ask:** What could you do to make these data easier to compare? Sample answers: use the same total as a baseline; use either 1,000 or 100,000 for both **Ask:** What do you get when you do this? Sample answers: 32 births out of 1,000 are twins, about 1.5 births out of 1,000 are triplets or more; 3,200 births out of 100,000 are twins, 153 births out of 100,000 are triplets or more

Sexual and Asexual Reproduction

Essential Question How do organisms reproduce?

Professional Development

For more detailed information about the topics in this lesson, refer to the Content Refresher in the Unit Opener pages.

Opening Your Lesson

Begin the lesson by assessing students' prerequisite and prior knowledge.

Prerequisite Knowledge

- Cell structure and function
- Mitosis
- Meiosis

Accessing Prior Knowledge

Ask: What happens to a cell that will be part of sexual reproduction? Students should explain the process of meiosis, in which a cell doubles its genetic material, then divides in two and then divides again, producing four haploid cells.

Ask: How do cells divide during mitosis? Sample answer: Cells double their genetic material, and then divide into two cells, each a diploid cell.

Customize Your Opening

☐ **Accessing Prior Knowledge,** above

☐ **Print Path** Engage Your Brain, SE p. 113, #1–2

☐ **Print Path** Active Reading, SE p. 113, #3–4

☐ **Digital Path** Lesson Opener

Key Topics/Learning Goals

Asexual Reproduction

1 Define *asexual reproduction*.
2 Describe four ways by which organisms reproduce asexually.

Sexual Reproduction

1 Define *sexual reproduction*.
2 Describe the process of fertilization.

Comparing Asexual and Sexual Reproduction

1 Compare asexual and sexual reproduction.
2 Identify the advantages of both forms.
3 Relate why some organisms reproduce both ways.

Supporting Concepts

- Asexual reproduction requires one parent and results in genetically identical offspring.
- Four common ways: binary fission, budding, spore formation, vegetative reproduction
- During binary fission, an organism divides to form two identical organisms.
- During budding, a new organism grows from the outside surface of the parent.
- Spores can survive harsh conditions and later develop into multicellular organisms.
- During vegetative reproduction, plants develop from modified stems or roots, or from plantlets.

- Sexual reproduction involves two parents. It results in offspring that have characteristics of both parents but that are not identical to either one.
- During fertilization, the male gamete and female gamete, each of which has half the full set of chromosomes, combine to form a zygote. The zygote has a full set of chromosomes.

- Advantages of asexual reproduction include rapid increase in numbers and no energy expended to attract a mate.
- Sexual reproduction provides genetic diversity, increasing the chance that at least some offspring will survive.
- An organism may reproduce asexually until unfavorable conditions cause it to undergo sexual reproduction, increasing diversity and improving the chance of survival.

Options for Instruction

Two parallel paths provide coverage of the Essential Questions, with a strong Inquiry strand woven into each. Follow the Print Path, the Digital Path, or your customized combination of print, digital, and inquiry.

 Print Path
Teaching support for the Print Path appears with the Student Pages.

 Inquiry Labs and Activities

Digital Path
Digital Path shortcut: TS673220

One Becomes Two,
SE pp. 114–115
What is asexual reproduction?
How do organisms reproduce asexually?
- Binary Fission
- Budding
- Spores
- Vegetative Reproduction

Field Lab
Investigate Asexual Reproduction

Daily Demo
Budding Yeast

Activity
Growing Plants

Activity
Class Plant Display

Asexual Reproduction
Interactive Graphics

Two Make One, SE p. 116
What is sexual reproduction?
- Fertilization

Quick Lab
Egg versus Sperm

Sexual Reproduction
Interactive Graphics

Added Advantage,
SE pp. 118–119
What are the advantages of each type of reproduction?
- Advantages of Asexual Reproduction
- Advantages of Sexual Reproduction
- Advantages of Using Both Types of Reproduction

Quick Lab
Reproduction and Diversity

Quick Lab
Create a Classification System

Activity
Ways Organisms Reproduce

Sexual vs. Asexual Reproduction
Interactive Graphics

Options for Assessment

See the Evaluate page for options, including Formative Assessment, Summative Assessment, and Unit Review.

Engage and Explore

Activities and Discussion

Probing Question *How Do Plants Reproduce?*

 Engage

Sexual Reproduction

 whole class
 10 min
Inquiry **GUIDED** inquiry

Ask: How do plants reproduce? Sample answers: seeds, runners, spores **Ask:** Do plants reproduce asexually or sexually? both
If students think that plants only reproduce asexually, they may not understand that pollination is sexual reproduction. Explain that pollen is a male sex cell that contains half the plant's genetic information. The pollen combines with the female sex cell in the flower or cone to form a seed, which contains the complete set of genetic information—half from a male cell and half from a female cell.

Ask: What are the two main differences between sexual reproduction and asexual reproduction? Sample answer: Sexual reproduction involves two parents, and the offspring has a new genetic combination that is different from either parent. Asexual reproduction involves only one parent, and the offspring is a genetic copy of the parent.

Activity *Ways Organisms Reproduce*

Comparing Asexual and Sexual Reproduction

 individuals, then pairs
 20 min
Inquiry **GUIDED** inquiry

Think, Pair, Share Give students three minutes to write down as many examples as they can of organisms that reproduce in different ways. Remind students that not all animals reproduce one way and not all plants reproduce in another way. Then have students choose three examples from their list and pair up. Pairs should justify examples to each other by identifying the type of reproduction in each example they have chosen. Call on pairs to discuss their examples with the class.

Activity *Growing Plants*

Asexual Reproduction

 individuals or small groups
 ongoing
Inquiry **GUIDED** inquiry

Have a contest! Students can try to propagate offspring from a potato, a geranium, or another vegetative reproducer. As they work, students will begin to understand that certain parts of the plant (cambium) are required for asexual propagation.

Activity *Class Plant Display*

 Engage

Asexual Reproduction

 individuals
 varies
Inquiry **GUIDED** inquiry

Bring in, or invite students to bring in, plants that reproduce asexually. Examples might include cuttings from plants that have developed roots; a spider plant, a plant that has visible runners; and a cactus plant with baby cacti.

Take It Home *Plants at Home*

Introducing Key Topics

 adult-student pairs
 ongoing
Inquiry **GUIDED** inquiry

Have students work with an adult to identify plants in and near their home. The pair might go on a walk, look through a window, visit a park, or look at plants in their kitchen (such as carrots, potatoes, lettuce, strawberries, and corn).

Customize Your Labs

 See the Lab Manual for lab datasheets.

Go Online for editable lab datasheets.

©Science Pictures Limited/Photo Researchers, Inc.

Levels of  **Inquiry**

DIRECTED inquiry	**GUIDED** inquiry	**INDEPENDENT** inquiry
introduces inquiry skills within a structured framework.	develops inquiry skills within a supportive environment.	deepens inquiry skills with student-driven questions or procedures.

Labs and Demos

Daily Demo *Budding Yeast*

Engage

Asexual Reproduction

👥 whole class
🕐 10 min
Inquiry **GUIDED** inquiry

PURPOSE **To observe the asexual reproductive process budding**

MATERIALS

- microscope
- petri dish
- slide plate
- sugar, 1 mL
- toothpick
- water, warm, 4 mL
- yeast grains, 2 mL

To help students better understand the ways plants can reproduce asexually, let students observe yeast buds.

1. Place 2 mL of yeast grains and 1 mL of sugar into a petri dish.
2. Add 4 mL of warm water.
3. Let the petri dish sit, covered, in a warm place for 10 min.
4. Smear a yeast sample on a slide plate with a sterile toothpick. Cover.
5. Have students take turns looking under a 40× microscope at the budding yeast (or project the image onto a computer using a microscope hookup).
6. Have students make drawings of what they observe.

Quick Lab *Egg vs. Sperm*

PURPOSE **To compare the size, structure, and function of human sperm cells and human egg cells**

See the Lab Manual or go Online for planning information.

Field Lab *Investigate Asexual Reproduction*

Asexual Reproduction

👥 pairs
🕐 three 45-min periods
Inquiry **GUIDED/INDEPENDENT** inquiry

Students take cuttings of plants to bring back to the lab for propagation.

PURPOSE **To test various plant parts to observe whether they will grow into new plants**

MATERIALS

- containers
- cuttings from local native plants
- geranium plant
- notebook
- scissors
- soil, potting
- sweet potato tuber

⚫ ▣ Quick Lab *Reproduction and Diversity*

PURPOSE **To compare the effects of sexual and asexual reproduction on genetic diversity**

See the Lab Manual or go Online for planning information.

⚫ ▣ Quick Lab *Create a Classification System*

PURPOSE **To create systems to classify organisms by their reproductive processes**

See the Lab Manual or go Online for planning information.

Activities and Discussion

- ☐ **Probing Question** How Do Plants Reproduce?
- ☐ **Activity** Ways Organisms Reproduce
- ☐ **Activity** Growing Plants
- ☐ **Activity** Class Plant Display

Labs and Demos

- ☐ **Daily Demo** Budding Yeast
- ☐ **Quick Lab** Egg vs. Sperm
- ☐ **Field Lab** Investigating Asexual Reproduction
- ☐ **Quick Lab** Reproduction & Diversity
- ☐ **Quick Lab** Create a Classification System

Your Resources

_____

_____

_____

Explain Science Concepts

	📖 **Print Path**	🖥 **Digital Path**
Key Topics		
Asexual Reproduction	☐ **One Becomes Two,** SE pp. 114–115 • Active Reading, #5 • Think Outside the Book, #6 • Visualize It!, #7 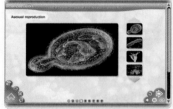	☐ **Asexual Reproduction** Learn about the function and process of asexual reproduction.
Sexual Reproduction	☐ **Two Make One,** SE p. 116 • Active Reading, #8 • Compare, #9 	☐ **Sexual Reproduction** Learn about the function and process of sexual reproduction.
Comparing Sexual and Asexual Reproduction	☐ **Added Advantage,** SE pp. 118–119 • Compare, #13 • List, #14 • Explain, #15 • Compare #16 🌐 *Optional Online support: Venn Diagram* 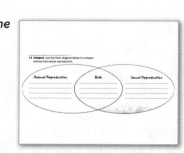	☐ **Sexual vs. Asexual Reproduction** Compare and contrast sexual and asexual reproduction. 

Differentiated Instruction

Basic *Concept Map*

Asexual Reproduction

 individuals

🕐 10 min

Help students organize the information on asexual reproduction by using a Concept Map. Let them write the words *Asexual Reproduction* in the center oval. In smaller ovals around the center oval, have them add *binary fission, budding, spores*, and *vegetative reproduction*. Around each of these ovals, have students add important details, such as examples of organisms that reproduce in each way.

Advanced *Writing an Essay*

Sexual Reproduction

 individuals

🕐 ongoing

Have students research a species that shows low genetic diversity, such as the Florida panther or the cheetah. Have them write an essay discussing how the species got into this situation, what threats the low genetic diversity presents, and what, if anything, might be done about it.

ELL *Fertilization Diagram*

Sexual Reproduction

 pairs

🕐 20 min

Have pairs of students work together to draw a diagram that shows the human fertilization process. Encourage students to label their diagrams with these terms: *sperm cell, egg cell, fertilization, 23 chromosomes, 46 chromosomes, zygote.*

ELL *Vocabulary*

Asexual Reproduction

 individuals or pairs

🕐 10 min

Have students write these words on index cards or in their journal: *binary fission, budding, spores, vegetative reproduction.* Underneath each term, have students write a definition using their own words. On the back of each card or below the journal entry, have students draw an illustration or diagram that helps them remember and understand each term.

Lesson Vocabulary

sexual reproduction   **asexual reproduction**   **fertilization**

Previewing Vocabulary

 whole class

🕐 10 min

Word Parts Write the vocabulary term *asexual reproduction* on the board. Explain to students that this kind of reproduction occurs when a parent cell divides to produce offspring exactly like the parent. Circle the prefix *a-* in *asexual* and explain that it means "not" —therefore, *asexual reproduction* means *not-sexual reproduction*. Ask students the meanings of other words with this prefix, such as *atypical* and *asocial*.

Reinforcing Vocabulary

 individuals

🕐 ongoing

Description Wheel To help students remember the vocabulary and any other terms they find difficult in this lesson, have them write the term in the center of a Description Wheel diagram. On the wheel's spokes, have students write words describing the term, such as a definition and examples. Encourage students to use as many spokes as they can to describe each term.

Customize Your Core Lesson

Core Instruction
- ☐ Print Path
- ☐ Digital Path

Vocabulary
- ☐ Previewing Vocabulary Word Parts
- ☐ Reinforcing Vocabulary Description Wheel

Your Resources

Differentiated Instruction
- ☐ **Basic** Concept Map
- ☐ **Advanced** Writing an Essay
- ☐ **ELL** Fertilization Diagram
- ☐ **ELL** Vocabulary

Extend Science Concepts

Reinforce and Review

Activity *Asexual Reproduction Game*

Asexual Reproduction   whole class   15 min

Four Corners Label each corner of the classroom either *binary fission*, *budding*, *spore formation*, or *vegetative reproduction*. Read the following descriptions to students. After each one, ask students to stand in the corner that names the type of asexual reproduction you just described. Give each student in the correct corner a point. You can continue the game with additional examples that are provided by student volunteers.

1 Prokaryotes reproduce by splitting in two. binary fission

2 Spider plants can reproduce by the division of cells from roots or runners. vegetative reproduction

3 A multicellular hydra forms a new, smaller hydra on its side that is an identical copy of its parent. The new hydra separates from the parent and becomes independent. budding

4 A mushroom produces specialized cells that survive harsh conditions. The specialized cells then develop into multicellular organisms. spore formation

5 A branch on a rhododendron plant becomes buried in leaf litter and eventually grows roots. vegetative reproduction

6 Blue-green algae split in two. binary fission

7 Moss releases specialized cells that can be carried by the wind. The specialized cells later develop into more moss when they land somewhere favorable. spore formation

8 A farmer grafts branches from one apple tree onto another apple tree. vegetative reproduction

Graphic Organizer

Comparing Sexual and Asexual Reproduction   individuals   15 min

Two-Panel Flip Chart After students have studied the lesson, have them make a Two-Panel Flip Chart to compare characteristics of sexual and asexual reproduction.

Going Further

Technology Connection

Asexual Reproduction   individuals   varied

Make a Plant Documentary Have students use a video camera to record images of different kinds of plants. Students should edit the video and add narration describing how each type of plant reproduces.

Social Studies Connection

Synthesizing Key Topics   pairs, or small groups   varied

Have students find out more about Luther Burbank or George Washington Carver. Invite them to prepare an oral or PowerPoint presentation to share what they learned about the work of these plant scientists and their impact on American agriculture.

Customize Your Closing

 See the Assessment Guide for quizzes and tests.

Go Online to edit and create quizzes and tests.

Reinforce and Review

☐ **Activity** Asexual Reproduction Game

☐ **Graphic Organizer** Two-Panel Flip Chart

☐ **Print Path** Visual Summary, SE p. 120

☐ **Digital Path** Lesson Closer

Evaluate Student Mastery

See the teacher support below the Student Pages for additional Formative Assessment questions.

Have students describe in their own words what happens during fertilization. **Ask:** What happens during fertilization? Sample answer: A sperm and an egg join together to form a zygote with a full set of chromosomes. The offspring has characteristics of each parent but is identical to neither. **Ask:** Describe one way in which organisms reproduce asexually. Sample answer: A cell divides in two, producing two new cells that are identical to the parent cell.

Reteach

Formative assessment may show that students need reinforcement for certain topics. The resources below are recommended for reteaching. If students were introduced to a topic through the Print Path, you can also use the Digital Path to reteach, and vice versa.
🎧 *Can be assigned to individual students*

Asexual Reproduction
Activity Growing Plants 🎧
Daily Demo Budding Yeast 🎧

Sexual Reproduction
ELL Fertilization Diagram 🎧

Comparing Asexual and Sexual Reproduction
Quick Lab Reproduction and Diversity

Alternative Assessment
Reproduction

⊘ *Online resources: student worksheet, optional rubrics*

Sexual and Asexual Reproduction

Tic-Tac-Toe: *Reproduction*

1. Work on your own, with a partner, or with a small group.
2. Choose three quick activities from the game. Check the boxes you plan to complete. They must form a straight line in any direction.
3. Have your teacher approve your plan.
4. Do each activity, and turn in your results.

__ **Plant Detective**	__ **Parent Clone**	__ **Sporific!**
Suppose you find a strange plant. How does it reproduce? Write the steps you would take to figure out whether the plant reproduces sexually or asexually.	Write a journal entry for a plant that is exactly the same as its parent. Describe the advantages of being genetically identical to your parent.	Make an illustration that shows the life cycle of a plant that produces spores. In which stage can the plant best survive harsh conditions?
__ **Diagram It!**	__ **What're the Advantages?**	__ **News Flash!**
Draw a diagram that shows how organisms reproduce by mitosis.	Make a chart showing the advantages to each kind of reproduction. Which kind allows cells to reproduce quickly and efficiently? Which promotes genetic diversity?	Imagine that a giant plant has been discovered that reproduces by budding. The buds are growing. You are a reporter. Report on what happens next.
__ **Plan a Garden**	__ **Switching Roles**	__ **Explain It!**
Design and sketch a garden. In the garden, grow some plants that reproduce sexually and some that reproduce asexually. Describe the conditions in which each type of plant will best succeed.	You notice that one of your plants usually grows new roots, but under certain conditions, it blooms. Explain why the plant may be changing types of reproduction.	Draw an explanation of fertilization for a person who is learning English. Add labels to your drawing.

Going Further
- ☐ Technology Connection
- ☐ Social Studies Connection
- ☐ Print Path Why It Matters, SE p. 117

Formative Assessment
- ☐ Strategies Throughout TE
- ☐ Lesson Review SE

Summative Assessment
- ☐ Alternative Assessment Reproduction
- ☐ Lesson Quiz
- ☐ Unit Tests A and B
- ☐ Unit Review SE End-of-Unit

Your Resources

_____

_____

Answers

Answers for 1–3 should represent students' current thoughts, even if incorrect.

1. F; T; T; F

2. Sample answer: The young wolf has a nose, two ears, two eyes, and four legs like its mother. It also has fur, but the fur is a different color.

3. Sample answer: Reproduction is the process by which organisms make offspring.

4. Students should define or sketch each vocabulary term in the lesson.

Opening Your Lesson

Discuss students' answers to #1 to assess their understanding of sexual and asexual reproduction. Explain that in sexual reproduction, organisms get half their genetic material from one parent and half from the other parent. In asexual reproduction, one parent produces offspring that are genetically identical to the parent.

Prerequisites: Students should already understand what happens during mitosis and meiosis.

Learning Alert

Difficult Concept Students may need to be reminded that an organism that reproduces by sexual reproduction gets half of its genetic material from one parent and half from the other parent. Even if an offspring looks more like one parent than the other, students should remember that many genes do not contribute to an organism's appearance, and so the offspring still gets half of its genetic material from each parent. Students may also be surprised to learn that not all types of reproduction require two parents.

One Becomes Two

What is asexual reproduction?

An individual organism does not live forever. The survival of any species depends on the ability to reproduce. Reproduction lets genetic information be passed on to new organisms. Reproduction involves various kinds of cell division.

Most single-celled organisms and some multicellular organisms reproduce asexually. In **asexual reproduction** (ay•SEHK•shoo•uhl ree•pruh•DUHK•shuhn), one organism produces one or more new organisms that are identical to itself. These organisms live independently of the original organism. The organism that produces the new organism or organisms is called a *parent*. Each new organism is called an *offspring*. The parent passes on all of its genetic information to the offspring. So, the offspring produced by asexual reproduction are genetically identical to their parents. They may differ only if a genetic mutation happens.

Active Reading

5 Relate Describe the genetic makeup of the offspring of asexual reproduction.

Dandelions usually reproduce asexually. The dandelions in this field may all be genetically identical!

Think Outside the Book Inquiry

6 Summarize Research five organisms that reproduce asexually. Make informative flash cards that describe how each organism reproduces asexually. When you have finished, trade flashcards with a classmate to learn about five more organisms.

114

How do organisms reproduce asexually?

Organisms reproduce asexually in many ways. In prokaryotes, which include bacteria and archaea, asexual reproduction happens by cell division. In eukaryotes, which include single-celled and multicellular organisms, asexual reproduction is a more involved process. It often involves a type of cell division called *mitosis* (my•TOH•sis). Mitosis produces genetically identical cells.

Binary Fission

Binary fission (BY•nuh•ree FISH•uhn) is the form of asexual reproduction in prokaryotes. It is a type of cell division. During binary fission, the parent organism splits in two, producing two new cells. Genetically, the new cells are exactly like the parent cell.

Budding

During *budding*, an organism develops tiny buds on its body. A bud grows until it forms a new full-sized organism that is genetically identical to the parent. Budding is the result of mitosis. Eukaryotes such as single-celled yeasts and multicellular hydras reproduce by budding.

Spores

A *spore* is a specialized cell that can survive harsh conditions. Both prokaryotes and eukaryotes can form spores. Spores are produced asexually by one parent. Spores are light and can be carried by the wind. In the right conditions, a spore develops into an organism, such as a fungus.

Vegetative Reproduction

Some plants are able to reproduce asexually by *vegetative reproduction*. Mitosis makes vegetative reproduction possible. New plants may grow from stems, roots, or leaves. Runners are aboveground stems from which a new plant can grow. Tubers are underground stems from which new plants can grow. Plantlets are tiny plants that grow along the edges of a plant's leaves. They drop off the plant and grow on their own.

Visualize It!

7 Infer Pick one of the pictures below. Describe how the type of asexual reproduction can help the organism reproduce quickly.

Bacteria reproduce by binary fission.

Hydras reproduce by budding.

Spores can survive long periods of time in harsh conditions.

New potato plants can grow from tubers.

115

Answers

5. Sample answer: The offspring of asexual reproduction are genetically identical to the parent.

6. Students' annotations will vary. Students should accurately present the ways by which five different organisms reproduce asexually.

7. Sample answer: In binary fission, the organism splits in two. The resulting cells can each split in two and so forth until there are many new organisms.

Probing Questions

Analyze How can mitosis accomplish reproduction? Sample answer: If mitosis results in two new organisms, there has been asexual reproduction. **Ask:** What is the difference between mitosis that causes organisms to grow and mitosis that creates new organisms? Sample answer: When a cell divides during mitosis, two cells are produced that are identical to the parent. If an organism is single celled, for example, it makes a complete new organism when the cell is copied.

Learning Alert ⚡ MISCONCEPTION ⚡

How Plants Reproduce Some students may hold the misconception that plants can only reproduce asexually. They may not understand that pollination is a form of sexual reproduction. Find out if students hold this misconception. **Ask:** Can plants reproduce only asexually? If students answer yes, explain that pollen is a male sex cell with half the plant's genetic information. **Ask:** If pollen has half the plant's genetic material, where is the other half of the plant's genetic material? Sample answer: in the plant's female sex cells Explain that a sperm cell from a pollen grain combines with an egg cell to form a zygote. The new zygote is diploid because it was formed by the union of a haploid sperm cell with a haploid egg cell.

Two Make One

What is sexual reproduction?

Most multicellular organisms can reproduce sexually. In **sexual reproduction** (SEHK•shoo•uhl ree•pruh•DUHK•shuhn), two parents each contribute a sex cell to the new organism. Half the genes in the offspring come from each parent. So, the offspring are not identical to either parent. Instead, they have a combination of traits from each parent.

Active Reading

8 Identify As you read, underline the male and female sex cells.

Fertilization

Usually, one parent is male and the other is female. Males produce sex cells called *sperm cells*. Females produce sex cells called *eggs*. Sex cells are produced by a type of cell division called *meiosis* (my•OH•sis). Sex cells have only half of the full set of genetic material found in body cells.

A sperm cell and an egg join together in a process called **fertilization** (fer•tl•i•ZAY•shuhn). When an egg is fertilized by a sperm cell, a new cell is formed. This cell is called a *zygote* (ZY•goht). It has a full set of genetic material. The zygote develops into a new organism. The zygote divides by mitosis, which increases the number of cells. This increase in cells produces growth. You are the size that you are today because of mitosis.

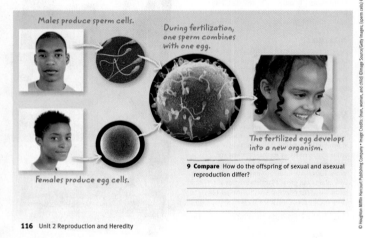

Males produce sperm cells.

During fertilization, one sperm combines with one egg.

The fertilized egg develops into a new organism.

Females produce egg cells.

9 Compare How do the offspring of sexual and asexual reproduction differ?

116 Unit 2 Reproduction and Heredity

Why It Matters

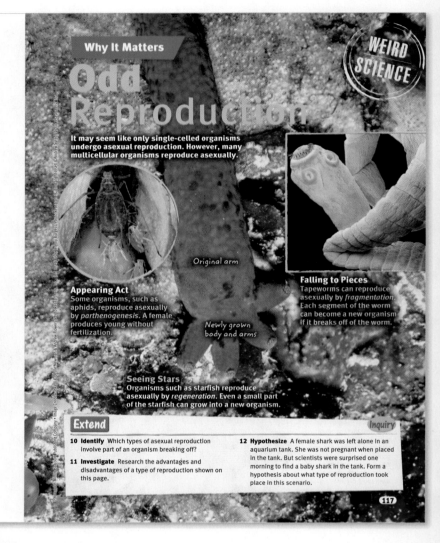

WEIRD SCIENCE

Odd Reproduction

It may seem like only single-celled organisms undergo asexual reproduction. However, many multicellular organisms reproduce asexually.

Appearing Act
Some organisms, such as aphids, reproduce asexually by *parthenogenesis*. A female produces young without fertilization.

Original arm

Newly grown body and arms

Falling to Pieces
Tapeworms can reproduce asexually by *fragmentation*. Each segment of the worm can become a new organism if it breaks off of the worm.

Seeing Stars
Organisms such as starfish reproduce asexually by *regeneration*. Even a small part of the starfish can grow into a new organism.

Extend   Inquiry

10 Identify Which types of asexual reproduction involve part of an organism breaking off?

11 Investigate Research the advantages and disadvantages of a type of reproduction shown on this page.

12 Hypothesize A female shark was left alone in an aquarium tank. She was not pregnant when placed in the tank. But scientists were surprised one morning to find a baby shark in the tank. Form a hypothesis about what type of reproduction took place in this scenario.

117

Answers

8. *See student pages for annotations.*

9. Sample answer: The offspring of asexual reproduction have one parent, and they are identical to the parent. The offspring of sexual reproduction have two parents, and they are not identical to either parent.

10. regeneration and fragmentation

11. Students' annotations will vary. Students should identify advantages such as quick reproduction and the fact that a parent does not need to find a partner. They may cite a disadvantage such as lack of genetic diversity.

12. Sample answer: The female shark reproduced asexually by parthenogenesis.

Probing Questions

Interpret In what way is meiosis important in sexual reproduction? Sample answer: Meiosis results in the production of sex cells that have half the number of chromosomes of body cells. When a male and female sex cell join, they form a diploid zygote that can grow into a new organism.

Why It Matters

Have students look at each example of asexual reproduction. **Ask:** What are some of the advantages of each type of reproduction shown? Sample answers: In parthenogenesis, a female animal does not use energy to find a mate. In regeneration and fragmentation, an injured animal doesn't die but rather regrows. **Ask:** In the past, people tried to stop the spread of starfish by chopping them up and throwing them back into the sea. What do you think was the result? Sample answer: This action led to more starfish, not fewer, because the pieces regenerated into new, complete organisms.

Added Advantage

What are the advantages of each type of reproduction?

Organisms reproduce asexually, sexually, or both. Each type of reproduction has advantages. For example, sexual reproduction involves complex structures, such as flowers and other organs. These are not needed for asexual reproduction. But the offspring of sexual reproduction may be more likely to survive in certain situations. Read on to find out more about the advantages of each.

13 Compare Use the Venn diagram below to compare asexual and sexual reproduction.

Asexual Reproduction   Both   Sexual Reproduction

Advantages of Asexual Reproduction

Asexual reproduction has many advantages. First, an organism can reproduce very quickly. Offspring are identical to the parent. So, it also ensures that any favorable traits the parent has are passed on to offspring. Also, a parent organism does not need to find a partner to reproduce. Finally, all offspring—not just females—are able to produce more offspring.

14 List Identify four advantages of asexual reproduction.

Cholla cactuses reproduce asexually by vegetative reproduction. They drop off small pieces that grow into new plants.

Cats reproduce sexually. Offspring are similar to, but not exactly like, their parents.

Advantages of Sexual Reproduction

Sexual reproduction is not as quick as asexual reproduction. Nor does it produce as many offspring. However, it has advantages. First, it increases genetic variation. Offspring have different traits that improve the chance that at least some offspring will survive. This is especially true if the environment changes. Offspring are not genetically identical to the parents. So, they may have a trait that the parents do not have, making them more likely to survive.

15 Explain How can increased genetic variation help some offspring survive?

Advantages of Using Both Types of Reproduction

Some organisms can use both types of reproduction. For example, when conditions are favorable, many plants and fungi will reproduce asexually. Doing so lets them spread quickly and take over an area. When the environment changes, these organisms will switch to sexual reproduction. This strategy increases the chance that the species will survive. Because of genetic variation, at least some of the offspring may have traits that help them make it through the environmental change.

16 Compare In the table below, place a check mark in the cells that describe a characteristic of asexual or sexual reproduction.

	Quick	Increases chance of survival in changing environments	Produces genetic variation	Doesn't need a partner	Requires complex structures
Asexual reproduction					
Sexual reproduction					

© Houghton Mifflin Harcourt Publishing Company • Image Credits: ©Petra Wegner/Alamy

---

Answers

13. Sample answer: Asexual reproduction: one parent, offspring are identical to parent, involves cell division such as mitosis; Both: produces offspring; Sexual reproduction: two parents, involves fertilization, meiosis produces sex cells

14. Asexual reproduction is quick, ensures offspring inherit favorable traits from the parent, doesn't require a partner, and all offspring can reproduce.

15. Offspring may have a trait the parents lack that may make offspring more likely to survive if the environment changes.

16. Check marks in Row 1 under Quick and Doesn't need a partner; in Row 2, under Increases chance of survival, Produces genetic variation, and Requires complex structures.

Formative Assessment

Ask: What are the advantages to some organisms of reproducing asexually? Sample answers: These organisms can produce large populations quickly; only one individual is needed to continue a species. **Ask:** What are the advantages to an organism of reproducing sexually? Sample answer: More genetic diversity is created, which can help survival if conditions change. **Ask:** What are the advantages to an organism of reproducing either sexually or asexually, depending on environmental conditions? Sample answer: Organisms can reproduce rapidly asexually, but when conditions change, they can reproduce sexually to ensure genetic diversity, which is helpful to survival when the environment changes.

Interpreting Visuals

Analyze Have students look at the photos on these pages. **Ask:** For the cactus, what are the possible advantages of asexual reproduction? Sample answer: When conditions in the desert are favorable, the cactus can produce many offspring. **Ask:** What advantages might sexual reproduction hold for the cat? Sample answer: There is more genetic diversity among the offspring, so if environmental conditions change, there is a greater likelihood that at least some of the offspring will survive.

Visual Summary

To complete this summary, circle the correct word that completes each statement. Then use the key below to check your answers. You can use this page to review the main concepts of the lesson.

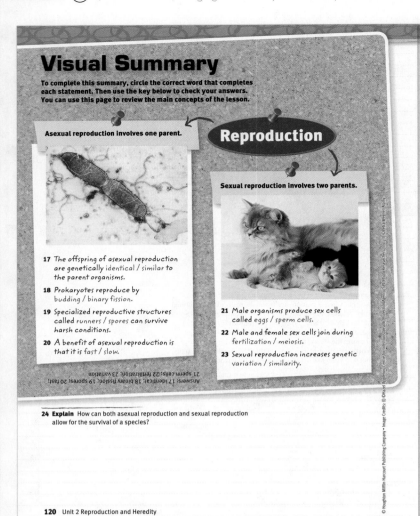

Asexual reproduction involves one parent.

Reproduction

Sexual reproduction involves two parents.

17 The offspring of asexual reproduction are genetically **identical / similar** to the parent organisms.

18 Prokaryotes reproduce by **budding / binary fission.**

19 Specialized reproductive structures called **runners / spores** can survive harsh conditions.

20 A benefit of asexual reproduction is that it is **fast / slow.**

21 Male organisms produce sex cells called **eggs / sperm cells.**

22 Male and female sex cells join during **fertilization / meiosis.**

23 Sexual reproduction increases genetic **variation / similarity.**

Answers: 17 identical; 18 binary fission; 19 spores; 20 fast; 21 sperm cells; 22 fertilization; 23 variation

24 Explain How can both asexual reproduction and sexual reproduction allow for the survival of a species?

Lesson Review

Lesson ③

Vocabulary

Fill in the blanks with the term that best completes the following sentences.

1 After _____ , the zygote develops into a larger organism.

2 An advantage of _____ reproduction is the ability to reproduce quickly.

3 The offspring of _____ reproduction are more likely to survive changes in the environment.

Key Concepts

4 Identify What are some advantages of asexual and sexual reproduction?

5 Compare In sexual reproduction, how do the offspring compare to the parents?

6 Identify List four types of asexual reproduction.

7 Explain Why do some organisms use both types of reproduction?

Critical Thinking

Use the graph to answer the following questions.

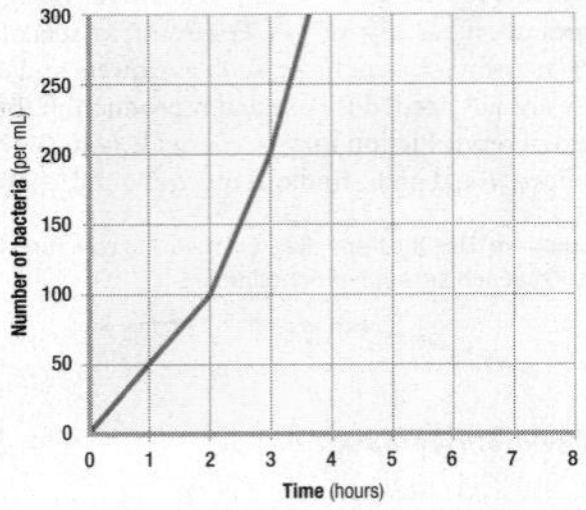

Growth of a Bacterial Population Over Time

(graph: y-axis "Number of bacteria (per mL)" 0–300; x-axis "Time (hours)" 0–8)

8 Infer What type of reproduction is most likely taking place?

9 Analyze Which advantage of reproduction does the graph show? Explain.

10 Predict How might the graph change if the environmental conditions of the bacteria suddenly change? Explain.

Visual Summary Answers

17. identical

18. binary fission

19. spores

20. fast

21. sperm cells

22. fertilization

23. variation

24. Sample answer: Both asexual reproduction and sexual reproduction produce offspring, which are necessary for the survival of a species.

Lesson Review Answers

1. fertilization

2. asexual

3. sexual

4. Sample answer: Asexual reproduction is quick, produces a large number of offspring, ensures favorable traits are passed on, and all offspring can reproduce. Sexual reproduction increases genetic variation.

5. Sample answer: Offspring are genetically different from the parents.

6. binary fission, budding, spores, and vegetative reproduction

7. Sample answer: When conditions are favorable, some organisms reproduce asexually to spread quickly. When conditions are unfavorable, they reproduce sexually to increase genetic variation. This ensures that some of the offspring are more likely to survive.

8. asexual reproduction

9. Sample answer: The graph shows quick reproduction. In 3.5 hours, the population has increased from 1 bacterium to about 275 bacteria.

10. Sample answer: The line will likely fall. All of the bacteria are genetically identical unless a mutation takes place. If they don't have the trait that ensures survival, the population will decrease.

Heredity

Essential Question How are traits inherited?

For more detailed information about the topics in this lesson, refer to the Content Refresher in the Unit Opener pages.

Opening Your Lesson

Begin the lesson by assessing students' prerequisite and prior knowledge.

Prerequisite Knowledge

- Meiosis
- Mitosis

Accessing Prior Knowledge

Write the vocabulary words on the board. Have students copy the words and write as much as they know about each term. Explain that students will learn about each of these terms in the lesson. Revisit student lists at the end of the lesson. Have students add additional information to their lists.

Customize Your Opening

- ☐ **Accessing Prior Knowledge,** above
- ☐ **Print Path** Engage Your Brain, SE p. 123, #1–2
- ☐ **Print Path** Active Reading, SE p. 123, #3–4
- ☐ **Digital Path** Lesson Opener

Key Topics/Learning Goals	Supporting Concepts
Mendel's Work **1** Summarize Mendel's findings. **2** Explain how dominant and recessive traits differ.	• Gregor Mendel crossed pea plants that had certain traits. • Mendel observed that some traits were always present from one generation to the next; he called these dominant traits. • Other traits seemed to disappear between generations; he called these recessive traits. • Mendel's theory explains the pattern of inheritance called complete dominance.
DNA's Role in Inheritance **1** Describe DNA's role in determining traits. **2** Identify the relationship between genes and alleles. **3** Identify the relationship between genotype and phenotype.	• Every organism has a set of instructions (DNA) that determines its traits. • A gene is an instruction for a characteristic. • An allele is one of the alternative forms of a gene that governs a trait. • A genotype is the alleles inherited; a phenotype is the observable traits that result.
Genes, Traits, and Characteristics **1** Describe the relationship among genes, traits, and characteristics. **2** Discuss complete and incomplete dominance and codominance. **3** Distinguish between inherited and acquired characteristics. **4** Provide examples of environmental factors that may affect phenotype.	• One gene can be responsible for many different characteristics, and many genes may contribute to a single characteristic. • In complete dominance, only the dominant allele contributes to the phenotype of the heterozygous individual, but in incomplete dominance and codominance, both alleles contribute to the phenotype of an individual. • While many characteristics are inherited through DNA, some characteristics are acquired or learned. • Environmental factors can affect the phenotype of some characteristics.

Options for Instruction

Two parallel paths provide coverage of the Essential Questions, with a strong **Inquiry** strand woven into each.
Follow the **Print Path,** the **Digital Path,** or your customized combination of print, digital, and inquiry.

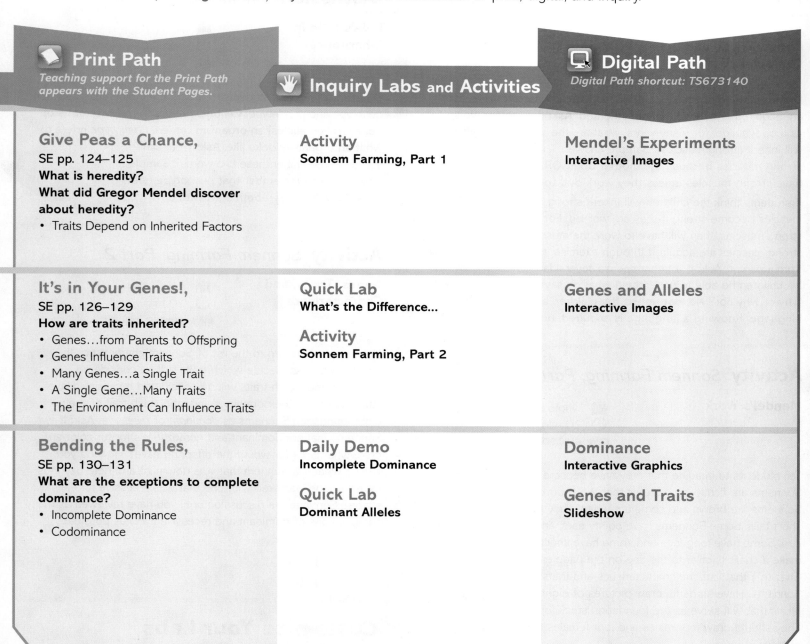

Print Path	Inquiry Labs and Activities	Digital Path
Teaching support for the Print Path appears with the Student Pages.		Digital Path shortcut: TS673140
Give Peas a Chance, SE pp. 124–125 **What is heredity? What did Gregor Mendel discover about heredity?** • Traits Depend on Inherited Factors	**Activity** **Sonnem Farming, Part 1**	**Mendel's Experiments** **Interactive Images**
It's in Your Genes!, SE pp. 126–129 **How are traits inherited?** • Genes…from Parents to Offspring • Genes Influence Traits • Many Genes…a Single Trait • A Single Gene…Many Traits • The Environment Can Influence Traits	**Quick Lab** **What's the Difference...** **Activity** **Sonnem Farming, Part 2**	**Genes and Alleles** **Interactive Images**
Bending the Rules, SE pp. 130–131 **What are the exceptions to complete dominance?** • Incomplete Dominance • Codominance	**Daily Demo** **Incomplete Dominance** **Quick Lab** **Dominant Alleles**	**Dominance** **Interactive Graphics** **Genes and Traits** **Slideshow**

Options for Assessment

See the Evaluate page for options, including Formative Assessment, Summative Assessment, and Unit Review.

Engage and Explore

Activities and Discussion

Probing Question *What's Your Inheritance?*

Engage

Genes, Traits, and Characteristics

 whole class
 15 min
 GUIDED inquiry

Distinguishing Invite students to think about characteristics that are acquired and those that are inherited. **Ask:** If a mother works out as a bodybuilder for many years, what are the chances her offspring will inherit strong muscles? Sample answer: The children will have strong muscles because the mother does. OR, The children won't have strong muscles unless they work out, too.

If students think the children will inherit strong muscles, explain that muscles become strong if they are worked. For the children to get strong muscles, they will have to work the muscles, too. Explain that strong muscles are acquired through exercise; they are not inherited from a parent. **Ask:** If a father speaks several languages fluently, will his children be able to understand what he says in each language? Why or why not? No, not unless the children already know each language. Knowing a language is acquired, not inherited.

Activity *Sonnem Farming, Part 1*

Mendel's Work

 whole class
 20 min
 GUIDED inquiry

Tell students to imagine that they have become Sonnem farmers. Sonnems are fictitious creatures that are about the size of cats. Some Sonnems are brown and some are white. They may have long tails or short tails. Some Sonnems have pointy ears, and some have ears that curl. Some have long legs and some have short legs. Have students make a chart (similar to the one on the page entitled "Give Peas a Chance") that lists the characteristics and traits found among the Sonnems. Have students draw pictures of eight Sonnems on their farms that will serve as the foundation stock for the next generation. They should draw four males and four females that display a variety of traits.

Discussion *Mnemonic*

DNA's Role in Inheritance

 whole class
 10 min
 GUIDED inquiry

Differentiating Ask students to describe the difference between genotype and phenotype. *Genotype* refers to the two forms of genes (called alleles) an organism carries. *Phenotype* refers to what an organism looks like. **Ask:** What can you do to remember these two words? Sample answers: I can remember that *phenotype* refers to *physical* features—both start with *ph*.

Activity *Sonnem Farming, Part 2*

Genes, Traits, and Characteristics

 whole class
🕐 20 min
GUIDED inquiry

Have students return to the list of Sonnem charactistics they made. As a class, decide which traits will be considered dominant and which traits will be considered recessive. Have students review their drawings and label each trait of their eight foundation Sonnems as *dominant* or *recessive*. **Ask:** If two Sonnems that are dominant and homozygous for fur color are bred, what color fur would the offspring have? How do you know? What if a Sonnem that was dominant and heterozygous for ear shape was bred with one that was recessive for ear shape? Continue the discussion until you have reviewed as many combinations of dominant and recessive traits as possible.

Customize Your Labs

 See the Lab Manual for lab datasheets.

 Go Online for editable lab datasheets.

Levels of

DIRECTED inquiry
introduces inquiry skills within a structured framework.

GUIDED inquiry
develops inquiry skills within a supportive environment.

INDEPENDENT inquiry
deepens inquiry skills with student-driven questions or procedures.

Labs and Demos

Daily Demo *Incomplete Dominance*

 Engage

Genes, Traits, and Characteristics

👥 whole class
🕐 10 min
Inquiry **GUIDED** inquiry

PURPOSE **To show how two alleles can exert influence in incomplete dominance**

MATERIALS

- beaker, half full of water colored with blue food coloring
- beaker, half full of water colored with yellow food coloring

Explain that each beaker represents an allele for a color gene. Have students predict what will happen if you mix the yellow water with the blue water.

Pour the blue water into the yellow water. Discuss what happened. Lead students to understand that when one trait is not completely dominant over another, each allele has some influence. In this case, the water is neither blue nor yellow, but halfway in between.

Ask: What would have happened to the water if the blue was dominant and the yellow was recessive? The water would have been blue after the two alleles mixed.

Ask: What would have happened if the alleles both exerted influence, or were codominant? Sample answer: The water would be partly blue and partly yellow, but not halfway in between.

Quick Lab *What's the Difference Between a Dominant Trait and a Recessive Trait?*

DNA's Role in Inheritance

👥 small groups
🕐 20 min
Inquiry **DIRECTED** inquiry

PURPOSE **To study patterns of inheritance that involve dominant and recessive traits**

MATERIALS

- bag, paper lunch
- beads, 2 colors (6 of each color)
- paper
- pencil

Quick Lab *Dominant Alleles*

Genes, Traits, and Characteristics

👥 small groups
🕐 20 min
Inquiry **GUIDED** inquiry

PURPOSE **To demonstrate patterns of inheritance**

MATERIALS

- 5 index cards or pieces of card stock
- red and yellow markers
- clear plastic wrap
- white paper
- ruler
- scissors
- tape

Activities and Discussion

☐ **Probing Question** What's Your Inheritance?

☐ **Discussion** Mnemonic

☐ **Activity** Sonnem Farming, 1 and 2

Labs and Demos

☐ **Daily Demo** Incomplete Dominance

☐ **Quick Lab** What's the Difference…

☐ **Quick Lab** Dominant Alleles

Your Resources

Explain Science Concepts

	📘 **Print Path**	🖥 **Digital Path**
Key Topics		
Mendel's Work	☐ **Give Peas a Chance,** SE pp. 124–125 • Apply, #5 • Active Reading, #6 • Visualize It!, #7	☐ **Mendel's Experiments** Learn about Gregor Mendel and the observations he made during his genetic experiments.
DNA's Role in Inheritance	☐ **It's in Your Genes!,** SE pp. 126–129 • Visualize It!, #8 • Apply, #9 • Think Outside the Book, #10 • Active Reading, #11 • Visualize It!, #12 • Active Reading, #13 • Predict, #14	☐ **Genes and Alleles** Learn about genes and alleles and the relationship between them.
Genes, Traits, and Characteristics	☐ **Bending the Rules,** SE pp. 130–131 • Active Reading, #15 • Visualize It!, #16 • Think Outside the Book, #17 • Active Reading, #18 • Visualize It!, #19	☐ **Dominance** Explore the different types of dominance. ☐ **Genes and Traits** Learn about genes and traits and the relationship between them.

Basic *Inherited or Acquired?*

Genes, Traits, and Characteristics

 individuals
 10 min

Have students draw a picture of a person. The picture should show some traits that are inherited from parents and some that are not inherited. Students should label each trait *Inherited* or *Acquired*. For example, students might draw a person with black, curly hair and a big smile, running across a finish line. The hair would be labeled *Inherited,* but being happy or a fast runner would be labeled *Acquired.*

Advanced *Dominance Over Generations*

Genes, Traits, and Characteristics

 individuals
10 min

Have students make a drawing showing a cross between two imaginary creatures, such as the Sonnems from earlier activities. Have them make some characteristics dominant and recessive, incompletely dominant, or codominant. Ask them to draw what the offspring of the two imaginary creatures would look like after several generations.

ELL *Mendel Comic*

Mendel's Work

 pairs
20 min

Have pairs of students work together to create a comic book biography of Gregor Mendel. They should do their own research to uncover information not included in their books. Students may want to make a timeline first to help them remember the sequence of events in Mendel's life. Have them include diagrams that show the rules of heredity that Mendel discovered.

Lesson Vocabulary

heredity	genotype	dominant
genes	phenotype	recessive
allele	incomplete dominance	codominance

Previewing Vocabulary

 whole class
 10 min

Word Origins Write the word *genotype* on the board and circle *geno.* Explain that this word part comes from the Greek word *genos* that means "race, kind." Note that the word *gene,* which comes from the Greek *genea* meaning "generation, race" has a similar origin.

Reinforcing Vocabulary

 individuals
ongoing

Word Triangles Have students make Word Triangles for the vocabulary terms to help them remember meanings.

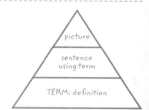

Customize Your Core Lesson

Core Instruction
- ☐ **Print Path** choices
- ☐ **Digital Path** choices

Vocabulary
- ☐ **Previewing Vocabulary** Word Origins
- ☐ **Reinforcing Vocabulary** Word Triangles

Your Resources

Differentiated Instruction
- ☐ **Basic** Inherited or Acquired?
- ☐ **Advanced** Dominance Over Generations
- ☐ **ELL** Mendel Comic

_____

_____

_____

Extend Science Concepts

Reinforce and Review

Activity *Heredity Game*

Genes, Traits, and Characteristics	whole class
	🕐 15 min

Four Corners Label each corner of the classroom either *complete dominance, incomplete dominance, codominance,* or *none of these.* Read the following patterns of heredity to students. After each one is read, ask the students to stand in the corner they think describes the pattern. Give each student in the correct corner a point. You can continue the game with additional examples that are provided by student volunteers.

1 One animal parent has black fur. The other animal parent has white fur. The offspring has black and white fur. codominance

2 One parent plant has dark blue flowers. The other parent has white flowers. The offspring has light blue flowers. incomplete dominance

3 One parent has brown eyes. The other parent has blue eyes. The offspring has brown eyes. complete dominance

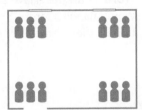

4 One parent has red hair. The other parent has brown hair. The offspring has brown hair. complete dominance

Graphic Organizer

Synthesizing Key Topics	individuals
	🕐 15 min

Combination Notes After students have studied the lesson, ask them to write Combination Notes to summarize what they learned. Have them include these terms in their notes: *heredity, dominant, recessive, gene, allele, phenotype, genotype, incomplete dominance, codominance.*

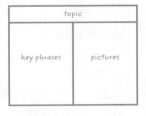

🔘 *Optional Online resource: Combination Notes support*

Going Further

Life Science Connection

Genes, Traits, and Characteristics	individuals
	🕐 ongoing

Analyze Relationships Have students find out how one or more of the following are affected by genes: human height; comb shape in chickens; or human eye color (all of which are polygenic, or affected by several genes); or the frizzle-feather trait in chickens; the link between coat color, eye color, and deafness in cats; or sickle cell anemia (all of which are pleiotropic, or involve single genes with multiple effects). Allow time for students to share their findings with the class.

Language Arts Connection

Mendel's Work	👥 individuals
	🕐 ongoing

Blog Entries Ask students to imagine that they are assistants to Gregor Mendel. As part of their work, they write the monk's daily blog entry—although neither computers nor blogs existed during Mendel's time! Have them write a blog entry that tells about one aspect of Mendel's discoveries.

Customize Your Closing

📖 *See the Assessment Guide for quizzes and tests.*

🔘 *Go Online to edit and create quizzes and tests.*

Reinforce and Review

☐ **Activity** Heredity Game

☐ **Graphic Organizer** Combination Notes

☐ **Print Path** Visual Summary, SE p. 132

☐ **Digital Path** Lesson Closer

Evaluate Student Mastery

Formative Assessment

See the teacher support below the Student Pages for additional Formative Assessment questions.

Lead students in a discussion of dominance and recessiveness. **Ask:** How are dominance and recessiveness expressed? Sample answers: A dominant trait will be expressed even if there is only one allele for the trait present. A recessive trait will only be expressed if both alleles are the same.

Reteach

Formative assessment may show that students need reinforcement for certain topics. The resources below are recommended for reteaching. If students were introduced to a topic through the Print Path, you can also use the Digital Path to reteach, or vice versa.

🎧 *Can be assigned to individual students*

Mendel's Work
Activity Sonnem Farming, Part 1 🎧
ELL Mendel Comic 🎧

DNA's Role in Inheritance
Quick Lab What's the Difference...
Basic Inherited or Acquired? 🎧

Genes, Traits, and Characteristics
Daily Demo Incomplete Dominance
Quick Lab Dominant Alleles 🎧
Activity Sonnem Farming, Part 2 🎧

Summative Assessment

Alternative Assessment
It's Hereditary

🔘 *Online resources: student worksheet, optional rubrics*

Heredity

Climb the Ladder: *It's Hereditary*
Complete the activities below to show what you know about heredity.

1. Work on your own, with a partner, or with a small group.
2. Choose one item from each rung of the ladder. Check your choices.
3. Have your teacher approve your plan.
4. Submit or present your results.

__ **Alien Eyes**	__ **DNA's Role**
Imagine that an alien mother has purple eyes, which are recessive. The alien father has red eyes, which are dominant. What color are the offspring's eyes if aliens inherit genes in the same way as humans? _____ Explain what alleles the father might have.	Make a diagram or sketch that explains DNA's role in determining human traits. Add labels and descriptions to your diagram to make the explanation clear.
__ **Dominance Differences**	__ **Dominance Differences**
Write an entry for an encyclopedia that summarizes Mendel's findings. Include diagrams or illustrations as needed.	Make a chart that explains how complete dominance, incomplete dominance, and co-dominance are alike and different.
__ **Type Casting**	__ **Genes and Traits**
Make a poster for younger people that identifies the relationship between genotype and phenotype. Include a catchy way to remember what each term means.	Write a paragraph that explains how one gene can be responsible for many traits, and how many genes can be responsible for one trait.

Going Further
- [ ] Life Science Connection
- [ ] Language Arts Connection

Formative Assessment
- [ ] Strategies Throughout TE
- [ ] Lesson Review SE

Summative Assessment
- [ ] Alternative Assessment It's Hereditary
- [ ] Lesson Quiz
- [ ] Unit Tests A and B
- [ ] Unit Review SE End-of-Unit

Your Resources

_____   _____

_____   _____

Lesson ④

Heredity

ESSENTIAL QUESTION

How are traits inherited?

By the end of this lesson, you should be able to analyze the inheritance of traits in individuals.

Members of the same family share certain traits. Can you think of some traits that family members share?

Lesson Labs

Quick Labs
• Dominant Alleles
• What's the Difference between a Dominant Trait and a Recessive Trait?

Engage Your Brain

1 Predict Check T or F to show whether you think each statement is true or false.

T F
☐ ☐ Siblings look similar because they each have some traits of their parents.
☐ ☐ Siblings always have the same hair color.
☐ ☐ Siblings have identical DNA.

2 Describe Do you know any identical twins? How are they similar? How are they different?

Active Reading

3 Infer Use context clues to write your own definition for the words *exhibit* and *investigate*.

Example sentence
A person with brown hair may also <u>exhibit</u> the trait of brown eye color.

exhibit:

Example sentence
Gregor Mendel began to <u>investigate</u> the characteristics of pea plants.

investigate:

Vocabulary Terms

• heredity   • dominant
• gene   • recessive
• allele   • incomplete
• genotype   dominance
• phenotype   • codominance

4 Identify This list contains the key terms you'll learn in this lesson. As you read, circle the definition of each term.

Answers

Answers for 1–3 should represent students' current thoughts, even if incorrect.

1. T; F; F

2. Sample answer: Yes. They look the same, but they have different personalities.

3. to show or express; to research

4. Students' annotations will vary.

Opening Your Lesson

Discuss students' answers to the caption question to assess their understanding of inherited traits. Explain that some traits are inherited from parents and some traits aren't. Explain that in this lesson they will learn what traits are inherited, as well as some genetic principles governing how traits are inherited.

Prerequisites: Students should already understand the processes of mitosis and meiosis.

Learning Alert   GUIDED Inquiry

Classifying Traits Help students to understand that an organism obtains traits from its parents (inherited traits) or through learning or through interacting with the environment (acquired traits). Make a list on the board of traits that students think are acquired and traits that students think are inherited. Have students add to the list as they read the lesson. If, after reading, they think a trait should be moved to a different category, discuss the reasons they think the trait should be reclassified.

Give Peas a Chance

What is heredity?

Imagine a puppy. The puppy has long floppy ears like his mother has, and the puppy has dark brown fur like his father has. How did the puppy get these traits? The traits are a result of information stored in the puppy's genetic material. The passing of genetic material from parents to offspring is called **heredity**.

What did Gregor Mendel discover about heredity?

The first major experiments investigating heredity were performed by a monk named Gregor Mendel. Mendel lived in Austria in the 1800s. Before Mendel became a monk, he attended a university and studied science and mathematics. This training served him well when he began to study the inheritance of traits among the pea plants in the monastery's garden. Mendel studied seven different characteristics of pea plants: plant height, flower and pod position, seed shape, seed color, pod shape, pod color, and flower color. A *characteristic* is a feature that has different forms in a population. Mendel studied each pea plant characteristic separately, always starting with plants that were true-breeding for that characteristic. A true-breeding plant is one that will always produce offspring with a certain trait when allowed to self-pollinate. Each of the characteristics that Mendel studied had two different forms. For example, the color of a pea could be green or yellow. These different forms are called *traits*.

5 Apply Is flower color a characteristic or a trait?

Characteristics of Pea Plants

Characteristic	Traits
Seed color	
Seed shape	
Pod color	
Flower position	

Traits Depend on Inherited Factors

In his experiments with seed pod color, Mendel took two sets of plants, one true-breeding for plants that produce yellow seed pods and the other true-breeding for plants that produce green seed pods. Instead of letting the plants self-pollinate as they do naturally, he paired one plant from each set. He did this by fertilizing one plant with the pollen of another plant. Mendel called the plants that resulted from this cross the first generation. All of the plants from this first generation produced green seed pods. Mendel called this trait the *dominant* trait. Because the yellow trait seemed to recede, or fade away, he called it the *recessive* trait.

Then Mendel let the first-generation plants self-pollinate. He called the offspring that resulted from this self-pollination the second generation. About three-fourths of the second-generation plants had green seed pods, but about one-fourth had yellow pods. So the trait that seemed to disappear in the first generation reappeared in the second generation. Mendel hypothesized that each plant must have two heritable "factors" for each trait, one from each parent. Some traits, such as yellow seed pod color, could only be observed if a plant received two factors—one from each parent—for yellow pod color. A plant with one yellow factor and one green factor would produce green pods because producing green pods is a dominant trait. However, this plant could still pass on the yellow factor to the next generation of plants.

6 Identify As you read, underline Mendel's hypothesis about how traits are passed from parents to offspring.

Visualize It!

7 Apply Which pod color is recessive?

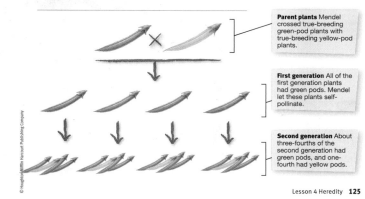

Parent plants Mendel crossed true-breeding green-pod plants with true-breeding yellow-pod plants.

First generation All of the first generation plants had green pods. Mendel let these plants self-pollinate.

Second generation About three-fourths of the second generation had green pods, and one-fourth had yellow pods.

124 Unit 2 Reproduction and Heredity

Lesson 4 Heredity 125

Answers

5. a characteristic
6. *See students' pages for annotations.*
7. yellow

Interpreting Visuals

Have students look at the visual of the first- and second-generation pea pods and use their own words to describe what has occurred. **Ask:** What trait is dominant? green coloration **Ask:** How do you know? I know because all the pea pods in the first generation are green. **Ask:** What trait is recessive? yellow coloration **Ask:** How do you know? There are no yellow pea pods in the first generation, but in the second generation, one in four pea pods is yellow.

Probing Questions GUIDED Inquiry

Synthesizing Sketch a green seed and a yellow seed on the board. **Ask:** What will the seeds produced by the next two generations of plants look like if the two true-breeding (homozygous) plants are crossed? In the first generation, all offspring will produce green seeds; in the second generation, about one in four plants will produce yellow seeds.

It's in your genes!

Genes are made up of DNA.

How are traits inherited?

Mendel's experiments and conclusions have been the basis for much of the scientific thought about heredity. His ideas can be further explained by our modern understanding of the genetic material DNA. What Mendel called "factors" are actually segments of DNA known as genes!

Genes Are Passed from Parents to Offspring

Genes are segments of DNA found in chromosomes that give instructions for producing a certain characteristic. Humans, like many other organisms, inherit their genes from their parents. Each parent gives one set of genes to the offspring. The offspring then has two versions, or forms, of the same gene for every characteristic—one version from each parent. The different versions of a gene are known as **alleles** (uh•LEELZ). Genes are often represented by letter symbols. Dominant alleles are shown with a capital letter, and recessive alleles are shown with a lowercase version of the same letter. An organism with two dominant or two recessive alleles is said to be *homozygous* for that gene. An organism that has one dominant and one recessive allele is *heterozygous*.

Humans have 23 pairs of chromosomes.

In humans, cells contain pairs of chromosomes. One chromosome of each pair comes from each of two parents. Each chromosome contains sites where specific genes are located.

A gene occupies a specific location on both chromosomes in a pair.

Visualize It!

8 Apply Circle a gene pair for which this person is heterozygous.

Alleles are alternate forms of the same gene.

126 Unit 2 Reproduction and Heredity

9 Apply The girls in this photograph have different types of hair. Is hair type a genotype or a phenotype?

This girl has dimples.

This girl does not have dimples.

Genes Influence Traits

The alternate forms of genes, called alleles, determine the traits of all living organisms. The combination of alleles that you inherited from your parents is your **genotype** (JEEN•uh•typ). Your observable traits make up your **phenotype** (FEEN•uh•typ). The phenotypes of some traits follow patterns similar to the ones that Mendel discovered in pea plants. That is, some traits are dominant over others. For example, consider the gene responsible for producing dimples, or creases in the cheeks. This gene comes in two alleles: one for dimples and one for no dimples. If you have even one copy of the allele for dimples, you will have dimples. This happens because the allele for producing dimples is dominant. The **dominant** allele contributes to the phenotype if one or two copies are present in the genotype. The no-dimples allele is recessive. The **recessive** allele contributes to the phenotype only when two copies of it are present. If one chromosome in the pair contains a dominant allele and the other contains a recessive allele, the phenotype will be determined by the dominant allele. If you do not have dimples, it is because you inherited two no-dimples alleles—one from each parent. This characteristic shows *complete dominance*, because one trait is completely dominant over another. However, not all characteristics follow this pattern.

Active Reading

11 Identify What is the phenotype of an individual with one allele for dimples and one allele for no dimples?

_____

Think Outside the Book Inquiry

10 Imagine Write a short story about a world in which you could change your DNA and your traits. What would be the advantages? What would be the disadvantages?

127

Answers

8. Students should draw a circle around A a, c C, E e, g G, or h H.

9. a phenotype

10. Students should describe advantages and disadvantages of a world in which DNA could be changed.

11. dimples

Interpreting Visuals

Have students look at the visual that shows chromosomes, genes, and alleles. **Ask:** How are chromosomes, genes, and alleles related to each other? Alleles are a form of a gene, such as a form of a color gene that passes on brown eyes. Genes are found in chromosomes. **Ask:** How does DNA relate to chromosomes? Genes are segments of DNA in the chromosomes.

Using Annotations

Have students discuss the gene they circled that has two different alleles. **Ask:** How do you know this gene has two alleles? Sample answer: Alleles are forms of a gene, and in the illustration, these different forms are depicted by the same letter in different cases, such as capital *E* and lowercase *e*.

Many Genes Can Influence a Single Trait

Some characteristics, such as the color of your skin, hair, and eyes, are the result of several genes acting together. Different combinations of alleles can result in different shades of eye color. Because there is not always a one-to-one relationship between a trait and a gene, many traits do not have simple patterns of inheritance.

A Single Gene Can Influence Many Traits

Sometimes, one gene influences more than one trait. For example, a single gene causes the tiger shown below to have white fur. If you look closely, you will see that the tiger also has blue eyes. The gene that affects fur color also influences eye color.

Many genetic disorders in humans are linked to a single gene but affect many traits. For example, the genetic disorder sickle cell anemia occurs in individuals who have two recessive alleles for a certain gene. This gene carries instructions for producing a protein in red blood cells. When a person has sickle cell anemia alleles, the body makes a different protein. This protein causes red blood cells to be sickle or crescent shaped when oxygen levels are low. Sickle-shaped blood cells can stick in blood vessels, sometimes blocking the flow of blood. These blood cells are also more likely to damage the spleen. With fewer healthy red blood cells, the body may not be able to deliver oxygen to the body's organs. All of the traits associated with sickle cell anemia are due to a single gene.

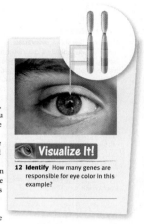

Visualize It!

12 Identify How many genes are responsible for eye color in this example?

This single gene affects the tiger's fur color and eye color.

128 Unit 2 Reproduction and Heredity

The Environment Can Influence Traits

Sometimes, the environment influences an organism's phenotype. For example, the arctic fox has a gene that is responsible for coat color. This gene is affected by light. In the winter, there are fewer hours of daylight, and the hairs that make up the arctic fox's coat grow in white. In the summer, when there are more daylight hours, the hairs in the coat grow in brown. In this case, both genes and the environment contribute to the organism's phenotype. The environment can influence human characteristics as well. For example, your genes may make it possible for you to grow to be tall, but you need a healthy diet to reach your full height potential.

Traits that are learned in one's environment are not inherited. For example, your ability to read and write is an acquired trait—a skill you learned. You were not born knowing how to ride a bike, and if you have children, they will not be born knowing how to do it either. They will have to learn the skill just as you did.

Active Reading

13 Identify Give an example of an acquired trait.

In the summer, the arctic fox has a brown coat.

In the winter, the arctic fox has a white coat.

14 Predict What advantage does white fur give the arctic fox in winter?

Lesson 4 Heredity 129

Answers

12. 2

13. Sample answer: ability to read

14. It can blend in with its environment.

Learning Alert 🍀 MISCONCEPTION 🍀

Inherited or Acquired? Students may not understand completely which traits are passed down through genes and which are acquired. They may think that acquired traits, such as muscle mass built through exercise, language, or scars, are passed on through genes. Look for signs of confusion by asking if being a good hitter in baseball is acquired or passed on through genes. Students should realize that hitters become good through practice, not because they have inherited a good hitting gene. Review further examples as needed.

Interpreting Visuals

Analyzing Information Have students look at the photos of the Arctic fox in winter and in summer. Explain that some Arctic foxes are a blue-gray year-round, but most are white in winter and brown in summer. **Ask:** What role has the environment played in the color of Arctic foxes? Sample answer: Foxes with white fur have a survival advantage in the winter, because they are harder for predators to see and catch. Over time, foxes that developed white coats in winter became more common than foxes whose fur didn't change. The environment made it more likely that more white foxes survived.

Bending the Rules

What are the exceptions to complete dominance?

The characteristics that Mendel chose to study demonstrated complete dominance, meaning that heterozygous individuals show the dominant trait. Some human traits, such as freckles and dimples, follow the pattern of complete dominance, too. However, other traits do not. For traits that show incomplete dominance or codominance, one trait is not completely dominant over another.

Incomplete Dominance

In **incomplete dominance**, each allele in a heterozygous individual influences the phenotype. The result is a phenotype that is a blend of the phenotypes of the parents. One example of incomplete dominance is found in the snapdragon flower, shown below. When a true-breeding red snapdragon is crossed with a true-breeding white snapdragon, all the offspring are pink snapdragons. Both alleles of the gene have some influence. Hair texture is an example of incomplete dominance in humans. A person with one straight-hair allele and one curly-hair allele will have wavy hair.

Active Reading
15 Identify As you read, underline examples of incomplete dominance and codominance.

Visualize It!
16 Analyze How can you tell that these snapdragons do not follow the pattern of complete dominance?

_____
_____
_____

Pink snapdragons are produced by a cross between a red snapdragon and a white snapdragon.

130

Codominance

For a trait that shows **codominance**, both of the alleles in a heterozygous individual contribute to the phenotype. Instead of having a blend of the two phenotypes, heterozygous individuals have both of the traits associated with their two alleles. An example of codominance is shown in the genes that determine human blood types. There are three alleles that play a role in determining a person's blood type: A, B, and O. The alleles are responsible for producing small particles on the surface of red blood cells called antigens. The A allele produces red blood cells coated with A antigens. The B allele produces red blood cells coated with B antigens. The O allele does not produce antigens. The A and B alleles are codominant. So, someone with one A allele and one B allele will have blood cells that are coated with A antigens and B antigens. This person would have type AB blood.

Active Reading **18 Identify** What antigens coat the red blood cells of a person with type AB blood?

_____

Think Outside the Book Inquiry
17 Research Blood type is an important factor when people give or receive blood. Research the meanings of the phrases "universal donor" and "universal recipient." What are the genotypes of each blood type?

Visualize It!
19 Predict The color of these imaginary fish is controlled by a single gene. Sketch or describe their offspring if the phenotypes follow the pattern of complete dominance, incomplete dominance, or codominance.

Complete dominance (Blue is dominant to yellow.)	Incomplete dominance	Codominance

Answers

15. *See students' pages for annotations.*

16. The offspring are neither red nor white.

17. Students should find that a universal donor has type O blood and can donate to people with any of the blood types. A universal recipient has type AB blood and can get blood from people with any of the blood types.

18. A and B

19. Students' first sketch or description should be of a solid blue fish. Their second sketch or description should be of a green fish. Their third sketch or description should be of a fish that has blue and yellow portions.

Formative Assessment

Write *complete dominance, incomplete dominance,* and *codominance* on the board. **Ask:** What are examples of each type of inheritance? Sample answers: complete dominance: Mendel's peas, which would be green if they contained a dominant green allele and a recessive allele for another color; incomplete dominance: snapdragons, which will be pink if one parent has a red allele and the other has a white allele; codominance: human blood types: if a person has an A allele and a B allele, his or her blood type will be AB.

Building Reading Skills

Combination Notes Have students use Combination Notes to help them remember the three types of dominance they have read about. Have them title their notes "Types of Dominance." On the left side of a sheet of paper, students can list the types of dominance and write a brief description of each. On the right side, they can draw a simple sketch or drawing that helps them remember each type of dominance.

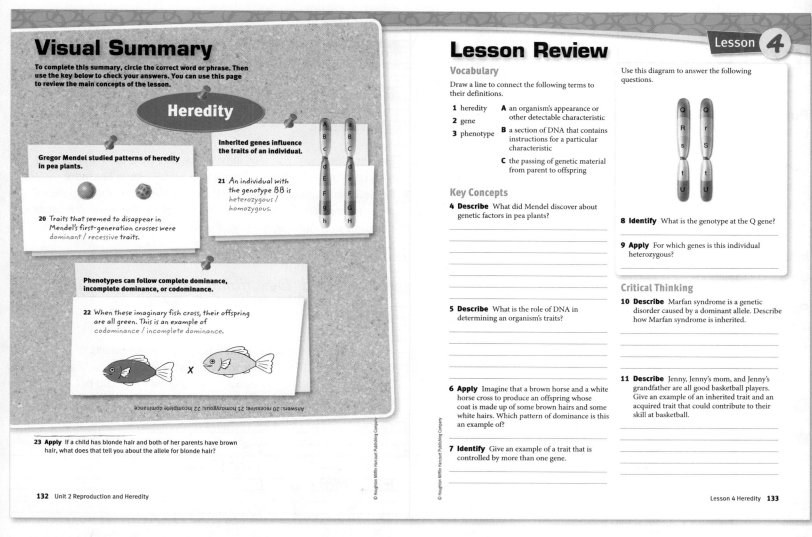

Visual Summary

To complete this summary, circle the correct word or phrase. Then use the key below to check your answers. You can use this page to review the main concepts of the lesson.

Heredity

Gregor Mendel studied patterns of heredity in pea plants.

20 Traits that seemed to disappear in Mendel's first-generation crosses were dominant / recessive traits.

Inherited genes influence the traits of an individual.

21 An individual with the genotype BB is heterozygous / homozygous.

Phenotypes can follow complete dominance, incomplete dominance, or codominance.

22 When these imaginary fish cross, their offspring are all green. This is an example of codominance / incomplete dominance.

X

Answers: 20 recessive; 21 homozygous; 22 incomplete dominance

23 **Apply** If a child has blonde hair and both of her parents have brown hair, what does that tell you about the allele for blonde hair?

132 Unit 2 Reproduction and Heredity

© Houghton Mifflin Harcourt Publishing Company

Lesson Review

Lesson 4

Vocabulary

Draw a line to connect the following terms to their definitions.

1 heredity   **A** an organism's appearance or other detectable characteristic

2 gene

3 phenotype   **B** a section of DNA that contains instructions for a particular characteristic

   C the passing of genetic material from parent to offspring

Key Concepts

4 **Describe** What did Mendel discover about genetic factors in pea plants?

5 **Describe** What is the role of DNA in determining an organism's traits?

6 **Apply** Imagine that a brown horse and a white horse cross to produce an offspring whose coat is made up of some brown hairs and some white hairs. Which pattern of dominance is this an example of?

7 **Identify** Give an example of a trait that is controlled by more than one gene.

Use this diagram to answer the following questions.

8 **Identify** What is the genotype at the Q gene?

9 **Apply** For which genes is this individual heterozygous?

Critical Thinking

10 **Describe** Marfan syndrome is a genetic disorder caused by a dominant allele. Describe how Marfan syndrome is inherited.

11 **Describe** Jenny, Jenny's mom, and Jenny's grandfather are all good basketball players. Give an example of an inherited trait and an acquired trait that could contribute to their skill at basketball.

Lesson 4 Heredity 133

© Houghton Mifflin Harcourt Publishing Company

Visual Summary Answers

20. recessive
21. homozygous
22. incomplete dominance
23. It is recessive.

Lesson Review Answers

1. C
2. B
3. A
4. Mendel discovered that for each trait, the plants got one factor from each parent. Two recessive factors resulted in a recessive trait. One or two dominant factors resulted in a dominant trait.
5. DNA is the genetic material that contains genes. Genes contain information about an organism's traits.
6. codominance
7. Sample answer: skin color
8. QQ

9. R, S
10. A person will have Marfan syndrome if he or she inherits at least one dominant allele from a parent.
11. An inherited trait that could contribute to skill at basketball is the ability to grow tall. An acquired trait that could contribute is good coordination.

Interpreting Tables

Purpose
To interpret and analyze data contained in scientific tables

Learning Goals
- Identify and analyze the features of a scientific table.
- Analyze the data in a scientific table to observe trends.
- Summarize the information contained in a scientific table.

Informal Vocabulary
trends, combinations

Prerequisite Knowledge
- Basic knowledge that traits are passed from parent to offspring
- How scientists represent data

Discussion *The Importance of Tables*

 whole class   10 min

 GUIDED inquiry

Encourage students to think about what they already know about tables. **Ask:** Why is it helpful to organize the data you collect in a table? Sample answers: It helps make the data easier to read. It can help you see patterns in the data. **Ask:** What else might you do with your data after you have organized them in a table? Sample answer: You might graph certain data in the table to highlight important information or to illustrate any patterns.

Optional Online rubric: Class Discussion

Differentiated Instruction

Basic *Clear Titles*

individuals   10 min

Help students write a clear, informative title for a table that shows the colors of the offspring from a cross of a brown Labrador Retriever and a black and white Border Collie. Then have students make up three more titles for tables that show the results of other breeding experiments, such as crosses of mice of various colors.

Advanced *Describing Data*

individuals   15 min

Have students write a paragraph to describe the results of the data shown in the table about heredity in Brittanies. Then encourage them to think about what information could be discovered from additional crosses between similar dogs.

Optional Online rubric: Written Pieces

ELL *Make a Table*

pairs or small groups   15 min

Help pairs or small groups collect data about the first names of students in the classroom. Then have them put their data in a table. After they have finished making their tables, guide them to analyze the data. Which names are most popular? Which letter of the alphabet do the most names start with? Then have students share their finding with the class.

Optional Online resources: Collecting and Organizing Data, Analyzing Data support

Customize Your Feature

- ☐ **Discussion** The Importance of Tables
- ☐ **Basic** Clear Titles
- ☐ **Advanced** Describing Data
- ☐ **ELL** Make a Table
- ☐ **Take It Home**

Think Science

Interpreting Tables

Visual displays, such as diagrams, tables, or graphs, are useful ways to show data collected in an experiment. A table is the most direct way to communicate this information. Tables are also used to summarize important trends in scientific data. Making a table may seem easy. However, if tables are not clearly organized, people will have trouble reading them. Below are a few strategies to help you improve your skills in interpreting scientific tables.

Tutorial

Use the following instructions to study the parts of a table about heredity in Brittanies and to analyze the data shown in the table.

Offspring from Cross of Black Solid and Liver Tricolor Brittanies		
Color	**Pattern**	**Number of Offspring**
orange and white	solid	1
black and white	solid	1
	tricolor	3
liver and white	solid	1
	tricolor	3

Reading the Title
Every table should have an informative title. By reading the title of the table to the left, we know that the table contains data about the offspring of a cross between a black solid Brittany and a liver tricolor Brittany.

Summarizing the Title
Sometimes it is helpful to write a sentence to summarize a table's title. For example, you could write, "This table shows how puppies that are the offspring of a black solid Brittany and a liver tricolor Brittany might look."

Analyzing the Headings
Row and column headings describe the data in the cells. Headings often appear different from the data in the cells, such as being larger, bold, or being shaded. The row headings in the table to the left organize three kinds of data: the coat color of the puppies, the coat pattern of the puppies, and the number of puppies that have each combination of coat color and pattern.

Describing the Data
In complete sentences, record the information that you read in the table. For example, you could write, "There are five different kinds of offspring. Tricolor puppies are most common, and puppies with a solid coat pattern are least common. There are twice as many tricolor puppies as solid puppies."

Analyzing the Data
Now that you have seen how the table is organized, you can begin to look for trends in the data. Which combinations are most common? Which combinations are least common?

134 Unit 2 Reproduction and Heredity

You Try It!

The table below shows the characteristics of Guinea pig offspring. Look at the table, and answer the questions that follow.

Characteristics of Guinea Pig Offspring from Controlled Breeding			
Hair Color	**Coat Texture**	**Hair Length**	**Number of Guinea Pigs**
black	rough	short	27
		long	9
	smooth	short	9
		long	3
white	rough	short	9
		long	3
	smooth	short	3
		long	1

1 Summarizing the Title Circle the title of the table. Write a one-sentence description of the information shown in the table.

2 Analyzing the Headings Shade the column headings in the table. What information do they show? How many combinations of hair color, coat texture, and hair length are shown?

3 Analyzing the Data Circle the most common type of Guinea pig. Box the least common type of Guinea pig. Write sentences to describe the characteristics of each.

4 Applying Mathematics Calculate the total number of Guinea pig offspring. Write this total at the bottom of the table. What percentage of the total number of Guinea pigs has short hair? What percentage of the total number of Guinea pigs has long hair?

5 Observing Trends Based on your data from Step 4, which characteristic is dominant in Guinea pigs: long hair or short hair?

6 Applying Concepts What is one advantage of displaying data in tables? What is one advantage of describing data in writing?

Take It Home

With an adult, practice making tables. You can categorize anything that interests you. Make sure your table has a title and clearly and accurately organizes your data using headings. If possible, share your table with your class.

Unit 2 Think Science 135

Answers

1. The title of the table should be circled and a one-sentence summary produced. For example: "This table shows what the coat texture, hair length and hair color of Guinea pig offspring from controlled breeding might be like."

2. Students should shade the column headings and explain that they show the possible hair characteristics of Guinea pig offspring and the number of Guinea pigs that can be expected for each combination. There are 8 combinations shown.

3. Students should circle the 27 and box the 1. The most common type of Guinea pig (27) has black, rough, short hair. The least common type (1) has white, smooth, long hair.

4. There are a total of 64 Guinea pig offspring. 75% of the total number of Guinea pigs have short hair, and 25% have long hair.

5. Short hair is the dominant characteristic in Guinea pigs.

6. Possible answer: Tables are more organized and easy to read. Describing data in writing allows for more detail in an explanation.

Take It Home

As an alternative, students may want to find a table from a magazine, newspaper, or other source and interpret the table for the class.

⊙ Optional Online rubric: Oral Presentations

Punnett Squares and Pedigrees

Essential Question How are patterns of inheritance studied?

 Professional Development

For more detailed information about the topics in this lesson, refer to the Content Refresher in the Unit Opener pages.

Opening Your Lesson

Begin the lesson by assessing students' prerequisite and prior knowledge.

Prerequisite Knowledge

- A basic understanding of Mendel's work
- An understanding of how dominant and recessive traits differ
- An understanding of the relationship between genes and alleles

Accessing Prior Knowledge

Invite students to use a KWL chart to access what they know about how dominant and recessive traits are passed on to offspring. Have them put what they know in the first column and what they want to know in the second column. After the lesson, they can complete the third column with what they have learned.

🌐 *Optional Online resource: KWL chart support*

Customize Your Opening

☐ **Accessing Prior Knowledge,** above

☐ **Print Path** Engage Your Brain, SE p. 137, #1–2

☐ **Print Path** Active Reading, SE p. 137, #3–4

☐ **Digital Path** Lesson Opener

Key Topics/Learning Goals

Punnett Squares

1 Define *Punnett square*.
2 Use a Punnett square to find combinations of alleles in potential offspring.
3 Define *ratio*.
4 Define *probability*.

Pedigrees

1 Define *pedigree*.
2 Explain what a sex-linked disorder is.
3 Give examples of sex-linked disorders.
4 Use a pedigree to trace a genetic trait.

Supporting Concepts

- A Punnett square illustrates how the parents' alleles may be passed on to offspring.
- The top of the Punnett square shows one parent's alleles for the trait; the side of the Punnett square shows the other parent's alleles for the same trait. Each box in the Punnett square shows a way the alleles from each parent could combine in offspring.
- A ratio compares, or shows the relationship between, two quantities.
- Probability is the likelihood, or chance, of a specific outcome in relation to the total number of possible outcomes.

- A pedigree is a diagram of family relationships that includes two or more generations.
- A sex-linked disorder is associated with an allele on a sex chromosome. Females can be carriers and not express the gene as they may have a normal allele that gives them a normal phenotype.
- Sex-linked disorders include hemophilia, sickle cell anemia, and color blindness.
- In a typical pedigree, boxes represent males and circles represent females. Shading indicates that a person shows the trait; white indicates that a person does not. Half-shaded shows that a person carries the trait. Lines connect mates and children.

Options for Instruction

Two parallel paths provide coverage of the Essential Questions, with a strong Inquiry strand woven into each. Follow the Print Path, the Digital Path, or your customized combination of print, digital, and inquiry.

 Print Path
Teaching support for the Print Path appears with the Student Pages.

 Inquiry Labs and Activities

 Digital Path
Digital Path shortcut: TS673190

Squared Away, SE pp. 138–141
How are Punnett squares used to predict patterns of heredity?
How can a Punnett square be used to make predictions about offspring?

S.T.E.M. Lab
Matching Punnett Square Predictions

Quick Labs
Completing a Punnett Square
Gender Determination

Daily Demos
Coding for Traits
Multi-trait Punnett Squares

 Virtual Lab
Crossing Pea Plants

Punnett Squares
Interactive Graphics

Ratios and Probabilities
Slideshow

Squared Away, SE p. 142
How can a pedigree trace a trait through generations?

Quick Lab
Interpreting Pedigree Charts

Pedigrees
Interactive Image

Options for Assessment

See the Evaluate page for options, including Formative Assessment, Summative Assessment, and Unit Review.

Engage and Explore

Activities and Discussion

Activity *What's the Probability?*

 Engage

Punnett Squares

 individuals, pairs
 10 min
Inquiry **GUIDED** inquiry

Explain that human parents have a 1:2 probability of having a boy or a girl with each pregnancy. **Ask:** If the first child is a girl, what is the probability that the second child will be a girl? Have students think about the answer to this question individually. Then have them work with a partner to share and trade their ideas. Finally, have pairs share their answer with the class. The probability for the second child is the same, 1:2. Explain to students that the probability of something happening is not affected by what has happened before.

Activity *Sonnem Farming, Part 3*

Punnett Squares

 pairs
 20 min
Inquiry **GUIDED** inquiry

Return to the activity from earlier in the unit, in which students imagined that they were farmers raising cat-sized fictitious creatures called Sonnems. Write the genotype of a homozygous, brown-furred, long-tailed Sonnem on the board (BBTT), as well as the genotype for a homozygous, white-furred, short-tailed Sonnem (bbtt). Show students how to complete a Punnett square that shows the possible outcomes of this cross. Then, have them work in pairs. Repeat this activity for straight ears (SS)/curly ears (ss), long legs (LL)/short legs (ll), and any combinations of the alleles. Challenge students to tell the phenotypes of Sonnems with the following genotypes: BbttSsll (brown fur, short tail, straight ears, short legs); BBTTssLL (brown fur, long tail, curly ears, long legs), bbTTssll (white fur, long tail, curly ears, short legs), bbTtSSLl (white fur, long tail, straight ears, long legs), BbttssLl (brown fur, short tail, curly ears, long legs), and BBttssll (brown fur, short tail, curly ears, short legs).

Labs and Demos

Daily Demo *Coding for Traits*

Punnett Squares

 whole class
 15 min
Inquiry **GUIDED** inquiry

PURPOSE **To show how alleles code for different traits**
MATERIALS

- **building blocks of various shapes and various colors**

Show two different colored blocks of the same shape (such as circles). Explain that these two blocks represent different alleles of the same gene. Then show two more blocks of one shape (such as triangles), but again of different colors. Place these pairs of blocks on a table, and model a Punnett square by placing more blocks on the table to show the four ways these alleles could combine in the offspring. Have students explain what the offspring would look like if one trait was dominant (for example, red circles). Repeat the process with other dominant traits.

Daily Demo *Multi-trait Punnett Squares*

Punnett Squares

 pairs
 20 min
Inquiry **GUIDED** inquiry

Make a multi-trait Punnett square. Use as an example a plant homozygous for green seeds (GG) and heterozygous for purple flowers (Ff) crossed with a plant heterozygous for green seeds (Gg) and homozygous for white flowers (ff). First, write the genotypes on the board. Then, write down the possible combinations of alleles that would be in the gametes (Plant 1: GF, Gf, GF, Gf; plant 2: Gf, gf, Gf, gf). Write these combinations along the top and side of a 16-cell Punnett square and complete it. Four genotypes will result: GGFf, GGff, GgFf, and Ggff.

Customize Your Labs

 See the Lab Manual for lab datasheets.

 Go Online for editable lab datasheets.

Levels of **Inquiry**	**DIRECTED** inquiry	**GUIDED** inquiry	**INDEPENDENT** inquiry
introduces inquiry skills within a structured framework.	develops inquiry skills within a supportive environment.	deepens inquiry skills with student-driven questions or procedures.

Quick Lab *Gender Determination*

PURPOSE **To explain how gender is inherited**

See the Lab Manual or Go Online for planning information.

Quick Lab *Completing a Punnett Square*

Punnett Squares

   individuals
   15 min
Inquiry **DIRECTED** inquiry

Students construct a Punnett square to predict the genotypes of the offspring resulting from a cross of two heterozygous plants.

PURPOSE **To use a Punnett square to predict the probabilities of genotypes and phenotypes**

MATERIALS

• **no materials needed**

Quick Lab *Interpreting Pedigree Charts*

PURPOSE **To predict patterns of inheritance of a recessive trait**

See the Lab Manual or Go Online for planning information.

S.T.E.M. Lab *Matching Punnett Square Predictions*

Punnett Squares

   pairs
   45 min
Inquiry **DIRECTED/GUIDED** inquiry

Students flip pennies to determine whether the actual outcomes of a genetic cross can be expected to match the outcomes predicted by a Punnett square analysis.

PURPOSE **To compare the results of a simulated genetic cross to the outcomes predicted by a Punnett square**

MATERIALS

• **marker**
• **2 pennies**
• **blank paper**
• **graphing paper**
• **masking tape**

Virtual Lab *Crossing Pea Plants*

DNA's Role in Inheritance

   individuals
   10 min
Inquiry **DIRECTED** inquiry

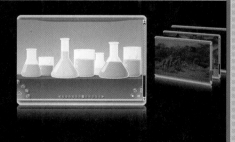

Students use Punnett squares to determine genotypes of various crosses.

PURPOSE **To study how Punnett squares are used to determine the genetic outcome of offspring.**

Activities and Discussion

☐ **Activity** Sonnem Farming, Part 3
☐ **Activity** What's the Probability?

Labs and Demos

☐ **Daily Demo** Coding for Traits

☐ **Daily Demo** Multi-trait Squares
☐ **Quick Lab** Gender Determination
☐ **S.T.E.M. Lab** Matching Predictions
☐ **Quick Lab** Completing/Punnett
☐ **Quick Lab** Interpreting Pedigrees
☐ **Virtual Lab** Crossing Pea Plants

Your Resources

Explain Science Concepts

Key Topics

Punnett Squares

Print Path

☐ **Squared Away,** SE pp. 138–141
- Active Reading, #5
- Visualize It!, #6
- Visualize It!, #7
- Do the Math #8, #9

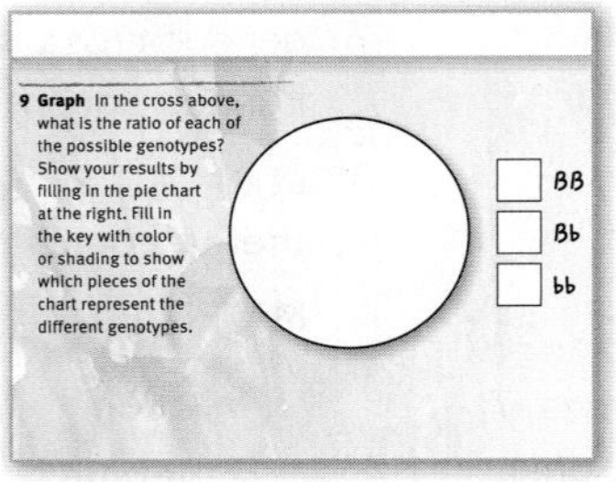

> **9 Graph** In the cross above, what is the ratio of each of the possible genotypes? Show your results by filling in the pie chart at the right. Fill in the key with color or shading to show which pieces of the chart represent the different genotypes.
>
> ☐ BB
> ☐ Bb
> ☐ bb

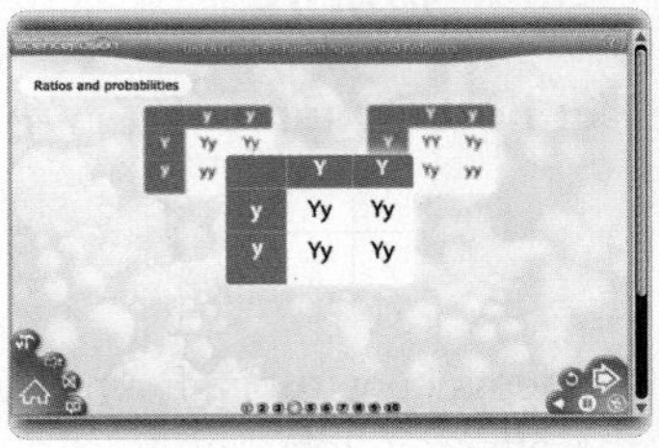

Digital Path

☐ **Punnett Squares**
Learn about Punnett squares and how they are used to predict the genetic makeup of offspring.

☐ **Ratios**
Examine how ratios and probability are calculated with the use of Punnett squares.

Ratios and probabilities

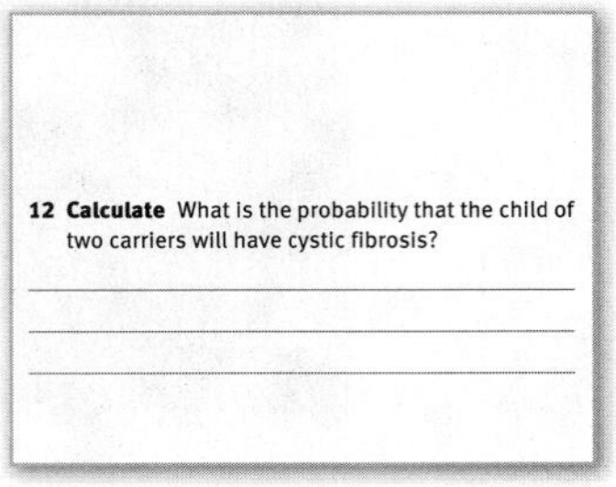

Pedigrees

Print Path

☐ **Squared Away,** SE p. 142
- Think Outside the Book, #10
- Visualize It!, #11
- Calculate, #12

> **12 Calculate** What is the probability that the child of two carriers will have cystic fibrosis?

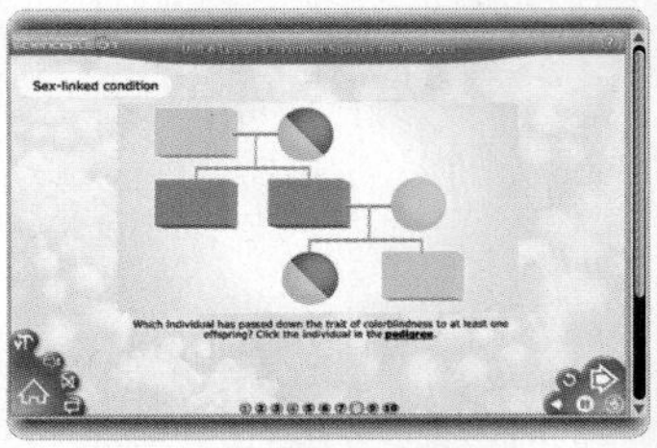

Digital Path

☐ **Pedigrees**
Learn about pedigrees and how they are used to trace a genetic trait through multiple generations.

Sex-linked condition

Basic *Fictional Punnett Squares*

Punnett Squares

 individuals
 10 min

Have students draw a Punnett square for a fictional creature, such as a dragon. Let students identify what each allele codes for and assign dominant or recessive qualities to each allele. Then invite students to draw a picture to show what each of the offspring would look like for generations 1 and 2.

Advanced *Pet Pedigrees*

Pedigrees

 individuals
 15 min

Have students create a pedigree for several generations of guinea pigs (or other pet of their choosing), tracing dominant fur color through several generations. Have students display and explain their pedigree.

ELL *Probability*

Punnett Squares

 pairs
 20 min

Have pairs of students work together to create Punnett squares that show different combinations of recessive and dominant alleles. After they have completed each Punnett square, have students use it to write the ratio of offspring that will have various traits.

ELL *Ratios and Percentages*

Punnett Squares

 pairs
 10 min

Have pairs of students draw a two-column chart. At the top of the first column, have students write the word *Ratio*. At the top of the second column, have them write the word *Percentage*. Then have students write 2:4, 1:4, 3:4, and 4:4. In the second column, have students write these ratios as percentages. **Answers: 50%, 25%, 75%, 100%**

Lesson Vocabulary

Punnett square **ratio**
probability **pedigree**

Previewing Vocabulary

 whole class ⏱ 10 min

Word Origins Explain to students that some terms come from people's names, as is the case with *Punnett square*. This tool was developed by English scientist Reginald Punnett (1875–1967). Not only did Punnett develop his famous square, but he also co-discovered (with William Bateson) genetic linkage and wrote the first book that introduced Gregor Mendel's work to the general public.

Reinforcing Vocabulary

👥 individuals ⏱ ongoing

Key-Term FoldNotes Have students make a Key-Term FoldNote to help them remember the meanings of the vocabulary terms. They can write the term on the outside, and on the inside include definitions or helpful illustrations.

Customize Your Core Lesson

Core Instruction
☐ **Print Path** choices
☐ **Digital Path** choices

Vocabulary
☐ **Previewing Vocabulary** Word Origins
☐ **Reinforcing Vocabulary** Key-Term FoldNote

Your Resources

Differentiated Instruction
☐ **Basic** Fictional Punnett Squares
☐ **Advanced** Pet Pedigrees
☐ **ELL** Probability
☐ **ELL** Ratios and Percentages

Extend Science Concepts

Reinforce and Review

Activity *Carousel Review*

Synthesizing Key Topics whole class
 20–40 min

1 Arrange chart paper in different parts of the room. On each piece of paper, write a question to review the content.

2 Divide students into small groups and assign each group a chart. Give each group a different colored marker.

3 Groups review their question, discuss their answer, and write a response.

4 After 5 to 10 min, each group rotates to the next station. Groups put a check mark by each answer they agree with, comment on answers they don't agree with, and add their own answers. Continue until all groups have reviewed all charts.

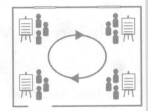

5 Invite each group to share information with the class.

Graphic Organizer

Synthesizing Key Topics individuals
🕐 15 min

Description Wheel Have students make Description Wheels about Punnett squares and pedigrees to clarify the function of each.

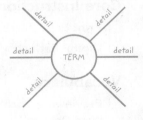

Going Further

Life Science Connection

Pedigrees individuals
🕐 ongoing

Analyze Genes Have students conduct research to find out more about sex-linked traits. Encourage students to make a chart or poster about their findings. Allow time for students to share their findings with the class.

Math Connection

Punnett Squares individuals
🕐 ongoing

Ask students to use Punnett squares to figure out the probability of each of the following:

1 The allele for short hair is dominant in cats. Two short-haired cats are bred; both carry the recessive allele for long hair, and their genotypes are Ss. What is the probability that one of the offspring will have short hair? **75%** What is the probability that one of the offspring will have long hair? **25%**

2 A cat with two dominant alleles for short hair (SS) is bred with a short-haired cat that has a recessive allele for long hair (Ss). What is the probability of a kitten having the SS genotype? **50%** The Ss genotype? **50%** What percentage of the kittens would have long hair? **0%**

Customize Your Closing

📔 *See the Assessment Guide for quizzes and tests.*

🌐 *Go Online to edit and create quizzes and tests.*

Reinforce and Review

☐ **Activity** Carousel Review

☐ **Graphic Organizer** Description Wheel

☐ **Print Path** Visual Summary, SE p. 144

☐ **Digital Path** Lesson Closer

Evaluate Student Mastery

Formative Assessment

See the teacher support below the Student Pages for additional Formative Assessment questions.

Set up one Punnett square with one parent having both dominant alleles and the other having both recessive, and another square with each parent having a dominant and a recessive allele. Have students fill in the squares and predict the ratios and percentages.

Reteach

Formative assessment may show that students need reinforcement for certain topics. The resources below are recommended for reteaching. If students were introduced to a topic through the Print Path, you can also use the Digital Path to reteach, or vice versa.

🎧 *Can be assigned to individual students*

Punnett Squares
S.T.E.M. Lab Matching Punnett Square Predictions

Quick Lab Completing a Punnett Square 🎧

Activity What's the Probability?

Daily Demo Multi-trait Punnett Squares

Pedigrees
Quick Lab Interpreting Pedigree Charts 🎧

Advanced Pet Pedigrees 🎧

Summative Assessment

Alternative Assessment
Make a Flower

💿 *Online resources: student worksheet, optional rubrics*

Punnett Squares and Pedigrees

Climb the Pyramid: *Make a Flower*
Fill in three Punnett squares, at least one from each layer of the pyramid. After you have completed them, circle one trait in each Punnett square. List these traits at the bottom of the page. Then draw a flower that has all these traits.

1. Work on your own, with a partner, or with a small group.

2. Choose one or more items from each layer of the pyramid. Check your choices.

3. Have your teacher approve your plan.

4. Submit or present your results.

```
      __  R = red flower
          r = pink flower

          R              r

      r _____   _____

      r _____   _____
```

```
 __ L = long stem         __ T = thick stem
    l = short stem            t = thin stem

      L        L              T        t

 l _____ _____      T _____ _____

 l _____ _____      t _____ _____
```

```
 __ O = oval leaf    __ G = solid green leaf   __ B = big leaf
    o = round leaf      g = spotted green leaf     b = small leaf

    O       O          G         g              B        B

 O ____ ____       G ____ ____              B ____ ____

 o ____ ____       g ____ ____              b ____ ____
```

Going Further
☐ **Life Science Connection**

☐ **Math Connection**

☐ **Print Path** Why It Matters, SE p. 143

Formative Assessment
☐ **Strategies** Throughout TE

☐ **Lesson Review** SE

Summative Assessment
☐ **Alternative Assessment** Make a Flower

☐ **Lesson Quiz**

☐ **Unit Tests A and B**

☐ **Unit Review** SE End-of-Unit

Your Resources

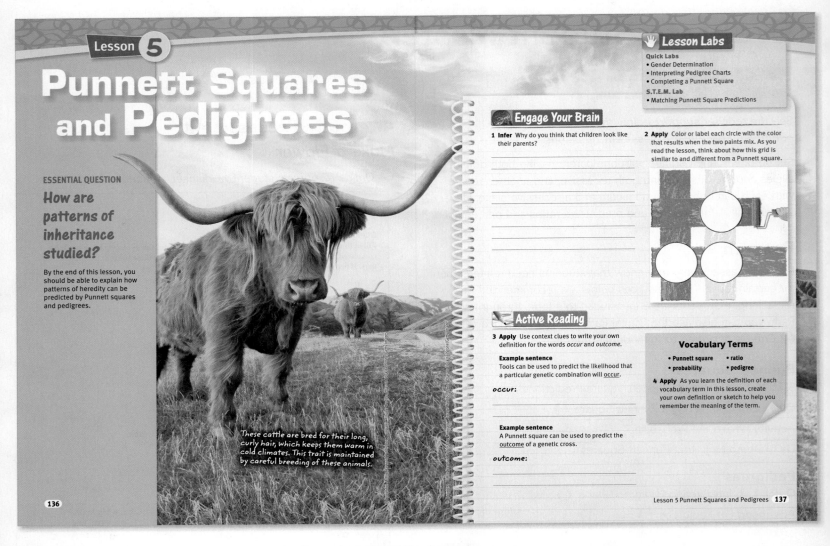

Lesson 5

Punnett Squares and Pedigrees

ESSENTIAL QUESTION

How are patterns of inheritance studied?

By the end of this lesson, you should be able to explain how patterns of heredity can be predicted by Punnett squares and pedigrees.

These cattle are bred for their long, curly hair, which keeps them warm in cold climates. This trait is maintained by careful breeding of these animals.

136

Lesson Labs

Quick Labs
- Gender Determination
- Interpreting Pedigree Charts
- Completing a Punnett Square

S.T.E.M. Lab
- Matching Punnett Square Predictions

Engage Your Brain

1 Infer Why do you think that children look like their parents?

2 Apply Color or label each circle with the color that results when the two paints mix. As you read the lesson, think about how this grid is similar to and different from a Punnett square.

Active Reading

3 Apply Use context clues to write your own definition for the words *occur* and *outcome*.

Example sentence
Tools can be used to predict the likelihood that a particular genetic combination will <u>occur</u>.

occur:

Example sentence
A Punnett square can be used to predict the <u>outcome</u> of a genetic cross.

outcome:

Vocabulary Terms
- Punnett square
- ratio
- probability
- pedigree

4 Apply As you learn the definition of each vocabulary term in this lesson, create your own definition or sketch to help you remember the meaning of the term.

Lesson 5 Punnett Squares and Pedigrees 137

Answers

Answers for 1–3 should represent students' current thoughts, even if incorrect.

1. Sample answer: Children look like their parents because children inherit genetic material from their parents.

2. Students should fill in circles with orange *(top)*, purple *(bottom left)*, and green *(bottom right)*.

3. to happen; a result

4. Students should define or sketch each vocabulary term in the lesson.

Opening Your Lesson

In discussing answers to #2, consider the idea of the grid shape and that two different paints contribute to the result in the appropriate compartment of the grid. Similarly, alleles from two parents contribute to the genotype of offspring in a Punnett square grid. After students have completed the lesson, ask students how the image is different from a Punnett square. The paint example is different from a Punnett square in that the alleles do not blend together like paint does. They are both present in an organism's cells.

Prerequisites: Students should already know about Gregor Mendel's principles of heredity. In addition, they should know that an organism has two copies of the alleles for each inherited trait. To be expressed, a completely dominant trait requires only one copy of the allele to be present; a recessive trait requires two copies of the allele to be present.

Learning Alert ⚠ MISCONCEPTION ⚠

Some students may hold the misconception that one parent contributes more genes than the other. Have students look at a Punnett square. **Ask:** How many alleles for this gene does each parent have? **two Ask:** Even if an offspring resembles one parent more than the other, how many alleles did the offspring get from each parent? **one**

Squared Away

How are Punnett squares used to predict patterns of heredity?

When Gregor Mendel studied pea plants, he noticed that traits are inherited in patterns. One tool for understanding the patterns of heredity is a diagram called a *Punnett square*. A **Punnett square** is a graphic used to predict the possible genotypes of offspring in a given cross. Each parent has two alleles for a particular gene. An offspring receives one allele from each parent. A Punnett square shows all of the possible allele combinations in the offspring.

The Punnett square below shows how alleles are expected to be distributed in a cross between a pea plant with purple flowers and a pea plant with white flowers. The top of the Punnett square shows one parent's alleles for this trait (*F* and *F*). The left side of the Punnett square shows the other parent's alleles (*f* and *f*). Each compartment within the Punnett square shows an allele combination in potential offspring. You can see that in this cross, all offspring would have the same genotype (*Ff*). Because purple flower color is completely dominant to white flower color, all of the offspring would have purple flowers.

Active Reading

5 Identify In a Punnett square, where are the parents' alleles written?

_____

_____

_____

_____

This Punnett square shows the possible offspring combinations in pea plants with different flower colors.

Key:
F Purple flower allele
f White flower allele

Genotype: FF
Phenotype: purple flower

One parent's alleles

The other parent's alleles

	F	F
f	Ff	Ff
f	Ff	Ff

Genotype: ff
Phenotype: white flower

© Houghton Mifflin Harcourt Publishing Company

138 Unit 2 Reproduction and Heredity

Visualize It!

6 Apply Fill in the genotypes and phenotypes of the parents and offspring in this Punnett square. Sketch the resulting offspring possibilities in the white boxes below. (Hint: Assume complete dominance.)

Key:
R Round pea allele
r Wrinkled pea allele

Genotype: _____
Phenotype: _____

	R	r
R	Genotype: _____ Phenotype: _____	Genotype: _____ Phenotype: _____
r	Genotype: _____ Phenotype: _____	Genotype: _____ Phenotype: _____

Genotype: _____
Phenotype: _____

7 Analyze What does each compartment of the Punnett square represent?

_____

_____

_____

_____

139

Answers

5. The parents' alleles are along the top and left of the Punnett square.

6. At top and to the left of Punnet square, answers are Genotype: Rr; Phenotype: round pea. Within the Punnett square, answers are *(top left)* Genotype: RR, Phenotype: round pea; *(top right)* Genotype: Rr, Phenotype: round pea; *(bottom left)* Genotype: Rr, Phenotype: round pea; *(bottom right)* Genotype: rr, Phenotype: wrinkled pea. Students should sketch a round pea in boxes that have the round pea phenotype and a wrinkled pea in boxes that have the wrinkled pea phenotype.

7. Each compartment represents a possible allele combination in offspring.

Interpreting Visuals

Help students interpret the diagram of the Punnett square showing the pea flowers. **Ask:** How is the symbol for each allele the same? Each allele is symbolized by the same letter, *F.* **Ask:** How can you tell which allele is dominant and which allele is recessive? A capital *F* is used for the dominant allele, and a lowercase *f* is used for the recessive allele. **Ask:** In this Punnett square, which trait is dominant? purple flowers, F **Ask:** Which trait is recessive? white flowers, f **Ask:** What does each box show? the alleles of one possible cross

Interpreting Visuals

Help students understand the Punnett square showing round and wrinkled peas. **Ask:** What kinds of alleles do both parents have? Both parents have one dominant and one recessive allele. **Ask:** What does the dominant allele produce? round peas **Ask:** What does the recessive allele produce? wrinkled peas **Ask:** What two genotypes (pairs of alleles) will produce a phenotype (physical appearance) of a round pea? RR and Rr **Ask:** What genotype will produce a phenotype of a wrinkled pea? rr

How can a Punnett square be used to make predictions about offspring?

A Punnett square does not tell you what the exact results of a certain cross will be. A Punnett square only helps you find the probability that a certain genotype will occur. **Probability** is the mathematical chance of a specific outcome in relation to the total number of possible outcomes.

Probability can be expressed in the form of a **ratio** (RAY•shee•oh), an expression that compares two quantities. A ratio written as 1:4 is read as "one to four." The ratios obtained from a Punnett square tell you the probability that any one offspring will get certain alleles. Another way of expressing probability is as a *percentage*. A percentage is like a ratio that compares a number to 100. A percentage states the number of times a certain outcome might happen out of a hundred chances.

1:4 is the ratio of red squares to total squares.

Do the Math Sample Problem

In guinea pigs, the dominant *B* allele is responsible for black fur, while the recessive *b* allele is responsible for brown fur. Use the Punnett square to find the probability of this cross resulting in offspring with brown fur.

	B	b
b	Bb	bb
b	Bb	bb

Identify

A. What do you know?
Parent genotypes are Bb and bb. Possible offspring genotypes are Bb and bb.

B. What do you want to find out?
Probability of the cross resulting in offspring with brown fur

Plan

C. Count the total number of offspring allele combinations: 4

D. Count the number of allele combinations that will result in offspring with brown fur: 2

Solve

E. Write the probability of offspring with brown fur as a ratio: 2:4

F. Rewrite the ratio to express the probability out of 100 offspring by multiplying each side of the ratio by the same number (such as 25): 50:100

G. Convert the ratio to a percentage: 50%

Answer: 50% chance of offspring with brown fur

Do the Math You Try It

8 Calculate This Punnett square shows a cross between two *Bb* guinea pigs. What is the probability of the cross resulting in offspring with black fur?

	B	b
B	BB	Bb
b	Bb	bb

Identify

A. What do you know?

B. What do you want to find out?

Plan

C. Count the total number of offspring allele combinations:

D. Count the number of allele combinations that will result in offspring with black fur:

Solve

E. Write the probability of offspring with black fur as a ratio:

F. Rewrite the ratio to express the probability out of 100 offspring by multiplying each side of the ratio by the same number:

G. Convert the ratio to a percentage:

Answer:

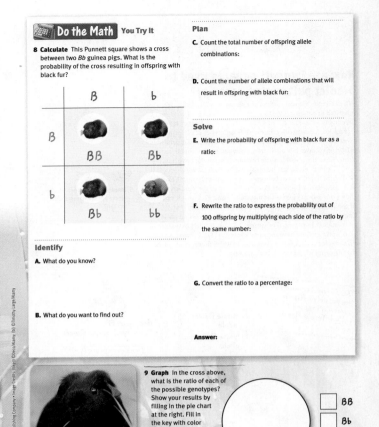

9 Graph In the cross above, what is the ratio of each of the possible genotypes? Show your results by filling in the pie chart at the right. Fill in the key with color or shading to show which pieces of the chart represent the different genotypes.

☐ BB
☐ Bb
☐ bb

Answers

8. A: Parent genotypes are *Bb* and *Bb*. Possible offspring genotypes are *BB*, *Bb*, and *bb*; B: Probability of the cross resulting in offspring with black fur; C: 4; D: 3; E: 3:4; F: 75:100; G: 75%; Answer: 75% chance of offspring with black fur.

9. Students should fill in circle chart to show *BB* with 25% of the chart, Bb with 50% of the chart, and bb with 25% of the chart. Students should have filled in key to indicate which pieces of the chart represent the different genotypes.

Learning Alert GUIDED Inquiry

Difficult Concepts Help students to understand that ratios and percentages can show the same information but in different ways. For example, if you tossed a coin in the air, and there is a 50% chance that the coin will land heads-up, this means that out of 100 times the coin is tossed, it landed heads-up 50 of those times. A ratio expresses this idea, too, but it is not necessarily based on 100. A 50% chance that a coin tossed will land heads-up can be expressed as a ratio of 1:2. The ratio indicates that, on average, the coin will land heads-up one of every two times it is tossed.

Learning Alert ⚠ MISCONCEPTION ⚠

Ask: If there is a 50% chance of having a boy baby, what is the ratio? 1:2 **Ask:** If the first child is a girl, what is the probability of the next child being a boy? 50% If students think there is now a higher probability that the child will be a boy, have them fill out a Punnett square using XX and XY to see the ratio of boys to girls during each pregnancy. Explain that human parents have a 50% probability of having a boy or a girl with each pregnancy.

How can a pedigree trace a trait through generations?

A pedigree is another tool used to study patterns of inheritance. A **pedigree** traces the occurrence of a trait through generations of a family. Pedigrees can be created to trace any inherited trait—even hair color!

Pedigrees can be useful in tracing a special class of inherited disorders known as *sex-linked disorders*. Sex-linked disorders are associated with an allele on a sex chromosome. Many sex-linked disorders, such as hemophilia and colorblindness, are caused by an allele on the X chromosome. Women have two X chromosomes, so a woman can have one allele for colorblindness without being colorblind. A woman who is heterozygous for this trait is called a *carrier*, because she can carry or pass on the trait to her offspring. Men have just one X chromosome. In men, this single chromosome determines if the trait is present.

The pedigree below traces a disease called *cystic fibrosis*. Cystic fibrosis causes serious lung problems. Carriers of the disease have one recessive allele. They do not have cystic fibrosis, but they are able to pass the recessive allele on to their children. If a child receives a recessive allele from each parent, then the child will have cystic fibrosis. Other genetic conditions follow a similar pattern.

Think Outside the Book Inquiry

10 Design Create a pedigree chart that traces the occurrence of dimples in your family or in the family of a friend. Collect information for as many family members as you can.

Visualize It!

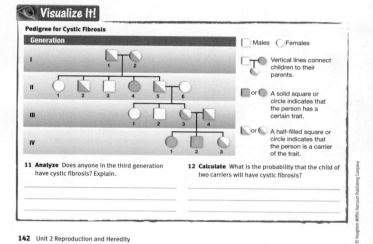

Pedigree for Cystic Fibrosis

☐ Males ◯ Females

Vertical lines connect children to their parents.

◼ or ● A solid square or circle indicates that the person has a certain trait.

◧ or ◑ A half-filled square or circle indicates that the person is a carrier of the trait.

11 Analyze Does anyone in the third generation have cystic fibrosis? Explain.

12 Calculate What is the probability that the child of two carriers will have cystic fibrosis?

142 Unit 2 Reproduction and Heredity

Why It Matters

EYE ON THE ENVIRONMENT

Saving the European Mouflon

The European mouflon is an endangered species of sheep. Scientists at the University of Teramo in Italy used genetic tools and techniques to show how the population of mouflon could be preserved.

Maintaining Genetic Diversity
When a very small population of animals interbreeds, there is a greater risk that harmful genetic conditions can appear in the animals. This is one issue that scientists face when trying to preserve endangered species. One way to lower this risk is to be sure that genetically-similar animals do not breed.

Genetics to the Rescue!
Researchers combined the sperm and egg of genetically-dissimilar European mouflons in a laboratory. The resulting embryo was implanted into a mother sheep. By controlling the combination of genetic material, scientists hope to lower the risk of inherited disorders.

Extend Inquiry

13 Explain Why are small populations difficult to preserve?

14 Research Research another population of animals that has been part of a captive breeding program.

15 Describe Describe these animals and the results of the breeding program by doing one of the following:
• make a poster
• write a short story
• write a song
• draw a graphic novel

143

Answers

10. Students' pedigrees should indicate the gender of each individual as well as whether individuals have, do not have, or are carriers for the trait. Lines should connect children to their parents.

11. No. No one in the third generation has two copies of the cystic fibrosis allele.

12. 25%

13. There is a greater risk that the animals will interbreed, resulting in harmful genetic conditions.

14. Students should research animals such as the giant panda or red wolf that have undergone captive breeding programs.

15. Students should describe the results of a captive breeding program.

Interpreting Visuals

Analyzing Information Have students look at the pedigree chart shown. **Ask:** What do the man and woman have in common in the first generation? They both are carriers of a trait. **Ask:** How do you know this? because both are shown as half shaded, which means they carry a trait **Ask:** In the second generation, who expresses the trait, and who carries the trait? The daughter expresses the trait. Two sons carry the trait. **Ask:** What happens to the trait in the third generation? One daughter is a carrier of the trait. The son and other daughter are not carriers. No one in the third generation has the trait. **Ask:** What happens to the trait in the fourth generation? One daughter is a carrier, and one daughter and a son have the trait.

Formative Assessment

Analyzing Traits Write Punnett squares on the board to examine the genotypes of organisms and to indicate which individuals will express dominant or recessive traits. Students should be able to explain that in complete dominance, the presence of one or two dominant alleles results in the expression of a dominant trait, while two recessive alleles are required for an offspring to express a recessive trait.

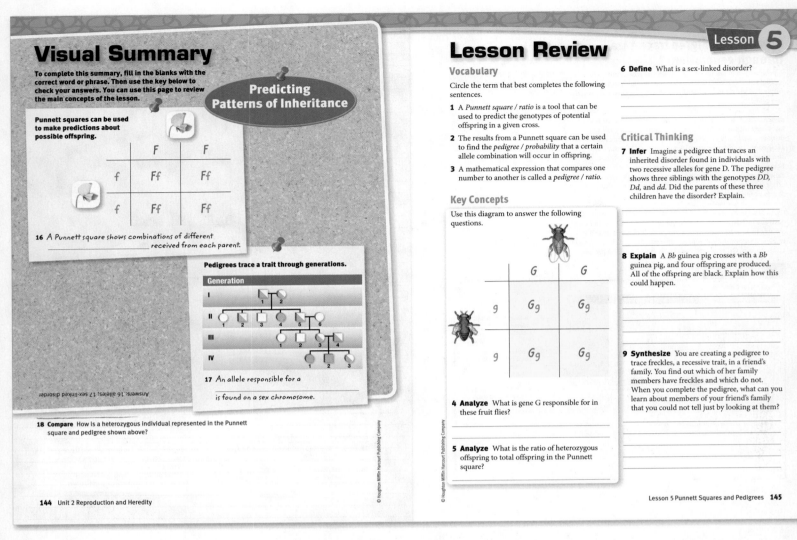

Visual Summary

To complete this summary, fill in the blanks with the correct word or phrase. Then use the key below to check your answers. You can use this page to review the main concepts of the lesson.

Predicting Patterns of Inheritance

Punnett squares can be used to make predictions about possible offspring.

	F	F
f	Ff	Ff
f	Ff	Ff

16 A Punnett square shows combinations of different _____ received from each parent.

Pedigrees trace a trait through generations.

17 An allele responsible for a _____ is found on a sex chromosome.

Answers: 16 alleles; 17 sex-linked disorder

18 Compare How is a heterozygous individual represented in the Punnett square and pedigree shown above?

144 Unit 2 Reproduction and Heredity

Lesson Review

Lesson 5

Vocabulary

Circle the term that best completes the following sentences.

1 A *Punnett square / ratio* is a tool that can be used to predict the genotypes of potential offspring in a given cross.

2 The results from a Punnett square can be used to find the *pedigree / probability* that a certain allele combination will occur in offspring.

3 A mathematical expression that compares one number to another is called a *pedigree / ratio*.

Key Concepts

Use this diagram to answer the following questions.

	G	G
g	Gg	Gg
g	Gg	Gg

4 Analyze What is gene G responsible for in these fruit flies?

5 Analyze What is the ratio of heterozygous offspring to total offspring in the Punnett square?

6 Define What is a sex-linked disorder?

Critical Thinking

7 Infer Imagine a pedigree that traces an inherited disorder found in individuals with two recessive alleles for gene D. The pedigree shows three siblings with the genotypes *DD*, *Dd*, and *dd*. Did the parents of these three children have the disorder? Explain.

8 Explain A *Bb* guinea pig crosses with a *Bb* guinea pig, and four offspring are produced. All of the offspring are black. Explain how this could happen.

9 Synthesize You are creating a pedigree to trace freckles, a recessive trait, in a friend's family. You find out which of her family members have freckles and which do not. When you complete the pedigree, what can you learn about members of your friend's family that you could not tell just by looking at them?

Lesson 5 Punnett Squares and Pedigrees **145**

Visual Summary Answers

16. alleles

17. sex-linked disorder

18. In the Punnett square, a heterozygous individual is represented by *Ff*. In the pedigree, a heterozygous individual is represented by a half-shaded shape.

Lesson Review Answers

1. Punnett square

2. probability

3. ratio

4. wing development

5. 4:4

6. a disorder in which the allele that is responsible for producing the disorder is found on a sex chromosome

7. No. Both parents had to have been heterozygous (carriers).

8. Punnett squares only show the probability that offspring will have a certain genotype. They do not predict actual outcomes.

9. I would be able to determine which family members are carriers of the freckle trait.

DNA Structure and Function

Essential Question **What Is DNA?**

 Professional Development

For more detailed information about the topics in this lesson, refer to the Content Refresher in the Unit Opener pages.

Opening Your Lesson

Begin the lesson by assessing students' prerequisite and prior knowledge.

Prerequisite Knowledge

- Definition and mechanics of heredity
- Process of cell division

Accessing Prior Knowledge

Ask: Why, with the exception of identical twins, do siblings have traits that differ from one another? Sample answer: Each sibling receives a unique combination of genes from its parents. These genes determine the traits the individual will have.

Ask: What happens to the genetic material prior to cell division? Before cell division, genetic material is duplicated.

Customize Your Opening

☐ **Accessing Prior Knowledge,** above

☐ **Print Path** Engage Your Brain, SE p. 147 #1–2

☐ **Print Path** Active Reading, SE p. 147 #3–4

☐ **Digital Path** Lesson Opener

Key Topics/Learning Goals

DNA Structure

1 Define *DNA* and list the components of DNA.
2 Describe Chargaff's rules concerning bases.
3 Explain Rosalind Franklin's and Watson and Crick's contributions to knowledge about the structure of DNA.

DNA Replication

1 Explain how DNA makes copies of itself.
2 Describe when DNA replication occurs.

Mutations

1 Define *mutation* and list three different types of mutations.
2 Describe some consequences of mutations.
3 Explain why mutations occur.

DNA Transcription and Translation

1 Define the role of *RNA*.
2 Compare RNA to DNA.

Supporting Concepts

- DNA is the material that determines inherited characteristics in all living things. DNA is made up of compounds called *nucleotides,* which consist of a sugar, a phosphate, and a base.
- Chargaff's rule states that in DNA, the base adenine (A) pairs with thymine (T) and the base cytosine (C) pairs with guanine (G).
- Franklin used x-ray diffraction to image the DNA molecule and show its spiral shape; Watson and Crick created the double-helix model of DNA.

- During replication, a DNA molecule separates into two strands; the bases on each side are used as a pattern for the two new strands.
- DNA replication occurs prior to cell division.

- A mutation is a change in the number, type, or order of bases. Mutations include deletions, substitutions, and insertions.
- A mutation may have no effect, a beneficial effect, or a deleterious effect.
- Mutations can be caused by random errors or by physical or chemical agents.

- RNA helps make proteins.
- RNA is a single-stranded molecule with a sugar-phosphate backbone and the bases adenine (A), guanine (G), cytosine (C), and uracil (U).

Options for Instruction

Two parallel paths provide coverage of the Essential Questions, with a strong Inquiry strand woven into each.
Follow the **Print Path**, the **Digital Path**, or your customized combination of print, digital, and inquiry.

 Print Path
Teaching support for the Print Path appears with the Student Pages.

 Inquiry Labs and Activities

 Digital Path
Digital Path shortcut: TS673120

Print Path	Inquiry Labs and Activities	Digital Path
Cracking the Code, SE pp. 148–149 **What is DNA?** **How was DNA discovered?** **Unraveling DNA,** SE pp. 150–151 **What does DNA look like?** • The Shape of DNA Is a Double Helix • DNA Is Made Up of Nucleotides	**Exploration Lab** **Extracting DNA** **Quick Labs** **Modeling DNA** **Building a DNA Sequence** **Activity** **Modeling Code**	**History of DNA Science** Interactive Graphics **What DNA Is Made Of** Interactive Images
Replication and Mutation, SE p. 152 **How are copies of DNA made?** **When are copies of DNA made?**	**Activity** **Human DNA Model**	**How Is DNA Copied?** Interactive Graphics
Replication and Mutation, SE p. 153 **What are mutations?**	**Quick Lab** **Mutations Cause Diversity**	**Mutations and Errors** Interactive Graphics
Protein Factory, SE pp. 154–155 **What is the role of DNA and RNA in building proteins?** • Transcription • Translation	**Activity** **Make Connections**	**DNA and RNA** Interactive Graphics **RNA and Proteins** Interactive Graphics

Options for Assessment

See the Evaluate page for options, including Formative Assessment,
Summative Assessment, and Unit Review.

Engage and Explore

Activities and Discussion

Activity *Modeling Code*

Introducing Key Topics

 pairs
20 min
Inquiry **GUIDED** inquiry

Create a code by pairing each letter of the alphabet with a numeral. For example, the numeral 1 could represent the letter *a*. Have students encode a brief message. Then, have them exchange and decode the message. Explain that a code is simply another way to represent information and that there are many types of codes. The genetic code is based on sequences of the four nucleotide bases of DNA.

For greater depth: Provide students with a copy of the Morse code. Have them decode a message written in Morse code. Ask them how Morse code is similar to the pairing of nucleotides in DNA and RNA. They should understand that mRNA is similar to the key that matches dots and dashes to letters. The translation of the code into words is comparable to translation of mRNA by tRNA and ribosomes.

Activity *Human DNA Model*

Engage

DNA Structure and DNA Replication

 whole class
10 min
Inquiry **DIRECTED** inquiry

Role Playing Have students stand in two lines. Each line should hold some string. Ask students to hold cards labeled A, T, C, or G to represent DNA bases. Have the two lines move away from each other to model how the DNA molecule separates into two strands. One at a time, have other students act as DNA bases, matching A, T, C, or G cards in a complementary fashion to model how the open strands replicate. Have the students forming each new complementary strand hold a piece of string to join them together. At the conclusion of the activity, two new strands of DNA should be formed.

Discussion *Mutating DNA*

Mutations

 whole class
15 min
Inquiry **GUIDED** inquiry

Quick Discussion Write a sequence of DNA on the board. Invite students to come to the board and make a change in the sequence. Discuss what type of change is made (insertion, deletion, substitution). Then, discuss the possible consequences of such mutations in DNA. Encourage them to brainstorm examples of both helpful and harmful mutations.

Reminder Most mutations are corrected, and even those that are not may have no apparent effect. For example, a mutation may occur in a cell that does not produce a particular protein or in a region of DNA that does not code for anything.

Take It Home *Extract DNA at Home*

Engage

DNA Structure

 adult-student pairs
varied
Inquiry **INDEPENDENT** inquiry

This activity expands the Extracting DNA Exploration Lab found in this lesson. Students work with an adult to extract DNA at home using common household materials. The pair should try extracting DNA from fruits, such as strawberries, or from legumes, such as split peas. They should experiment with adding a small amount of pineapple or papaya juice to one sample. Students should hypothesize about whether the extraction works better with or without the juice, and why.

Customize Your Labs

 See the Lab Manual for lab datasheets.

 Go Online for editable lab datasheets.

Labs and Demos

Exploration Lab *Extracting DNA*

DNA Structure

 pairs
🕐 45 min
Inquiry **DIRECTED or GUIDED** inquiry

Students use common household items to release, unravel, and collect DNA.

PURPOSE **To extract DNA and observe its structure**

MATERIALS

- glass rod, 8 cm long
- glass slide
- inoculating loop
- isopropyl alcohol (15 mL)
- liquid dish soap (1 mL)
- table salt

- test tube or beaker, 50 mL
- hot tap water (20 mL)
- wheat germ, raw (1 g)
- gloves
- lab apron
- safety goggles

Quick Lab *Building a DNA Sequence*

DNA Structure

 individuals
🕐 15 min
Inquiry **DIRECTED** inquiry

Students use clay to model base pairing in a DNA strand.

PURPOSE **To describe how DNA is made up of smaller molecules**

MATERIALS

- modeling clay, 4 colors
- gloves
- apron

Quick Lab *Modeling DNA*

DNA Structure

 pairs
🕐 15 min
Inquiry **DIRECTED** inquiry

Students construct a DNA model to illustrate the structure of genetic material.

PURPOSE **To make a model of DNA and learn pertinent terminology**

MATERIALS

- craft beads, 2 colors (8 each)
- paper, blank
- paper clips, 4 colors (2 each)

- pipe cleaners (2)
- safety goggles

Quick Lab *Mutations Cause Diversity*

Mutations

individuals
🕐 15 min
Inquiry **DIRECTED** inquiry

Students simulate the process of making proteins from RNA code in order to demonstrate how errors in translation lead to diversity.

PURPOSE **To explain how protein translation errors cause mutations**

MATERIALS

- stopwatch
- beads, blue, green, orange, and yellow
- safety goggles

- sewing needle
- string, 20 cm in length

Activities and Discussion

- ☐ **Activity** Modeling Code
- ☐ **Activity** Human DNA Model
- ☐ **Discussion** Mutating DNA
- ☐ **Take It Home** Extract DNA at Home

Labs and Demos

- ☐ **Exploration Lab** Extracting DNA
- ☐ **Quick Lab** Building a DNA Sequence
- ☐ **Quick Lab** Modeling DNA
- ☐ **Quick Lab** Mutations Cause Diversity

Your Resources

_____

_____

_____

Explain Science Concepts

	📙 Print Path	💻 Digital Path
Key Topics		

DNA Structure

📙 **Print Path**

☐ **Cracking the Code,** SE pp. 148–149
- Active Reading (Annotation Strategy), #5
- Analyze, #6
- Think Outside the Book, #7

☐ **Unraveling DNA,** SE pp. 150–151
- Active Reading, #8
- Compare, #9
- Apply, #10
- Devise, #11

💻 **Digital Path**

☐ **History of DNA Science**
Explore significant people and events to the discovery of DNA, its function, and its structure.

☐ **What DNA Is Made Of**
Learn about DNA's structure.

DNA Replication

☐ **Replication and Mutation,** SE p. 152
- Apply, #12

☐ **How Is DNA Copied?**
Learn how and when DNA replication occurs.

Mutations

☐ **Replication and Mutation,** SE p. 153
- Apply, #13
- Explain, #14

☐ **Mutations and Errors**
Learn about three different types of mutations in DNA and their consequences.

DNA Transcription and Translation

☐ **Protein Factory,** SE pp. 154–155
- Active Reading (Annotation Strategy) #15
- Apply, #16

☐ **DNA and RNA**
Learn about the process of transcription

☐ **RNA and Proteins**
Learn about the process of translation.

Differentiated Instruction

Basic *Complementary Code*

Synthesizing Key Topics

 individuals
🕐 20 min

Have students use index cards or construction paper to make and label DNA bases. The cards should have ends shaped like puzzle pieces, with the correct pairs having complementary ends. Encourage them to draw pictures of the DNA sequences they made to illustrate the structure of the DNA molecule.

Basic *A Place in History*

Synthesizing Key Topics

 small groups
🕐 25 min

Role Playing Have students imagine that they discovered the structure of DNA and must present their findings to a group of scientists. Have small groups use a model of DNA, a poster, or another visual aid to briefly describe the structure of DNA to their classmates. Then have them explain how DNA replicates.

Advanced *Genetic Disorders*

Mutations

 individuals
🕐 varied

Quick Research Have students select, research, and write a report about a genetic disorder. Suggest disorders such as hemophilia, diabetes type I, familial ALS (amyotrophic lateral sclerosis, or Lou Gehrig's disease), and Huntington's disease. Suggest that their reports focus on historical occurrence of the disease, famous persons who had or have the disease, and treatments that have been tried.

🌐 *Optional Online rubric: Written Pieces*

ELL *Protein Performance*

DNA Transcription and Translation

 small groups
🕐 15 min

Role Playing Have groups of students perform a short skit to demonstrate the formation of a protein. For example, students could play the roles of a ribosome, an amino acid, a tRNA, and an mRNA. Have EL learners verbally describe their actions as they perform them.

Lesson Vocabulary

| DNA | nucleotide | replication |
| mutation | RNA | ribosome |

Previewing Vocabulary

 whole class
🕐 10 min

Write the following abbreviations in the first column of a three-column chart: PM, MD, and DNA. Ask students to give the general meaning of the first two abbreviations. afternoon, doctor Write these meanings in a second column and write the meaning "genetic material" for DNA. In the third column, write what each letter in the abbreviations stands for (post meridian, medical doctor, deoxyribonucleic acid). Point out that it is not always important to remember the exact words that an abbreviation stands for, but to know what the abbreviation means.

Reinforcing Vocabulary

👥 individuals
🕐 20 min

Analogies The lesson contains many analogies about DNA's structure and function. To help students remember the concepts behind the terms introduced in the lesson, have them create their own analogies. Students write the term in the first column of an analogies table and the definition in the second column. In the third column, they write their analogy.

Customize Your Core Lesson

Core Instruction
- ☐ **Print Path** choices
- ☐ **Digital Path** choices

Vocabulary
- ☐ **Previewing Vocabulary**
- ☐ **Reinforcing Vocabulary** Analogies

Differentiated Instruction
- ☐ **Basic** Complementary Code
- ☐ **Basic** A Place in History
- ☐ **Advanced** Genetic Disorders
- ☐ **ELL** Protein Performance

Your Resources

Extend Science Concepts

Reinforce and Review

Activity *Make Connections*

Synthesizing Key Topics

 whole class
 varied

Write Fast Write the following on eight different pieces of paper: *transcription, translation, DNA, RNA, mRNA, tRNA, nucleotide,* and *gene.* Put these pieces of paper in a small container. Write the question *How are they linked?* on the board. Have a student pick two pieces of paper from the container. Show the terms to the class and give them a couple of minutes to write down the answer. Return the papers to the container and repeat as long as time will allow.

Activity *Standup DNA*

DNA Structure

 whole class
 10 min

Divide the class into four equal groups. Assign each group one of the base letters: A, T, G, or C. Ask each student to write his or her assigned letter on paper in large print. Then, have students hold their papers up. Finally, tell them that when you call out, "Mix it up," they should find and stand next to someone with whom they could form a base pair.

Graphic Organizer

Synthesizing Key Topics

 individuals
 ongoing

Venn Diagram After students have studied the lesson, have them create a Venn diagram to compare DNA and RNA. Emphasize that they should use the diagram to compare and contrast both the structure and the function of the two molecules.

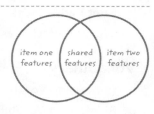

item one features | shared features | item two features

⟳ *Optional Online resource: Venn Diagram support*

Going Further

Environmental Science Connection

Mutations

 pairs, then whole class
 varied

Research and Discuss Many environmental factors (such as x-rays and gamma rays) and chemicals can cause mutations. Have pairs of students research a specific mutagen. Among other things, they should discover the mechanism by which the mutagen causes mutations, the type of mutation caused, and the ill effects of the mutation on the human body. Have pairs discuss their findings with the class.

Real World Connection

Synthesizing Key Topics

 whole class
 15 min

Discussion Only one-tenth of a percent of DNA varies from person to person. However, with current DNA sequencing technology, forensic scientists can focus on regions of human DNA that do differ and can use DNA evidence to help solve crimes or to clear people who have been wrongly convicted of a crime. Discuss with students the advantages of using DNA evidence over other evidence, such as fingerprints and blood type. Also discuss the potential privacy concerns of collecting DNA, such as the ability to learn if a person has a genetic disorder.

Customize Your Closing

🗂 *See the Assessment Guide for quizzes and tests.*

⟳ *Go Online to edit and create quizzes and tests.*

Reinforce and Review

☐ **Activity** Make Connections

☐ **Activity** Standup DNA

☐ **Graphic Organizer** Venn Diagram

☐ **Print Path** Visual Summary, SE p. 156

☐ **Digital Path** Lesson Closer

Evaluate Student Mastery

Formative Assessment

See the teacher support below the Student Pages for additional Formative Assessment questions.

Ask: What must happen to DNA in both replication and transcription? The two strands of a DNA molecule must separate. How do replication and transcription differ? In replication, the two strands of DNA gradually unwind and complementary bases are added to each strand to form two identical DNA molecules. In transcription, only part of the DNA template strand opens up and is read. Then, RNA bases match up to complementary bases on the DNA template.

Reteach

Formative assessment may show that students need reinforcement for certain topics. The resources below are recommended for reteaching. If students were introduced to a topic through the Print Path, you can also use the Digital Path to reteach, and vice versa.

🎧 *Can be assigned to individual students*

DNA Structure
Quick Lab Building a DNA Sequence 🎧

Activity Standup DNA

DNA Replication
Activity Human DNA Model

Mutations
Discussion Mutating DNA

Quick Lab Mutations Cause Diversity 🎧

DNA Transcription and Translation
Activity Make Connections 🎧

Summative Assessment

Alternative Assessment
Exploring the Double Helix

⊘ *Online resources: student worksheet, optional rubrics*

DNA Structure and Function

Points of View: *Exploring the Double Helix*
Your class will work together to show what you've learned about DNA from several different viewpoints.

1. Work in groups as assigned by your teacher. Each group will be assigned to one or two viewpoints.

2. Complete your assignment, and present your perspective to the class.

DNA

 Vocabulary Define *DNA* in your own words, and also write down a dictionary or textbook definition. Then write three sentences that use the word *DNA*.

 Details Describe the components of DNA. Make sure to use the word *nucleotide*.

 Illustrations Draw a picture of a DNA molecule and show how it replicates.

 Examples Give examples of what can happen when a mutation in a piece of DNA occurs. Explain how mutations can happen.

 Analysis Tell how the components of DNA work together.

Going Further
- [ ] **Environmental Science Connection**
- [ ] **Real World Connection**

Formative Assessment
- [ ] **Strategies** Throughout TE
- [ ] **Lesson Review** SE

Summative Assessment
- [ ] **Alternative Assessment** Exploring the Double Helix
- [ ] **Lesson Quiz**
- [ ] **Unit Tests A and B**
- [ ] **Unit Review** SE End-of-Unit

Your Resources

_____

_____

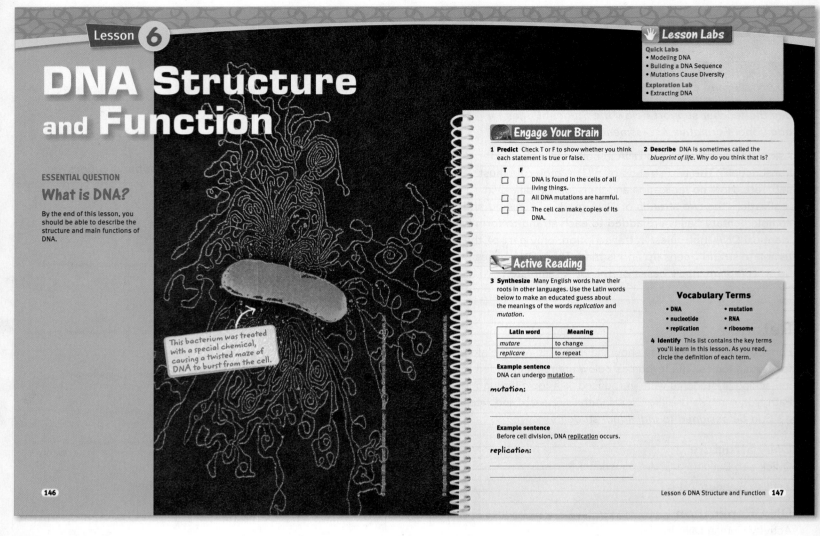

Answers

Answers for 1–3 should represent students' current thoughts, even if incorrect.

1. T; F; T

2. Sample answer: DNA contains the instructions that the body's cells need.

3. a change; the process of making a copy

4. Students' annotations will vary.

Opening Your Lesson

Discuss students' answers to items 1 and 2 to assess their prerequisite knowledge and to estimate what they already know about the key topics.

Preconceptions: Students may believe that each cell has a unique set of instructions, in the form of DNA, that code for the unique products of that cell. In fact, each cell (with the exception of egg and sperm) contains the entire set of chromosomes, which includes two copies of every gene. Only a small fraction of each chromosome contains genes, and only a small fraction of the genes are converted into proteins in any one cell.

Prerequisites: Students should already have a basic understanding of heredity, including that inherited traits are passed from parents to their offspring through their genes. Students should also know how and why cells divide and what happens to genetic material during cell division.

Learning Alert

Difficult Concepts The roles of DNA, RNA, and proteins in cells are very complex, and many puzzles remain. Students may tend to simplify their concept of the "rules" as they learn them. Students may also remain unconvinced of the role of random mutations in heredity.

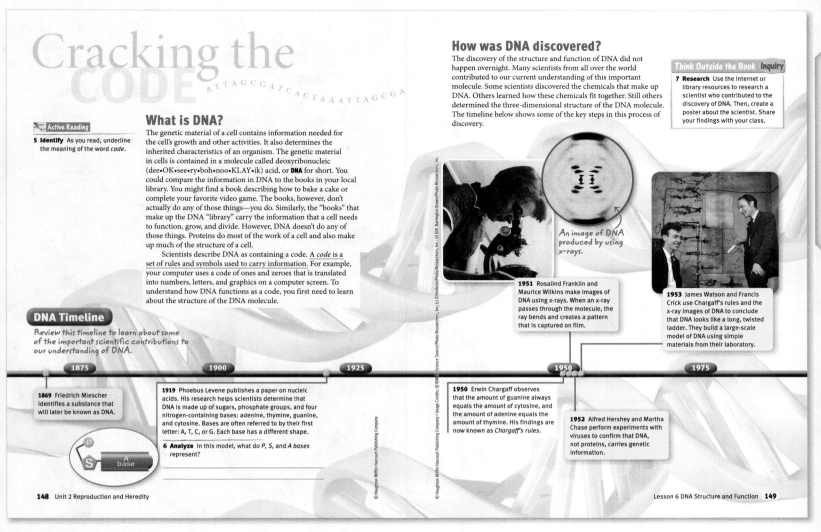

Cracking the CODE
ATTAGCGATCACTAAATTAGCGA

5 Identify As you read, underline the meaning of the word *code*.

What is DNA?

The genetic material of a cell contains information needed for the cell's growth and other activities. It also determines the inherited characteristics of an organism. The genetic material in cells is contained in a molecule called deoxyribonucleic (dee•OK•see•ry•boh•noo•KLAY•ik) acid, or **DNA** for short. You could compare the information in DNA to the books in your local library. You might find a book describing how to bake a cake or complete your favorite video game. The books, however, don't actually do any of those things—you do. Similarly, the "books" that make up the DNA "library" carry the information that a cell needs to function, grow, and divide. However, DNA doesn't do any of those things. Proteins do most of the work of a cell and also make up much of the structure of a cell.

Scientists describe DNA as containing a code. A *code* is a set of rules and symbols used to carry information. For example, your computer uses a code of ones and zeroes that is translated into numbers, letters, and graphics on a computer screen. To understand how DNA functions as a code, you first need to learn about the structure of the DNA molecule.

DNA Timeline

Review this timeline to learn about some of the important scientific contributions to our understanding of DNA.

1869 Friedrich Miescher identifies a substance that will later be known as DNA.

1919 Phoebus Levene publishes a paper on nucleic acids. His research helps scientists determine that DNA is made up of sugars, phosphate groups, and four nitrogen-containing bases: adenine, thymine, guanine, and cytosine. Bases are often referred to by their first letter: A, T, C, or G. Each base has a different shape.

6 Analyze In this model, what do *P, S,* and *A bases* represent?

P S A base

1875 1900 1925 1950 1975

How was DNA discovered?

The discovery of the structure and function of DNA did not happen overnight. Many scientists from all over the world contributed to our current understanding of this important molecule. Some scientists discovered the chemicals that make up DNA. Others learned how these chemicals fit together. Still others determined the three-dimensional structure of the DNA molecule. The timeline below shows some of the key steps in this process of discovery.

Think Outside the Book Inquiry

7 Research Use the Internet or library resources to research a scientist who contributed to the discovery of DNA. Then, create a poster about the scientist. Share your findings with your class.

An image of DNA produced by using x-rays.

1951 Rosalind Franklin and Maurice Wilkins make images of DNA using x-rays. When an x-ray passes through the molecule, the ray bends and creates a pattern that is captured on film.

1953 James Watson and Francis Crick use Chargaff's rules and the x-ray images of DNA to conclude that DNA looks like a long, twisted ladder. They build a large-scale model of DNA using simple materials from their laboratory.

1950 Erwin Chargaff observes that the amount of guanine always equals the amount of cytosine, and the amount of adenine equals the amount of thymine. His findings are now known as *Chargaff's rules.*

1952 Alfred Hershey and Martha Chase perform experiments with viruses to confirm that DNA, not proteins, carries genetic information.

Answers

5. *See students' pages for annotations.*

6. phosphate, sugar, and adenine base

7. Students should create a poster that contains biographical information about the scientist and his or her contribution to the study of DNA.

Building Reading Skills

Text Structure: Sequence Guide students as they read the DNA timeline. Emphasize how later discoveries build on earlier ones. **Ask:** What important discovery about DNA happened in 1950? Erwin Chargaff observed that the amount of guanine always equals the amount of cytosine, and the amount of adenine equals the amount of thymine. **Ask:** What later discovery about DNA depended on Chargaff's findings? Watson and Crick used Chargaff's rules to conclude that DNA looks like a long, twisted ladder.

Learning Alert

The Genetic Material Most scientists initially thought that the genetic material was protein because proteins are made from 20 different amino acids, which can be combined in many more ways. Scientists also knew that proteins were important to many aspects of cell structure and metabolism, but they knew very little about DNA. Although earlier experiments pointed to DNA as the genetic material, Hershey and Chase provided more conclusive evidence. They infected bacteria with a virus. Scientists knew that viruses are composed of DNA or RNA surrounded by a protein coat, and that when viruses infect bacterial cells, they produce more viruses. When Hershey and Chase examined the infected bacteria, they found that viral DNA, not viral protein, had been injected into the bacterial cells, proving that DNA is the genetic material.

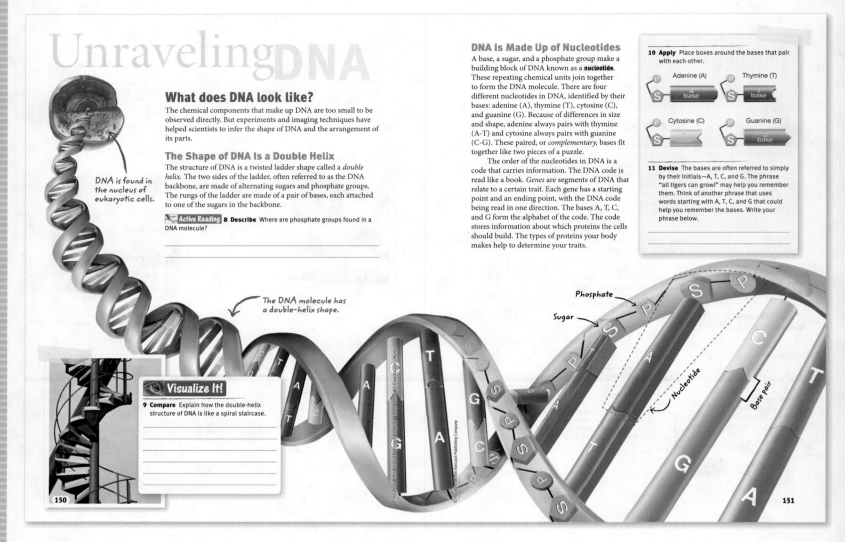

Unraveling DNA

What does DNA look like?

The chemical components that make up DNA are too small to be observed directly. But experiments and imaging techniques have helped scientists to infer the shape of DNA and the arrangement of its parts.

The Shape of DNA Is a Double Helix

The structure of DNA is a twisted ladder shape called a *double helix*. The two sides of the ladder, often referred to as the DNA backbone, are made of alternating sugars and phosphate groups. The rungs of the ladder are made of a pair of bases, each attached to one of the sugars in the backbone.

Active Reading 8 **Describe** Where are phosphate groups found in a DNA molecule?

_____

_____

DNA is found in the nucleus of eukaryotic cells.

The DNA molecule has a double-helix shape.

Visualize It!

9 **Compare** Explain how the double-helix structure of DNA is like a spiral staircase.

_____

_____

_____

150

DNA Is Made Up of Nucleotides

A base, a sugar, and a phosphate group make a building block of DNA known as a **nucleotide**. These repeating chemical units join together to form the DNA molecule. There are four different nucleotides in DNA, identified by their bases: adenine (A), thymine (T), cytosine (C), and guanine (G). Because of differences in size and shape, adenine always pairs with thymine (A-T) and cytosine always pairs with guanine (C-G). These paired, or *complementary*, bases fit together like two pieces of a puzzle.

The order of the nucleotides in DNA is a code that carries information. The DNA code is read like a book. *Genes* are segments of DNA that relate to a certain trait. Each gene has a starting point and an ending point, with the DNA code being read in one direction. The bases A, T, C, and G form the alphabet of the code. The code stores information about which proteins the cells should build. The types of proteins your body makes help to determine your traits.

10 **Apply** Place boxes around the bases that pair with each other.

Adenine (A)   Thymine (T)

Cytosine (C)   Guanine (G)

11 **Devise** The bases are often referred to simply by their initials—A, T, C, and G. The phrase "all tigers can growl" may help you remember them. Think of another phrase that uses words starting with A, T, C, and G that could help you remember the bases. Write your phrase below.

_____

Phosphate

Sugar

Nucleotide

Base pair

151

Answers

8. on the sides of the twisted-ladder shape of DNA

9. DNA and a spiral staircase both have a spiral shape. The "steps" of DNA are the base pairs. The "rails" of DNA are the sugar-phosphate backbones.

10. Students should draw boxes around adenine and thymine and around cytosine and guanine.

11. Students should create a phrase that contains four words that begin with the letters A, T, C, and G, in any order. Sample answer: Graham crackers are tasty.

Building Reading Skills

Student Vocabulary Strategy Help students understand the meaning of the word *helix* from context. **Prompt:** If a double helix is shaped like a twisted ladder, what would a single helix be shaped like? a spiral

Formative Assessment

Ask: If one strand of DNA has the nucleotide sequence TCGAACT, what must the matching sequence on the other strand be? AGCTTGA. Now invent your own sequence of base pairs. Remember to pair bases correctly. Answers will vary, but should have adenine paired with thymine and cytosine paired with guanine.

Building Math Skills

Ask: A given sequence of three bases codes for one amino acid. For example, AGT is one possible sequence. How many different sequences of the four DNA base types are possible? You can make a list to help you. $4 \times 4 \times 4 = 64$; There are 64 possible three-letter sequences. Explain that each combination of three nucleotides that codes for one amino acid is called a *codon*. Since there are 64 possible codons but cells use only 20 different amino acids to build proteins, most amino acids have several redundant corresponding, or synonymous, codons.

Replication and Mutation

How are copies of DNA made?

The cell is able to make copies of DNA molecules through a process known as **replication**. During replication, the two strands of DNA separate, almost like two threads in a string being unwound. The bases on each side of the molecule are used as a pattern for a new strand. As the bases on the original molecule are exposed, complementary nucleotides are added. For example, an exposed base containing adenine attaches to a nucleotide containing thymine. When replication is complete, there are two identical DNA molecules. Each new DNA molecule is made of one strand of old DNA and one strand of new DNA.

Visualize It!

12 Apply Fill in the blanks to complete the labels on this model of replicating DNA.

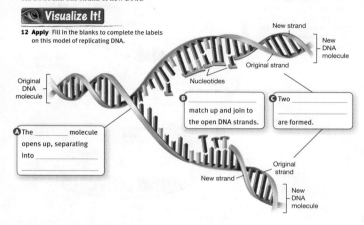

New strand

New DNA molecule

Original strand

Nucleotides

Original DNA molecule

B _____ match up and join to the open DNA strands.

C Two _____ are formed.

A The _____ molecule opens up, separating into _____

New strand

Original strand

New DNA molecule

When are copies of DNA made?

Before a cell divides, it copies the DNA so that each new daughter cell will have a complete set of instructions. Our cells can replicate DNA in just a few hours. How? Replication begins in many places along the DNA strand. So, many groups of proteins are working to replicate your DNA at the same time.

152 Unit 2 Reproduction and Heredity

What are mutations?

Changes in the number, type, or order of bases on a piece of DNA are known as **mutations**. Sometimes, a base is left out. This kind of change is known as a *deletion*. Or, an extra base might be added. This kind of change is an *insertion*. The most common mutation happens when one base replaces another. This kind of change is known as a *substitution*.

How do mutations happen? Given the large number of bases in an organism's DNA, it is not surprising that random errors can occur during replication. However, DNA can also be damaged by physical or chemical agents called *mutagens*. Ultraviolet light and the chemicals in cigarette smoke are examples of mutagens.

Cells make proteins that can fix errors in DNA. But sometimes a mistake isn't corrected, and it becomes part of the genetic code. Mutations to DNA may be beneficial, neutral, or harmful. A *genetic disorder* results from mutations that harm the normal function of a cell. Some of these disorders, such as Tay-Sachs disease and sickle-cell anemia, are *inherited*, or passed on from parent to offspring. Other genetic disorders result from mutations that occur during a person's lifetime. Most cancers fall into this category.

Visualize It!

13 Apply Place a check mark in the box to indicate which type of mutation is being shown.

Original sequence

☐ deletion ☐ insertion ☐ substitution

☐ deletion ☐ insertion ☐ substitution

☐ deletion ☐ insertion ☐ substitution

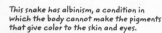

☐ deletion ☐ insertion ☐ substitution

This snake has albinism, a condition in which the body cannot make the pigments that give color to the skin and eyes.

14 Explain Albinism is an inherited genetic disorder. Explain what is meant by "inherited genetic disorder."

Lesson 6 DNA Structure and Function **153**

Answers

12. A: DNA; two strands; B: Nucleotides; C: identical molecules

13. A: substitution; B: insertion; C: deletion

14. The change in the DNA that causes albinism is passed on from parent to offspring.

Interpreting Visuals

Help students understand the diagram of replicating DNA. **Ask:** Why is one strand labeled "Original strand" and the other labeled "New strand"? The bases on each strand of the original molecule are used as a pattern for a new strand. **Ask:** Why are nucleotides joining at different places along the DNA strands? Replication is taking place at many places along the DNA strand.

Formative Assessment

Ask: What are two ways mutations can happen? Through random errors during replication; through damage to DNA by physical or chemical agents called *mutagens*.
Ask: If a sequence of DNA with the base pairs A-T, C-G, G-C, A-T, T-A is replicated as A-T, G-C, G-C, T-A, what kinds of mutations have occurred? substitution and deletion

Learning Alert

Error Correction Nucleotides can be added to a growing DNA strand only if the previous nucleotide is correctly paired to its complementary base. In the event of a mismatched nucleotide, the incorrect nucleotide is removed and replaced with the correct one. This "proofreading" reduces errors in replication to about one error per 1 billion nucleotides.

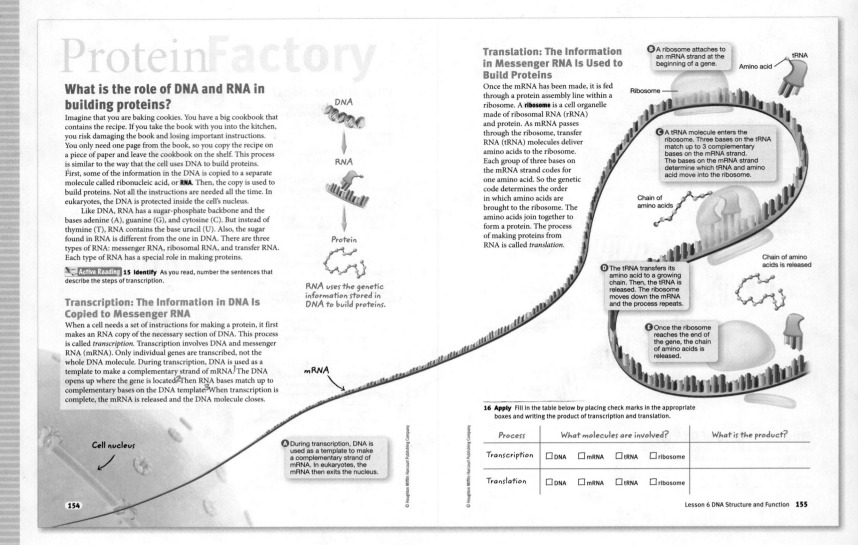

Protein Factory

What is the role of DNA and RNA in building proteins?

Imagine that you are baking cookies. You have a big cookbook that contains the recipe. If you take the book with you into the kitchen, you risk damaging the book and losing important instructions. You only need one page from the book, so you copy the recipe on a piece of paper and leave the cookbook on the shelf. This process is similar to the way that the cell uses DNA to build proteins. First, some of the information in the DNA is copied to a separate molecule called ribonucleic acid, or **RNA**. Then, the copy is used to build proteins. Not all the instructions are needed all the time. In eukaryotes, the DNA is protected inside the cell's nucleus.

Like DNA, RNA has a sugar-phosphate backbone and the bases adenine (A), guanine (G), and cytosine (C). But instead of thymine (T), RNA contains the base uracil (U). Also, the sugar found in RNA is different from the one in DNA. There are three types of RNA: messenger RNA, ribosomal RNA, and transfer RNA. Each type of RNA has a special role in making proteins.

Active Reading 15 **Identify** As you read, number the sentences that describe the steps of transcription.

Transcription: The Information in DNA Is Copied to Messenger RNA

When a cell needs a set of instructions for making a protein, it first makes an RNA copy of the necessary section of DNA. This process is called *transcription*. Transcription involves DNA and messenger RNA (mRNA). Only individual genes are transcribed, not the whole DNA molecule. During transcription, DNA is used as a template to make a complementary strand of mRNA. The DNA opens up where the gene is located. Then RNA bases match up to complementary bases on the DNA template. When transcription is complete, the mRNA is released and the DNA molecule closes.

DNA

RNA

Protein

RNA uses the genetic information stored in DNA to build proteins.

mRNA

Cell nucleus

A During transcription, DNA is used as a template to make a complementary strand of mRNA. In eukaryotes, the mRNA then exits the nucleus.

154

© Houghton Mifflin Harcourt Publishing Company

Translation: The Information in Messenger RNA Is Used to Build Proteins

Once the mRNA has been made, it is fed through a protein assembly line within a ribosome. A **ribosome** is a cell organelle made of ribosomal RNA (rRNA) and protein. As mRNA passes through the ribosome, transfer RNA (tRNA) molecules deliver amino acids to the ribosome. Each group of three bases on the mRNA strand codes for one amino acid. So the genetic code determines the order in which amino acids are brought to the ribosome. The amino acids join together to form a protein. The process of making proteins from RNA is called *translation*.

B A ribosome attaches to an mRNA strand at the beginning of a gene.

Amino acid

tRNA

Ribosome

C A tRNA molecule enters the ribosome. Three bases on the tRNA match up to 3 complementary bases on the mRNA strand. The bases on the mRNA strand determine which tRNA and amino acid move into the ribosome.

Chain of amino acids

Chain of amino acids is released

D The tRNA transfers its amino acid to a growing chain. Then, the tRNA is released. The ribosome moves down the mRNA and the process repeats.

E Once the ribosome reaches the end of the gene, the chain of amino acids is released.

16 **Apply** Fill in the table below by placing check marks in the appropriate boxes and writing the product of transcription and translation.

Process	What molecules are involved?				What is the product?
Transcription	☐ DNA	☐ mRNA	☐ tRNA	☐ ribosome	
Translation	☐ DNA	☐ mRNA	☐ tRNA	☐ ribosome	

© Houghton Mifflin Harcourt Publishing Company

Lesson 6 DNA Structure and Function   **155**

Answers

15. *See students' pages for annotations.*
16. Transcription: mRNA, DNA; complementary strand of mRNA; Translation: mRNA, tRNA, ribosome; protein

Learning Alert

Proteins Proteins have many functions in organisms. Some, such as hormones, serve as chemical messengers. Proteins act as transport molecules in cells, allowing only specific molecules in. Proteins on cell surfaces act as receptors to determine what materials can enter a cell and when foreign substances are present. For example, proteins in the immune system immobilize foreign molecules so they can be destroyed. Proteins also help maintain blood pH and serve as the oxygen-carrying molecule (hemoglobin) in blood.

Eukaryotes and Prokaryotes Remind students that eukaryotes are organisms whose cells have a nucleus and prokaryotes are organisms whose cells do not. The DNA of prokaryotes has a circular shape and remains in a region of the cell called the nucleoid at all times, including during transcription and translation.

Building Reading Skills

Text Structure: Compare/Contrast Help students understand the differences between RNA and DNA. **Ask:** How are RNA and DNA alike and different? Like DNA, RNA has a sugar and phosphate backbone, and the bases adenine, guanine, and cytosine. The sugar-phosphate backbone of RNA has a different structure than that of DNA, and RNA contains uracil instead of thymine.

🌐 *Optional Online resource: Text Structure: Comparison/Contrast support*

Visual Summary

To complete this summary, fill in the blanks with the correct word or phrase. Then use the key below to check your answers. You can use this page to review the main concepts of the lesson.

DNA Structure and Function

DNA has a double-helix shape and is made up of nucleotides.

17 The four bases in DNA nucleotides are _____

The cell can make copies of DNA.

18 DNA replication happens before cells _____

DNA and RNA are involved in making proteins.

20 The two processes involved in making proteins from the DNA code are _____

DNA can mutate.

19 Three types of DNA mutations are _____

Answers: 17 adenine, guanine, cytosine, and thymine; 18 divide; 19 insertion, deletion, and substitution; 20 transcription; translation

21 Explain How could a mutation in the DNA affect what proteins are made by the cell?

© Houghton Mifflin Harcourt Publishing Company

Lesson Review

Vocabulary

In your own words, define the following terms.

1 A(n) _____ of DNA consists of a sugar, a phosphate, and a nitrogen-containing base.

2 A(n) _____ is a change in the base sequence of a DNA molecule.

Key Concepts

Draw a line to connect the following scientists to their contributions to our understanding of DNA.

3 Erwin Chargaff

4 Rosalind Franklin and Maurice Wilkins

5 James Watson and Francis Crick

A took x-ray images of DNA molecule

B proposed a double-helix model of DNA

C found that the amount of adenine equals the amount of thymine and that the amount of guanine equals the amount of cytosine

6 Identify How does the structure of RNA differ from the structure of DNA?

7 Identify When does DNA replication occur?

8 Describe Name the three types of RNA and list their roles in making proteins.

9 Identify What can cause DNA mutations?

Critical Thinking

Use this diagram to answer the following questions.

10 Describe What is the sequence of bases on DNA strand *b*, from left to right?

11 Apply This segment of DNA is transcribed to form a complementary strand of mRNA. The mRNA then undergoes translation. How many amino acids would the RNA code for?

12 Infer After many cell divisions, a segment of DNA has more base pairs than it originally did. Explain what has happened.

13 Explain Why must DNA replicate?

© Houghton Mifflin Harcourt Publishing Company

Visual Summary Answers

17. adenine, guanine, cytosine, and thymine

18. divide

19. insertion, deletion, and substitution

20. transcription; translation

21. A mutation in the DNA could result in a different sequence of bases. These bases will cause different amino acids to be brought to the ribosome by tRNA. Different amino acids would make a different protein.

Lesson Review Answers

1. nucleotide

2. mutation

3. C

4. A

5. B

6. RNA contains uracil instead of thymine and has a different type of sugar in its backbone.

7. before cell division

8. mRNA: provides instructions for building a protein; rRNA: makes up the ribosome; tRNA: transfers amino acids to the ribosome during translation

9. random errors in replication and mutagens such as ultraviolet light

10. TGAGGACTT

11. 3

12. An insertion mutation has occurred.

13. The body is constantly generating new cells. Each cell must contain a copy of the instructions needed to build proteins. So, each cell needs a DNA molecule.

Identifying Variables

Purpose To identify the variables in a scientific experiment

Learning Goals
- Identify the independent variable and the dependent variable in an experiment.
- Analyze a graph showing the relationship between variables in order to identify the effects of the variables.

Informal Vocabulary
independent variable, dependent variable, **x**-axis, **y**-axis

Prerequisite Knowledge
- Scientific investigations
- How scientists represent data
- Structure and function of DNA

Discussion *What Variables Show*

 whole class   10 min
                                           GUIDED inquiry

Encourage students to think about what they already know about variables. **Ask:** In an experiment, what is the independent variable? Sample answer: It is the variable that is purposely changed in an experiment. **Ask:** What is the dependent variable? Sample answer: It is the factor that changes in response to the independent variable.

For greater depth, provide students with descriptions of simple experiments, and guide them to identify the independent and dependent variables in each one.

○ *Optional Online resource: Identifying Variables and Constants support*

○ *Optional Online rubric: Class Discussion*

Differentiated Instruction

Basic *Experiment Summary*

 pairs   ○ 15 min

Tell students to describe an experiment that clearly shows the independent and dependent variables without identifying them. Then direct students to exchange summaries with a partner. Tell partners to identify the dependent and independent variables based on the information contained in the summary.

○ *Optional Online resource: Identifying Variables and Constants support*

Advanced *Plan an Experiment*

 individuals   ○ 20 min

Allow students to plan and write a design for an experiment they could conduct. They should clearly describe the methods they would use and identify the variables. Encourage students to also explain how they would display the results of their experiment.

○ *Optional Online rubrics: Design Your Own Investigations: Experiments, Written Pieces*

ELL *Make a Graph*

 pairs or small groups   ○ 10 min

Tell students that an experimenter wants to see how tall corn plants will grow when they are given different amounts of water. In the experiment, plants are given either 1 mL, 2 mL, or 3 mL of water per day. Have students draw a graph that presents the hypothetical results of this experiment.

○ *Optional Online resource: Graphing Data support*

Customize Your Feature

☐ **Discussion** What Variables Show

☐ **Basic** Experiment Summary

☐ **Advanced** Plan an Experiment

☐ **ELL** Make a Graph

☐ **Take It Home**

Think Science

Identifying Variables

When you are analyzing or designing a scientific experiment, it is important to identify the variables in the experiment. Usually, an experiment is designed to discover how changing one variable affects another variable. In a scientific investigation, the independent variable is the factor that is purposely changed. The dependent variable is the factor that changes in response to the independent variable.

Tutorial

Use the following strategies to help you identify the variables in an experiment.

Summary: We genetically modified corn plants to increase growth in low-light conditions.

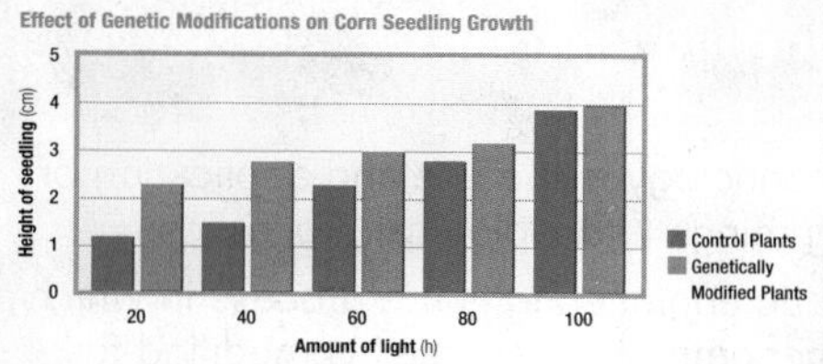

Effect of Genetic Modifications on Corn Seedling Growth

(bar graph: Height of seedling (cm) vs Amount of light (h), with Control Plants and Genetically Modified Plants)

Reading a Summary The published results of an experiment usually include a brief summary. You should be able to identify the variables from it. In the summary to the left, the independent variable is the DNA of the corn plants, and the dependent variable is the height of the plants.

Analyzing a Graph Making a graph can be a very effective way to show the relationship between variables. For a line graph, the independent variable is usually shown on the x-axis, or the horizontal axis. The dependent variable is usually shown on the y-axis, or the vertical axis.

Describing the Data When you read a graph, describing the information in complete sentences can help you to identify the variables. For example, you could write, "In the first 80 hours, the genetically modified corn plants grew much more quickly than the control plants grew. But by 100 hours, both kinds of plants were about the same height. This shows that the effect of the independent variable was greatest during the first 80 hours of plant growth."

Identifying the Effects of Variables Look closely at the graph. Notice that the genetically modified seedlings grew more quickly than the control seedlings, but the effects were greatest in the early part of the experiment. A variable's effect is not always constant throughout an experiment.

158

You Try It!

The passage below describes the process of gel electrophoresis. Use the description to answer the question that follows.

During gel electrophoresis, DNA is broken into separate fragments. These fragments are added to a gel. When an electric current is applied to the gel, the fragments travel different distances through the gel. The size of the DNA fragments determines how far they travel. Smaller fragments travel farther than larger fragments do. Scientists can use these data to identify unknown samples of DNA.

1 Reading a Summary Identify the variables described in the passage.

_____

_____

The graph below shows the results of DNA analysis using gel electrophoresis. Look at the graph, and answer the questions that follow.

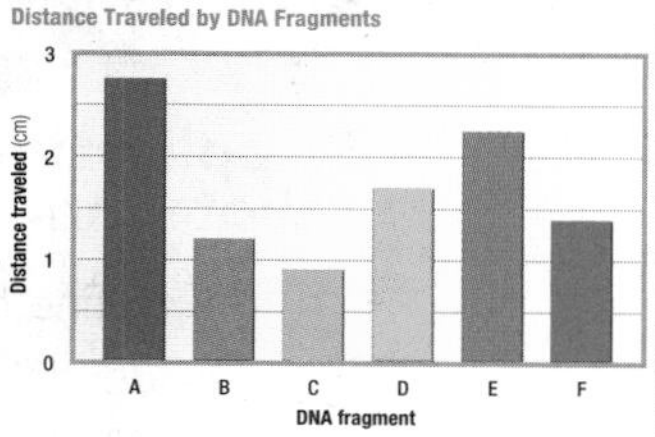

Distance Traveled by DNA Fragments

(bar graph: Distance traveled (cm) vs DNA fragment A–F)

2 Analyzing a Graph Which variables are shown in the graph? Circle the axis that shows the dependent variable.

_____

_____

3 Analyzing the Data What is the relationship between the size of the DNA fragments and the distance they traveled? Circle the DNA fragment that is the smallest.

_____

_____

4 Applying Mathematics Calculate the average distance that the DNA fragments traveled. How much farther than the average distance did the smallest DNA fragment travel?

5 Applying Concepts Why is it important to limit the number of variables in an experiment?

_____

_____

_____

Take It Home

With an adult, plan and conduct a simple experiment that includes an independent variable and a dependent variable. Record your results and graph your data if possible. Then share your results with the class.

Unit 2 Think Science 159

Answers

1. The independent variable described in the passage is the size of the DNA fragment. The dependent variable is the distance that the fragment travels.

2. The dependent variable (distance traveled) is on the vertical axis (y-axis), and the independent variable (DNA fragment) on the horizontal axis (x-axis).

3. The DNA fragment with the smallest size will travel the farthest distance. The larger DNA fragments will travel a shorter distance. Students should circle fragment A as the smallest because it has travelled the farthest.

4. Students should estimate the distance each fragment has travelled based on the graph. The average distance travelled by the DNA fragments is 1.7 cm. The smallest DNA fragment travelled 1.1 cm farther than the average distance.

5. It is important to limit the number of variables in an experiment so that you can be sure to identify the specific variable that is affecting your results. If you have more than one variable that you are testing, it will be much more difficult to determine which of the variables is the one affecting the results.

Take It Home

Simple experiments may use time as the independent variable. For example, how many seconds (t) does it take a marble to roll down a 2-ft ramp when one end is held x inches above the other?

Optional Online rubric: Design Your Own Investigations: Experiments

Biotechnology

Essential Question How does biotechnology impact our world?

For more detailed information about the topics in this lesson, refer to the Content Refresher in the Unit Opener pages.

Opening Your Lesson

Begin the lesson by assessing students' prerequisite and prior knowledge.

Prerequisite Knowledge

• Structure and function of DNA

Accessing Prior Knowledge

Help students review what they know about key topics. Have students write whether or not they agree with the following statements.

1 Biotechnology has existed for only the past 40 years.

2 The dog breed varieties that exist today are products of artificial selection.

3 A gene from one species can be transferred to the DNA of another species.

4 People can clone only cells, not whole organisms.

Customize Your Opening

☐ **Accessing Prior Knowledge,** above

☐ **Print Path** Engage Your Brain, SE p. 161 #1–2

☐ **Print Path** Active Reading, SE p. 161 #3–4

☐ **Digital Path** Lesson Opener

Key Topics/Learning Goals

Applications of Biotechnology

1 Define *biotechnology*.

2 Identify examples of biotechnology, including cloning, genetic engineering, and artificial selection (selective breeding).

Biotechnology and Society

1 Identify biotechnology's impact on individuals, society, and the environment.

Supporting Concepts

• Biotechnology is the use and application of living things and biological processes.

• Genetic engineering is the process in which the genome of a living cell is modified for medical or industrial use.

• Artificial selection, also called selective breeding, is the human practice of breeding animals or plants to have certain desired traits. It is used to develop new varieties of plants and domesticated animals.

• A clone is an organism, cell, or piece of genetic material that is genetically identical to one from which it was derived. *Cloning* refers to any process in which a genetic duplicate is made.

• Biotechnology can affect individuals, society, and the environment. Scientists, policymakers, and citizens weigh these impacts and consider the risks, benefits, and ethical concerns associated with different forms of biotechnology.

Options for Instruction

Two parallel paths provide coverage of the Essential Questions, with a strong **Inquiry** strand woven into each.
Follow the **Print Path,** the **Digital Path,** or your customized combination of print, digital, and inquiry.

 Print Path
Teaching support for the Print Path appears with the Student Pages.

 Inquiry Labs and Activities

 Digital Path
Digital Path shortcut: TS673280

Biotechnology, SE pp. 162–165
What is biotechnology?
What are some applications of biotechnology?
- Artificial Selection
- Genetic Engineering
- Cloning

Quick Lab
Observing Selective Breeding

Quick Lab
How Can a Simple Code Be Used to Make a Product?

Activity
History of Corn

Activity
Genetically Engineered Plants

Activity
Biotechnology Types

Artificial Selection
Interactive Images

The Process of Genetic Engineering
Animation

Three Make One
Slideshow

Feel the Impact!,
SE pp. 166–167
How does biotechnology impact our world?

Positive and Negative Effects of Biotechnology
Video

Options for Assessment

See the Evaluate page for options, including Formative Assessment, Summative Assessment, and Unit Review.

Engage and Explore

Activities and Discussion

Discussion *Fruit Fancies*

Engage

Applications of Biotechnology

 whole class
🕐 10 min
 DIRECTED inquiry

Quick Discussion Have students identify their favorite fruits and vegetables. Then ask them what characteristics they would change in their favorites, if they could. Discuss how scientists manipulate characteristics of many fruits and vegetables using artificial selection or genetic engineering techniques.

Activity *History of Corn*

Engage

Applications of Biotechnology

👥 small groups
🕐 40 min
GUIDED inquiry

Timeline Corn is thought to have first been domesticated in Mexico more than 8,700 years ago from a wild grass that bears little resemblance to modern corn. Today there are many varieties of corn, from the sweet corn eaten as corn on the cob to that used as livestock feed. Corn is also used to make products such as corn syrup, corn starch, plastics, and ethanol. Many corn varieties are genetically modified. Divide the class into two groups. Have one group use library and Internet resources to research the history of corn domestication, cultivation, and use through artificial selection. Have the other group research the more recent history of corn, including how it has been genetically modified and how it is refined to make different products. Then, direct the class to work together to create an illustrated timeline of the history of corn from ancient times to the present.

Discussion *Ethics Debate*

Engage

Biotechnology and Society

👥 whole class
🕐 30 min
GUIDED inquiry

Class Debate Have students debate what regulations should be placed on genetic manipulation practices. Consider issues such as transferring genes between species, forensic uses of DNA, cloning, and genetic patents. Questions concerning these topics include: What are the environmental and health risks of transgenic organisms? When is it acceptable to collect DNA samples from a person? Should those DNA samples be kept in a database? Is it ethical to clone entire animals?

Activity *Genetically Engineered Plants*

Applications of Biotechnology

👥 small groups
🕐 45 min
INDEPENDENT inquiry

Oral Presentations Have students work in small groups to research genetically engineered plants. Assign each group a plant that is engineered for one of these reasons: to enhance its nutritional value, to be resistant to herbicides, to improve its resistance to insects or other pests, or to enhance its aesthetic value. Have each group present their findings, including a description and picture of the plant, the methods used to develop it, the cost and time involved in engineering it, the public's acceptance of the plant, and any problems associated with producing or marketing it.

Customize Your Labs

📒 *See the Lab Manual for lab datasheets.*

💿 *Go Online for editable lab datasheets.*

Levels of  **Inquiry** | **DIRECTED** inquiry | **GUIDED** inquiry | **INDEPENDENT** inquiry

| introduces inquiry skills within a structured framework. | develops inquiry skills within a supportive environment. | deepens inquiry skills with student-driven questions or procedures. |

Take It Home *Weird Produce*

Applications of Biotechnology

  adult-student pairs
🕐 varied
Inquiry **INDEPENDENT** inquiry

Have students and adults purchase a broccoflower or a tangelo from a supermarket. The pair can observe the produce and describe how it looks, tastes, and smells. They can also identify what pair of plants were crossed to make the produce and what characteristics come from each parent species. Students may also research the kind of biotechnology used to make the cross.

🌐 *Optional Online resource: student worksheet*

Discussion *Ancient DNA*

Synthesizing Key Topics

   whole class
🕐 20 min
Inquiry **GUIDED** inquiry

Dinosaurs went extinct millions of years ago, and it is not likely dinosaur DNA will be found. But, DNA of more recent species has been discovered. In fact, scientists have determined the woolly mammoth genome from DNA preserved in a frozen 27,000-year-old specimen. Some people speculate that this DNA can be used to clone mammoths and bring them back from extinction. Scientists are now using DNA to establish the chronology and genealogy of ancient Egyptian mummies. Discuss the benefits of using ancient DNA to study humans and other species and the ethical and environmental concerns related to cloning extinct species.

Labs and Demos

Quick Lab *Observing Selective Breeding*

Applications of Biotechnology

 individuals
🕐 20 min
Inquiry **DIRECTED** inquiry

Students study a diagram of wild cabbage and analyze how other vegetable species were bred from it using selective breeding.

PURPOSE **To describe how new species of plants have been produced through selective breeding**

MATERIALS
- colored pencils
- reference materials

Quick Lab *How Can a Simple Code Be Used to Make a Product?*

Applications of Biotechnology

👤 individuals
🕐 30 min
Inquiry **GUIDED** inquiry

Students decipher a numeric code in order to make sand sculptures with the colors in the correct order.

PURPOSE **To observe how a code can be used to make a product**

MATERIALS
- bottle, clear plastic
- code sheet
- colored pencils
- cups, paper (4)
- funnel
- sand, colored (4 colors)
- spoon

Activities and Discussion

☐ **Discussion** Fruit Fancies
☐ **Activity** History of Corn
☐ **Discussion** Ethics Debate
☐ **Activity** Genetically Engineered Plants
☐ **Take It Home** Weird Produce

☐ **Discussion** Ancient DNA

Labs and Demos

☐ **Quick Lab** Observing Selective Breeding
☐ **Quick Lab** How Can a Simple Code Be Used to Make a Product?

Your Resources

Explain Science Concepts

Key Topics	📖 Print Path	🖥 Digital Path
Applications of Biotechnology	☐ **Biotechnology,** SE pp. 162–165 • Think Outside the Book, #5 • Active Reading, #6 • Visualize It!, #7 • Active Reading, #8 • Infer, #9 • Apply, #10	☐ **Artificial Selection** Learn how artificial selection is used by scientists. ☐ **The Process of Genetic Engineering** Explore how scientists use genetic engineering to insert genes with desired traits into host organisms. ☐ **Three Make One** Learn how scientists are able to clone an organism.
Biotechnology and Society	☐ **Feel the Impact!,** SE pp. 166–167 • Evaluate, #11 • Think Outside the Book, #12	☐ **Positive and Negative Effects of Biotechnology** Learn about the positive and negative effects of biotechnology on the environment, society, and individuals.

Differentiated Instruction

Basic *Biotechnology Compare and Contrast*

Applications of Biotechnology

👥 individuals
🕐 20 min

Venn Diagram Have students develop a Venn diagram to compare and contrast artificial selection and genetic engineering. Guide them to include information about how each type of biotechnology works and what each is used for. Encourage them to also include advantages or disadvantages of each technique.

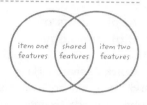

🌐 *Optional Online resource: Venn Diagram support*

Advanced *Interview a Scientist*

Synthesizing Key Topics

👥 individuals
🕐 varied

Instruct students to prepare for a visit to a pharmaceutical company or university that uses genetic engineering techniques. Have them write a list of questions about the research conducted, the staff and resources available, the techniques and equipment used, and any applications of the research that are currently in use.

To extend the activity, have students actually conduct their interviews and report their findings to the class.

ELL *Biotechnology Terms*

Applications of Biotechnology

👥 individuals
🕐 20 min

Cluster Diagram Struggling or EL learners may not know the words *artificial* or *engineering*, both of which are key to understanding biotechnology. Define these words for students (artificial: "made by humans," "not natural"; engineering: "the application of science and math to practical purposes"). Then have them create one cluster diagram for *artificial* and one for *engineering*. Provide students with examples for each word from outside the lesson as necessary to aid their understanding.

🌐 *Optional Online resource: Cluster Diagram support*

Lesson Vocabulary

biotechnology
genetic engineering
artificial selection
clone

Previewing Vocabulary

👥 whole class
🕐 ongoing

Magnet Word Use the Magnet Word strategy to help students understand the relationships among the terms in this lesson. Write the word *biotechnology* in a Word Magnet. Then, write the terms *genetic engineering, artificial selection,* and *clone* on lines around the magnet. Explain that each term relates to a type of biotechnology. As students read the lesson, encourage them to suggest other terms to add to the magnet.

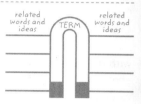

Reinforcing Vocabulary

👥 individuals
🕐 25 min

Description Wheel To help students learn the lesson vocabulary, have them make a description wheel for each lesson vocabulary term. Students write the term in the center of the wheel, and on the spokes, they write words describing the term, including definitions and examples.

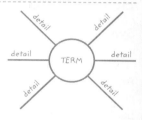

Customize Your Core Lesson

Core Instruction

☐ **Print Path** choices
☐ **Digital Path** choices

Vocabulary

☐ **Previewing Vocabulary** Magnet Word
☐ **Reinforcing Vocabulary** Description Wheel

Your Resources

Differentiated Instruction

☐ **Basic** Biotechnology Compare and Contrast
☐ **Advanced** Interview a Scientist
☐ **ELL** Biotechnology Terms

Extend Science Concepts

Reinforce and Review

Activity *Biotechnology Types*

Applications of Biotechnology

 whole class
🕐 20 min

Card Responses Have students make answer cards for questions you will ask. Each student should have three cards, one with *artificial selection,* one with *genetic engineering,* and one with *cloning*. Provide examples of biotechnology. At a signal from you, students hold up their cards to answer. Every few questions, include an example of biotechnology directly from the lesson and have students answer by holding up a card. If the class's accuracy rate is less than 90%, it might be time to reteach another way. This technique also helps pinpoint those who need individual help.

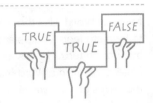

Booklet FoldNote

Synthesizing Key Topics

 individuals
🕐 ongoing

Booklet Have students create a Booklet FoldNote to summarize what they learned from the lesson. Each page of the booklet can contain a key topic from the lesson. Students should write the details of each key topic on the appropriate page to create an outline of the lesson.

🌐 *Online resource: Booklet FoldNote support*

Going Further

Health Connection

Applications of Biotechnology

 small groups
🕐 varied

Quick Research Have students work in small groups to research diseases that are more common in people of specific ethnic or racial backgrounds. Examples include sickle cell anemia, thalassemia, Tay-Sachs disease, and tyrosinemia. Have each group write a report on the disease, including its prevalence in the specific population and the general population; its symptoms and severity; current treatments available; and current genetic engineering research being conducted as part of efforts to prevent, control, and/or treat the disease.

🌐 *Optional Online rubric: Written Pieces*

Real World Connection

Applications of Biotechnology

 small groups
🕐 varied

Multimedia Presentations In 2003, the Human Genome Project (HGP) had mapped 99% of the 3 billion base pairs that make up human DNA. Many benefits are predicted to result from the HGP, and some have already been realized. For example, scientists working on the HGP developed faster methods of determining the DNA sequences in samples, making it easier to study the genetics of all kinds of organisms and to find the genetic indicators of specific kinds of diseases. Have small groups research one advancement in biotechnology resulting from the HGP, and prepare a multimedia presentation about the advancement to present to the class.

Customize Your Closing

🔶 *See the Assessment Guide for quizzes and tests.*

🌐 *Go Online to edit and create quizzes and tests.*

Reinforce and Review

- ☐ **Activity** Biotechnology Types
- ☐ **Activity** Booklet
- ☐ **Print Path** Visual Summary, SE p. 168
- ☐ **Digital Path** Lesson Closer

Evaluate Student Mastery

See the teacher support below the Student Pages for additional Formative Assessment questions.

Ask: How has biotechnology affected our world? Sample answer: For thousands of years, artificial selection has allowed humans to breed plants and animals to have desirable traits. More recently, genetic engineering and cloning have allowed further advancements in our understanding of genetics and have led to new applications of biotechnology, such as genetically modifying crops to make them resistant to plant-eating insects. But biotechnology also raises issues and could have a negative impact if not used wisely. For example, people must carefully consider genetically modified crops' impact on the environment before planting them. **Prompt:** Think about all aspects of biotechnology's impact, both positive and negative.

Reteach

Formative assessment may show that students need reinforcement for certain topics. The resources below are recommended for reteaching. If students were introduced to a topic through the Print Path, you can also use the Digital Path to reteach, and vice versa.
🎧 *Can be assigned to individual students*

Applications of Biotechnology

Activity Genetically Engineered Plants 🎧

Quick Lab Observing Selective Breeding 🎧

Activity Biotechnology Types

Biotechnology and Society

Discussion Ethics Debate

Discussion Ancient DNA

Alternative Assessment
The World of Biotechnology

🌐 Online resources: student worksheet, optional rubrics

Biotechnology

Climb the Pyramid: *The World of Biotechnology*
Climb the pyramid to show what you have learned about biotechnology.

1. Work on your own, with a partner, or with a small group.
2. Choose one item from each layer of the pyramid. Check your choices.
3. Have your teacher approve your plan.
4. Submit or present your results.

___ Assess the Impact
Choose one application of biotechnology you learned about. Create a list of pros and cons about it. You might consider the ethical, legal, social, financial, or environmental issues surrounding this technology.

___ Comic Strip
Draw a comic strip to show how humans have changed the animal or plant over time. Show the differences between the modern organism and its ancestors.

___ Just the Facts
Make a short presentation about how biotechnology is used in forensics or how transgenic organisms are used in scientific research.

___ Forensics
Research the technology behind DNA fingerprinting or other ways forensic scientists use biotechnology to help solve crimes.

___ Transgenic Organisms
Research a transgenic organism. Find out how the organism's genes were modified and for what purpose.

___ Breeding the Best
Find out about organism that has been bred by humans. It could be a pet, such as a dog, a farm animal, such as a chicken, or a crop, such as corn. How does it differ from its wild ancestors? What qualities have humans promoted through selective breeding?

Going Further
- [ ] **Health Connection**
- [ ] **Real World Connection**

Formative Assessment
- [ ] **Strategies** Throughout TE
- [ ] **Lesson Review** SE

Summative Assessment
- [ ] **Alternative Assessment** The World of Biotechnology
- [ ] **Lesson Quiz**
- [ ] **Unit Tests A and B**
- [ ] **Unit Review** SE End-of-Unit

Your Resources

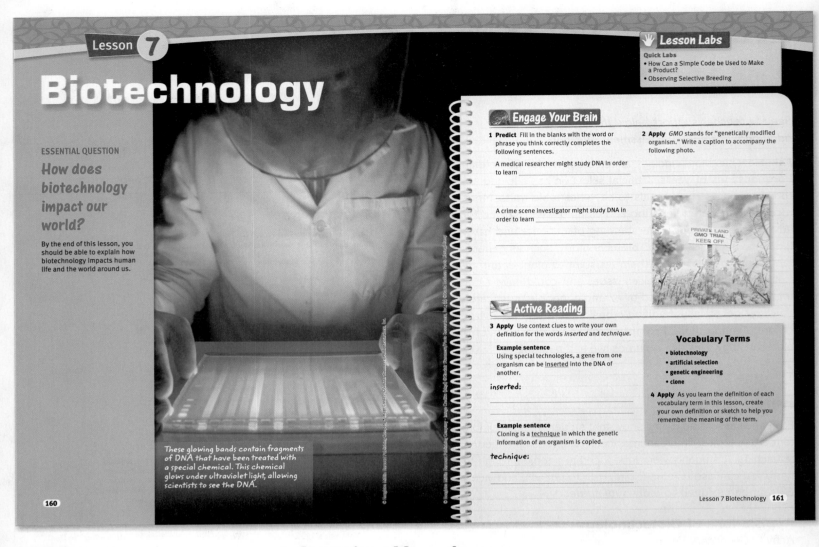

Lesson 7

Biotechnology

ESSENTIAL QUESTION

How does biotechnology impact our world?

By the end of this lesson, you should be able to explain how biotechnology impacts human life and the world around us.

These glowing bands contain fragments of DNA that have been treated with a special chemical. This chemical glows under ultraviolet light, allowing scientists to see the DNA.

160

Lesson Labs

Quick Labs
• How Can a Simple Code be Used to Make a Product?
• Observing Selective Breeding

Engage Your Brain

1 Predict Fill in the blanks with the word or phrase you think correctly completes the following sentences.

A medical researcher might study DNA in order to learn _____

A crime scene investigator might study DNA in order to learn _____

2 Apply *GMO* stands for "genetically modified organism." Write a caption to accompany the following photo.

_____

PRIVATE LAND
GMO TRIAL
KEER OFF

Active Reading

3 Apply Use context clues to write your own definition for the words *inserted* and *technique*.

Example sentence
Using special technologies, a gene from one organism can be <u>inserted</u> into the DNA of another.

inserted:

_____

Example sentence
Cloning is a <u>technique</u> in which the genetic information of an organism is copied.

technique:

_____

Vocabulary Terms
• biotechnology
• artificial selection
• genetic engineering
• clone

4 Apply As you learn the definition of each vocabulary term in this lesson, create your own definition or sketch to help you remember the meaning of the term.

Lesson 7 Biotechnology **161**

Answers

Answers for 1–3 should represent students' current thoughts, even if incorrect.

1. Sample answer: how to treat inherited disorders; who was at the scene of a crime

2. Sample answer: The DNA of these plants has been modified.

3. added into; a method

4. Students should define or sketch each vocabulary term in the lesson.

Opening Your Lesson

As students read the lesson, have them revisit their answers to item 1 and check if their answers were correct.

Preconceptions Technology is always electronic.

Prerequisites Students should already understand the structure and function of DNA, including that DNA is the genetic material and that genes in DNA code for proteins.

Learning Alert

Electrophoresis The photograph shows an example of gel electrophoresis, a technique for analyzing DNA. Electrophoresis applies an electric current that travels from one end of a depression filled with a gel material to the other. DNA samples that have been cut by digestive enzymes are placed in wells near the end of the gel where the electric current is applied. As the current moves toward the opposite end of the gel, fragments of the DNA also move. Smaller fragments move farther through the gel than larger fragments. After a set amount of time, the electric current is turned off. Ethidium bromide is used to stain the DNA, making it visible under ultraviolet light, as seen in the photograph. Electrophoresis can be used to help isolate particular genes for study or to create a DNA fingerprint that can be used to identify individuals, such as for use as forensic evidence.

BioTECHNOLOGY

Protective clothing keeps this geneticist safe as he works with infectious particles.

This scientist works inside of a greenhouse. He breeds potato plants.

What is biotechnology?

A forensic scientist makes copies of DNA from a crime scene. A botanist breeds flowers for their bright red blooms. A geneticist works to place a human gene into the DNA of bacteria. What do these processes have in common? They are all examples of biotechnology. **Biotechnology** is the use and application of living things and biological processes. In the past 40 years, new technologies have allowed scientists to directly change DNA. But biotechnology is not a new scientific field. For thousands of years, humans have been breeding plants and animals and using bacteria and yeast to ferment foods. These, too, are examples of biotechnology.

Active Reading 6 **Identify** Name three examples of biotechnology.

_____

_____

Think Outside the Book

5 **Research** Research careers in biotechnology. Choose a career that you might like to have and share it with your class. You may choose to present your findings in one of the following ways:
- a poster
- a computer presentation
- a play
- a short essay

162 Unit 2 Reproduction and Heredity

What are some applications of biotechnology?

Biotechnology processes fall into some broad categories. Artificial selection, genetic engineering, and cloning are some of the most common techniques.

Artificial Selection

For thousands of years, humans have been carefully selecting and breeding certain plants and animals that have desirable traits. Over many generations, horses have gotten faster, pigs have gotten leaner, and corn has become sweeter. **Artificial selection** is the process of selecting and breeding organisms that have certain desired traits. Artificial selection is also known as *selective breeding.*

Artificial selection can be successful as long as the desirable traits are controlled by genes. Animal and plant breeders select for alleles, which are different versions of a gene. The alleles being selected must already be present in the population. People do not change DNA during artificial selection. Instead, they cause certain alleles to become more common in a population. The different dog breeds are a good example of artificial selection. All dogs share a common ancestor, the wolf. However, thousands of years of selection by humans have produced dogs with a variety of characteristics.

Different dog breeds are produced by artificial selection.

Visualize It!

These vegetables have been developed through artificial selection. Their common ancestor is the mustard plant.

7 **Infer** Why might farmers use artificial selection to develop different types of vegetables?

_____

_____

Lesson 7 Biotechnology 163

Answers

5. Students should describe a career in biotechnology and explain why the career interests them.

6. Sample answer: breeding plants, fermenting foods, copying DNA found at a crime scene

7. Sample answer: to produce vegetables with different colors, shapes, and tastes

Learning Alert

Everyday Definitions Many students may think only electronic or digital devices count as technology. Broadly defined, *technology* is the application of knowledge for practical purposes or any product of such application. For example, humans began breeding animals thousands of years before electronic devices were created, and this is an example of technology (in this case, biotechnology) because people applied their knowledge that animals pass on certain characteristics to their offspring to create new breeds of animals. Other examples of technology include devices as simple as pencils and pens.

Probing Questions GUIDED Inquiry

Comparing How does artificial selection differ from natural selection? In artificial selection, humans select and breed organisms to have certain desired traits. In natural selection, organisms that have traits that help them to survive in their environment are better able to reproduce and pass on those traits. In this way, the environment "selects" the traits.

Interpreting Visuals

Ask: What characteristics might have been selected for in these dog breeds? Sample answers: attractiveness, obedience, speed, sense of smell, sense of hearing

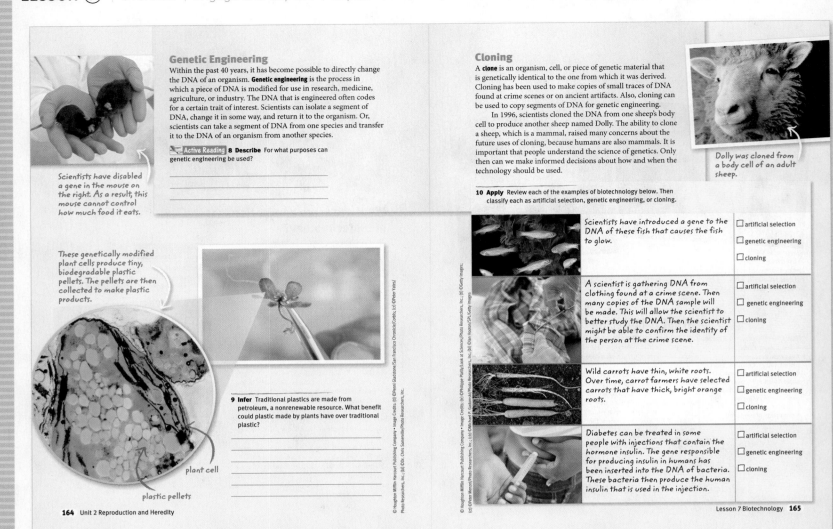

Genetic Engineering

Within the past 40 years, it has become possible to directly change the DNA of an organism. **Genetic engineering** is the process in which a piece of DNA is modified for use in research, medicine, agriculture, or industry. The DNA that is engineered often codes for a certain trait of interest. Scientists can isolate a segment of DNA, change it in some way, and return it to the organism. Or, scientists can take a segment of DNA from one species and transfer it to the DNA of an organism from another species.

Active Reading 8 Describe For what purposes can genetic engineering be used?

Scientists have disabled a gene in the mouse on the right. As a result, this mouse cannot control how much food it eats.

These genetically modified plant cells produce tiny, biodegradable plastic pellets. The pellets are then collected to make plastic products.

plant cell

plastic pellets

9 Infer Traditional plastics are made from petroleum, a nonrenewable resource. What benefit could plastic made by plants have over traditional plastic?

164   Unit 2 Reproduction and Heredity

Cloning

A **clone** is an organism, cell, or piece of genetic material that is genetically identical to the one from which it was derived. Cloning has been used to make copies of small traces of DNA found at crime scenes or on ancient artifacts. Also, cloning can be used to copy segments of DNA for genetic engineering.

In 1996, scientists cloned the DNA from one sheep's body cell to produce another sheep named Dolly. The ability to clone a sheep, which is a mammal, raised many concerns about the future uses of cloning, because humans are also mammals. It is important that people understand the science of genetics. Only then can we make informed decisions about how and when the technology should be used.

Dolly was cloned from a body cell of an adult sheep.

10 Apply Review each of the examples of biotechnology below. Then classify each as artificial selection, genetic engineering, or cloning.

Scientists have introduced a gene to the DNA of these fish that causes the fish to glow.	☐ artificial selection ☐ genetic engineering ☐ cloning
A scientist is gathering DNA from clothing found at a crime scene. Then many copies of the DNA sample will be made. This will allow the scientist to better study the DNA. Then the scientist might be able to confirm the identity of the person at the crime scene.	☐ artificial selection ☐ genetic engineering ☐ cloning
Wild carrots have thin, white roots. Over time, carrot farmers have selected carrots that have thick, bright orange roots.	☐ artificial selection ☐ genetic engineering ☐ cloning
Diabetes can be treated in some people with injections that contain the hormone insulin. The gene responsible for producing insulin in humans has been inserted into the DNA of bacteria. These bacteria then produce the human insulin that is used in the injection.	☐ artificial selection ☐ genetic engineering ☐ cloning

Lesson 7 Biotechnology   165

Answers

8. research, medicine, agriculture, or industry

9. Sample answer: Plastics grown in plant cells would be more sustainable because plants are a renewable resource.

10. genetic engineering; cloning; artificial selection; genetic engineering

Probing Questions   GUIDED Inquiry

Inferring Read the caption under the photograph of the mice. Why might scientists perform this kind of experiment on mice? Sample answer: It might help them learn about possible causes of obesity in humans. **Prompt:** Think about how their findings might apply to humans.

Learning Alert ▨ MISCONCEPTION ▨

Dino DNA Can ancient DNA be used to produce dinosaurs? In some science fiction books and movies, scientists make dinosaurs by combining fragments of ancient DNA with DNA from modern organisms. In reality, less-ancient fragments of DNA have indeed been found. Point out to students that a fragment of DNA does not provide enough information to make an entire organism. And identifying the owner of a given DNA fragment is difficult.

Feel the IMPACT!

How does biotechnology impact our world?

Scientists are aware that there are many ethical, legal, and social issues that arise from the ability to use and change living things. Biotechnology can impact both our society and our environment. We must decide how and when it is acceptable to use biotechnology. The examples that follow show some concerns that might be raised during a classroom debate about biotechnology.

11 Evaluate Read the first two examples of biotechnology and what students had to say about their effects on individuals, society, and the environment. Then complete Example 3 by filling in questions or possible effects of the technology.

Example 1

A Glowing Mosquito?

This is the larva of a genetically engineered mosquito. Its DNA includes a gene from a glowing jellyfish that causes the engineered mosquito to glow. Scientists hope to use this same technology to modify the mosquito's genome in other ways. For example, it is thought that the DNA of the mosquito could be changed so that the mosquito could not spread malaria.

Effects on Individuals and Society

"If the mosquito could be engineered so that it does not spread malaria, many lives could be saved."

Effects on Environment

"Mosquitoes are a food source for birds and fish. Are there health risks to animals that eat genetically modified mosquitoes?"

Think Outside the Book Inquiry

12 Debate As a class, choose a current event that involves biotechnology. Then hold a debate to present the benefits and risks of this technology.

Example 2

Cloning the Gaur

The gaur is an endangered species. In 2001, a gaur was successfully cloned. The clone, named Noah, died of a bacterial infection 2 days after birth.

Effects on Individuals and Society

"How will we decide when it is appropriate to clone other types of organisms?"

Effects on Environment

"Cloning could help increase small populations of endangered species like the gaur and save them from extinction."

Example 3

Tough Plants!

Much of the corn and soybeans grown in the United States is genetically engineered. The plants have bacterial genes that make them more resistant to plant-eating insects.

Effects on Individuals and Society

Effects on Environment

166 Unit 2 Reproduction and Heredity

Lesson 7 Biotechnology **167**

Answers

11. Sample answer: Effects on Individuals and Society: If corn is more resistant to pests, corn will be more readily available for people to eat; Effects on Environment: How might this affect the insects that feed on corn and, in turn, the organisms that feed on the insects?

12. Students should explore two sides of a current issue involving biotechnology in their debate. Students should consider impacts on individuals, society, and the environment.

Formative Assessment

Ask: Choose an example of biotechnology, either from the lesson or from prior knowledge. Describe one of the ethical, legal, social, or environmental issues surrounding that example of biotechnology. Sample answer: Many organisms, including plants, insects, and bacteria, have been genetically modified. An environmental issue that concerns the potential consequences of genetically modified organisms breeding with their wild relatives. If genetically modified genes are passed on to wild organisms, could that harm the environment?

Learning Alert

Malaria Malaria is caused by a mosquito-borne parasite called *Plasmodium*. This deadly disease causes high fever and flu-like symptoms. Prompt treatment with antimalarial drugs can prevent the disease from becoming fatal, and preventive measures such as spraying insect repellent and sleeping under netting can help prevent infection. However, at least 250 million people are infected with malaria and more than 1 million die of the disease every year, largely in sub-Saharan Africa and other warm climates. For this reason, malaria prevention is an important area of scientific research.

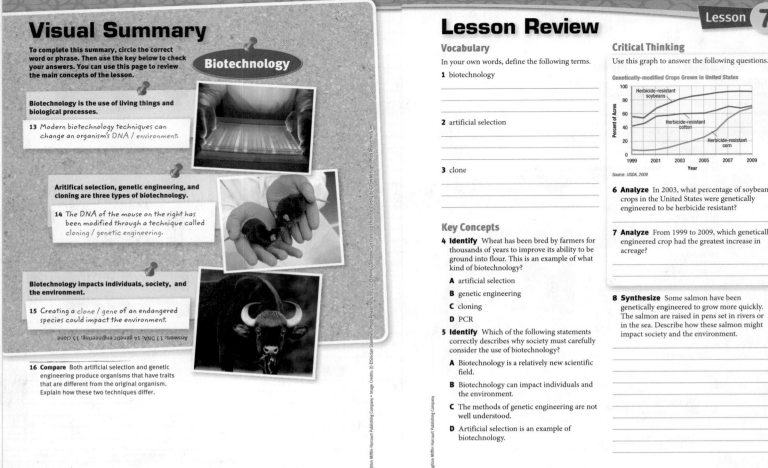

Visual Summary

To complete this summary, circle the correct word or phrase. Then use the key below to check your answers. You can use this page to review the main concepts of the lesson.

Biotechnology

Biotechnology is the use of living things and biological processes.

13 Modern biotechnology techniques can change an organism's DNA / environment.

Aritifical selection, genetic engineering, and cloning are three types of biotechnology.

14 The DNA of the mouse on the right has been modified through a technique called cloning / genetic engineering.

Biotechnology impacts individuals, society, and the environment.

15 Creating a clone / gene of an endangered species could impact the environment.

Answers: 13 DNA; 14 genetic engineering; 15 clone

16 Compare Both artificial selection and genetic engineering produce organisms that have traits that are different from the original organism. Explain how these two techniques differ.

168 Unit 2 Reproduction and Heredity

Lesson Review

Lesson 7

Vocabulary

In your own words, define the following terms.

1 biotechnology

_____

2 artificial selection

_____

3 clone

_____

Key Concepts

4 Identify Wheat has been bred by farmers for thousands of years to improve its ability to be ground into flour. This is an example of what kind of biotechnology?

A artificial selection

B genetic engineering

C cloning

D PCR

5 Identify Which of the following statements correctly describes why society must carefully consider the use of biotechnology?

A Biotechnology is a relatively new scientific field.

B Biotechnology can impact individuals and the environment.

C The methods of genetic engineering are not well understood.

D Artificial selection is an example of biotechnology.

Critical Thinking

Use this graph to answer the following questions.

Genetically-modified Crops Grown in United States

Source: USDA, 2009

6 Analyze In 2003, what percentage of soybean crops in the United States were genetically engineered to be herbicide resistant?

7 Analyze From 1999 to 2009, which genetically engineered crop had the greatest increase in acreage?

8 Synthesize Some salmon have been genetically engineered to grow more quickly. The salmon are raised in pens set in rivers or in the sea. Describe how these salmon might impact society and the environment.

_____

Lesson 7 Biotechnology 169

Visual Summary Answers

13. DNA

14. genetic engineering

15. clone

16. Sample answer: Artificial selection cannot introduce new genes into an organism, but genetic engineering can. Artificial selection can only act on DNA that already exists in a population.

Lesson Review Answers

1. Sample answer: the use of living things and processes

2. Sample answer: the crossing of selected organisms that have certain traits

3. Sample answer: an organism or part of an organism that is made genetically identical to another

4. A

5. B

6. 80%

7. herbicide-resistant corn

8. Sample answer: Faster-growing salmon could increase the number available to feed people. If the fish escape their pens, they could breed with fish from wild populations.

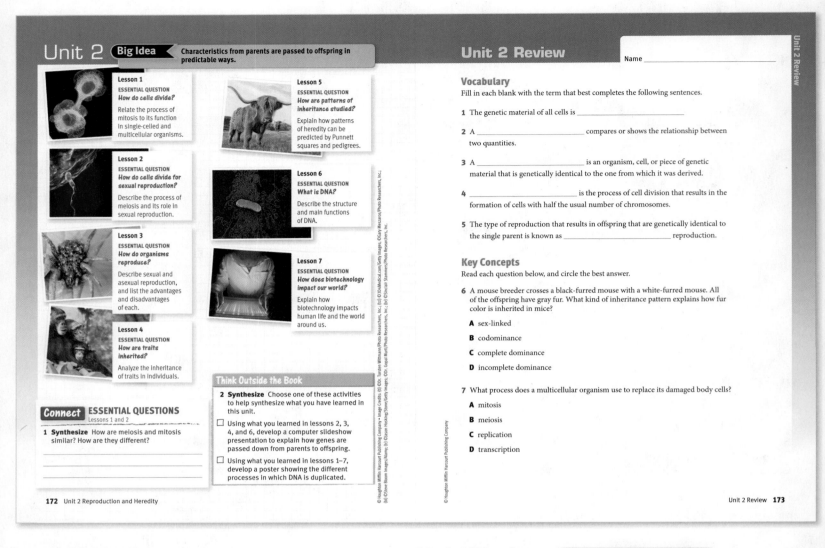

Unit 2

Big Idea Characteristics from parents are passed to offspring in predictable ways.

Lesson 1
ESSENTIAL QUESTION
How do cells divide?
Relate the process of mitosis to its function in single-celled and multicellular organisms.

Lesson 2
ESSENTIAL QUESTION
How do cells divide for sexual reproduction?
Describe the process of meiosis and its role in sexual reproduction.

Lesson 3
ESSENTIAL QUESTION
How do organisms reproduce?
Describe sexual and asexual reproduction, and list the advantages and disadvantages of each.

Lesson 4
ESSENTIAL QUESTION
How are traits inherited?
Analyze the inheritance of traits in individuals.

Lesson 5
ESSENTIAL QUESTION
How are patterns of inheritance studied?
Explain how patterns of heredity can be predicted by Punnett squares and pedigrees.

Lesson 6
ESSENTIAL QUESTION
What is DNA?
Describe the structure and main functions of DNA.

Lesson 7
ESSENTIAL QUESTION
How does biotechnology impact our world?
Explain how biotechnology impacts human life and the world around us.

Think Outside the Book

2 Synthesize Choose one of these activities to help synthesize what you have learned in this unit.

☐ Using what you learned in lessons 2, 3, 4, and 6, develop a computer slideshow presentation to explain how genes are passed down from parents to offspring.

☐ Using what you learned in lessons 1–7, develop a poster showing the different processes in which DNA is duplicated.

Connect ESSENTIAL QUESTIONS
Lessons 1 and 2

1 Synthesize How are meiosis and mitosis similar? How are they different?

_____
_____
_____

172 Unit 2 Reproduction and Heredity

Unit 2 Review

Name _____

Vocabulary
Fill in each blank with the term that best completes the following sentences.

1 The genetic material of all cells is _____

2 A _____ compares or shows the relationship between two quantities.

3 A _____ is an organism, cell, or piece of genetic material that is genetically identical to the one from which it was derived.

4 _____ is the process of cell division that results in the formation of cells with half the usual number of chromosomes.

5 The type of reproduction that results in offspring that are genetically identical to the single parent is known as _____ reproduction.

Key Concepts
Read each question below, and circle the best answer.

6 A mouse breeder crosses a black-furred mouse with a white-furred mouse. All of the offspring have gray fur. What kind of inheritance pattern explains how fur color is inherited in mice?

A sex-linked

B codominance

C complete dominance

D incomplete dominance

7 What process does a multicellular organism use to replace its damaged body cells?

A mitosis

B meiosis

C replication

D transcription

Unit 2 Review 173

Unit Summary Answers

1. Mitosis results in two cells that have the same number of chromosomes the parent cell had. Meiosis results in four cells that each have half the number of chromosomes the parent cell had. Sex cells are formed by meiosis.

2. Option 1: Students' computer presentations will likely focus on inheritance in offspring produced by sexual reproduction. Presentations should include topics such as the combination of the parents' sex cells to produce a full set of chromosomes, the relationship between chromosomes, genes, and alleles, and an explanation of how different alleles are responsible for different heritable traits.

   Option 2: Students' poster presentations should include diagrams or explanatory texts that highlight the replication of DNA in mitosis and meiosis. Students should refer to the steps of DNA replication. Some students may also include biotechnological applications, such as cloning, in their posters.

Unit Review [Response to Intervention]

A Quick Grading Chart follows the Answers. See the Assessment Guide for more detail about correct and incorrect answer choices. Refer back to the Lesson Planning pages for activities and assignments that can be used as remediation for students who answer questions incorrectly.

Answers

1. DNA DNA, the genetic material, determines the traits of an organism. (Lesson 4)

2. ratio Ratios are often used in describing the outcomes of genetic crosses (for example, the ratio of predicted and/or observed brown-eyed offspring to blue-eyed offspring). (Lesson 5)

3. clone A clone is an exact genetic duplicate of a parent or sister cell (or organism). It is made in the process of cloning. (Lesson 7)

Unit 2 Review continued

Name _____

8 The following diagram shows one way a mutation can form during DNA replication.

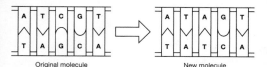

Original molecule → New molecule

What kind of mutation has occurred during the DNA replication shown in the diagram?

A deletion   **C** substitution

B insertion   **D** transcription

9 How does a sex cell differ from a body cell?

A A sex cell does not contain chromosomes.

B A sex cell contains homologous chromosomes.

C A sex cell has the same number of chromosomes as a body cell.

D A sex cell has half the amount of genetic material as a body cell.

10 How do the chromosomes at the end of meiosis I compare with the chromosomes at the end of meiosis II?

A Chromosomes have one chromatid at the end of both meiosis I and meiosis II.

B Chromosomes have two chromatids at the end of both meiosis I and meiosis II.

C Chromosomes have one chromatid at the end of meiosis I and two chromatids at the end of meiosis II.

D Chromosomes have two chromatids at the end of meiosis I and one chromatid at the end of meiosis II.

11 The following table shows the percentage of each base in a sample of DNA.

Base	Percentage of total bases
A	12%
C	38%
T	12%
G	38%

Which of the following statements explains the data in the table?

A A pairs only with C, and T pairs only with G.

B A pairs only with T, and C pairs only with G.

C DNA is made up of nucleotides that consist of a sugar, a phosphate, and a base.

D The bases in DNA are arranged in the interior of a double helix, like rungs of a ladder.

12 Which of the following is an advantage of asexual reproduction?

A It is a slow process.   **C** The organism can increase in number quickly.

B Two parents are needed.   **D** It introduces genetic diversity in the offspring.

13 The diagram below shows a cross that is similar to one of Mendel's pea plant crosses.

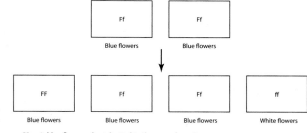

How is blue flower color inherited in the cross shown?

A as a codominant trait   **C** as a dominant trait

B as a recessive trait   **D** as an incompletely dominant trait

174 Unit 2 Reproduction and Heredity

Unit 2 Review 175

© Houghton Mifflin Harcourt Publishing Company

Answers (continued)

4. Meiosis Meiosis takes place only in reproductive structures of an organism. (Lesson 2)

5. asexual Four types of asexual reproduction are binary fission, budding, spore formation, and vegetative reproduction. (Lesson 3)

6. Answer D is correct because both alleles contribute to the phenotype of a heterozygote in incomplete dominance, producing an intermediate phenotype. (Lesson 4)

7. Answer A is correct because the new cells that form from mitosis are genetically identical to the parent cells, and they replace the damaged cells. (Lesson 1)

8. Answer C is correct because adenine (A) has been substituted for cytosine (C) in the third position. Thymine (T) is now paired with the substituted adenine (A). Originally, guanine (G) was at that position. (Lesson 6)

9. Answer D is correct because fertilization and formation of the zygote restores the full set of chromosomes found in body cells. (Lesson 2)

10. Answer D is correct because chromatids remain together during meiosis I and separate during meiosis II. (Lesson 2)

11. Answer B is correct because this pairing, A with T and C with G, results in equal amounts of A and T, and C and G. This is known as Chargaff's rule. (Lesson 6)

12. Answer C is correct because large numbers of organisms are produced in a relatively short period of time. (Lesson 3)

13. Answer C is correct because only one allele of the blue flower trait needs to be inherited for the gene to be expressed in the phenotype (so it is dominant). Therefore, each parent must have one allele for blue flowers if the ratio of blue to white flowers in the offspring is 3:1. (Lesson 4)

14. Answer B is correct because reproduction is the formation of two organisms from a single parent cell that are genetically identical to the parent. (Lesson 1)

Unit 2 Review continued

Name _____

14 Which of the following statements correctly describes the function of cell division in unicellular organisms?

A Cell division allows the organism to grow.

B Cell division allows the organism to reproduce.

C Cell division allows the organism to produce sex cells.

D Cell division allows the organism to repair damage to the cell.

15 Which statement about zygotes, which form by fertilization, is correct?

A Zygotes have a full set of chromosomes, receiving half from each parent.

B Zygotes have half the set of chromosomes from one parent only.

C Zygotes have two full sets of chromosomes, one set from each parent.

D Zygotes have half the set of chromosomes, one-fourth from each parent.

16 The diagram shows a cell during the anaphase stage of mitosis.

Justin's teacher showed him this slide of a stage of mitosis. He noticed the slide contains two homologous pairs of chromosomes. How would this diagram be different if it showed anaphase I of meiosis instead of anaphase of mitosis?

A Each chromosome would still have two chromatids.

B The chromosomes would look the same as in mitosis.

C You would be able to see DNA in the chromosomes during meiosis.

D Homologous chromosomes would be moving to the same end of the cell.

17 If the sequence of bases in one strand of DNA is ATTCGAC, what will be the base sequence on the strand that is formed during replication?

A ATTCGAC   **C** UAAGCUG

B TAAGCTG   **D** AUUCGAC

Critical Thinking

Answer the following questions in the space provided.

18 Describe the major steps of gene transcription and translation. What molecules and organelles are involved in the processes?

_____

_____

_____

_____

_____

19 Jake made a pedigree to trace the traits of straight and curly hair in his family.

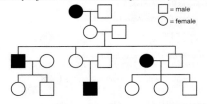

A shaded circle or square in Jake's pedigree represents a person with straight hair. Is straight hair controlled by a dominant allele or a recessive allele? What led to your conclusion? How do you know that straight hair is not sex-linked?

_____

_____

_____

_____

_____

_____

Answers (continued)

15. Answer A is correct because the diploid number is restored by fertilization. (Lesson 3)

16. Answer A is correct because the two chromatids of each chromosome have not yet separated in anaphase I. Only homologous pairs separate during meiosis I. (Lesson 2)

17. Answer B is correct because a strand of DNA serves as a template by adding complementary bases when a new strand is made during replication. (Lesson 6)

18. Key Elements:

- *The genetic information is transferred in the nucleus from DNA to mRNA during transcription.*

- *mRNA carries the information to rRNA in the ribosome. tRNA brings amino acids to the ribosome, where protein chains are assembled during translation.*

- *Transcription takes place in the nucleus, and translation takes place in the cytoplasm, in the ribosomes.* (Lesson 6)

19. Key Elements:

- *Straight hair is controlled by a recessive allele because the offspring of a parent with straight hair and a parent with curly hair will most likely have curly hair.*

- *A recessive trait can appear in an offspring of two parents who do not exhibit the trait.*

- *The trait cannot be sex-linked because both males and females express the straight hair phenotype in equal proportions.* (Lesson 5)

20. Key Elements:

- *Biotechnology has advantages and disadvantages.*

- Positive effect: *Mosquitoes can be genetically engineered so they do not spread malaria.*

- Negative effect: *If a gene from a plant that people are allergic to is inserted into a different kind of plant, people could become allergic to that plant.* (Lesson 7)

Unit 2 Review continued

20 Rachel's class is debating the impact of biotechnology on people, society, and the environment. Give one example of how biotechnology can have a positive impact. Give one example of how biotechnology can have a negative impact.

_____

_____

_____

Connect **ESSENTIAL QUESTIONS**
Lessons 4 and 5

Answer the following question in the space provided.

21 The following diagram shows a Punnett square made to predict the earlobe shape of the offspring of two parents.

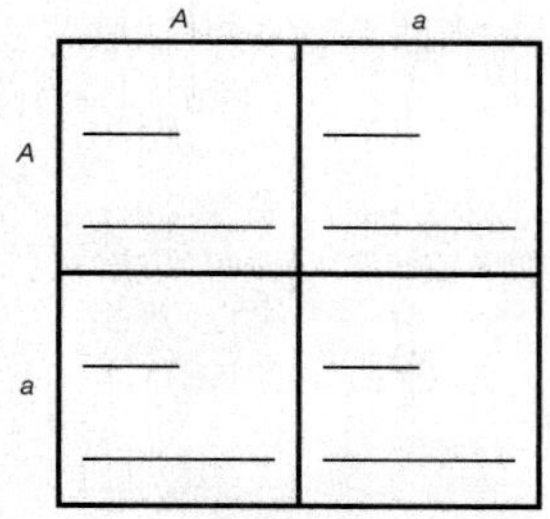

A stands for the trait of free-hanging earlobes and *a* stands for the trait of attached earlobes. Write the genotype of each offspring on the first line in each box of the Punnett square. What will be the phenotype of each offspring? Write either *attached* or *free-hanging* on the second line in each box. Describe how the trait of free-hanging earlobes is inherited. What is the expected ratio of free-hanging earlobes to attached earlobes in the offspring?

_____

_____

_____

_____

© Houghton Mifflin Harcourt Publishing Company

178 Unit 2 Reproduction and Heredity

Answers *(continued)*

21. Key Elements:

- *The genotype in the first box is* AA. *The genotype in the top right and bottom left boxes is* Aa. *The genotype of the bottom right box is* aa.

- *The phenotype in the first three boxes is free-hanging earlobes. The phenotype of the* aa *genotype is attached.*

- *Free-hanging earlobes are inherited as a simple dominant trait.*

- *There will be an expected ratio of 3 free-hanging earlobes phenotypes to 1 attached earlobes phenotype.* (Lesson 5)

Quick Grading Chart

Use the chart below for quick test grading. The lesson correlations can help you target reteaching for missed items.

Item	Answer	Cognitive Complexity	Lesson
1.	—	Low	4
2.	—	Low	5
3.	—	Low	7
4.	—	Low	2
5.	—	Low	3
6.	D	Moderate	4
7.	A	Low	1
8.	C	Moderate	6
9.	D	Moderate	2
10.	D	High	2
11.	B	High	6
12.	C	Moderate	3
13.	C	Moderate	4
14.	B	Moderate	1
15.	A	Low	3
16.	A	High	2
17.	B	Moderate	6
18.	—	Moderate	6
19.	—	Moderate	5
20.	—	Moderate	7
21.	—	Low	5

Cognitive Complexity refers to the demand on thinking associated with an item, and may vary with the answer choices, the number of steps required to arrive at an answer, and other factors, but not the ability level of the student.

Teacher Notes

Resources

Handbook

References

Mineral Properties

Here are five steps to take in mineral identification:

1. Determine the color of the mineral. Is it light-colored, dark-colored, or a specific color?
2. Determine the luster of the mineral. Is it metallic or non-metallic?
3. Determine the color of any powder left by its streak.
4. Determine the hardness of your mineral. Is it soft, hard, or very hard? Using a glass plate, see if the mineral scratches it.
5. Determine whether your sample has cleavage or any special properties.

TERMS TO KNOW	DEFINITION
adamantine	a non-metallic luster like that of a diamond
cleavage	how a mineral breaks when subject to stress on a particular plane
luster	the state or quality of shining by reflecting light
streak	the color of a mineral when it is powdered
submetallic	between metallic and nonmetallic in luster
vitreous	glass-like type of luster

Silicate Minerals

Mineral	Color	Luster	Streak	Hardness	Cleavage and Special Properties
Beryl	deep green, pink, white, bluish green, or yellow	vitreous	white	7.5–8	1 cleavage direction; some varieties fluoresce in ultraviolet light
Chlorite	green	vitreous to pearly	pale green	2–2.5	1 cleavage direction
Garnet	green, red, brown, black	vitreous	white	6.5–7.5	no cleavage
Hornblende	dark green, brown, or black	vitreous	none	5–6	2 cleavage directions
Muscovite	colorless, silvery white, or brown	vitreous or pearly	white	2–2.5	1 cleavage direction
Olivine	olive green, yellow	vitreous	white or none	6.5–7	no cleavage
Orthoclase	colorless, white, pink, or other colors	vitreous	white or none	6	2 cleavage directions
Plagioclase	colorless, white, yellow, pink, green	vitreous	white	6	2 cleavage directions
Quartz	colorless or white; any color when not pure	vitreous or waxy	white or none	7	no cleavage

Nonsilicate Minerals

Mineral	Color	Luster	Streak	Hardness	Cleavage and Special Properties
Native Elements					
Copper	copper-red	metallic	copper-red	2.5–3	no cleavage
Diamond	pale yellow or colorless	adamantine	none	10	4 cleavage directions
Graphite	black to gray	submetallic	black	1–2	1 cleavage direction
Carbonates					
Aragonite	colorless, white, or pale yellow	vitreous	white	3.5–4	2 cleavage directions; reacts with hydrochloric acid
Calcite	colorless or white to tan	vitreous	white	3	3 cleavage directions; reacts with weak acid; double refraction
Halides					
Fluorite	light green, yellow, purple, bluish green, or other colors	vitreous	none	4	4 cleavage directions; some varieties fluoresce
Halite	white	vitreous	white	2.0–2.5	3 cleavage directions
Oxides					
Hematite	reddish brown to black	metallic to earthy	dark red to red-brown	5.6–6.5	no cleavage; magnetic when heated
Magnetite	iron-black	metallic	black	5.5–6.5	no cleavage; magnetic
Sulfates					
Anhydrite	colorless, bluish, or violet	vitreous to pearly	white	3–3.5	3 cleavage directions
Gypsum	white, pink, gray, or colorless	vitreous, pearly, or silky	white	2.0	3 cleavage directions
Sulfides					
Galena	lead-gray	metallic	lead-gray to black	2.5–2.8	3 cleavage directions
Pyrite	brassy yellow	metallic	greenish, brownish, or black	6–6.5	no cleavage

References

Geologic Time Scale

Geologists developed the geologic time scale to represent the 4.6 billion years of Earth's history that have passed since Earth formed. This scale divides Earth's history into blocks of time. The boundaries between these time intervals (shown in millions of years ago or mya in the table below), represent major changes in Earth's history. Some boundaries are defined by mass extinctions, major changes in Earth's surface, and/or major changes in Earth's climate.

The four major divisions that encompass the history of life on Earth are Precambrian time, the Paleozoic era, the Mesozoic era, and the Cenozoic era. The largest divisions are eons. **Precambrian time** is made up of the first three eons, over 4 billion years of Earth's history.

The **Paleozoic era** lasted from 542 mya to 251 mya. All major plant groups, except flowering plants, appeared during this era. By the end of the era, reptiles, winged insects, and fishes had also appeared. The largest known mass extinction occurred at the end of this era.

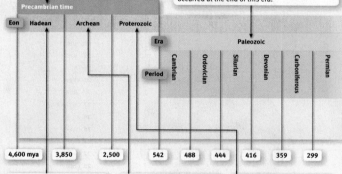

The **Hadean eon** lasted from about 4.6 billion years ago (bya) to 3.85 bya. It is described based on evidence from meteorites and rocks from the moon.

The **Archean eon** lasted from 3.85 bya to 2.5 bya. The earliest rocks from Earth that have been found and dated formed at the start of this eon.

The **Proterozoic eon** lasted from 2.5 bya to 542 mya. The first organisms, which were single-celled organisms, appeared during this eon. These organisms produced so much oxygen that they changed Earth's oceans and Earth's atmosphere.

© Houghton Mifflin Harcourt Publishing Company

Divisions of Time

The divisions of time shown here represent major changes in Earth's surface and when life developed and changed significantly on Earth. As new evidence is found, the boundaries of these divisions may shift. The Phanerozoic eon is divided into three eras. The beginning of each of these eras represents a change in the types of organisms that dominated Earth. And, each era is commonly characterized by the types of organisms that dominated the era. These eras are divided into periods, and periods are divided into epochs.

The **Mesozoic era** lasted from 251 mya to 65.5 mya. During this era, many kinds of dinosaurs dominated land, and giant lizards swam in the ocean. The first birds, mammals, and flowering plants also appeared during this time. About two-thirds of all land species went extinct at the end of this era.

The **Phanerozoic eon** began 542 mya. We live in this eon.

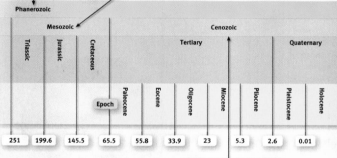

The **Cenozoic era** began 65.5 mya and continues today. Mammals dominate this era. During the Mesozoic era, mammals were small in size but grew much larger during the Cenozoic era. Primates, including humans, appeared during this era.

© Houghton Mifflin Harcourt Publishing Company

References

Star Charts for the Northern Hemisphere

A star chart is a map of the stars in the night sky. It shows the names and positions of constellations and major stars. Star charts can be used to identify constellations and even to orient yourself using Polaris, the North Star.

Because Earth moves through space, different constellations are visible at different times of the year. The star charts on these pages show the constellations visible during each season in the Northern Hemisphere.

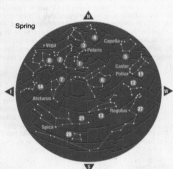

Spring

Autumn

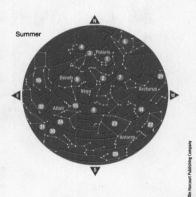

Summer

Winter

Constellations

1 Ursa Minor
2 Draco
3 Cepheus
4 Cassiopeia
5 Auriga
6 Ursa Major
7 Boötes
8 Hercules
9 Cygnus
10 Perseus
11 Gemini
12 Cancer
13 Leo
14 Serpens
15 Sagitta
16 Pegasus
17 Pisces

Constellations

18 Aries
19 Taurus
20 Orion
21 Virgo
22 Libra
23 Ophiuchus
24 Aquila
25 Lepus
26 Canis Major
27 Hydra
28 Corvus
29 Scorpius
30 Sagittarius
31 Capricornus
32 Aquarius
33 Cetus
34 Columba

References

World Map

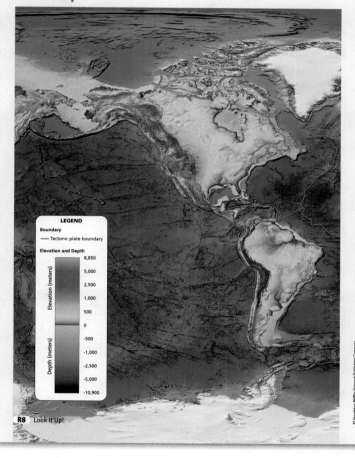

LEGEND

Boundary
— Tectonic plate boundary

Elevation and Depth

Elevation (meters)
- 8,850
- 5,000
- 2,500
- 1,000
- 500
- 0

Depth (meters)
- -500
- -1,000
- -2,500
- -5,000
- -10,900

R8   Look It Up!

Look It Up!   R9

© Houghton Mifflin Harcourt Publishing Company

© Houghton Mifflin Harcourt Publishing Company

Classification of Living Things

Domains and Kingdoms

All organisms belong to one of three domains: Domain Archaea, Domain Bacteria, or Domain Eukarya. Some of the groups within these domains are shown below. (Remember that genus names are italicized.)

Domain Archaea

The organisms in this domain are single-celled prokaryotes, many of which live in extreme environments.

Archaea		
Group	**Example**	**Characteristics**
Methanogens	*Methanococcus*	produce methane gas; can't live in oxygen
Thermophiles	*Sulpholobus*	require sulphur; can't live in oxygen
Halophiles	*Halococcus*	live in very salty environments; most can live in oxygen

Domain Bacteria

Organisms in this domain are single-celled prokaryotes and are found in almost every environment on Earth.

Bacteria		
Group	**Example**	**Characteristics**
Bacilli	*Escherichia*	rod shaped; some bacilli fix nitrogen; some cause disease
Cocci	*Streptococcus*	spherical shaped; some cause disease; can form spores
Spirilla	*Treponema*	spiral shaped; cause diseases such as syphilis and Lyme disease

Domain Eukarya

Organisms in this domain are single-celled or multicellular eukaryotes.

Kingdom Protista Many protists resemble fungi, plants, or animals, but are smaller and simpler in structure. Most are single celled.

Protists		
Group	**Example**	**Characteristics**
Sarcodines	*Amoeba*	radiolarians; single-celled consumers
Ciliates	*Paramecium*	single-celled consumers
Flagellates	*Trypanosoma*	single-celled parasites
Sporozoans	*Plasmodium*	single-celled parasites
Euglenas	*Euglena*	single celled; photosynthesize
Diatoms	*Pinnularia*	most are single celled; photosynthesize
Dinoflagellates	*Gymnodinium*	single celled; some photosynthesize
Algae	*Volvox*	single celled or multicellular; photosynthesize
Slime molds	*Physarum*	single celled or multicellular; consumers or decomposers
Water molds	powdery mildew	single celled or multicellular; parasites or decomposers

Kingdom Fungi Most fungi are multicellular. Their cells have thick cell walls. Fungi absorb food from their environment.

Fungi		
Group	**Examples**	**Characteristics**
Threadlike fungi	bread mold	spherical; decomposers
Sac fungi	yeast; morels	saclike; parasites and decomposers
Club fungi	mushrooms; rusts; smuts	club shaped; parasites and decomposers
Lichens	British soldier	a partnership between a fungus and an alga

Kingdom Plantae Plants are multicellular and have cell walls made of cellulose. Plants make their own food through photosynthesis. Plants are classified into divisions instead of phyla.

Plants		
Group	**Examples**	**Characteristics**
Bryophytes	mosses; liverworts	no vascular tissue; reproduce by spores
Club mosses	*Lycopodium*; ground pine	grow in wooded areas; reproduce by spores
Horsetails	rushes	grow in wetland areas; reproduce by spores
Ferns	spleenworts; sensitive fern	large leaves called fronds; reproduce by spores
Conifers	pines; spruces; firs	needlelike leaves; reproduce by seeds made in cones
Cycads	*Zamia*	slow growing; reproduce by seeds made in large cones
Gnetophytes	*Welwitschia*	only three living families; reproduce by seeds
Ginkgoes	*Ginkgo*	only one living species; reproduce by seeds
Angiosperms	all flowering plants	reproduce by seeds made in flowers; fruit

Kingdom Animalia Animals are multicellular. Their cells do not have cell walls. Most animals have specialized tissues and complex organ systems. Animals get food by eating other organisms.

Animals		
Group	**Examples**	**Characteristics**
Sponges	glass sponges	no symmetry or specialized tissues; aquatic
Cnidarians	jellyfish; coral	radial symmetry; aquatic
Flatworms	planaria; tapeworms; flukes	bilateral symmetry; organ systems
Roundworms	*Trichina*; hookworms	bilateral symmetry; organ systems
Annelids	earthworms; leeches	bilateral symmetry; organ systems
Mollusks	snails; octopuses	bilateral symmetry; organ systems
Echinoderms	sea stars; sand dollars	radial symmetry; organ systems
Arthropods	insects; spiders; lobsters	bilateral symmetry; organ systems
Chordates	fish; amphibians; reptiles; birds; mammals	bilateral symmetry; complex organ systems

References

Periodic Table of the Elements

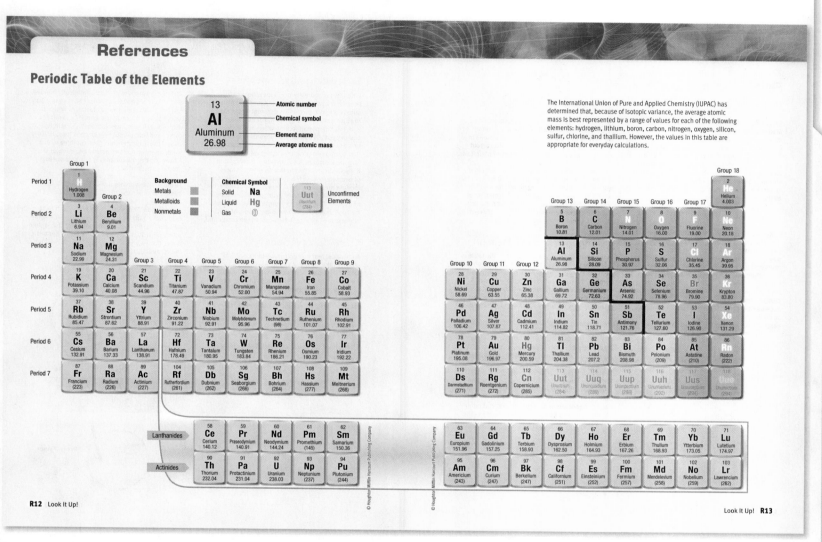

The International Union of Pure and Applied Chemistry (IUPAC) has determined that, because of isotopic variance, the average atomic mass is best represented by a range of values for each of the following elements: hydrogen, lithium, boron, carbon, nitrogen, oxygen, silicon, sulfur, chlorine, and thallium. However, the values in this table are appropriate for everyday calculations.

© Houghton Mifflin Harcourt Publishing Company

References

Physical Science Refresher

Atoms and Elements

Every object in the universe is made of matter. **Matter** is anything that takes up space and has mass. All matter is made of atoms. An **atom** is the smallest particle into which an element can be divided and still be the same element. An **element**, in turn, is a substance that cannot be broken down into simpler substances by chemical means. Each element consists of only one kind of atom. An element may be made of many atoms, but they are all the same kind of atom.

Atomic Structure

Atoms are made of smaller particles called **electrons**, **protons**, and **neutrons**. Electrons have a negative electric charge, protons have a positive charge, and neutrons have no electric charge. Together, protons and neutrons form the **nucleus**, or small dense center, of an atom. Because protons are positively charged and neutrons are neutral, the nucleus has a positive charge. Electrons move within an area around the nucleus called the **electron cloud**. Electrons move so quickly that scientists cannot determine their exact speeds and positions at the same time.

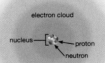

electron cloud

nucleus → ← proton

← neutron

Atomic Number

To help distinguish one element from another, scientists use the atomic numbers of atoms. The **atomic number** is the number of protons in the nucleus of an atom. The atoms of a certain element always have the same number of protons.

When atoms have an equal number of protons and electrons, they are uncharged, or electrically neutral. The atomic number equals the number of electrons in an uncharged atom. The number of neutrons, however, can vary for a given element. Atoms of the same element that have different numbers of neutrons are called **isotopes**.

Periodic Table of the Elements

In the periodic table, each element in the table is in a separate box. And the elements are arranged from left to right in order of increasing atomic number. That is, an uncharged atom of each element has one more electron and one more proton than an uncharged atom of the element to its left. Each horizontal row of the table is called a **period**. Changes in chemical properties of elements across a period correspond to changes in the electron arrangements of their atoms.

Each vertical column of the table is known as a **group.** A group lists elements with similar physical and chemical properties. For this reason, a group is also sometimes called a family. The elements in a group have similar properties because their atoms have the same number of electrons in their outer energy level. For example, the elements helium, neon, argon, krypton, xenon, and radon all have similar properties and are known as the noble gases.

Molecules and Compounds

When two or more elements join chemically, they form a **compound**. A compound is a new substance with properties different from those of the elements that compose it. For example, water, H_2O, is a compound formed when hydrogen (H) and oxygen (O) combine. The smallest complete unit of a compound that has the properties of that compound is called a **molecule**. A chemical formula indicates the elements in a compound. It also indicates the relative number of atoms of each element in the compound. The chemical formula for water is H_2O. So, each water molecule consists of two atoms of hydrogen and one atom of oxygen. The subscript number after the symbol for an element shows how many atoms of that element are in a single molecule of the compound.

Chemical Equations

A chemical reaction occurs when a chemical change takes place. A chemical equation describes a chemical reaction using chemical formulas. The equation indicates the substances that react and the substances that are produced. For example, when carbon and oxygen combine, they can form carbon dioxide, shown in the equation below: $C + O_2 \longrightarrow CO_2$

Acids, Bases, and pH

An **ion** is an atom or group of chemically bonded atoms that has an electric charge because it has lost or gained one or more electrons. When an acid, such as hydrochloric acid, HCl, is mixed with water, it separates into ions. An **acid** is a compound that produces hydrogen ions, H^+, in water. The hydrogen ions then combine with a water molecule to form a hydronium ion, H_3O^+. A **base**, on the other hand, is a substance that produces hydroxide ions, OH^-, in water.

To determine whether a solution is acidic or basic, scientists use pH. The **pH** of a solution is a measure of the hydronium ion concentration in a solution. The pH scale ranges from 0 to 14. Acids have a pH that is less than 7. The lower the number, the more acidic the solution. The middle point, pH = 7, is neutral, neither acidic nor basic. Bases have a pH that is greater than 7. The higher the number is, the more basic the solution.

The pH of Some Common Materials

0 1 2 3 4 5 6 7 8 9 10 11 12 13 14

Stomach Acid

Antacid (dissolved in water)

Drain Cleaner

apple juice

Baking Soda

Hand Soap

References

Physical Laws and Useful Equations

Law of Conservation of Mass

Mass cannot be created or destroyed during ordinary chemical or physical changes.

The total mass in a closed system is always the same no matter how many physical changes or chemical reactions occur.

Law of Conservation of Energy

Energy can be neither created nor destroyed.

The total amount of energy in a closed system is always the same. Energy can be changed from one form to another, but all of the different forms of energy in a system always add up to the same total amount of energy, no matter how many energy conversions occur.

Law of Universal Gravitation

All objects in the universe attract each other by a force called gravity. The size of the force depends on the masses of the objects and the distance between the objects.

The first part of the law explains why lifting a bowling ball is much harder than lifting a marble. Because the bowling ball has a much larger mass than the marble does, the amount of gravity between Earth and the bowling ball is greater than the amount of gravity between Earth and the marble.

The second part of the law explains why a satellite can remain in orbit around Earth. The satellite is placed at a carefully calculated distance from Earth. This distance is great enough to keep Earth's gravity from pulling the satellite down, yet small enough to keep the satellite from escaping Earth's gravity and wandering off into space.

Newton's Laws of Motion

Newton's first law of motion states that an object at rest remains at rest, and an object in motion remains in motion at constant speed and in a straight line unless acted on by an unbalanced force.

The first part of the law explains why a football will remain on a tee until it is kicked off or until a gust of wind blows it off. The second part of the law explains why a bike rider will continue moving forward after the bike comes to an abrupt stop. Gravity and the friction of the sidewalk will eventually stop the rider.

Newton's second law of motion states that the acceleration of an object depends on the mass of the object and the amount of force applied.

The first part of the law explains why the acceleration of a 4 kg bowling ball will be greater than the acceleration of a 6 kg bowling ball if the same force is applied to both balls. The second part of the law explains why the acceleration of a bowling ball will be greater if a larger force is applied to the bowling ball. The relationship of acceleration (a) to mass (m) and force (F) can be expressed mathematically by the following equation:

$$\text{acceleration} = \frac{\text{force}}{\text{mass}}, \text{ or } a = \frac{F}{m}$$

This equation is often rearranged to read force = mass × acceleration, or $F = m \times a$

Newton's third law of motion states that whenever one object exerts a force on a second object, the second object exerts an equal and opposite force on the first.

This law explains that a runner is able to move forward because the ground exerts an equal and opposite force on the runner's foot after each step.

Average speed

$$\text{average speed} = \frac{\text{total distance}}{\text{total time}}$$

Example:
A bicycle messenger traveled a distance of 136 km in 8 h. What was the messenger's average speed?

$$\frac{136 \text{ km}}{8 \text{ h}} = 17 \text{ km/h}$$

The messenger's average speed was **17 km/h.**

Average acceleration

$$\text{average acceleration} = \frac{\text{final velocity} - \text{starting velocity}}{\text{time it takes to change velocity}}$$

Example:
Calculate the average acceleration of an Olympic 100 m dash sprinter who reached a velocity of 20 m/s south at the finish line. The race was in a straight line and lasted 10 s.

$$\frac{20 \text{ m/s} - 0 \text{ m/s}}{10 \text{ s}} = 2 \text{ m/s/s}$$

The sprinter's average acceleration was **2 m/s/s south.**

Pressure

Pressure is the force exerted over a given area. The SI unit for pressure is the pascal. Its symbol is Pa.

$$\text{pressure} = \frac{\text{force}}{\text{area}}$$

Net force
Forces in the Same Direction

When forces are in the same direction, add the forces together to determine the net force.

Example:
Calculate the net force on a stalled car that is being pushed by two people. One person is pushing with a force of 13 N northwest, and the other person is pushing with a force of 8 N in the same direction.

$$13 \text{ N} + 8 \text{ N} = 21 \text{N}$$

The net force is **21 N northwest.**

Forces in Opposite Directions

When forces are in opposite directions, subtract the smaller force from the larger force to determine the net force. The net force will be in the direction of the larger force.

Example:
Calculate the net force on a rope that is being pulled on each end. One person is pulling on one end of the rope with a force of 12 N south. Another person is pulling on the opposite end of the rope with a force of 7 N north.

$$12 \text{ N} - 7 \text{ N} = 5 \text{ N}$$

The net force is **5 N south.**

Example:
Calculate the pressure of the air in a soccer ball if the air exerts a force of 10 N over an area of 0.5 m².

$$\text{pressure} = \frac{10N}{0.5 \, m^2} = \frac{20N}{m^2} = 20 \text{ Pa}$$

The pressure of the air inside the soccer ball is **20 Pa.**

R16 Look It Up!

Look It Up! R17

Reading and Study Skills

A How-To Manual for Active Reading

This book belongs to you, and you are invited to write in it. In fact, the book won't be complete until you do. Sometimes you'll answer a question or follow directions to mark up the text. Other times you'll write down your own thoughts. And when you're done reading and writing in the book, the book will be ready to help you review what you learned and prepare for tests.

Active Reading Annotations

Before you read, you'll often come upon an Active Reading prompt that asks you to underline certain words or number the steps in a process. Here's an example.

> **Active Reading**
>
> **12 Identify** In this paragraph, number the sequence of sentences that describe replication.

Marking the text this way is called **annotating,** and your marks are called **annotations.** Annotating the text can help you identify important concepts while you read.

There are other ways that you can annotate the text. You can draw an asterisk (*) by vocabulary terms, mark unfamiliar or confusing terms and information with a question mark (?), and mark main ideas with a double underline. And you can even invent your own marks to annotate the text!

Other Annotating Opportunities

Keep your pencil, pen, or highlighter nearby as you read, so you can make a note or highlight an important point at any time. Here are a few ideas to get you started.

- Notice the headings in red and blue. The blue headings are questions that point to the main idea of what you're reading. The red headings are answers to the questions in the blue ones. Together these headings outline the content of the lesson. After reading a lesson, you could write your own answers to the questions.

- Notice the bold-faced words that are highlighted in yellow. They are highlighted so that you can easily find them again on the page where they are defined. As you read or as you review, challenge yourself to write your own sentence using the bold-faced term.

- Make a note in the margin at any time. You might
  - Ask a "What if" question
  - Comment on what you read
  - Make a connection to something you read elsewhere
  - Make a logical conclusion from the text

Use your own language and abbreviations. Invent a code, such as using circles and boxes around words to remind you of their importance or relation to each other. Your annotations will help you remember your questions for class discussions, and when you go back to the lesson later, you may be able to fill in what you didn't understand the first time you read it. Like a scientist in the field or in a lab, you will be recording your questions and observations for analysis later.

Active Reading Questions

After you read, you'll often come upon Active Reading questions that ask you to think about what you've just read. You'll write your answer underneath the question. Here's an example.

> **Active Reading**
>
> **8 Describe** Where are phosphate groups found in a DNA molecule?
> _____
> _____

This type of question helps you sum up what you've just read and pull out the most important ideas from the passage. In this case the question asks you to **describe** the structure of a DNA molecule that you have just read about. Other times you may be asked to do such things as **apply** a concept, **compare** two concepts, **summarize** a process, or **identify a cause-and-effect** relationship. You'll be strengthening those critical thinking skills that you'll use often in learning about science.

Reading and Study Skills

Using Graphic Organizers to Take Notes

Graphic organizers help you remember information as you read it for the first time and as you study it later. There are dozens of graphic organizers to choose from, so the first trick is to choose the one that's best suited to your purpose. Following are some graphic organizers to use for different purposes.

To remember lots of information	To relate a central idea to subordinate details	To describe a process	To make a comparison
• Arrange data in a Content Frame • Use Combination Notes to describe a concept in words and pictures	• Show relationships with a Mind Map or a Main Idea Web • Sum up relationships among many things with a Concept Map	• Use a Process Diagram to explain a procedure • Show a chain of events and results in a Cause-and-Effect Chart	• Compare two or more closely related things in a Venn Diagram

Content Frame

1 Make a four-column chart.

2 Fill the first column with categories (e.g., snail, ant, earthworm) and the first row with descriptive information (e.g., group, characteristic, appearance).

3 Fill the chart with details that belong in each row and column.

4 When you finish, you'll have a study aid that helps you compare one category to another.

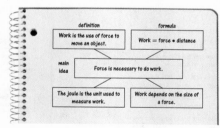

Invertebrates			
NAME	**GROUP**	**CHARACTERISTICS**	**DRAWING**
snail	mollusks	mantle	
ant	arthropods	six legs, exoskeleton	
earthworm	segmented worms	segmented body, circulatory and digestive systems	
heartworm	roundworms	digestive system	
sea star	echinoderms	spiny skin, tube feet	
jellyfish	cnidarians	stinging cells	

© Houghton Mifflin Harcourt Publishing Company

Combination Notes

1 Make a two-column chart.

2 Write descriptive words and definitions in the first column.

3 Draw a simple sketch that helps you remember the meaning of the term in the second column.

Mind Map

1 Draw an oval, and inside it write a topic to analyze.

2 Draw two or more arms extending from the oval. Each arm represents a main idea about the topic.

3 Draw lines from the arms on which to write details about each of the main ideas.

Main Idea Web

1 Make a box and write a concept you want to remember inside it.

2 Draw boxes around the central box, and label each one with a category of information about the concept (e.g., definition, formula, descriptive details).

3 Fill in the boxes with relevant details as you read.

Reading and Study Skills

Concept Map

1 Draw a large oval, and inside it write a major concept.

2 Draw an arrow from the concept to a smaller oval, in which you write a related concept.

3 On the arrow, write a verb that connects the two concepts.

4 Continue in this way, adding ovals and arrows in a branching structure, until you have explained as much as you can about the main concept.

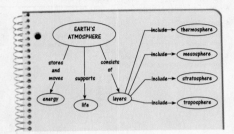

Venn Diagram

1 Draw two overlapping circles or ovals—one for each topic you are comparing—and label each one.

2 In the part of each circle that does not overlap with the other, list the characteristics that are unique to each topic.

3 In the space where the two circles overlap, list the characteristics that the two topics have in common.

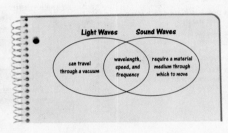

Cause-and-Effect Chart

1 Draw two boxes and connect them with an arrow.

2 In the first box, write the first event in a series (a cause).

3 In the second box, write a result of the cause (the effect).

4 Add more boxes when one event has many effects, or vice versa.

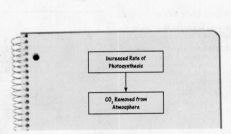

Process Diagram

A process can be a never-ending cycle. As you can see in this technology design process, engineers may backtrack and repeat steps, they may skip steps entirely, or they may repeat the entire process before a useable design is achieved.

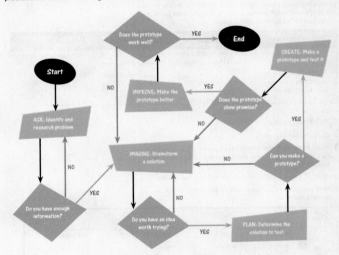

Reading and Study Skills

Using Vocabulary Strategies

Important science terms are highlighted where they are first defined in this book. One way to remember these terms is to take notes and make sketches when you come to them. Use the strategies on this page and the next for this purpose. You will also find a formal definition of each science term in the Glossary at the end of the book.

Description Wheel

1 Draw a small circle.

2 Write a vocabulary term inside the circle.

3 Draw several arms extending from the circle.

4 On the arms, write words and phrases that describe the term.

5 If you choose, add sketches that help you visualize the descriptive details or the concept as a whole.

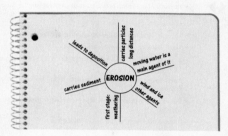

Four Square

1 Draw a small oval and write a vocabulary term inside it.

2 Draw a large rectangle around the oval, and divide the rectangle into four smaller squares.

3 Label the smaller squares with categories of information about the term, such as: definition, characteristics, examples, non-examples, appearance, and root words.

4 Fill the squares with descriptive words and drawings that will help you remember the overall meaning of the term and its essential details.

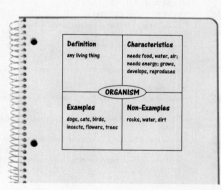

Frame Game

1 Draw a small rectangle, and write a vocabulary term inside it.

2 Draw a larger rectangle around the smaller one. Connect the corners of the larger rectangle to the corners of the smaller one, creating four spaces that frame the word.

3 In each of the four parts of the frame, draw or write details that help define the term. Consider including a definition, essential characteristics, an equation, examples, and a sentence using the term.

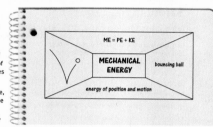

Magnet Word

1 Draw horseshoe magnet, and write a vocabulary term inside it.

2 Add lines that extend from the sides of the magnet.

3 Brainstorm words and phrases that come to mind when you think about the term.

4 On the lines, write the words and phrases that describe something essential about the term.

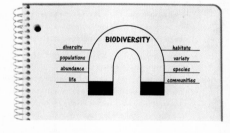

Word Triangle

1 Draw a triangle, and add lines to divide it into three parts.

2 Write a term and its definition in the bottom section of the triangle.

3 In the middle section, write a sentence in which the term is used correctly.

4 In the top section, draw a small picture to illustrate the term.

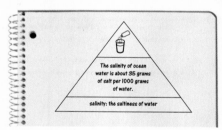

Science Skills

Safety in the Lab

Before you begin work in the laboratory, read these safety rules twice. Before starting a lab activity, read all directions and make sure that you understand them. Do not begin until your teacher has told you to start. If you or another student are injured in any way, tell your teacher immediately.

Dress Code

Eye Protection

Hand Protection

Clothing Protection

- Wear safety goggles at all times in the lab as directed.
- If chemicals get into your eyes, flush your eyes immediately.
- Do not wear contact lenses in the lab.
- Do not look directly at the sun or any intense light source or laser.
- Do not cut an object while holding the object in your hand.
- Wear appropriate protective gloves as directed.
- Wear an apron or lab coat at all times in the lab as directed.
- Tie back long hair, secure loose clothing, and remove loose jewelry.
- Do not wear open-toed shoes, sandals, or canvas shoes in the lab.

Glassware and Sharp Object Safety

Glassware Safety

Sharp Objects Safety

- Do not use chipped or cracked glassware.
- Use heat-resistant glassware for heating or storing hot materials.
- Notify your teacher immediately if a piece of glass breaks.
- Use extreme care when handling all sharp and pointed instruments.
- Cut objects on a suitable surface, always in a direction away from your body.

Chemical Safety

Chemical Safety

- If a chemical gets on your skin, on your clothing, or in your eyes, rinse it immediately (shower, faucet or eyewash fountain) and alert your teacher.
- Do not clean up spilled chemicals unless your teacher directs you to do so.
- Do not inhale any gas or vapor unless directed to do so by your teacher.
- Handle materials that emit vapors or gases in a well-ventilated area.

Electrical Safety

Electrical Safety

- Do not use equipment with frayed electrical cords or loose plugs.
- Do not use electrical equipment near water or when clothing or hands are wet.
- Hold the plug housing when you plug in or unplug equipment.

Heating and Fire Safety

Heating Safety

- Be aware of any source of flames, sparks, or heat (such as flames, heating coils, or hot plates) before working with any flammable substances.
- Know the location of lab fire extinguishers and fire-safety blankets.
- Know your school's fire-evacuation routes.
- If your clothing catches on fire, walk to the lab shower to put out the fire.
- Never leave a hot plate unattended while it is turned on or while it is cooling.
- Use tongs or appropriate insulated holders when handling heated objects.
- Allow all equipment to cool before storing it.

Plant and Animal Safety

Plant Safety

Animal Safety

- Do not eat any part of a plant.
- Do not pick any wild plants unless your teacher instructs you to do so.
- Handle animals only as your teacher directs.
- Treat animals carefully and respectfully.
- Wash your hands thoroughly after handling any plant or animal.

Cleanup

Proper Waste Disposal

Hygienic Care

- Clean all work surfaces and protective equipment as directed by your teacher.
- Dispose of hazardous materials or sharp objects only as directed by your teacher.
- Keep your hands away from your face while you are working on any activity.
- Wash your hands thoroughly before you leave the lab or after any activity.

Wafting

Science Skills

Designing, Conducting, and Reporting an Experiment

An experiment is an organized procedure to study something under specific conditions. Use the following steps of the scientific method when designing or conducting a controlled experiment.

1 Identify a Research Problem

Every day, you make observations by using your senses to gather information. Careful observations lead to good questions, and good questions can lead you to an experiment. Imagine, for example, that you pass a pond every day on your way to school, and you notice green scum beginning to form on top of it. You wonder what it is and why it seems to be growing. You list your questions, and then you do a little research to find out what is already known. A good place to start a research project is at the library. A library catalog lists all of the resources available to you at that library and often those found elsewhere. Begin your search by using:

- keywords or main topics.
- similar words, or synonyms, of your keyword.

The types of resources that will be helpful to you will depend on the kind of information you are interested in. And, some resources are more reliable for a given topic than others. Some different kinds of useful resources are:

- magazines and journals (or periodicals)—articles on a topic.
- encyclopedias—a good overview of a topic.
- books on specific subjects—details about a topic.
- newspapers—useful for current events.

The Internet can also be a great place to find information. Some of your library's reference materials may even be online. When using the Internet, however, it is especially important to make sure you are using appropriate and reliable sources. Websites of universities and government agencies are usually more accurate and reliable than websites created by individuals or businesses. Decide which sources are relevant and reliable for your topic. If in doubt, check with your teacher.

Take notes as you read through the information in these resources. You will probably come up with many questions and ideas for which you can do more research as needed. Once you feel you have enough information, think about the questions you have on the topic. Then, write down the problem that you want to investigate. Your notes might look like these.

© Houghton Mifflin Harcourt Publishing Company

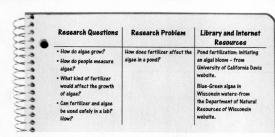

Research Questions	Research Problem	Library and Internet Resources
• How do algae grow? • How do people measure algae? • What kind of fertilizer would affect the growth of algae? • Can fertilizer and algae be used safely in a lab? How?	How does fertilizer affect the algae in a pond?	Pond fertilization: initiating an algal bloom – from University of California Davis website. Blue-Green algae in Wisconsin waters–from the Department of Natural Resources of Wisconsin website.

As you gather information from reliable sources, record details about each source, including author name(s), title, date of publication, and/or web address. Make sure to also note the specific information that you use from each source. Staying organized in this way will be important when you write your report and create a bibliography or works cited list. Recording this information and staying organized will help you credit the appropriate author(s) for the information that you have gathered.

Representing someone else's ideas or work as your own, (without giving the original author credit), is known as plagiarism. Plagiarism can be intentional or unintentional. The best way to make sure that you do not commit plagiarism is to always do your own work and to always give credit to others when you use their words or ideas.

Current scientific research is built on scientific research and discoveries that have happened in the past. This means that scientists are constantly learning from each other and combining ideas to learn more about the natural world through investigation. But, a good scientist always credits the ideas and research that they have gathered from other people to those people. There are more details about crediting sources and creating a bibliography under step 9.

2 Make a Prediction

A prediction is a statement of what you expect will happen in your experiment. Before making a prediction, you need to decide in a general way what you will do in your procedure. You may state your prediction in an if-then format.

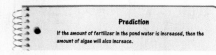

Prediction

If the amount of fertilizer in the pond water is increased, then the amount of algae will also increase.

© Houghton Mifflin Harcourt Publishing Company

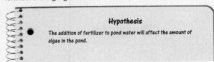

Science Skills

3 Form a Hypothesis

Many experiments are designed to test a hypothesis. A hypothesis is a tentative explanation for an expected result. You have predicted that additional fertilizer will cause additional algae growth in pond water; your hypothesis should state the connection between fertilizer and algal growth.

Hypothesis

The addition of fertilizer to pond water will affect the amount of algae in the pond.

4 Identify Variables to Test the Hypothesis

The next step is to design an experiment to test the hypothesis. The experimental results may or may not support the hypothesis. Either way, the information that results from the experiment may be useful for future investigations.

Experimental Group and Control Group

An experiment to determine how two factors are related has a control group and an experimental group. The two groups are the same, except that the investigator changes a single factor in the experimental group and does not change it in the control group.

Experimental Group: two containers of pond water with one drop of fertilizer solution added to each

Control Group: two containers of the same pond water sampled at the same time but with no fertilizer solution added

Variables and Constants

In a controlled experiment, a variable is any factor that can change. Constants are all of the variables that are kept the same in both the experimental group and the control group.

The independent variable is the factor that is manipulated or changed in order to test the effect of the change on another variable. The dependent variable is the factor the investigator measures to gather data about the effect.

Independent Variable	Dependent Variable	Constants
Amount of fertilizer in pond water	Growth of algae in the pond water	• Where and when the pond water is obtained • The type of container used • Light and temperature conditions where the water is stored

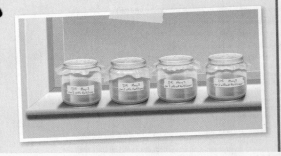

5 Write a Procedure

Write each step of your procedure. Start each step with a verb, or action word, and keep the steps short. Your procedure should be clear enough for someone else to use as instructions for repeating your experiment.

Procedure

1. Use the masking tape and the marker to label the containers with your initials, the date, and the identifiers "Jar 1 with Fertilizer," "Jar 2 with Fertilizer," "Jar 1 without Fertilizer," and "Jar 2 without Fertilizer."

2. Put on your gloves. Use the large container to obtain a sample of pond water.

3. Divide the water sample equally among the four smaller containers.

4. Use the eyedropper to add one drop of fertilizer solution to the two containers labeled, "Jar 1 with Fertilizer," and "Jar 2 with Fertilizer".

5. Cover the containers with clear plastic wrap. Use the scissors to punch ten holes in each of the covers.

6. Place all four containers on a window ledge. Make sure that they all receive the same amount of light.

7. Observe the containers every day for one week.

8. Use the ruler to measure the diameter of the largest clump of algae in each container, and record your measurements daily.

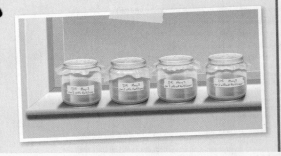

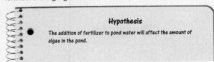

© Houghton Mifflin Harcourt Publishing Company

© Houghton Mifflin Harcourt Publishing Company

Science Skills

6 Experiment and Collect Data

Once you have all of your materials and your procedure has been approved, you can begin to experiment and collect data. Record both quantitative data (measurements) and qualitative data (observations), as shown below.

Algal Growth and Fertilizer

Date and Time	Experimental Group		Control Group		Observations
	Jar 1 with Fertilizer (diameter of algal clump in mm)	Jar 2 with Fertilizer (diameter of algal clump in mm)	Jar 1 without Fertilizer (diameter of algal clump in mm)	Jar 2 without Fertilizer (diameter of algal clump in mm)	
5/3 4:00 p.m.	0	0	0	0	condensation in all containers
5/4 4:00 p.m.	0	3	0	0	tiny green blobs in Jar 2 with fertilizer
5/5 4:15 p.m.	4	5	0	3	green blobs in Jars 1 and 2 with fertilizer and Jar 2 without fertilizer
5/6 4:00 p.m.	5	6	0	4	water light green in Jar 2 with fertilizer
5/7 4:00 p.m.	8	10	0	6	water light green in Jars 1 and 2 with fertilizer and Jar 2 without fertilizer
5/8 3:30 p.m.	10	18	0	6	cover off of Jar 2 with fertilizer
5/9 3:30 p.m.	14	23	0	8	drew sketches of each container

Drawings of Samples Viewed Under Microscope on 5/9 at 100x

Jar 1 with Fertilizer Jar 2 with Fertilizer Jar 1 without Fertilizer Jar 2 without Fertilizer

7 Analyze Data

After you complete your experiment, you must analyze all of the data you have gathered. Tables, statistics, and graphs are often used in this step to organize and analyze both the qualitative and quantitative data. Sometimes, your qualitative data are best used to help explain the relationships you see in your quantitative data.

Computer graphing software is useful for creating a graph from data that you have collected. Most graphing software can make line graphs, pie charts, or bar graphs from data that has been organized in a spreadsheet. Graphs are useful for understanding relationships in the data and for communicating the results of your experiment.

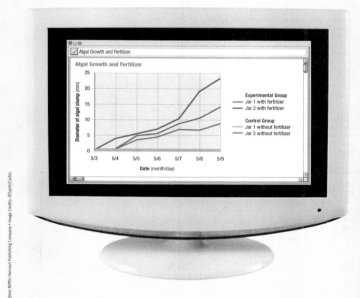

Science Skills

8 Make Conclusions

To draw conclusions from your experiment, first, write your results. Then, compare your results with your hypothesis. Do your results support your hypothesis? What have you learned?

Conclusion

More algae grew in the pond water to which fertilizer had been added than in the pond water to which fertilizer had not been added. My hypothesis was supported. I conclude that it is possible that the growth of algae in ponds can be influenced by the input of fertilizer.

9 Create a Bibliography or Works Cited List

To complete your report, you must also show all of the newspapers, magazines, journals, books, and online sources that you used at every stage of your investigation. Whenever you find useful information about your topic, you should write down the source of that information. Writing down as much information as you can about the subject can help you or someone else find the source again. You should at least record the author's name, the title, the date and where the source was published, and the pages in which the information was found. Then, organize your sources into a list, which you can title Bibliography or Works Cited.

Usually, at least three sources are included in these lists. Sources are listed alphabetically, by the authors' last names. The exact format of a bibliography can vary, depending on the style preferences of your teacher, school, or publisher. Also, books are cited differently than journals or websites. Below is an example of how different kinds of sources may be formatted in a bibliography.

BOOK: Hauschultz, Sara. *Freshwater Algae*. Brainard, Minnesota: Northwoods Publishing, 2011.

ENCYCLOPEDIA: Lasure, Sedona. "Algae is not all just pond scum." *Encyclopedia of Algae*. 2009.

JOURNAL: Johnson, Keagan. "Algae as we know it." *Sci Journal*, vol 64. (September 2010): 201-211.

WEBSITE: Dout, Bill. "Keeping algae scum out of birdbaths." *Help Keep Earth Clean*. News. January 26, 2011. <www.SaveEarth.org>.

Using a Microscope

Scientists use microscopes to see very small objects that cannot easily be seen with the eye alone. A microscope magnifies the image of an object so that small details may be observed. A microscope that you may use can magnify an object 400 times—the object will appear 400 times larger than its actual size.

Eyepiece Objects are viewed through the eyepiece. The eyepiece contains a lens that commonly magnifies an image ten times.

Body The body separates the lens in the eyepiece from the objective lenses below.

Coarse Adjustment This knob is used to focus the image of an object when it is viewed through the low-power lens.

Nosepiece The nosepiece holds the objective lenses above the stage and rotates so that all lenses may be used.

Fine Adjustment This knob is used to focus the image of an object when it is viewed through the high-power lens.

High-Power Objective Lens This is the largest lens on the nosepiece. It magnifies an image approximately 40 times.

Low-Power Objective Lens This is the smallest lens on the nosepiece. It magnifies images about 10 times.

Stage The stage supports the object being viewed.

Arm The arm supports the body above the stage. Always carry a microscope by the arm and base.

Diaphragm The diaphragm is used to adjust the amount of light passing through the slide and into an objective lens.

Stage Clip The stage clip holds a slide in place on the stage.

Mirror or Light Source Some microscopes use light that is reflected through the stage by a mirror. Other microscopes have their own light sources.

Base The base supports the microscope.

Science Skills

Measuring Accurately

Precision and Accuracy

When you do a scientific investigation, it is important that your methods, observations, and data be both precise and accurate.

Low precision: The darts did not land in a consistent place on the dartboard.

Precision, but not accuracy: The darts landed in a consistent place, but did not hit the bull's eye.

Precision and accuracy: The darts landed consistently on the bull's eye.

Precision

In science, *precision* is the exactness and consistency of measurements. For example, measurements made with a ruler that has both centimeter and millimeter markings would be more precise than measurements made with a ruler that has only centimeter markings. Another indicator of precision is the care taken to make sure that methods and observations are as exact and consistent as possible. Every time a particular experiment is done, the same procedure should be used. Precision is necessary because experiments are repeated several times and if the procedure changes, the results might change.

Example

Suppose you are measuring temperatures over a two-week period. Your precision will be greater if you measure each temperature at the same place, at the same time of day, and with the same thermometer than if you change any of these factors from one day to the next.

Accuracy

In science, it is possible to be precise but not accurate. *Accuracy* depends on the difference between a measurement and an actual value. The smaller the difference, the more accurate the measurement.

Example

Suppose you look at a stream and estimate that it is about 1 meter wide at a particular place. You decide to check your estimate by measuring the stream with a meter stick, and you determine that the stream is 1.32 meters wide. However, because it is difficult to measure the width of a stream with a meter stick, it turns out that your measurement was not very accurate. The stream is actually 1.14 meters wide. Therefore, even though your estimate of about 1 meter was less precise than your measurement, your estimate was actually more accurate.

Graduated Cylinders

How to Measure the Volume of a Liquid with a Graduated Cylinder

- Be sure that the graduated cylinder is on a flat surface so that your measurement will be accurate.

- When reading the scale on a graduated cylinder, be sure to have your eyes at the level of the surface of the liquid.

- The surface of the liquid will be curved in the graduated cylinder. Read the volume of the liquid at the bottom of the curve, or meniscus (muh-NIHS-kuhs).

- You can use a graduated cylinder to find the volume of a solid object by measuring the increase in a liquid's level after you add the object to the cylinder.

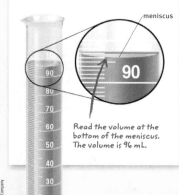

meniscus

Read the volume at the bottom of the meniscus. The volume is 96 mL.

Metric Rulers

How to Measure the Length of a Leaf with a Metric Ruler

1 Lay a ruler flat on top of the leaf so that the 1-centimeter mark lines up with one end. Make sure the ruler and the leaf do not move between the time you line them up and the time you take the measurement.

2 Look straight down on the ruler so that you can see exactly how the marks line up with the other end of the leaf.

3 Estimate the length by which the leaf extends beyond a marking. For example, the leaf below extends about halfway between the 4.2-centimeter and 4.3-centimeter marks, so the apparent measurement is about 4.25 centimeters.

4 Remember to subtract 1 centimeter from your apparent measurement, since you started at the 1-centimeter mark on the ruler and not at the end. The leaf is about 3.25 centimeters long (4.25 cm − 1 cm = 3.25 cm).

Science Skills

Triple Beam Balance

This balance has a pan and three beams with sliding masses, called riders. At one end of the beams is a pointer that indicates whether the mass on the pan is equal to the masses shown on the beams.

How to Measure the Mass of an Object

1 Make sure the balance is zeroed before measuring the mass of an object. The balance is zeroed if the pointer is at zero when nothing is on the pan and the riders are at their zero points. Use the adjustment knob at the base of the balance to zero it.

2 Place the object to be measured on the pan.

3 Move the riders one notch at a time away from the pan. Begin with the largest rider. If moving the largest rider one notch brings the pointer below zero, begin measuring the mass of the object with the next smaller rider.

4 Change the positions of the riders until they balance the mass on the pan and the pointer is at zero. Then add the readings from the three beams to determine the mass of the object.

300 g	position of largest rider
90 g	position of middle rider
+ 3 g	position of smallest rider
393 g	mass of beaker and water

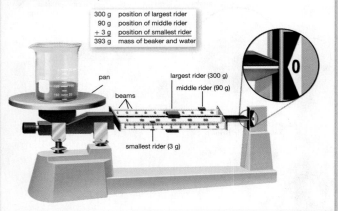

pan

beams

largest rider (300 g)

middle rider (90 g)

smallest rider (3 g)

Using the Metric System and SI Units

Scientists use International System (SI) units for measurements of distance, volume, mass, and temperature. The International System is based on powers of ten and the metric system of measurement.

Basic SI Units		
Quantity	**Name**	**Symbol**
length	meter	m
volume	liter	L
mass	gram	g
temperature	kelvin	K

SI Prefixes		
Prefix	**Symbol**	**Power of 10**
kilo-	k	1000
hecto-	h	100
deca-	da	10
deci-	d	0.1 or $\frac{1}{10}$
centi-	c	0.01 or $\frac{1}{100}$
milli-	m	0.001 or $\frac{1}{1000}$

Changing Metric Units

You can change from one unit to another in the metric system by multiplying or dividing by a power of 10.

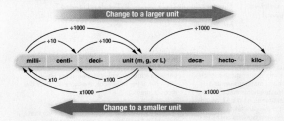

Change to a larger unit

÷1000   ÷1000

÷10   ÷100

milli-   centi-   deci-   unit (m, g, or L)   deca-   hecto-   kilo-

×10   ×100

×1000   ×1000

Change to a smaller unit

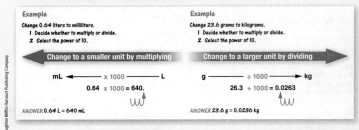

Example

Change 0.64 liters to milliliters.
  1 Decide whether to multiply or divide.
  2 Select the power of 10.

Change to a smaller unit by multiplying

mL ◄──── × 1000 ──── L

0.64 × 1000 = 640.

ANSWER 0.64 L = 640 mL

Example

Change 23.6 grams to kilograms.
  1 Decide whether to multiply or divide.
  2 Select the power of 10.

Change to a larger unit by dividing

g ──── ÷ 1000 ──► kg

26.3 ÷ 1000 = 0.0263

ANSWER 23.6 g = 0.0236 kg

Science Skills

Converting Between SI and U.S. Customary Units

Use the chart below when you need to convert between SI units and U.S. customary units.

SI Unit	From SI to U.S. Customary			From U.S. Customary to SI		
Length	When you know	multiply by	to find	When you know	multiply by	to find
kilometer (km) = 1000 m	kilometers	0.62	miles	miles	1.61	kilometers
meter (m) = 100 cm	meters	3.28	feet	feet	0.3048	meters
centimeter (cm) = 10 mm	centimeters	0.39	inches	inches	2.54	centimeters
millimeter (mm) = 0.1 cm	millimeters	0.04	inches	inches	25.4	millimeters
Area	When you know	multiply by	to find	When you know	multiply by	to find
square kilometer (km²)	square kilometers	0.39	square miles	square miles	2.59	square kilometers
square meter (m²)	square meters	1.2	square yards	square yards	0.84	square meters
square centimeter (cm²)	square centimeters	0.155	square inches	square inches	6.45	square centimeters
Volume	When you know	multiply by	to find	When you know	multiply by	to find
liter (L) = 1000 mL	liters	1.06	quarts	quarts	0.95	liters
	liters	0.26	gallons	gallons	3.79	liters
	liters	4.23	cups	cups	0.24	liters
	liters	2.12	pints	pints	0.47	liters
milliliter (mL) = 0.001 L	milliliters	0.20	teaspoons	teaspoons	4.93	milliliters
	milliliters	0.07	tablespoons	tablespoons	14.79	milliliters
	milliliters	0.03	fluid ounces	fluid ounces	29.57	milliliters
Mass	When you know	multiply by	to find	When you know	multiply by	to find
kilogram (kg) = 1000 g	kilograms	2.2	pounds	pounds	0.45	kilograms
gram (g) = 1000 mg	grams	0.035	ounces	ounces	28.35	grams

Temperature Conversions

Even though the kelvin is the SI base unit of temperature, the degree Celsius will be the unit you use most often in your science studies. The formulas below show the relationships between temperatures in degrees Fahrenheit (°F), degrees Celsius (°C), and kelvins (K).

$$°C = \frac{5}{9} \, (°F - 32) \qquad °F = \frac{9}{5} \, °C + 32 \qquad K = °C + 273$$

Examples of Temperature Conversions		
Condition	**Degrees Celsius**	**Degrees Fahrenheit**
Freezing point of water	0	32
Cool day	10	50
Mild day	20	68
Warm day	30	86
Normal body temperature	37	98.6
Very hot day	40	104
Boiling point of water	100	212

© Houghton Mifflin Harcourt Publishing Company

Math Refresher

Performing Calculations

Science requires an understanding of many math concepts. The following pages will help you review some important math skills.

Mean

The mean is the sum of all values in a data set divided by the total number of values in the data set. The mean is also called the *average*.

Example

Find the mean of the following set of numbers: 5, 4, 7, and 8.

Step 1   Find the sum.

5 + 4 + 7 + 8 = 24

Step 2   Divide the sum by the number of numbers in your set. Because there are four numbers in this example, divide the sum by 4.

24 ÷ 4 = 6

Answer The average, or mean, is 6.

Median

The median of a data set is the middle value when the values are written in numerical order. If a data set has an even number of values, the median is the mean of the two middle values.

Example

To find the median of a set of measurements, arrange the values in order from least to greatest. The median is the middle value.

13 mm   14 mm   16 mm   21 mm   23 mm

Answer The median is 16 mm.

Mode

The mode of a data set is the value that occurs most often.

Example

To find the mode of a set of measurements, arrange the values in order from least to greatest and determine the value that occurs most often.

13 mm, 14 mm, 14 mm, 16 mm, 21 mm, 23 mm, 25 mm

Answer The mode is 14 mm.

A data set can have more than one mode or no mode. For example, the following data set has modes of 2 mm and 4 mm:

2 mm   2 mm   3 mm   4 mm   4 mm

The data set below has no mode, because no value occurs more often than any other.

2 mm   3 mm   4 mm   5 mm

© Houghton Mifflin Harcourt Publishing Company

Math Refresher

Ratios

A **ratio** is a comparison between numbers, and it is usually written as a fraction.

Example
Find the ratio of thermometers to students if you have 36 thermometers and 48 students in your class.

Step 1 Write the ratio.

$$\frac{36 \text{ thermometers}}{48 \text{ students}}$$

Step 2 Simplify the fraction to its simplest form.

$$\frac{36}{48} = \frac{36 \div 12}{48 \div 12} = \frac{3}{4}$$

The ratio of thermometers to students is 3 to 4 or 3:4.

Proportions

A **proportion** is an equation that states that two ratios are equal.

$$\frac{3}{1} = \frac{12}{4}$$

To solve a proportion, you can use cross-multiplication. If you know three of the quantities in a proportion, you can use cross-multiplication to find the fourth.

Example
Imagine that you are making a scale model of the solar system for your science project. The diameter of Jupiter is 11.2 times the diameter of the Earth. If you are using a plastic-foam ball that has a diameter of 2 cm to represent the Earth, what must the diameter of the ball representing Jupiter be?

$$\frac{11.2}{1} = \frac{x}{2 \text{ cm}}$$

Step 1 Cross-multiply.

$$\frac{11.2}{1} = \frac{x}{2}$$

$$11.2 \times 2 = x \times 1$$

Step 2 Multiply.

$$22.4 = x \times 1$$

$$x = 22.4 \text{ cm}$$

You will need to use a ball that has a diameter of 22.4 cm to represent Jupiter.

Rates

A **rate** is a ratio of two values expressed in different units. A unit rate is a rate with a denominator of 1 unit.

Example
A plant grew 6 centimeters in 2 days. The plant's rate of growth was $\frac{6 \text{ cm}}{2 \text{ days}}$. To describe the plant's growth in centimeters per day, write a unit rate.

Divide numerator and denominator by 2:

$$\frac{6 \text{ cm}}{2 \text{ days}} = \frac{6 \text{ cm} \div 2}{2 \text{ days} \div 2}$$

Simplify:

$$= \frac{3 \text{ cm}}{1 \text{ day}}$$

Answer The plant's rate of growth is 3 centimeters per day.

Percent

A **percent** is a ratio of a given number to 100. For example, 85% = 85/100. You can use percent to find part of a whole.

Example
What is 85% of 40?

Step 1 Rewrite the percent as a decimal by moving the decimal point two places to the left.

$$0.85$$

Step 2 Multiply the decimal by the number that you are calculating the percentage of.

$$0.85 \times 40 = 34$$

85% of 40 is 34.

Decimals

To **add** or **subtract decimals**, line up the digits vertically so that the decimal points line up. Then, add or subtract the columns from right to left. Carry or borrow numbers as necessary.

Example
Add the following numbers: 3.1415 and 2.96.

Step 1 Line up the digits vertically so that the decimal points line up.

$$\begin{array}{r} 3.1415 \\ + 2.96 \\ \hline \end{array}$$

Step 2 Add the columns from right to left, and carry when necessary.

$$\begin{array}{r} 3.1415 \\ + 2.96 \\ \hline 6.1015 \end{array}$$

The sum is 6.1015.

Fractions

A **fraction** is a ratio of two nonzero whole numbers.

Example
Your class has 24 plants. Your teacher instructs you to put 5 plants in a shady spot. What fraction of the plants in your class will you put in a shady spot?

Step 1 In the denominator, write the total number of parts in the whole.

$$\frac{?}{24}$$

Step 2 In the numerator, write the number of parts of the whole that are being considered.

$$\frac{5}{24}$$

So, $\frac{5}{24}$ of the plants will be in the shade.

Math Refresher

Simplifying Fractions

It is usually best to express a fraction in its simplest form. Expressing a fraction in its simplest form is called **simplifying a fraction.**

Example

Simplify the fraction $\frac{30}{45}$ to its simplest form.

Step 1 Find the largest whole number that will divide evenly into both the numerator and denominator. This number is called the greatest common factor (GCF).

Factors of the numerator 30:
1, 2, 3, 5, 6, 10, 15, 30

Factors of the denominator 45:
1, 3, 5, 9, 15, 45

Step 2 Divide both the numerator and the denominator by the GCF, which in this case is 15.

$$\frac{30}{45} = \frac{30 \div 15}{45 \div 15} = \frac{2}{3}$$

Thus, $\frac{30}{45}$ written in its simplest form is $\frac{2}{3}$.

Adding and Subtracting Fractions

To **add** or **subtract fractions** that have the same denominator, simply add or subtract the numerators.

Examples

$$\frac{3}{5} + \frac{1}{5} = ? \text{ and } \frac{3}{4} - \frac{1}{4} = ?$$

Step 1 Add or subtract the numerators.

$$\frac{3}{5} + \frac{1}{5} = \frac{4}{5} \text{ and } \frac{3}{4} - \frac{1}{4} = \frac{2}{4}$$

Step 2 Write in the common denominator, which remains the same.

$$\frac{3}{5} + \frac{1}{5} = \frac{4}{5} \text{ and } \frac{3}{4} - \frac{1}{4} = \frac{2}{4}$$

Step 3 If necessary, write the fraction in its simplest form.

$\frac{4}{5}$ cannot be simplified, and $\frac{2}{4} = \frac{1}{2}$.

To **add** or **subtract** fractions that have **different denominators**, first find the least common denominator (LCD).

Examples

$$\frac{1}{2} + \frac{1}{6} = ? \text{ and } \frac{3}{4} - \frac{2}{6} = ?$$

Step 1 Write the equivalent fractions that have a common denominator.

$$\frac{3}{6} + \frac{1}{6} = ? \text{ and } \frac{9}{12} - \frac{8}{12} = ?$$

Step 2 Add or subtract the fractions.

$$\frac{3}{6} + \frac{1}{6} = \frac{4}{6} \text{ and } \frac{9}{12} - \frac{8}{12} = \frac{1}{12}$$

Step 3 If necessary, write the fraction in its simplest form.

$\frac{4}{6} = \frac{2}{3}$, and $\frac{1}{12}$ cannot be simplified.

Multiplying Fractions

To **multiply fractions**, multiply the numerators and the denominators together, and then simplify the fraction to its simplest form.

Example

$$\frac{5}{9} \times \frac{7}{10} = ?$$

Step 1 Multiply the numerators and denominators.

$$\frac{5}{9} \times \frac{7}{10} = \frac{5 \times 7}{9 \times 10} = \frac{35}{90}$$

Step 2 Simplify the fraction.

$$\frac{35}{90} = \frac{35 \div 5}{90 \div 5} = \frac{7}{18}$$

Dividing Fractions

To **divide fractions**, first rewrite the divisor (the number you divide by) upside down. This number is called the reciprocal of the divisor. Then multiply and simplify if necessary.

Example

$$\frac{5}{8} \div \frac{3}{2} = ?$$

Step 1 Rewrite the divisor as its reciprocal.

$$\frac{3}{2} \rightarrow \frac{2}{3}$$

Step 2 Multiply the fractions.

$$\frac{5}{8} \times \frac{2}{3} = \frac{5 \times 2}{8 \times 3} = \frac{10}{24}$$

Step 3 Simplify the fraction.

$$\frac{10}{24} = \frac{10 \div 2}{24 \div 2} = \frac{5}{12}$$

Using Significant Figures

The **significant figures** in a decimal are the digits that are warranted by the accuracy of a measuring device.

When you perform a calculation with measurements, the number of significant figures to include in the result depends in part on the number of significant figures in the measurements. When you multiply or divide measurements, your answer should have only as many significant figures as the measurement with the fewest significant figures.

Examples

Using a balance and a graduated cylinder filled with water, you determined that a marble has a mass of 8.0 grams and a volume of 3.5 cubic centimeters. To calculate the density of the marble, divide the mass by the volume.

Write the formula for density: $\text{Density} = \frac{\text{mass}}{\text{volume}}$

Substitute measurements: $\frac{8.0\,g}{3.5\,cm^3}$

Use a calculator to divide: $\approx 2.285714286\,g/cm^3$

Answer Because the mass and the volume have two significant figures each, give the density to two significant figures. The marble has a density of 2.3 grams per cubic centimeter.

Using Scientific Notation

Scientific notation is a shorthand way to write very large or very small numbers. For example, 73,500,000,000,000,000,000,000 kg is the mass of the moon. In scientific notation, it is 7.35×10^{22} kg. A value written as a number between 1 and 10, times a power of 10, is in scientific notation.

Examples

You can convert from standard form to scientific notation.

Standard Form	Scientific Notation
720,000	7.2×10^5
5 decimal places left	Exponent is 5.
0.000291	2.91×10^{-4}
4 decimal places right	Exponent is −4.

You can convert from scientific notation to standard form.

Scientific Notation	Standard Form
4.63×10^7	46,300,000
Exponent is 7.	7 decimal places right
1.08×10^{-6}	0.00000108
Exponent is −6.	6 decimal places left

© Houghton Mifflin Harcourt Publishing Company

Math Refresher

Making and Interpreting Graphs

Circle Graph

A circle graph, or pie chart, shows how each group of data relates to all of the data. Each part of the circle represents a category of the data. The entire circle represents all of the data. For example, a biologist studying a hardwood forest in Wisconsin found that there were five different types of trees. The data table at right summarizes the biologist's findings.

Wisconsin Hardwood Trees	
Type of tree	Number found
Oak	600
Maple	750
Beech	300
Birch	1,200
Hickory	150
Total	3,000

How to Make a Circle Graph

1 To make a circle graph of these data, first find the percentage of each type of tree. Divide the number of trees of each type by the total number of trees, and multiply by 100%.

$$\frac{600 \text{ oak}}{3,000 \text{ trees}} \times 100\% = 20\%$$

$$\frac{750 \text{ maple}}{3,000 \text{ trees}} \times 100\% = 25\%$$

$$\frac{300 \text{ beech}}{3,000 \text{ trees}} \times 100\% = 10\%$$

$$\frac{1,200 \text{ birch}}{3,000 \text{ trees}} \times 100\% = 40\%$$

$$\frac{150 \text{ hickory}}{3,000 \text{ trees}} \times 100\% = 5\%$$

A Community of Wisconsin Hardwood Trees

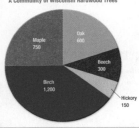

2 Now, determine the size of the wedges that make up the graph. Multiply each percentage by 360°. Remember that a circle contains 360°.

$20\% \times 360° = 72°$ $25\% \times 360° = 90°$

$10\% \times 360° = 36°$ $40\% \times 360° = 144°$

$5\% \times 360° = 18°$

3 Check that the sum of the percentages is 100 and the sum of the degrees is 360.

$20\% + 25\% + 10\% + 40\% + 5\% = 100\%$

$72° + 90° + 36° + 144° + 18° = 360°$

4 Use a compass to draw a circle and mark the center of the circle.

5 Then, use a protractor to draw angles of 72°, 90°, 36°, 144°, and 18° in the circle.

6 Finally, label each part of the graph, and choose an appropriate title.

Line Graphs

Line graphs are most often used to demonstrate continuous change. For example, Mr. Smith's students analyzed the population records for their hometown, Appleton, between 1910 and 2010. Examine the data at right.

Because the year and the population change, they are the variables. The population is determined by, or dependent on, the year. Therefore, the population is called the **dependent variable,** and the year is called the **independent variable.** Each year and its population make a **data pair.** To prepare a line graph, you must first organize data pairs into a table like the one at right.

Population of Appleton, 1910–2010	
Year	Population
1910	1,800
1930	2,500
1950	3,200
1970	3,900
1990	4,600
2010	5,300

How to Make a Line Graph

1 Place the independent variable along the horizontal (x) axis. Place the dependent variable along the vertical (y) axis.

2 Label the x-axis "Year" and the y-axis "Population." Look at your greatest and least values for the population. For the y-axis, determine a scale that will provide enough space to show these values. You must use the same scale for the entire length of the axis. Next, find an appropriate scale for the x-axis.

3 Choose reasonable starting points for each axis.

4 Plot the data pairs as accurately as possible.

5 Choose a title that accurately represents the data.

How to Determine Slope

Slope is the ratio of the change in the y-value to the change in the x-value, or "rise over run."

1 Choose two points on the line graph. For example, the population of Appleton in 2010 was 5,300 people. Therefore, you can define point A as (2010, 5,300). In 1910, the population was 1,800 people. You can define point B as (1910, 1,800).

2 Find the change in the y-value.
(y at point A) − (y at point B) = 5,300 people − 1,800 people = 3,500 people

3 Find the change in the x-value.
(x at point A) − (x at point B) = 2010 − 1910 = 100 years

4 Calculate the slope of the graph by dividing the change in y by the change in x.

$$slope = \frac{change \ in \ y}{change \ in \ x}$$

$$slope = \frac{3,500 \text{ people}}{100 \text{ years}}$$

$$slope = 35 \text{ people per year}$$

In this example, the population in Appleton increased by a fixed amount each year. The graph of these data is a straight line. Therefore, the relationship is **linear.** When the graph of a set of data is not a straight line, the relationship is **nonlinear.**

Math Refresher

Bar Graphs

Bar graphs can be used to demonstrate change that is not continuous. These graphs can be used to indicate trends when the data cover a long period of time. A meteorologist gathered the precipitation data shown here for Summerville for April 1–15 and used a bar graph to represent the data.

Precipitation in Summerville, April 1–15			
Date	Precipitation (cm)	Date	Precipitation (cm)
April 1	0.5	April 9	0.25
April 2	1.25	April 10	0.0
April 3	0.0	April 11	1.0
April 4	0.0	April 12	0.0
April 5	0.0	April 13	0.25
April 6	0.0	April 14	0.0
April 7	0.0	April 15	6.50
April 8	1.75		

How to Make a Bar Graph

1 Use an appropriate scale and a reasonable starting point for each axis.

2 Label the axes, and plot the data.

3 Choose a title that accurately represents the data.

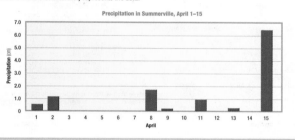

Precipitation in Summerville, April 1–15

Glossary

Pronunciation Key							
Sound	Symbol	Example	Respelling	Sound	Symbol	Example	Respelling
ă	a	pat	PAT	ŏ	ah	bottle	BAHT'l
ā	ay	pay	PAY	ō	oh	toe	TOH
âr	air	care	KAIR	ô	aw	caught	KAWT
ä	ah	father	FAH•ther	ôr	ohr	roar	ROHR
är	ar	argue	AR•gyoo	oi	oy	noisy	NOYZ•ee
ch	ch	chase	CHAYS	ŏŏ	u	book	BUK
ĕ	e	pet	PET	ōō	oo	boot	BOOT
ē (at end of a syllable)	eh	settee lessee	seh•TEE leh•SEE	ou	ow	pound	POWND
				s	s	center	SEN•ter
ĕr	ehr	merry	MEHR•ee	sh	sh	cache	CASH
ē	ee	beach	BEECH	ŭ	uh	flood	FLUHD
g	g	gas	GAS	ûr	er	bird	BERD
ĭ	i	pit	PIT	z	z	xylophone	ZY•luh•fohn
ĭ (at end of a syllable)	ih	guitar	gih•TAR	z	z	bags	BAGZ
ī	y eye (only for a complete syllable)	pie island	PY EYE•luhnd	zh	zh	decision	dih•SIZH•uhn
				ə	uh	around broken focus	uh•ROWND BROH•kuhn FOH•kuhs
îr	ir	hear	HIR	ər	er	winner	WIN•er
j	j	germ	JERM	th	th	thin they	THIN THAY
k	k	kick	KIK				
ng	ng	thing	THING	w	w	one	WUHN
ngk	ngk	bank	BANGK	wh	hw	whether	HWETH•er

Student Edition

Glossary

active transport (AK-tiv TRANS-pohrt) the movement of substances across the cell membrane that requires the cell to use energy (57)
transporte activo el movimiento de sustancias a través de la membrana celular que requiere que la célula gaste energía

allele (uh-LEEL) one of the alternative forms of a gene that governs a characteristic, such as hair color (126)
alelo una de las formas alternativas de un gene que rige un carácter, como por ejemplo, el color del cabello

artificial selection (ar-tuh-FISH-uhl sih-LEK-shuhn) the human practice of breeding animals or plants that have certain desired traits (163)
selección artificial la práctica humana de criar animales o cultivar plantas que tienen ciertos caracteres deseados

asexual reproduction (ay-SEK-shoo-uhl ree-pruh-DUHK-shuhn) reproduction that does not involve the union of sex cells and in which one parent produces offspring that are genetically identical to the parent (114)
reproducción asexual reproducción que no involucra la unión de células sexuales, en la que un solo progenitor produce descendencia que es genéticamente igual al progenitor

atom (AT-uhm) the smallest unit of an element that maintains the properties of that element (16)
átomo la unidad más pequeña de un elemento que conserva las propiedades de ese elemento

biotechnology (by-oh-tek-NAHL-uh-jee) the use and application of living things and biological processes (162)
biotecnología el uso y la aplicación de seres vivos y procesos biológicos

carbohydrate (kar-boh-HY-drayt) a class of molecules that includes sugars, starches, and fiber; contains carbon, hydrogen, and oxygen (19)
carbohidrato una clase de moléculas entre las que se incluyen azúcares, almidones y fibra; contiene carbono, hidrógeno y oxígeno

cell (SEL) in biology, the smallest unit that can perform all life processes; cells are covered by a membrane and contain DNA and cytoplasm (6)
célula en biología, la unidad más pequeña que puede realizar todos los procesos vitales; las células están cubiertas por una membrana y tienen ADN y citoplasma

cell cycle (SEL SY-kuhl) the life cycle of a cell (94)
ciclo celular el ciclo de vida de una célula

cell membrane (SEL MEM-brayn) a phospholipid layer that covers a cell's surface and acts as a barrier between the inside of a cell and the cell's environment (10)
membrana celular una capa de fosfolípidos que cubre la superficie de la célula y funciona como una barrera entre el interior de la célula y el ambiente de la célula

cell wall (SEL WAWL) a rigid structure that surrounds the cell membrane and provides support to the cell (30)
pared celular una estructura rígida que rodea la membrana celular y le brinda soporte a la célula

cellular respiration (SEL-yuh-luhr res-puh-RAY-shuhn) the process by which cells use oxygen to produce energy from food (54, 72)
respiración celular el proceso por medio del cual las células utilizan oxígeno para producir energía a partir de los alimentos

chlorophyll (KLOHR-uh-fil) a green pigment that captures light energy for photosynthesis (71)
clorofila un pigmento verde que capta la energía luminosa para la fotosíntesis

chloroplast (KLOHR-uh-plast) an organelle found in plant and algae cells where photosynthesis occurs (31)
cloroplasto un organelo que se encuentra en las células vegetales y en las células de las algas, en el cual se lleva a cabo la fotosíntesis

chromosome (KROH-muh-sohm) in a eukaryotic cell, one of the structures in the nucleus that are made up of DNA and protein; in a prokaryotic cell, the main ring of DNA (93)
cromosoma en una célula eucariótica, una de las estructuras del núcleo que está hecha de ADN y proteína; en una célula procariótica, el anillo principal de ADN

clone (KLOHN) an organism, cell, or piece of genetic material that is genetically identical to one from which it was derived; to make a genetic duplicate (165)
clon un organismo, una célula o una muestra de material genético que es genéticamente idéntico a aquél del cual deriva; hacer un duplicado genético

codominance (koh-DAHM-uh-nuhns) a condition in which two alleles are expressed such that the phenotype of a heterozygous individual is a combination of the phenotypes of the two homozygous parents (131)
codominancia una condición en la que dos alelos están expresados de modo que el fenotipo de un individuo heterocigoto es una combinación de los fenotipos de los dos padres homocigotos

cytokinesis (sy-toh-kuh-NEE-sis) the division of the cytoplasm of a cell (95)
citocinesis la división del citoplasma de una célula

cytoplasm (sy-toh-PLAZ-uhm) the region of the cell within the membrane that includes the fluid, the cytoskeleton, and all of the organelles except the nucleus (10)
citoplasma la región de la célula dentro de la membrana, que incluye el líquido, el citoesqueleto y los organelos, pero no el núcleo

cytoskeleton (sy-toh-SKEL-ih-tn) the cytoplasmic network of protein filaments that plays an essential role in cell movement, shape, and division (27)
citoesqueleto la red citoplásmica de filamentos de proteínas que juega un papel esencial en el movimiento, forma y división de la célula

diffusion (dih-FYOO-zhuhn) the movement of particles from regions of higher density to regions of lower density (56)
difusión el movimiento de partículas de regiones de mayor densidad a regiones de menor densidad

DNA (dee-en-AY) deoxyribonucleic acid, a molecule that is present in all living cells and that contains the information that determines the traits that a living thing inherits and needs to live (93, 148)
ADN ácido desoxirribonucleico, una molécula que está presente en todas las células vivas y que contiene la información que determina los caracteres que un ser vivo hereda y necesita para vivir

dominant (DAHM-uh-nuhnt) in genetics, describes an allele that is fully expressed whenever the allele is present in an individual (127)
dominante en la genética, término que describe a un alelo que se expresa por completo siempre que el alelo está presente en un individuo

endocytosis (en-doh-sy-TOH-sis) the process by which a cell membrane surrounds a particle and encloses the particle in a vesicle to bring the particle into the cell (58)
endocitosis el proceso por medio del cual la membrana celular rodea una partícula y la encierra en una vesícula para llevarla al interior de la célula

endoplasmic reticulum (en-doh-PLAZ-mik ri-TIK-yuh-luhm) a system of membranes that is found in a cell's cytoplasm and that assists in the production, processing, and transport of proteins and in the production of lipids (29)
retículo endoplásmico un sistema de membranas que se encuentra en el citoplasma de la célula y que tiene una función en la producción, procesamiento y transporte de proteínas y en la producción de lípidos

eukaryote (yoo-KAIR-ee-oht) an organism made up of cells that have a nucleus enclosed by a membrane; eukaryotes include protists, animals, plants, and fungi but not archaea or bacteria (11)
eucariote un organismo cuyas células tienen un núcleo contenido en una membrana; entre los eucariotes se encuentran protistas, animales, plantas y hongos, pero no arqueas ni bacterias

exocytosis (ek-soh-sy-TOH-sis) the process in which a cell releases a particle by enclosing the particle in a vesicle that then moves to the cell surface and fuses with the cell membrane (58)
exocitosis el proceso por medio del cual una célula libera una partícula encerrándola en una vesícula que luego se traslada a la superficie de la célula y se fusiona con la membrana celular

fertilization (fer-tl-ih-ZAY-shuhn) the union of a male and female gamete to form a zygote (116)
fecundación la unión de un gameto masculino y femenino para formar un cigoto

function (FUNGK-shuhn) the special, normal, or proper activity of an organ or part (44)
función la actividad especial, normal o adecuada de un órgano o parte

gene (JEEN) one set of instructions for an inherited trait (126)
gene un conjunto de instrucciones para un carácter heredado

genetic engineering (juh-NET-ik en-juh-NIR-ing) a technology in which the genome of a living cell is modified for medical or industrial use (164)
ingeniería genética una tecnología en la que el genoma de una célula viva se modifica con fines médicos o industriales

genotype (JEEN-uh-typ) the entire genetic makeup of an organism; also the combination of genes for one or more specific traits (127)
genotipo la constitución genética completa de un organismo; también, la combinación de genes para uno o más caracteres específicos

Golgi complex (GOHL-jee KAHM-pleks) a cell organelle that helps make and package materials to be transported out of the cell (29)
aparato de Golgi un organelo celular que ayuda a hacer y a empacar los materiales que serán transportados al exterior de la célula

© Houghton Mifflin Harcourt Publishing Company

© Houghton Mifflin Harcourt Publishing Company

heredity (huh·RED·ih·tee) the passing of genetic material from parent to offspring (124)
herencia la transmisión de material genético de padres a hijos

homeostasis (hoh·mee·oh·STAY·sis) the maintenance of a constant internal state in a changing environment (52)
homeostasis la capacidad de mantener un estado interno constante en un ambiente en cambio

homologous chromosomes (hoh·MAHL·uh·guhs KROH·muh·sohmz) chromosomes that have the same sequence of genes and the same structure (102)
cromosomas homólogos cromosomas con la misma secuencia de genes y la misma estructura

incomplete dominance (in·kuhm·PLEET DAHM·uh·nuhns) a condition in which two alleles are expressed such that the phenotype of a heterozygous individual is an intermediate of the phenotypes of the two homozygous parents (130)
dominancia incompleta una condición en la que dos alelos se expresan de modo que el fenotipo de un individuo heterocigoto es intermedio entre los fenotipos de sus dos padres homocigotos

interphase (IN·ter·fayz) the period of the cell cycle during which activities such as cell growth and protein synthesis occur without visible signs of cell division (94)
interfase el período del ciclo celular durante el cual las actividades como el crecimiento celular y la síntesis de proteínas existen sin signos visibles de división celular

L

lipid (LIP·id) a fat molecule or a molecule that has similar properties; examples include oils, waxes, and steroids (18)
lípido una molécula de grasa o una molécula que tiene propiedades similares; algunos ejemplos son los aceites, las ceras y los esteroides

lysosome (LY·suh·sohm) a cell organelle that contains digestive enzymes (32)
lisosoma un organelo celular que contiene enzimas digestivas

M

meiosis (my·OH·sis) a process in cell division during which the number of chromosomes decreases to half the original number by two divisions of the nucleus, which results in the production of sex cells (gametes or spores) (103)
meiosis un proceso de división celular durante el cual el número de cromosomas disminuye a la mitad del número original por medio de dos divisiones del núcleo, lo cual resulta en la producción de células sexuales (gametos o esporas)

mitochondrion (my·toh·KAHN·dree·uhn) in eukaryotic cells, the organelle that is the site of cellular respiration, which releases energy for use by the cell (28)
mitocondria en las células eucarióticas, el organelo donde se lleva a cabo la respiración celular, la cual libera energía para que utilice la célula

mitosis (my·TOH·sis) in eukaryotic cells, a process of cell division that forms two new nuclei, each of which has the same number of chromosomes (55, 95)
mitosis en las células eucarióticas, un proceso de división celular que forma dos núcleos nuevos, cada uno de los cuales posee el mismo número de cromosomas

molecule (MAHL·ih·kyool) a group of atoms that are held together by chemical forces; a molecule is the smallest unit of a compound that keeps all the properties of that compound (17)
molécula un grupo de átomos unidos por fuerzas químicas; una molécula es la unidad más pequeña de un compuesto que conserva todas las propiedades de ese compuesto

mutation (myoo·TAY·shuhn) a change in the nucleotide-base sequence of a gene or DNA molecule (153)
mutación un cambio en la secuencia de la base de nucleótidos de un gene o de una molécula de ADN

nucleic acid (noo·KLAY·ik AS·id) a molecule made up of subunits called nucleotides (19)
ácido nucleico una molécula formada por subunidades llamadas nucleótidos

nucleotide (NOO·klee·oh·tyd) in a nucleic-acid chain, a subunit that consists of a sugar, a phosphate, and a nitrogenous base (151)
nucleótido en una cadena de ácidos nucleicos, una subunidad formada por un azúcar, un fosfato y una base nitrogenada

nucleus (NOO·klee·uhs) in a eukaryotic cell, a membrane-bound organelle that contains the cell's DNA and that has a role in processes such as growth, metabolism, and reproduction (10)
núcleo en una célula eucariótica, un organelo cubierto por una membrana, el cual contiene el ADN de la célula y participa en procesos tales como el crecimiento, metabolismo y reproducción

organ (OHR·guhn) a collection of tissues that carry out a specialized function of the body (42)
órgano un conjunto de tejidos que desempeñan una función especializada en el cuerpo

organ system (OHR·guhn SIS·tuhm) a group of organs that work together to perform body functions (43)
aparato (o sistema) de órganos un grupo de órganos que trabajan en conjunto para desempeñar funciones corporales

organelle (ohr·guhn·EL) one of the small bodies in a cell's cytoplasm that are specialized to perform a specific function (10)
organelo uno de los cuerpos pequeños del citoplasma de una célula que están especializados para llevar a cabo una función específica

organism (OHR·guh·niz·uhm) a living thing; anything that can carry out life processes independently (6, 40)
organismo un ser vivo; cualquier cosa que pueda llevar a cabo procesos vitales independientemente

osmosis (ahz·MOH·sis) the diffusion of water through a semipermeable membrane (56)
ósmosis la difusión del agua a través de una membrana semipermeable

passive transport (PAS·iv TRANS·pohrt) the movement of substances across a cell membrane without the use of energy by the cell (56)
transporte pasivo el movimiento de sustancias a través de una membrana celular sin que la célula tenga que usar energía

pedigree (PED·ih·gree) a diagram that shows the occurrence of a genetic trait in several generations of a family (142)
pedigrí un diagrama que muestra la incidencia de un carácter genético en varias generaciones de una familia

phenotype (FEE·nuh·typ) an organism's appearance or other detectable characteristic (127)
fenotipo la apariencia de un organismo u otra característica perceptible

phospholipid (fahs·foh·LIP·id) a lipid that contains phosphorus and that is a structural component in cell membranes (20)
fosfolípido un lípido que contiene fósforo y que es un componente estructural de la membrana celular

photosynthesis (foh·toh·SIN·thih·sis) the process by which plants, algae, and some bacteria use sunlight, carbon dioxide, and water to make food (54, 70)
fotosíntesis el proceso por medio del cual las plantas, las algas y algunas bacterias utilizan la luz solar, el dióxido de carbono y el agua para producir alimento

probability (prahb·uh·BIL·ih·tee) the likelihood that a possible future event will occur in any given instance of the event (140)
probabilidad la probabilidad de que ocurra un posible suceso futuro en cualquier caso dado del suceso

prokaryote (proh·KAIR·ee·oht) a single-celled organism that does not have a nucleus or membrane-bound organelles; examples are archaea and bacteria (11)
procariote un organismo unicelular que no tiene núcleo ni organelos cubiertos por una membrana, por ejemplo, las arqueas y las bacterias

protein (PROH·teen) a molecule that is made up of amino acids and that is needed to build and repair body structures and to regulate processes in the body (18)
proteína una molécula formada por aminoácidos que es necesaria para construir y reparar estructuras corporales y para regular procesos del cuerpo

Punnett square (PUH·nuht SKWAIR) a graphic used to predict the results of a genetic cross (138)
cuadro de Punnett una gráfica que se usa para predecir los resultados de una cruza genética

R

ratio (RAY·shee·oh) a comparison of two numbers using division (140)
razón comparación de dos números mediante la división

recessive (ree·SES·iv) describes an allele that will be masked unless the organism is homozygous for the trait (127)
recesivo término que describe un alelo que no se expresa a menos que el organismo sea homocigoto para el carácter

replication (rep·lih·KAY·shuhn) the duplication of a DNA molecule (152)
replicación la duplicación de una molécula de ADN

ribosome (RY·buh·sohm) a cell organelle composed of RNA and protein; the site of protein synthesis (28, 155)
ribosoma un organelo celular compuesto de ARN y proteína; el sitio donde ocurre la síntesis de proteínas

RNA (ar·en·AY) ribonucleic acid, a molecule that is present in all living cells and that plays a role in protein production (154)
ARN ácido ribonucleico, una molécula que está presente en todas las células vivas y que juega un papel en la producción de proteínas

S

sexual reproduction (SEK·shoo·uhl ree·pruh·DUHK·shuhn) reproduction in which the sex cells from two parents unite to produce offspring that share traits from both parents (116)

reproducción sexual reproducción en la que se unen las células sexuales de los dos progenitores para producir descendencia que comparte caracteres de ambos progenitores

structure (STRUHK·cher) the arrangement of parts in an organism (44)

estructura el orden y distribución de las partes de un organismo

T–U

tissue (TISH·oo) a group of similar cells that perform a common function (41)

tejido un grupo de células similares que llevan a cabo una función común

V–Z

vacuole (VAK·yoo·ohl) a fluid-filled vesicle found in the cytoplasm of plant cells or protozoans (30)

vacuola una vesícula llena de líquido que se encuentra en el citoplasma de las células vegetales o de los protozoarios

State STANDARDS FOR ENGLISH LANGUAGE ARTS
Correlations

This table shows correlations to the *Reading Standards for Literacy in Science and Technical Subjects* for grades 6–8.

Go online at **thinkcentral.com** for correlations of all *ScienceFusion* Modules to Common Core State Standards for Mathematics and to the rest of the *Common Core State Standards for English Language Arts.*

Grade 6–8 Standard Code	Citations for Module K "Introduction to Science and Technology"
READING STANDARDS FOR LITERACY IN SCIENCE AND TECHNICAL SUBJECTS	
Key Ideas and Details	
RST.6–8.1 Cite specific textual evidence to support analysis of science and technical texts.	*Student Edition* pp. 25, 75, 113 *Teacher Edition* pp. 98, 117
RST.6–8.2 Determine the central ideas or conclusions of a text; provide an accurate summary of the text distinct from prior knowledge or opinions.	*Student Edition* pp. 25, 32, 60, 75, 113, 132, 137, 149, 157, 163, 171, 189 *Teacher Edition* pp. 17, 21, 22, 35, 51, 61, 62, 98, 106, 117, 128, 130, 161, 178, 179, 206, 213, 237, 240. Also use "Synthesizing Key Topics" items in the Extend Science Concepts sections of the Teacher Edition.
RST.6–8.3 Follow precisely a multistep procedure when carrying out experiments, taking measurements, or performing technical tasks.	*Student Edition* pp. 83, 90–91 *Teacher Edition* p. 94 *Other* Use the Lab Manual, Project-Based Assessments, Video-Based Projects, and the Virtual Labs.
Craft and Structure	
RST.6–8.4 Determine the meaning of symbols, key terms, and other domain-specific words and phrases as they are used in a specific scientific or technical context relevant to *grades 6–8 texts and topics.*	*Student Edition* pp. 5, 17, 31, 43, 63, 64, 77, 93, 115, 131, 141, 153, 169, 181 *Teacher Edition* p. 111. Also use "Previewing Vocabulary" and "Reinforcing Vocabulary" items in the Explain Science Concepts sections of the Teacher Edition.

Grade 6–8 Standard Code (continued)	Citations for Module K "Introduction to Science and Technology"
RST.6–8.5 Analyze the structure an author uses to organize a text, including how the major sections contribute to the whole and to an understanding of the topic.	*Student Edition* p. 75 *Teacher Edition* pp. 51, 128, 213, 237, 240
RST.6–8.6 Analyze the author's purpose in providing an explanation, describing a procedure, or discussing an experiment in a text.	*Student Edition* pp. 25, 75 *Teacher Edition* pp. 14, 47, 98

Integration of Knowledge and Ideas

RST.6–8.7 Integrate quantitative or technical information expressed in words in a text with a version of that information expressed visually (e.g., in a flowchart, diagram, model, graph, or table).	*Student Edition* pp. 3, 35, 54, 66–67, 81, 122–123, 144, 147, 158, 159 *Teacher Edition* pp. 21, 40, 53, 54, 123, 194, 201, 206, 208, 224, 237, 240. Also use the "Graphic Organizer" items in the Teacher Edition. *Other* Use the lessons in the Digital Path.
RST.6–8.8 Distinguish among facts, reasoned judgment based on research findings, and speculation in a text.	*Student Edition* pp. 13, 25, 74–75, 113 *Teacher Edition* pp. 14, 17, 98
RST.6–8.9 Compare and contrast the information gained from experiments, simulations, video, or multimedia sources with that gained from reading a text on the same topic.	*Student Edition* pp. 113, 137, 163 *Teacher Edition* pp. 40, 79, 117 *Other* Use the Lab Manual, Project-Based Assessments, Video-Based Projects, and the lessons in the Digital Path.

Range of Reading and Level of Text Complexity

RST.6–8.10 By the end of grade 8, read and comprehend science/technical texts in the grades 6–8 text complexity band independently and proficiently.	*Student Edition* pp. 3, 22, 75, 90, 113, 132, 137, 149, 157, 163, 171, 189. Also use all lessons in the Student Edition. *Teacher Edition* pp. 47, 48, 61, 62, 117

Science Trade Books

Bibliography

This bibliography is a compilation of trade books that can supplement the materials covered in *ScienceFusion* Grades 6–8. Many of the books are recommendations of the National Science Teachers Association (NSTA) and the Children's Book Council (CBC) as outstanding science trade books for children. These books were selected because they meet the following rigorous criteria: they are of literary quality and contain substantial science content; the theories and facts are clearly distinguished; they are free of gender, ethnic, and socioeconomic bias; and they contain clear, accurate, up-to-date information. Several selections are award-winning titles, or their authors have received awards.

As with all materials you share with your class, we suggest you review the books first to ensure their appropriateness. While titles are current at time of publication, they may go out of print without notice.

Grades 6–8

Acids and Bases (Material Matters/Express Edition) by Carol Baldwin (Heinemann-Raintree, 2005) focuses on the properties of acids and bases with photographs and facts.

Acids and Bases by Eurona Earl Tilley (Chelsea House, 2008) provides a thorough, basic understanding of acid and base chemistry, including such topics as naming compounds, writing formulas, and physical and chemical properties.

Across the Wide Ocean: The Why, How, and Where of Navigation for Humans and Animals at Sea by Karen Romano Young (Greenwillow, 2007) focuses on navigational tools, maps, and charts that researchers and explorers use to learn more about oceanography. AWARD-WINNING AUTHOR

Adventures in Sound with Max Axiom, Super Scientist (Graphic Science Series) by Emily Sohn (Capstone, 2007) provides information about sound through a fun graphic novel.

Air: A Resource Our World Depends on (Managing Our Resources) by Ian Graham (Heinemann-Raintree, 2005) examines this valuable natural resource and answers questions such as "How much does Earth's air weigh?" and "Why do plants need wind?"

The Alkaline Earth Metals: Beryllium, Magnesium, Calcium, Strontium, Barium, Radium (Understanding the Elements of the Periodic Table) by Bridget Heos (Rosen Central, 2009) describes the characteristics of these metals, including their similar physical and molecular properties.

All About Light and Sound (Mission: Science) by Connie Jankowski (Compass Point, 2010) focuses on the importance of light and sound and how without them we could not survive.

Alternative Energy: Beyond Fossil Fuels by Dana Meachen Rau (Compass Point, 2010) discusses the ways that water, wind, and sun provide a promising solution to our energy crisis and encourages readers to help the planet by conserving energy. AWARD-WINNING AUTHOR

Amazing Biome Projects You Can Build Yourself (Build it Yourself Series) by Donna Latham (Nomad, 2009) provides an overview of eight terrestrial biomes, including characteristics about climate, soil, animals, and plants.

Archaea: Salt-Lovers, Methane-Makers, Thermophiles, and Other Archaeans (A Class of Their Own) by David M. Barker (Crabtree, 2010) provides interesting facts about different types of archaeans.

The Art of Construction: Projects and Principles for Beginning Engineers and Architects by Mario Salvadori (Chicago Review, 2000) explains how tents, houses, stadiums, and bridges are built, and how to build models of such structures using materials found around the house. AWARD-WINNING AUTHOR

Astronomy: Out of This World! by Simon Basher and Dan Green (Kingfisher, 2009) takes readers on a journey of the universe and provides information about the planets, stars, galaxies, telescopes, space missions, and discoveries.

At the Sea Floor Café: Odd Ocean Critter Poems by Leslie Bulion (Peachtree, 2011) provides poetry to educate students about how ocean creatures search for food, capture prey, protect their young, and trick their predators.

Battery Science: Make Widgets That Work and Gadgets That Go by Doug Stillinger (Klutz, 2003) offers an array of activities and gadgets to get students excited about electricity.

The Biggest Explosions in the Universe by Sara Howard (BookSurge, 2009) tells the story of stars in our universe through fun text and captivating photographs.

Biology: Life as We Know It! by Simon Basher and Dan Green (Kingfisher, 2008) offers information about all aspects of life from the animals and plants to the minuscule cells, proteins, and DNA that bring them to life.

Birds of a Feather by Jane Yolen (Boyds Mills Press, 2011) offers facts and information about birds through fun poetry and beautiful photographs. AWARD-WINNING AUTHOR

Blackout!: Electricity and Circuits (Fusion) by Anna Claybourne (Heinemann-Raintree, 2005) provides an array of facts about electricity and how we rely on it for so many things in everyday life. AWARD-WINNING AUTHOR

Cell Division and Genetics by Robert Snedden (Heinemann, 2007) explains various aspects of cells and the living world, including what happens when cells divide and how characteristics are passed on from one generation to another. AWARD-WINNING AUTHOR

Chemistry: Getting a Big Reaction by Dan Green and Simon Basher (Kingfisher, 2010) acts as a guide about the chemical "characters" that fizz, react, and combine to make up everything around us.

Cool Stuff Exploded by Chris Woodford (Dorling Kindersley, 2008) focuses on today's technological marvels and tomorrow's jaw-dropping devices. OUTSTANDING SCIENCE TRADE BOOK

Disaster Deferred: How New Science Is Changing Our View of Earthquake Hazards in the Midwest by Seth Stein (Columbia University, 2010) discusses technological innovations that make earthquake prediction possible.

The Diversity of Species (Timeline: Life on Earth) by Michael Bright (Heinemann, 2008) explains how and why things on Earth have genetic and physical differences and how they have had and continue to have an impact on Earth.

Drip! Drop!: How Water Gets to Your Tap by Barbara Seuling (Holiday House, 2000) introduces students to JoJo and her dog, Willy, who explain the water cycle and introduce fun experiments about filtration, evaporation, and condensation. AWARD-WINNING AUTHOR

Eat Fresh Food: Awesome Recipes for Teen Chefs by Rozanne Gold (Bloomsbury, 2009) includes more than 80 recipes and places a strong emphasis on fresh foods throughout the book.

Eco-Tracking: On the Trail of Habitat Change (Worlds of Wonder) by Daniel Shaw (University of New Mexico, 2010) recounts success stories of young people involved in citizen science efforts and encourages others to join in to preserve nature's ecosystems.

Electric Mischief: Battery-Powered Gadgets Kids Can Build by Alan Bartholomew (Kids Can Press, 2002) offers a variety of fun projects that include making battery connections and switches and building gadgets such as electric dice and a bumper car.

Electricity (Why It Works) by Anna Claybourne (QED Publishing, 2008) provides information about electricity in an easy-to-follow manner. AWARD-WINNING AUTHOR

Electricity and Magnetism (Usborne Understand Science) by Peter Adamczyk (Usborne, 2008) explains the basics about electricity and magnetism, including information about static electricity, electric circuits, and electromagnetism.

Energy Transfers (Energy Essentials) by Nigel Saunders and Steven Chapman (Raintree, 2005) explains the different types of energy, how they can change, and how different forms of energy help us in our everyday lives.

The Everything Machine by Matt Novak (Roaring Brook, 2009) tells the silly story of a machine that does everything for a group of people until they wake up one day and discover that the machine has stopped working. AWARD-WINNING AUTHOR

Experiments with Plants and Other Living Things by Trevor Cook (PowerKids, 2009) provides fun, hands-on experiments to teach students about flowers, plants, and biology.

Exploring the Oceans: Seafloor by John Woodward (Heinemann, 2004) takes readers on a virtual tour through the bottom part of the ocean, highlighting the plants and animals that thrive in this environment.

Extreme Structures: Mega Constructions of the 21st Century (Science Frontiers) by David Jefferis (Crabtree, 2006) takes a look at how some of the coolest buildings in the world were built and what other kinds of structures are being planned for the future. AWARD-WINNING AUTHOR

Fascinating Science Projects: Electricity and Magnetism by Bobbi Searle (Aladdin, 2002) teaches the concepts of electricity and magnetism through dozens of projects and experiments and color illustrations.

Fizz, Bubble and Flash!: Element Explorations and Atom Adventures for Hands-on Science Fun! by Anita Brandolini, Ph.D. (Williamson, 2003) introduces chemistry to students in a nonintimidating way and focuses on the elements and the periodic table. PARENTS' CHOICE

Floods: Hazards of Surface and Groundwater Systems (The Hazardous Earth) by Timothy M. Kusky (Facts on File, 2008) explores the processes that control the development and flow in river and stream systems and when these processes become dangerous.

Fossils (Geology Rocks!) by Rebecca Faulkner (Raintree, 2008) educates students about rock formation and the processes and characteristics of rocks and fossils.

Friends: True Stories of Extraordinary Animal Friendships by Catherine Thimmesh (Houghton Mifflin Harcourt, 2011) depicts true stories of unlikely animal friendships, including a wild polar bear and a sled dog as well as a camel and a Vietnamese pig. AWARD-WINNING AUTHOR

The Frog Scientist (Scientists in the Field) by Pamela S. Turner (Houghton Mifflin Harcourt, 2009) follows a scientist and his protégés as they research the effects of atrazine-contaminated water on vulnerable amphibians. BOOKLIST EDITORS' CHOICE

From Steam Engines to Nuclear Fusion: Discovering Energy (Chain Reactions) by Carol Ballard (Heinemann-Raintree, 2007) tells the fascinating story of energy, from the heat produced by a simple fire to the extraordinary power contained in an atom.

Fully Charged (Everyday Science) by Steve Parker (Heinemann-Raintree, 2005) explains how electricity is generated, harnessed, and used and also the difference between electricity, including static electricity, and electronics. AWARD-WINNING AUTHOR

Galileo for Kids: His Life and Ideas by Richard Panchyk (Chicago Review, 2005) includes experiments that demonstrate scientific principles developed by the astronomer Galileo.

Genes and DNA by Richard Walker (Kingfisher, 2003) offers an abundance of information about characteristics of genes, gene function, DNA technology, and genetic engineering, as well as other fascinating topics. NSTA TRADE BOOK; OUTSTANDING SCIENCE TRADE BOOK

Hands-on Science Series: Simple Machines by Steven Souza and Joseph Shortell (Walch, 2001) investigates the concepts of work, force, power, efficiency, and mechanical advantage.

How Animals Work by David Burnie (Dorling Kindersley, 2010) provides vivid photographs and intriguing text to describe various animals and their characteristics, diets, and families. AWARD-WINNING AUTHOR

How Does an Earthquake Become a Tsunami? (How Does it Happen?) by Linda Tagliaferro (Heinemann-Raintree, 2009) describes the changes in water, waves, and tides that occur between an earthquake and a tsunami. AWARD-WINNING AUTHOR

How the Future Began: Machines by Clive Gifford (Kingfisher, 1999) acts as a guide to historical and current developments in the field of machinery, including mass production, computers, robots, microengineering, and communications technology. AWARD-WINNING AUTHOR

How Scientists Work (Simply Science) by Natalie M. Rosinsky (Compass Point, 2003) discusses the scientific method, equipment, and procedures and also describes how scientists compile information and answer questions.

How to Clean a Hippopotamus: A Look at Unusual Animal Partnerships by Steve Jenkins and Robin Page (Houghton Mifflin Harcourt, 2010) explores animal symbiosis with fun illustrations and a close-up, step-by-step view of some of nature's most fascinating animal partnerships. ALA NOTABLE BOOK

Human Spaceflight (Frontiers in Space) by Joseph A. Angelo (Facts on File, 2007) examines the history of space exploration and the evolution of space technology from the dawn of the space age to the present time.

The Hydrosphere: Agent of Change by Gregory L. Vogt, Ed.D. (Twenty-First Century, 2006) discusses the impact this 20-mile-thick sphere has had on the surface of the planet and the processes that go on there, including the ability of Earth to sustain life. AWARD-WINNING AUTHOR

In Rivers, Lakes, and Ponds (Under the Microscope) by Sabrina Crewe (Chelsea Clubhouse, 2010) educates readers about the microscopic critters that live in these various bodies of water.

A Kid's Guide to Climate Change and Global Warming: How to Take Action! by Cathryn Berger Kaye, M.A. (Free Spirit, 2009) encourages students to learn about the climate changes happening around the world and to get involved to help save our planet.

Lasers (Lucent Library of Science and Technology) by Don Nardo (Lucent, 2003) discusses the scientific discovery and development of lasers—high-intensity light—and their use in our daily lives. AWARD-WINNING AUTHOR

Leonardo's Horse by Jean Fritz (Putnam, 2001) tells the story of Leonardo da Vinci—the curious and inquisitive artist, engineer, and astronomer—who created a detailed horse sculpture for the city of Milan. ALA NOTABLE BOOK; NOTABLE SOCIAL STUDIES TRADE BOOK; NOTABLE CHILDREN'S BOOK IN THE LANGUAGE ARTS

Light: From Sun to Bulbs by Christopher Cooper (Heinemann, 2003) invites students to investigate the dazzling world of physical science and light through fun experiments. AWARD-WINNING AUTHOR

Magnetism and Electromagnets (Sci-Hi: Physical Science) by Eve Hartman (Raintree, 2008) offers colorful illustrations, photographs, quizzes, charts, graphs, and text to teach students about magnetism.

Making Good Choices About Nonrenewable Resources (Green Matters) by Paula Johanson (Rosen Central, 2009) focuses on the different types of nonrenewable natural resources, alternative resources, conservation, and making positive consumer choices.

Making Waves: Sound (Everyday Science) by Steve Parker (Heinemann-Raintree, 2005) describes what sound is, how it is formed and used, and properties associated with sound, such as pitch, speed, and volume. AWARD-WINNING AUTHOR

The Manatee Scientists: Saving Vulnerable Species (Scientists in the Field Series) by Peter Lourie (Houghton Mifflin Harcourt, 2011) discusses three species of manatees and the importance of preserving these mammals. AWARD-WINNING AUTHOR

The Man Who Named the Clouds by Julie Hannah and Joan Holub (Albert Whitman, 2006) tells the story of 18th-century English meteorologist Luke Howard and also discusses the ten classifications of clouds.

Medicine in the News (Science News Flash) by Brian R. Shmaefsky, Ph.D. (Chelsea House, 2007) focuses on medical advancements that are in the news today and the innovative tools that are used for diagnosis and treatment.

Metals and Metalloids (Periodic Table of the Elements) by Monica Halka, Ph.D., and Brian Nordstrom, Ed.D. (Facts on File, 2010), offers information about the physics, chemistry, geology, and biology of metals and metalloids.

Meteorology: Ferguson's Careers in Focus by Ferguson (Ferguson, 2011) profiles 18 different careers pertaining to the science of the atmosphere and its phenomena.

The Microscope (Great Medical Discoveries) by Adam Woog (Lucent, 2003) recounts how the microscope has had an impact on the history of medicine.

Microscopes and Telescopes: Great Inventions by Rebecca Stefoff (Marshall Cavendish Benchmark, 2007) describes the origin, history, development, and societal impact of the telescope and microscope. OUTSTANDING SCIENCE TRADE BOOK

Mighty Animal Cells by Rebecca L. Johnson (Millbrook, 2007) takes readers on a journey to discover how people and animals grow from just one single cell. AWARD-WINNING AUTHOR

Moon (Eyewitness Books) by Jacqueline Mitton (Dorling Kindersley, 2009) offers information about our planet's mysterious nearest neighbor, from the moon's waterless seas and massive craters to its effect on Earth's ocean tides and its role in solar eclipses. AWARD-WINNING AUTHOR

MP3 Players (Let's Explore Technology Communications) by Jeanne Sturm (Rourke, 2010) discusses the technological advances in music in our society.

Nanotechnologist (Cool Science Careers) by Ann Heinrichs (Cherry Lake, 2009) provides information about nanotechnologists—scientists who work with materials on a subatomic or atomic level.

Ocean: An Illustrated Atlas by Sylvia A. Earle (National Geographic, 2008) provides an overview on the ocean as a whole, each of the major ocean basins, and the future of the oceans. AWARD-WINNING AUTHOR

Oceans (Insiders) by Beverly McMillan and John A. Musick (Simon & Schuster, 2007) takes readers on a 3-D journey of the aquatic universe—exploring the formation of waves and tsunamis as well as the plant and animal species that live beneath the ocean's surface.

Organic Chemistry and Biochemistry (Facts at Your Fingertips) by Graham Bateman (Brown Bear, 2011) provides diagrams, experiments, and testing aids to teach students the basics about organic chemistry and biochemistry.

An Overcrowded World?: Our Impact on the Planet (21st Century Debates) by Rob Bowden (Heinemann, 2002) investigates how and why the world's population is growing so fast, the effects of this growth on wildlife and habitats, and the pressure on resources, and suggests ways of controlling growth.

The Pebble in My Pocket: A History of Our Earth by Meredith Hooper (Viking, 1996) follows the course of a pebble, beginning 480 million years ago, through a fiery volcano and primordial forest and along the icy bottom of a glacier and how it looks today as the result of its journey. AWARD-WINNING AUTHOR

The Periodic Table: Elements with Style! by Simon Basher and Adrian Dingle (Kingfisher, 2007) offers information about the different elements that make up the periodic table and their features and characteristics.

Phenomena: Secrets of the Senses by Donna M. Jackson (Little, Brown, 2008) focuses on the senses and how to interpret them and discusses ways that technology is changing how we experience the world around us. AWARD-WINNING AUTHOR

Pioneers of Light and Sound (Mission: Science) by Connie Jankowski (Compass Point, 2010) focuses on various scientists and their accomplishments and achievements.

Planet Animal: Saving Earth's Disappearing Animals by B. Taylor (Barron's, 2009) focuses on the planet's most endangered animals, their relationships to the environment, and steps that are being taken to try to save these animals from extinction.

Plant and Animal Science Fair Projects (Biology Science Projects Using the Scientific Method) by Yael Calhoun (Enslow, 2010) provides an array of experiments about plants and animals and describes the importance of the scientific method, forming a hypothesis, and recording data for any given project.

Plant Secrets: Plant Life Processes by Anna Claybourne (Heinemann-Raintree, 2005) includes informative text, vivid photographs, and detailed charts about characteristics of various plants. AWARD-WINNING AUTHOR

Polar Regions: Human Impacts (Our Fragile Planet) by Dana Desonie (Chelsea House, 2008) focuses on pollutants and global warming in the Arctic and Antarctic and future dangers that will occur if our planet continues on its current path.

Potato Clocks and Solar Cars: Renewable and Non-renewable Energy by Elizabeth Raum (Raintree, 2007) explores various topics, including alternative energy sources, fossil fuels, and sustainable energy.

The Power of Pressure (How Things Work) by Andrew Dunn (Thomson Learning, 1993) explains how water pressure and air work and how they are used in machines.

Protists and Fungi (Discovery Channel School Science) by Katie King and Jacqueline A. Ball (Gareth Stevens, 2003) focuses on the appearance, behavior, and characteristics of various protists and fungi, using examples of algae, mold, and mushrooms.

Protozoans, Algae and Other Protists by Steve Parker (Compass Point, 2010) introduces readers to the parts, life cycles, and reproduction of various types of protists, from microscopic protozoans to seaweedlike algae, and some of the harmful effects protists have on humans. AWARD-WINNING AUTHOR

Sally Ride: The First American Woman in Space by Tom Riddolls (Crabtree, 2010) focuses on the growth and impact of Sally Ride Science—an educational program founded by the astronaut to encourage girls to pursue hobbies and careers in science.

Science and Technology in 20th Century American Life by Christopher Cumo (Greenwood, 2008) takes readers on a history of technology from agricultural implements through modern computers, telecommunications, and skateboards.

Sedimentary Rock (Geology Rocks!) by Rebecca Faulkner (Raintree, 2008) educates students about rock formation and the processes and characteristics of sedimentary rock.

Shaping the Earth by Dorothy Hinshaw Patent (Clarion/Houghton Mifflin, 2000) combines vivid photographs with informative text to explain the forces that have created the geological features on Earth's surface. AWARD-WINNING AUTHOR

Silent Spring by Rachel Carson (Houghton Mifflin, 2002) celebrates marine biologist and environmental activist Rachel Carson's contribution to Earth through an array of essays.

Skywalkers: Mohawk Ironworkers Build the City by David Weitzman (Flash Point, 2010) focuses on the ironworkers who constructed bridges and skyscrapers in New York and Canada. AWARD-WINNING AUTHOR

Sustaining Earth's Energy Resources (Environment at Risk) by Ann Heinrichs (Marshall Cavendish, 2010) offers information on Earth's sources of nonrenewable and renewable energy, how they are used, and their disadvantages and benefits.

Team Moon: How 400,000 People Landed Apollo 11 on the Moon by Catherine Thimmesh (Houghton Mifflin, 2006) tells the story of the first moon landing and celebrates the dedication, ingenuity, and perseverance of the people who made this event happen. ALA NOTABLE BOOK; ORBIS PICTUS HONOR; NOTABLE CHILDREN'S BOOK IN THE LANGUAGE ARTS; ALA BEST BOOK FOR YOUNG ADULTS; GOLDEN KITE HONOR

The Top of the World: Climbing Mount Everest by Steve Jenkins (Houghton Mifflin, 1999) describes the conditions and terrain of Mount Everest, attempts that have been made to scale this peak, and information about the equipment and techniques of mountain climbing. ALA NOTABLE BOOK; SLJ BEST BOOK; BOSTON GLOBE–HORN BOOK AWARD; ORBIS PICTUS HONOR

Transmission of Power by Fluid Pressure: Air and Water by William Donaldson (Nabu, 2010) describes the transmission of fluid pressure as it pertains to the elements of air and water in the world of motion, forces, and energy.

Tsunami: The True Story of an April Fools' Day Disaster by Gail Langer Karwoski (Darby Creek, 2006) offers a variety of viewpoints about the wave that struck Hawaii in 1946. NOTABLE SOCIAL STUDIES TRADE BOOK

Vapor, Rain, and Snow: The Science of Clouds and Precipitation (Weatherwise) by Paul Fleisher (Lerner, 2010) answers an array of questions about water, such as "How does a cloud form?" and "Why do ice cubes shrink in the freezer?" AWARD-WINNING AUTHOR

Water Supplies in Crisis (Planet in Crisis) by Russ Parker (Rosen Central, 2009) describes a world where safe drinking water is not readily available, polluted water brings disease, and lakes are disappearing.

Weird Meat-Eating Plants (Bizarre Science) by Nathan Aaseng (Enslow, 2011) provides information about a variety of carnivorous plants, reversing the food chain's usual order. AWARD-WINNING AUTHOR

What Are Igneous Rocks? (Let's Rock!) by Molly Aloian (Crabtree, 2010) explains how granite, basalt, lava, silica, and quartz are formed after hot molten rock cools.

What's Living Inside Your Body? by Andrew Solway (Heinemann, 2004) offers information about an array of viruses, germs, and parasites that thrive inside the human body.

Why Should I Bother to Keep Fit? (What's Happening?) by Kate Knighton and Susan Meredith (Usborne, 2009) motivates students to get fit and stay fit.

The World of Microbes: Bacteria, Viruses, and Other Microorganisms (Understanding Genetics) by Janey Levy (Rosen Classroom, 2010) describes the world of microbes, a history of microbiology, and the characteristics of both harmful and beneficial bacteria.

Written in Bone: Buried Lives of Jamestown and Colonial Maryland by Sally M. Walker (Carolrhoda, 2009) describes the way that scientists used forensic anthropology to investigate colonial-era graves near Jamestown, Virginia. ALA NOTABLE BOOK; OUTSTANDING SCIENCE TRADE BOOK; NOTABLE SOCIAL STUDIES TRADE BOOK

You Blink Twelve Times a Minute and Other Freaky Facts About the Human Body by Barbara Seuling (Picture Window, 2009) provides fun and unusual facts about various ailments, medical marvels, and body parts and their functions. AWARD-WINNING AUTHOR

Correlation to
ScienceSaurus

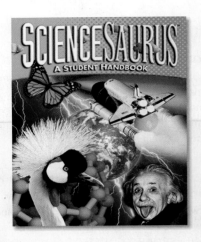

*ScienceSaurus, **A Student Handbook,*** is a "mini-encyclopedia" that students can use to find out more about unit topics. It contains numerous resources including concise content summaries, an almanac, many tables, charts, and graphs, history of science, and a glossary. ***ScienceSaurus*** is available from Houghton Mifflin Harcourt..

ScienceFusion **Page References**	**Topics**	*ScienceFusion* **Grades 6-8**
Scientific Investigation, pp. 1–19		
	Scientific Inquiry	Mod K, Unit 1, Lessons 1-3
		Mod K, Unit 2, Lessons 1, 3
	Designing Your Own Investigations	Mod K, Unit 1, Lessons 2, 4
Working in the Lab, pp. 20–72		
	Laboratory Safety	Mod K, Unit 2, Lesson 2
	Glassware and Microscopes	Mod K, Unit 2, Lesson 2
	Measurement	Mod K, Unit 2, Lesson 2
Life Science, pp. 73–164		
	Structure of Life	Mod A, Unit 1, Lessons 1-3
		Mod A, Unit 2, Lessons 1, 3
	Human Biology	Mod C, Unit 1, Lessons 1-6
		Mod C, Unit 2, Lesson 1
	Physiology and Behavior	Mod A, Unit 1, Lesson 5
		Mod B, Unit 2, Lessons 3-6
	Genes and Heredity	Mod A, Unit 2, Lessons 2-6
	Change and Diversity of Life	Mod B, Unit 1, Lessons 2-4

ScienceFusion Page References	Topics	*ScienceFusion* Grades 6-8
Life Science, pp. 73–164 (continued)		
	Ecosystems	Mod D, Unit 1, Lessons 1-4
		Mod D, Unit 2, Lessons 1-4
		Mod D, Unit 2, Lesson 5
	Classification	Mod B, Unit 1, Lesson 5
		Mod B, Unit 2, Lessons 3, 5
Earth Science, pp. 165–248		
	Geology	Mod E, Unit 4, Lesson 1
		Mod E, Unit 3, Lessons 1-3
		Mod E, Unit 4, Lessons 2-5
		Mod E, Unit 1, Lessons 2-4
		Mod E, Unit 2, Lessons 1-4
		Mod E, Unit 1, Lessons 3, 5
	Oceanography	Mod F, Unit 1, Lesson 1
		Mod F, Unit 2, Lessons 1, 3
	Meteorology	Mod F, Unit 3, Lesson 1
		Mod F, Unit 1, Lesson 2
		Mod F, Unit 4, Lesson 1, 2, 3, 6
	Astronomy	Mod G, Unit 3, Lessons 1-3
		Mod G, Unit 2, Lessons 2-6
		Mod G, Unit 1, Lessons 1-3
Physical Science, pp. 249–321		
	Matter	Mod H, Unit 1, Lessons 1-6
		Mod H, Unit 3, Lessons 1-4
		Mod H Unit 4, Lessons 1-3
		Mod H, Unit 5, Lessons 1-3

ScienceFusion Page References	Topics	ScienceFusion Grades 6-8
Physical Science, pp. 249–321 (continued)		
	Forces and Motion	Mod I, Unit 1, Lessons 1-5
		Mod I, Unit 2, Lessons 1-3
	Energy	Mod H, Unit 2, Lessons 1-4
		Mod I, Unit 3, Lessons 1-5
		Mod J, Unit 1, Lessons 1, 2
		Mod J, Unit 2, Lessons 1, 2
		Mod J, Unit 3, Lessons 1-4
Natural Resources and the Environment, pp. 322–353		
	Earth's Natural Resources	Mod D, Unit 3, Lessons 2-5
	Resource Conservation	Mod D, Unit 3, Lesson 5
	Solid Waste and Pollution	Mod D, Unit 4, Lessons 1-4 Mod F, Unit 4, Lesson 7
Science, Technology, and Society, pp. 354–373		
	Science and Technology	Mod A, Unit 2, Lesson 7
		Mod G, Unit 4, Lesson 2
		Mod I, Unit 3, Lesson 6
		Mod J, Unit 2, Lesson 3
		Mod J, Unit 3, Lesson 5
	Science and Society	Mod K, Unit 1, Lesson 4
		Mod K, Unit 3, Lesson 6

ScienceFusion Page References	Topics	*ScienceFusion* Grades 6-8
Almanac, pp. 374–438		
	Scientific Numbers	May be used with all units.
	Using Data Tables and Graphs	Mod K, Unit 2, Lesson 1
	Solving Math Problems in Science	May be used with all units.
	Classroom and Research Skills	May be used with all units.
	Test-Taking Skills	May be used with all units.
	References	May be used with all units.
Yellow Pages, pp. 439–524		
	History of Science Timeline	See People in Science features.
	Famous Scientists	See People in Science features.
	Greek and Latin Word Roots	Glossary
	Glossary of Scientific Terms	Glossary

Index

Key:

Teacher Edition page numbers follow the Student Edition page numbers and are printed in blue type.
Student Edition page numbers for highlighted definitions are printed in **boldface** type.
Student Edition page numbers for illustrations, maps, and charts are printed in *italics*.

Example:

| **Student Edition Pages** | **Teacher Edition Pages** |

atom, *352,* 352–355, 364–372, **367;** 355, 395, 397, 401, 443, 445

A

A (adenine), 148, 151, 154; 211, 212, 214
acquired trait, 129; 183
Active Reading, PD8–PD9
Active Reading, lesson opener page, 5, 15, 25, 39, 51, 67, 91, 101, 113, 123, 137, 147, 161; 24, 38, 52, 68, 82, 100, 136, 150, 166, 180, 196, 210, 226
active transport, 57, *57;* 12, 85
adenine (A), 148, 151, 154; 211, 212, 214
adenosine triphosphate (ATP), 72–73; 103
   anaerobic respiration and, 75; 104
   mitochondria and, 28; 54
   photosynthesis and, 31; 55
A How-To Manual for Active Reading, R18–R19; R10
albinism, 153; 212, 213
algae, 54; 84
allele, 126–128; 121, 122, 182
   artificial selection and, 163; 227
   codominance and, 131; 184
   dominant, **127;** 182
   incomplete dominance and, 130; 184
   Punnet square and, 138, *138;* 197
   recessive, **127;** 182
Alternative Assessment, 23, 37, 51, 67, 81, 99, 135, 149, 165, 179, 195, 209, 225
alveolus, 44, *44, 47;* 71, 72
amino acid, 18; 40
   ribosomes and, 28, 155; 54, 214
anaerobic respiration, 75; 104
anaphase
   in meiosis, 104–105, *104–105;* 119, 152
   in mitosis, 96, *96;* 118, 139

animal cell, 26, *26,* 32, *32;* 10, 44, 53, 56
   division, *55;* 84
   lysosome, **32,** *32;* 10, 56
animal
   artificial selection and, 163; 227
   cellular organization, *43;* 70
   cloning, 165, 167; 228, 229
   organ structure, 42; 70
   organ system, 46–47, *47;* 72
   tissue, 41, *41;* 69
aphid, *117;* 168
arctic fox, 129, *129;* 183
Art Connection, 50
artificial selection, 163, *165;* 218, 227, 228
asexual reproduction, 114–115, *115;* 120, 167
   binary fission, 115, *115;* 120, 167
   budding, 115, *115;* 120, 167
   compared to sexual reproduction, 118–119; 120, 160, 169
   fragmentation, 117, *117;* 168
   in multicellular animals, 117, *117;* 168
   parthenogenesis, 117; 168
   regeneration, 117; 168
   spore, 115, *115;* 167
   types of, 115; 167
   vegetative, 115, *115;* 120, 167
atom, 16–17; 9, 38, 39
   in molecule, 17; 32, 39
ATP (adenosine triphosphate), 72–73; 103
   anaerobic respiration and, 75; 104
   mitochondria and, 28; 54
   photosynthesis and, 31; 55

B

bacterial cell, 6, *115;* 25, 120
   photosynthesis and, 54; 84
balance, in cells, 53; 83. *See also* **homeostasis.**
base, nucleotide, 151, *151,* 154; 212, 214
Big Idea, 1, 80, 87, 172; PD1, 1, 14, 111, 126, 232
binary fission, 115, *115;* 120, 167
biotechnology, 162–167; 227–229
   artificial selection, 163; 227
   cloning and, 165, *165, 167;* 228, 229
   genetic engineering and, **164,** 166–167; 228, 229
   impact of, 166–167; 124, 218, 220, 229
blood, 53; 65, 83
blood type, 131; 184
blood vessel, 53; 83
breeding, 124–125. *See also* **heredity.**
budding, 115, *115;* 167
butterfly wing cell, *9;* 26

C

C (cytosine), 148, 151, 154; 211, 212, 214
Calorie, 63; 89
carbohydrate, 19; 40
carbon atom, 32
carbon dioxide
   cellular respiration and, 54, 73; 13, 84, 103
   photosynthesis and, 70, 71; 13, 102
cardiovascular system, 53; 83
carrier disease, 142; 199

DATE DUE

			PRINTED IN